P9-DWA-248

Women and Spiritual Equality
in Christian Tradition

Women and Spiritual Equality in Christian Tradition

Patricia Ranft

St. Martin's Press
New York

WOMEN AND SPIRITUAL EQUALITY IN CHRISTIAN TRADITION
Copyright © Patricia Ranft, 1998. All rights reserved. Printed in the United States of America. No part of this book may be used or reproduced in any manner whatsoever without written permission except in the case of brief quotations embodied in critical articles or reviews. For information, address St. Martin's Press, 175 Fifth Avenue, New York, N.Y. 10010.

ISBN 0-312-15911-0

Library of Congress Cataloging-in-Publication Data
Ranft, Patricia
  Women and spiritual equality in Christian tradition / Patricia
Ranft.
     p. cm.
  Includes bibliographical references and index.
  ISBN 0-312-15911-0
  1. Women in Christianity—History. 2. Spirituality—History of
doctrines. 3. Equality—Religious aspects—Christianity—History of
doctrines. I. Title.
BV639.W7R36 1998
270'.082—dc21   97-50397
                                                         CIP

Design by Acme Art, Inc.

First edition: July, 1998
10 9 8 7 6 5 4 3 2 1

To my parents
who so lovingly taught all their children about
spirituality and equality

Contents

Acknowledgments

This book truly would not have been possible were it not for my husband, Michael. Having his thorough grasp of theology and scripture available to me at all times has been indispensable in the preparation of this study, as was his willingness and patience when explaining to me for the umpteenth time why Aquinas argued thus-and-so. There is not a day that goes by that I do not realize how fortunate I am to have such a supportive husband. It is rather easy to be productive when you have such an unwavering, enthusiastic cheering section behind you.

I know I am also uniquely fortunate in the role my children play in my scholarly life. My daughter, Meredith, unselfishly took time away from her medical studies to edit and critique the manuscript. Her insight into historical matters, women's studies, theology, and her mastery of English grammar never ceases to amaze me, and I am deeply grateful for all her suggestions and all the blunders she saved me from. My son, Jeff, made a cross-country trip from Colorado to New Jersey to photograph Sts. Catherine and Clare for the front cover, thus making the book indeed a family effort.

The book would never have attained its final form were it not for Annette Davis's ever-present secretarial help. Slowly but surely she is inching me into the computer age, helping me out with every and any computer glitch I invent. That in itself deserves my gratitude, but I think I am more thankful for the warm and cheerful demeanor with which she always greets me, no matter how inane my request. I am indebted to many student workers who conscientiously helped type the manuscript and correct errors. I would like to thank in particular Lori Raquepaw, Liz Kiser, Treona Jones, and Jennifer Norman for their assistance. I owe a special debt of thanks to Kidada Williams, my teaching assistant in Spring 1997, for the extraordinarily competent manner in which she discharged her duties, thus allowing me to concentrate more fully on my writing.

Introduction

The origin of this study grew out of a certain frustration I experienced while researching Western women. Common to almost all studies was the thesis that because Christianity was primarily misogynist in theory and in practice, and because it was so influential in shaping Western ideas, Christianity was largely responsible for Western misogynism. What bothered me was the fact that nowhere could I find a study that established the validity of the assumption upon which the thesis rests, that Christianity was at its core misogynist.[1] Even when scholars unearthed evidence contradicting the thesis, they presented it as an exception to the rule. Dante, for example, is viewed as representative of medieval Christianity yet said to possess a unique rather than typical opinion of women. Many studies have, of course, documented misogynist statements of theologians and the hierarchy and traced the history of women's exclusion from specific rituals and actions. Certainly one cannot deny the presence of misogyny within Christianity, but the degree to which it was present is yet to be determined. What is lacking is a comprehensive study of all the various voices and discourses vying for attention. Is misogynism the only attitude toward women that Christianity embraced? Is it the dominant one? Did misogynism infiltrate all aspects of Christianity's treatment and opinion of women, or just a few? What is Christianity's theology of human nature? What was its perception of men, and how did that differ from its perceptions of women? Did Christianity's view of the spiritual nature of women differ from its view of women's physical and social nature, and, if so, did it try to alter society's perception to be more compatible with its own?

The fact that these questions have not been answered is not indicative of failure but rather of a need to move on. The anemic value of studies that analyze literary figures of woman as temptress without analyzing allusions to man as devil is now apparent to all. Just as male has no meaning without female, so too the history of women cannot be complete without the history of men; perspective comes through contrast and comparison. Likewise, today's scholars acknowledge the weakness of a history narrated solely through one voice or focused on one discourse. Indeed, a history predicated on a single, univocal tradition is no longer defensible in light of our current knowledge of the past. No longer must we be content with the identification of only one tradition within Christianity; we must push onward to discover other traditions within the public discourse. We must look at the literate discourse of male intellectuals but also beyond it into the world of devotion, liturgy, piety, monasticism, and into the visual and auricular worlds of the laity. Only then will we discover the plurality of voices that shaped and formed and influenced the thoughts and behavior of centuries of Christians.

Ideally this book should provide answers to all these questions, and I naively thought I actually could write such a book. Once immersed in the material, however, I realized how impractical my original goal was. My new goal is much more modest. I intend to contribute documentation of one particular voice within the discourse on women. Within Christianity there is a strong and enduring tradition that maintains the spiritual equality of women. It is this tradition that I will focus on here. The decision to limit the task in such a manner was made in part because of the overwhelming volume of material available concerning attitudes toward women in the Christian tradition, in part because men's history is not advanced enough to provide the data needed for proper perspective in women's history, and in part because a negative tradition already has been documented, albeit piecemeal. Even with these limitations I make no pretense of presenting a comprehensive, definitive work on the tradition of women's spiritual equality. Too much has been left out, again because of practical considerations. What has been included and excluded is based on arbitrary criteria. I have, for instance, emphasized those voices that were original to each period over continuing voices and excluded apocryphal literature and heretical groups in favor of the canonical and the orthodox. Much of the visual evidence was eliminated because inclusion would have entailed lengthy descriptive passages or innumerable illustrations, which in turn would mean exclusion of other evidence if the study was to remain one volume. Often inclusion was based on popularity of sources, or on their representational value. If there was one overriding principle of selection I tried to abide by throughout, it was to include material accessible to the majority of Christians and capable of influence. Hymns would be an example: They are audible, are sung by the whole congregation, are aesthetically appealing to both intellect and emotions, remain deeply embedded in the consciousness of singers and audiences alike, and induce a level of involvement beyond most forms of communication. Their content has tremendous potential for influence and thus receives due attention here.

While remembering at all times that premodern cultures were more visual and auricular than textual, I still have given a significant amount of attention to written evidence for several reasons. First, it is the historian's primary medium. Second, I agree with most historians today that new history must not replace traditional history but must complement it. Intellectual history remains an excellent mirror into the minds of those who summarized contemporary positions and forged new directions for society, and we would be foolish not to take advantage of its accessibility. Third, since historians of the misogynist Christian tradition concentrate on the intelligentsia, examination of the same pool of material for a positive tradition of women is necessary for balance and evaluation. Fourth, much of what is written also was read publicly and had a much greater audience than rates of literacy alone suggest. The vitae of saints are first and foremost written documents, but they were made familiar to the illiterate through oral recitation, sermons, sculpture, and paintings.

I defend my thesis—that within Christianity there exists a strong and enduring tradition that maintains the spiritual equality of women—with methodology that some may question. I assume that the mere presence, number, and popularity of sainted women had an effect on society and therefore is evidence of a positive tradition. I assume that by virtue of the fact that their world was surrounded by holy women of every class and situation who attained perfection, women believed they too could achieve perfection. Consequently, I am more interested in documenting incidences of woman's presence in Christianity than in analyzing the modes of her presence. I am fully conversant with recent scholarly literature whose goal it is to analyze historical images of women in literature and devotions; although analysis is present in this work, it is not the main goal. The main goal is to make sometimes neglected or muted voices within Christianity more vocal. I do not run away from analysis or from secondary sources, but I do use them sparingly. Moreover, I have problems with certain types of analysis, in particular psychological analysis of such phenomena as Mariology, Perpetua's dreams, or thirteenth-century hagiographical literature.[2] Such analyses are premised on a belief in the universality of symbols, relationships, physicality, gender, and biological sex, which, I argue, is incorrect. As Carolyn Walker Bynum comments, when we apply such approaches to past societies, each modern theory "appears less universal in conclusion and implication."[3] A medieval peasant woman going to Notre Dame cathedral at Chartres to celebrate the Annunciation gazed at Mary in the center of an exquisite rose window dedicated to Mary, while she sang the *Ave Maria*, listened to a sermon on Mary's role in redemption, and prayed the Hail Mary. Everything around her focused on the spiritual perfection of one creature, a woman. Throughout this study I approach such presence as a positive indication of Christianity's belief in women's spiritual equality. I do not deny distortions have been made of women's spiritual equality, nor do I exaggerate the presence of equality in realms other than spiritual. I intend merely to document the presence of a tradition of women's spiritual equality throughout the centuries.

Consequently, I try to allow the primary sources themselves tell as much of the story as possible, to use the very words of primary sources rather than paraphrases or modernized versions, and to rely infrequently on secondary sources; the goal is to let readers come into contact with the evidence without inference and thus experience the force of the tradition directly. I have used the King James Bible for all scriptural quotations because of its dominant influence in shaping scriptural images for English-speaking people throughout the centuries. I retain the original punctuation throughout, and only in chapter 11 do I modernize the spelling of certain quotes. This approach occasionally makes the presentation stylistically awkward. I have tried to integrate the primary sources into the narrative as best I could, although I am sure reading may at times still be tedious. I believe the primary sources will more than make up for my own failings, though, and I believe readers often will find themselves surprised at what the sources contain. I have taken great care not to edit the sources selectively to better serve my purposes or to quote out of context; those readers who do avail themselves to the sources will find, on the contrary, that I included only a small portion of the relevant evidence. When discussing art forms I have used familiar examples or ones readily available in most libraries. I also have been made aware in a new way just how much we all are indebted to Carolyn Walker Bynum's exceptional work and her almost uncanny insight into all things religious and female.

The chapters are arranged in chronological order, but not each period is given the same attention; the pivotal and most influential fourth century, for example, is treated in two chapters, while the entire Early Middle Ages is given only two chapters. The sources, of course, dictate the contents of each. I have employed the traditional theological periodization for the ancient church: ante-Nicene and post-Nicene. The Council of Nicea, held in 325, has long been perceived to be a watershed event, and, accordingly, I have found it best to organize the history of the tradition within these parameters. The first three chapters deal extensively with scripture and patristic theology; for those who find systematic theology dry, be forewarned! Later chapters that deal with periods rich in evidence, particularly the High Middle Ages, are more heavily laced with nontheological examples.

1

The Spiritual Nature of Woman in Scripture and Early Christian Writings

IT IS DIFFICULT TO OVEREMPHASIZE the importance of one's definition of *human being*. If fully adhered to, it determines what one thinks about oneself and consequently how one lives life. Are human beings inherently prone to evil or, left in their natural state, will they thrive in goodness? Is human behavior conditioned or even predetermined by environment, or is it ultimately the product of the individual's free will? Is race, gender, and age significant in the definition? In light of recent advances in medicine and genetic engineering, must we now define a human being in technical, scientific terms, or is there instead a more pressing need to define the essence of human beings in terms of personhood?

The answers to these and similar abstract questions have concrete, historical implications. The social and political programs a society promotes depend on the anthropological definition that dominates that society. Actions flow from beliefs. A society that holds that humans are by nature stratified according to economics, race, or heritage, for example, is more likely to engage in a caste system, or even a Holocaust, than a society that disavows such definitions. In American history the condition of African Americans did not improve until society's legal definition of human beings was expanded to include their legal equality.

It is well established that the acceptance of Christianity in the ancient world played a major role in the end of that civilization and the beginning of another. It is also acknowledged that part of what Christianity altered in antiquity was the definition of human being. Christianity adopted a potent Hebrew definition that had tremendous implications in all fields of human endeavor. Its first fundamental principle was the dependence of humans as creatures upon God as creator: "And the Lord God formed man of the dust of the ground, and breathed into his nostrils the breath of life; and man became a living soul" (Gen 2:7). This dependence is presupposed in all other doctrines of Christianity. It is, however, complicated by the second fundamental principle, that humans are persons who possess free will. The contradiction is not resolved but instead becomes one of Christianity's central mysteries. How can humans be both dependent and independent at the same time? The mystery enveloping humanity is deepened even further by a third principle: Humanity is made in the image of God. "God said, Let us make man [adam] in our image, after our likeness: and let them have dominion over the fish of the sea, and over the fowl of the air, and over the cattle, and over all the earth, and over every creeping thing that creepeth upon the earth. So God created man is his own image, in the image of God created he him; male and female created he them" (Gen 1:26-27).

This pregnant Old Testament definition of humanity was made the pivotal concept in Christianity's understanding of the nature of the human creature, yet for contemporary English readers the meaning of the passage is not always immediately accessible. Until very recently the word *man* was considered homonymous; it was a collective noun, understood either as humanity, and thus both men and women, or as a single male human being. Today the dominant connotation for *man* is the latter; hence the original meaning of the passage often is lost or debated. Is woman made in the image of God, or just the male human being? Does the lack of specific mention of woman infer that woman has no identity separate from man or that she is unworthy of notice?

Prior to the translation of the Bible in the vernacular during the early modern period, the meaning of scriptural verses that included the word *man* did not present the reader with such problems in interpretation. The meaning was clear in the original language of the Old Testament (Hebrew), in the primary language of the New Testament (Greek), and in the chief language of the Western Bible from the fourth to the sixteenth century (Latin). In Hebrew *adam* is used to designate the species human beings and *iysh-eesh* to refer to a male person. *Homo* is used in Latin when referring to humanity, *vir* when discussing a male, and *mulier* when discussing a female. Therefore, when people read the Old Testament in its original Hebrew, they read that *adam*—human beings, both male and female—are made in the image of God. Salvation is possible for all humans, because all are made in God's image. When they read the Old Testament in the Latin translation of Jerome's Vulgate, as most people of the West did for a millennium, they read that *homo*—human beings, both male and female—are made in the image of

God. The reader had no reason to question whether women were created spiritually equal to men; the text left no room for ambivalence.

There is a second Genesis creation story, although this narrative does not play as large a part in Christianity's definition of human beings. Still, it reinforces the central point of Genesis 1:26-27, that men and women share a common nature. Moreover, it emphasizes that humanity (*adam*) is the primary creation of God, that the division of humanity into male and female is secondary, and that humanity is best when undivided: "And the Lord God caused a deep sleep to fall upon Adam, and he slept: and he took one of his ribs, and closed up the flesh instead thereof; and the rib, which the Lord God had taken from man. And Adam said, This is now bone of my bones, and flesh of my flesh: she shall be called Woman, because she was taken out of man. Therefore shall a man leave his father and his mother, and shall cleave unto his wife; and they shall be one flesh" (Gen 2: 21-24).

In the New Testament two elements from both these creation stories are presupposed in all discussions of humans. First, in the eyes of God a common spiritual nature is humanity's (*anthropos* in Greek, the original language of Paul) most essential characteristic and takes precedence over the secondary characteristic of humans, their sexual division into male and female. Second, each human being—man (*aner*) and woman (*gune*)—is created in the image of God. The former is emphatically stated in Galatians 3:28: "There is neither Jew nor Greek, there is neither bond nor free; there is neither male nor female. For ye are all one in Christ Jesus." The latter is found in Colossians 3:9-10: "Seeing ye have put off the old man [*anthropos*] with his deeds and have put on the new man [*anthropos*] which is renewed in knowledge after the image of him that created him." The Genesis image doctrine is enhanced even further by Paul in 2 Corinthians 4:4 and Colossians 1:15. In these passages it is Christ who is the image of the invisible God; humans are more properly called the image of the Image. In Romans 8:28-29 Paul proclaims that those "that love God" are "to be made conformable to the image of his Son"; in 2 Corinthians 3:18 he states "but we all, with open face beholding as in a glass the glory of the Lord, are changes into the same image from glory to glory even as by the Spirit of the Lord"; and, last, in 1 Corinthians 15:47-49 Paul declares, "The first man [*anthropos*] is of the earth, earthly: the second man [*anthropos*] is the Lord from heaven . . . and as we have borne the image of the earthly, we shall also bear the image of the heavenly." In each of these passages human beings are being discussed, not exclusively male human beings.

In 1 Corinthians 11:7-12 the discussion becomes more complex. Concerned about the appropriateness of praying with uncovered heads, Paul writes, "For a man [aner] indeed ought not to cover his head, forasmuch as he is the image and glory of God: but the woman [gune] is the glory of the man [aner]" (1 Cor 11:7). There are two significant points to note in this passage. First, a male person, aner, is being discussed, not humanity, anthropos. Second, Paul has not repeated the original Genesis doctrine here but rather offered a variation of it. Genesis does not claim humans were made to the image and glory of God but "in our image after our likeness." Moreover, Paul is not claiming woman is the image of man; he leaves intact the scriptural statement that woman is made in the image of God, even while he focuses on the differences between man and woman.

Thus we have the definition of humanity Christianity offered to society. All Christian doctrine and behavior should ultimately rest on this biblical anthropology, and when we look at the first Christians we can see that they did indeed embrace this definition. New Testament authors always make it clear that women (gune) are full members of the fledging church and are the intended recipients of Christ's message. In Acts we are told that Saul "made havock of the church, entering every house, and haling men and women, committed them to prison" (Acts 8:3); that he rounded up the followers of "this way, whether they were men or women [to] bring them bound unto Jerusalem" (Acts 9:2); that "both men and women" were baptized after hearing Philip preach (Acts 8:12); and that "believers were the more added to the Lord, multitudes both of men and women" (Acts 5:14). Paul himself tells us, "I persecuted this way unto the death, binding and delivering into prisons both men and women" (Acts 22:4). There is no indication anywhere in the New Testament that women's spiritual nature excluded them from Christ's salvation. They could benefit from Christ's salvific act as much as men. Moreover, by their adherence to the spiritual message they could and many times did distinguish themselves in the spiritual realm: "And some of them believed and consorted with Paul and Silas; and of the devout Greeks a great multitude, and of the chief women not a few" (Acts 17:4); and, again, "Therefore many of them believed; also of honorable women which were Greeks, and of men, not a few" (Acts 17:12). Even in tales concerning the rejection of Christianity, it is clear that in spiritual matters women were as integral to the movement as men. When the Jews of Antioch rejected the preaching of Paul and Barnabas, "the Jews stirred up the devout and honorable women, and the chief men of the city" to help expel them (Acts 13:50).

When we look at the classic description of the first Christian community in Acts, we also find evidence of the inclusive, equalitarian nature of the first community: "And the multitude of them that believed were of one heart and one soul; neither said any of them, that ought of the things which he possessed was his own; but they had all things common. And with great power gave the apostles witness of the resurrection of the Lord Jesus: and great grace was upon them all" (Acts 4:32-33). There is no indication that women were considered inferior Christians. They were fully included within the Christian theology of community developed through the imagery of the Body of Christ (discussed in chapter 2). There are no descriptions of dual rites or obligations. No stories tell of a different set of commandments or expectations that women must fulfill above and beyond what men must fulfill. There is one spiritual standard that all must uphold, and only one. In all things spiritual, men and women are equal.

In matters other than spiritual, scripture does not offer a new standard for behavior but rather accepts the status quo, as in 1 Peter 3:1: "Likewise, ye wives, be in subjection to your own husbands." There is no scriptural mandate to overthrow traditional social norms. On the contrary, all are urged to accept those norms—in all areas except the spiritual realm. Here an abandonment of positions is demanded. "Likewise, ye husbands, dwell with them according to knowledge, giving honor unto the wife, as unto the weaker vessel, and as being heirs together of the grace of life" (1 Pet 3:7). Women are inferior physically and socially but are equal to men spiritually. Even after Paul pontificates about the necessity of maintaining women's subordinate position in the physical world in 1 Timothy 2:9-12, he ends by reminding us that ultimately women will be saved as men are saved "if they continue in faith and charity and holiness with sobriety" (1 Tim 2:15).[1] Thus even in Paul, whose misogynist voice was repeated so often by future generations to justify the inferior position of women in worldly matters, we must acknowledge the presence of another voice, one that helped form a tradition of women's spiritual equality within Christianity.

Scripture also mentions that women were members of two specific groups, prophets and widows. We are told Philip had four daughters who were prophets (Acts 21:9). In a most significant passage, Paul writes, "Every man praying or prophesying, having his head covered dishonoureth his head. But every women that prayeth or prophesieth with her head uncovered dishonoureth her head" (1 Cor 11:4-5). The passage, according to Elizabeth Schussler Fiorenza, reveals that women prophesying and praying in public was very much the norm and that early Christians made no distinction between the prophecy of a man or a woman.[2] Paul discusses both in the same manner, and there is nothing in the passage to imply that a woman prophesying was deemed unacceptable, unusual, or unique. Indeed, Paul's coupling of prophesy with prayer implies prophesy was an ordinary occurrence. What makes the presence of women prophets even more significant is that in his discourse on the Christian community as the Body of Christ, Paul allots to prophets a most exalted position: "Now ye are the body of Christ, and members in particular. And God hath set some in the church, first apostles, secondarily prophets, thirdly teachers, after that miracles, then gifts of healing, helps, governments, diversities of tongues" (1 Cor 12:27-28).

Paul also writes extensively about widows (1 Tim 5:2-14; Tit 2:3) and about their "good works" (1 Tim 5:10) as "teachers of good things" (Tit 2:3). Women are explicitly identified as part of the group of disciples gathered together in the upper room on Pentecost; the women "were all filled with the Holy Ghost, and began to speak with other tongues" (Acts 2:4), along with the men. After Pentecost these men and women were the witnesses chosen "to preach unto the people, and to testify" (Acts 10:41).

Finally, we should note the absence of any sayings of Jesus related to women, although in his actions he certainly treated women as spiritually indistinguishable from men. Jesus interacts with women on a regular basis and has much to say to individual women. He does not, unfortunately for our purposes here, have anything to say specifically about women's nature. Future generations were free to interpret his silence on the matter and his behavior toward women in whatever way they deemed proper.

The noncanonical literature of the apostolic age is also filled with references to the Genesis definition of humanity. In the *First Epistle of Clement to the Corinthians* (ca. 100), which Eusebius reported "was read aloud to the assembled worshippers in early days, as it is in our own,"[3] Clement of Rome made the *imago dei* metaphor his central argument for why Christians must "work the work of righteousness with our whole strength."

> Above all, with His holy and undefiled hands He formed man, the most excellent [of His creatures], and truly great through the understanding given him—the express likeness of His own image. For thus says God: "Let us make man in Our image, and after Our likeness. So God made man; male and female He created them." Having thus finished all these things, He approved them, and blessed them, and said, "Increase and multiply." We see, then, how all righteous men have been adorned with good works, and how the Lord Himself, adorning Himself with His works, rejoiced. Having therefore such an example, let us without delay accede to His will. . . .[4]

The author of *The Epistle of Barnabas* (written ca. 100) also believed the metaphor reveals that we have "in us wisdom and understanding of secret things," because "He hath made us after another pattern. . . . For Scripture says concerning us, while He speaks to the Son, 'Let Us made man after Our image, and after Our likeness.'"[5]

The immediate centrality of the doctrine may be due in part to Christianity's early merger with the Hellenistic culture of the day.[6] Many of the first Christian writers were quick to realize the compatibility of the metaphor with Greek philosophy and used it extensively. Clement of Alexandria was one such Christian. He adamantly believed that "before the advent of the Lord, philosophy was necessary to the Greeks for righteousness. And now it becomes conducive to piety; being a kind of preparatory training . . . paving the way for him who is perfected in Christ."[7]

Clement spent quite a bit of time expounding on the insights Christianity had concerning the nature of humanity. His starting point was Genesis 1:26. Man "was fashioned by Him, and after He [sic] likeness" and "is loved by God" who "breathed into him what was peculiar to Himself." Because of this privileged origin, "it is incumbent on us to return His love . . . and thus to perform the works of the Master according to His similitude, and so fulfill what Scripture says as to our being made in His image and likeness."[8] Here Clement paused and cautioned us. If we are to achieve our goal, we must be sure we understand this essential fact: "The virtue of man and woman is the same." Clement elaborated:

> For if the God of both is one, the master of both is also one; one church, one temperance, one modesty; their food is common, marriage an equal yoke; respiration, sight, hearing, knowledge, hope, obedience, love all alike. And those whose life is common have common graces and a common salvation; common to them are love and training. "For in this world," he says, "they marry, and are given in marriage," in which alone the female is distinguished from the male; "but in that world it is so no more." There the rewards of this social and holy life, which is based on conjugal union, are laid up, not for male and female, but for man, the sexual desire which divides humanity being removed. Common, therefore, too, to men and women, is the name of man.[9]

Clement's voice established the tradition of women's spiritual equality in the public discourse loud and clear. In other writings he reinforced the tradition. In the eyes of God and in all matters spiritual, women and men, whether Jew or Greek, bond or free, were the same: "We admit that the same nature exists in every race, and the same virtue." Lest someone persisted in maintaining a definition of duality, Clement was even more specific: "As far as respects human nature, the woman does not possess one nature, and the man exhibit another, but the same: so also with virtue." Clement became quite upset at the mere thought that some might claim that "it belongs to male alone to be virtuous," he finds it "offensive even to say this." Such a stance was indefensible when one contemplated those that had "reached the highest degree of excellence," martyrdom. "But as it is noble for a man to die for virtue, and for liberty, and for himself, so also is it for a woman. For this is not peculiar to the nature of males, but to the nature of the good." Consequently, women "if need be" die for their faith, alongside men and children.[10]

Besides this fundamental belief that woman's nature at its most basic level, the spiritual, is not distinct, peculiar, or modified in any way from man's, we also find another theme in Clement. While man and woman share the same spiritual nature, each possesses a physical nature that is sexually unique. "For undoubtedly it stands to reason that some difference should exist between each of them, in virtue of which one is male and the other female. Pregnancy and parturition, accordingly, we say belong to woman, as she is woman, and not as she is human being." In light of this "difference as respect the peculiar construction of the body, she is destined for childbearing and housekeeping." Paul thought it necessary to remind us that "the head of every man is Christ; and the head of the woman is the man" (1 Cor 11:3). For Clement, however, such stratification did not nullify the more basic rule guiding all relationships: "To the whole human race, then, discipline and virtue are a necessity, if they would pursue after happiness."[11]

In his *Exhortation to the Heathen*, Clement offered a variation of this theme. All differences, including sexual, were obliterated in "the one whole Christ [who] is not divided: There is neither barbarian, nor Jew, nor Greek, neither male nor female, but a new man transformed by God's Holy Spirit." Consequently all "counsel and precepts" that regulated humans' sexual nature "are unimportant" except for "the only command that is universal, and over the whole course of existence, at all times and in all circumstances, tends to the highest end, viz., life, is piety."[12] Ultimately, "in this perfection" that God ordained humanity's end to be, "it is possible for man and woman equally to share."[13]

Clement's interpretations and observations concerning the nature of women were not an exception in primitive Christianity; they were the norm. Irenaeus, a Greek-speaking bishop of Lyons, is often deemed the first systematic Christian theologian, and, like Clement of Alexandria, his understanding of humanity was grounded in the doctrine of *imago Dei*. In *Against Heresies*,

Irenaeus argued that the purpose of the "whole economy of salvation" was so the Lord "should save that very man who had been created after His image and likeness." This man was Adam, "the first formed man, of whom the Scripture says the Lord spake, 'Let Us make man after Our own image and likeness,'" Irenaeus repeated for emphasis.[14] He also used the metaphor to elucidate the Incarnation.

> [T]his Word was manifested when the Word of God was made man, assimilating Himself to man, and man to Himself, so that by means of his resemblance to the Son, man might become more precious to the Father. For in times long past, it was said that man was created after the image of God, but it was not [actually] shown; for the Word was as yet invisible, after whose image man was created. Wherefore also he did easily lose the similitude. When, however, the Word of God became flesh, He confirmed both these: for He both showed forth the image truly, since He became Himself what was His image; and He re-established the similitude after a sure manner, by assimilating man [anthropos] to the invisible Father through means of the visible Word.[15]

Like Clement, Irenaeus expanded on the Genesis passage to further his insights into the nature of humanity. Whereas Clement reflected more on the common nature of man and woman, Irenaeus concentrated on elements shared by man and woman within that common nature. He explained in detail:

> For by the hands of the Father, that is, by the Son and the Holy Spirit, man [anthropos], and not a part of man, was made in the likeness of God. Now the soul and the spirit are certainly a part of man but certainly not man; for the perfect man consists in the commingling and the union of the soul receiving the spirit of the Father, and the admixture of that fleshly nature which was moulded after the image of God. . . . For if anyone takes away the substance of flesh, that is, of the handiwork [of God], and understands that which is purely spiritual, such then would not be a spiritual man, but would be the spirit of man or the Spirit of God. But when the spirit here blended with the soul is united to [God's] handiwork, man is rendered spiritual and perfect because of the outpouring of the Spirit, and this is man who was made in the image and likeness of God.[16]

With this crucial distinction Irenaeus condemned attempts to portray the male as spirit or soul and the female as body. "For that flesh which has been moulded is not a perfect man in itself but the body of a man, and part of a man. Neither is the soul itself, considered apart by itself, the man; but it is the soul of a man, and part of a man. Neither is the spirit a man, for it is called the spirit, and not a man; but the commingling and union of all these constitutes the perfect man." It is precisely in humanity's imaging of God that they are indeed humans. Any identification of man or woman with only the body or only the soul rendered that person "as something else than a man."[17] Consequently, Irenaeus had true appreciation for the body being "the temple of God . . . in which the Spirit dwells" and the "members of Christ."[18]

This brings us to Irenaeus's second premise, that not only is body and soul united within each man and woman but that each man and woman have a source of unity in God. "He who contains all things, and is Himself contained by no one. Rightly also has Malachi said among the prophets: 'Is it not one God who hath established us? Have we not all one Father?'"[19] Irenaeus buttressed his argument by then citing Paul (Eph 4:6) and Matthew (Matt 11:27), and with a reminder of what this community in Christ is: "It is not possible to live apart from life, and the means of life is found in fellowship with God."[20] Christ came to save all and all are in Him.

Contemporaries Theophilus of Antioch and Athenagoras of Athens were of a similar mind as Irenaeus. In his treatise on the *Resurrection of the Dead*, Athenagoras stated perhaps even more emphatically than Irenaeus that body and soul are inseparable.

> For if the whole nature of men in general is composed of an immortal soul and a body which was fitted to it in the creation, and if neither to the nature of the soul by itself, nor to the nature of the body separately, has God assigned such a creation or such a life and an entire course of existence as this, but to men compounded of the two, in order that they may, when they have passed through their present existence, arrive at one common end, with the same elements of which they are composed at their birth and during life it unavoidably follows . . . that the whole series of these things must be referred to some one end. . . .[21]

While the unity of body and soul may not be important in gender issues today, it was very significant in ancient societies, which accepted medical theories on the physical inferiority of women's bodies without question. If a woman's soul was made in the image of God, and this soul was one with a woman's body, then blanket condemnation of woman was an attack on the image of God, regardless of what they had been taught about a woman's body.

The crowning glory of men and women, their intellectual powers, likewise resides in their universal nature: "But what which has received both understanding and reason is man, not the soul by itself."[22] or Theophilus of Antioch the uniqueness of man and woman rests in yet another characteristic: "God made man [*anthropos*] free, and with power over himself."[23] This gift was given by God to humanity, that is, both to man and to woman, whom he created together "lest then, it should be supposed that one God made the man and another the woman." Furthermore, "God made the woman together with the man . . . that their mutual affection might be greater."[24]

The voices of two other theologians in early Christianity are most commonly associated with the misogynist tradition: Tertullian and Origen. Both were preoccupied with the physical aspects of humanity, and both focused more on Genesis 2:7 than Genesis 1:26-27. Still, even within their works we find evidence of a positive tradition of women's spiritual nature.

Tertullian did not ignore Genesis 1:26-27, but it dominated his discussion of the Trinity more than his definition of humanity. "Remember," he cautioned, "that man is properly called flesh." This was the most fundamental fact guiding Tertullian's understanding of human nature.

> Besides, what else is man than flesh, since no doubt it was corporeal rather than the spiritual element from which the Author of man's nature gave him his designation? "And the Lord God made man of the dust of the ground," not of spiritual essence; this afterwards came from the divine afflatus: "and man became a living soul." What, then, is man? Made, no doubt of it, of the dust; and God placed him in paradise, because He moulded him, not breathed him, into being—a fabric of flesh, not of spirit.[25]

Reliance on Genesis 2:7 over Genesis 1:26-27 meant that in Tertullian's mind, to speak of women solely, or even predominately, in spiritual terms was not plausible. Tertullian's definition of humanity remained rooted in the material world, and, consequently, his opinion of women was rooted in materialism. It is, therefore, all the more surprising to see that Tertullian wrote about the spiritual aspects of marriage between man and woman in a treatise written for his wife. The bulk of the treatise concerned itself with fleshly and worldly concupiscence, "of human weakness which make marriages necessary,"[26]but at the very end of the treatise Tertullian wrote what Jean LaPorte calls "the most beautiful page among the ancient texts about marriage."[27]

What kind of yoke is that of two believers, (partakers) of one hope, one desire, one discipline, and one and the same service? Both (are) brethren, both fellow servants, no difference of spirit or of flesh; nay, (they are) truly "two in one flesh." Where the flesh is one, one is the spirit too. Together they pray, together prostrate themselves, together perform their fasts; mutually teaching, mutually exhorting, mutually sustaining. Equally (are they) both (found) in the Church of God; equally at the banquet of God; equally in straits, in persecutions, in refreshments.[28]

As eloquent as Tertullian was in his description of the spiritual union in marriage, he still had difficulty in allowing the spiritual aspects of a person dominate the physical. Nevertheless, when Tertullian did focus on the spiritual in this brief passage, his misogynist outlook was absent. The fact that both views occurred together is not a coincidence; it is cause and effect.

Like Tertullian, Origen's problem was with the corporeal nature of women. In his commentary on Genesis 1:26, Origen made an even stricter distinction than Tertullian between humanity's corporeal and spiritual natures: "The form of the body does not contain the image of God, nor is the corporeal man said to be 'made', but 'formed'. . . ."[29] He did not take advantage of the opportunity to discuss the sexual division of humanity in the following verse ("male and female created he them"), but instead focused on the blessing ("God blessed them saying: Increase and multiply"). Still, Origen did admit that ultimately "before God there is no distinction of sex."[30]

We can gain some insight into early Christians' perception of women as spiritual persons of equal dignity by looking next at their use of the female as symbol. While interpreting the impact a symbol has on a society is always a tenuous and difficult task, we must at least note the pervasive presence in early Christianity of the female as symbol even if we cannot offer a definitive interpretation. Woman personifies all that is essential to Christians. The church, Wisdom, virtue, the soul, the Holy Spirit, and the faithful are all spoken of in terms of the feminine. Attempts to dismiss the significance of the feminine personification of the Good as merely the product of inherent or inherited linguistic structures that feminize abstractions, as grammatical accidents,[31] or as means by which the patriarchy maintained women in inferior positions all fail to convince. Its presence in Scripture and its full-scale expansion into theology reveal it to be a deliberate and conscious choice beyond the realm of grammar and above the domain of secular structures.

The first fact to note is the inordinate amount of female imagery used in comparison to male imagery. The second striking fact is the disproportionate employment of the female image in a positive context in comparison to any negative context. The use of feminine symbols, feminine personifications of concepts, and attribution of female characteristics to theological terms and to desirous behavior is so widespread in the sources that it would take literally volumes to document. In an age where the skeptical must be persuaded by quantified analysis, this situation is almost to our disadvantage, for statistical analysis of the use of female imagery in Christian sources would be a full-time project in itself.

The use of the feminine as symbol and personification of spiritual values finds one of its fullest expressions in the Song of Solomon, a favorite Old Testament book throughout the centuries. While the extreme imagery of the work lends itself to numerous interpretations, most early Christian and medieval commentators read it as a religious allegory.[32] The love expressed in the Song of Solomon is literally the love between a faithful maiden and her betrothed shepherd, but allegorically it is between Yahweh and His Chosen People. The maiden, representing all men and women, is portrayed in this drama as the personification of virtue triumphant, the perfect example of how to stay faithful to one's original betrothed, no matter how tempting the love of another may be. The language describing this love affair is highly charged and physical, yet at all times it is a very positive presentation of the female, even at her most sexual level.

The female personification of Wisdom is found throughout Old Testament Wisdom literature, particularly in Proverbs, Ecclesiastes, and Job. Female imagery of Wisdom was not unique to Israel; many neighbors had similar literary traditions, but Israel's interpretation of Wisdom was not traditional. Wisdom's status in God's creation is awesome in its power, for Wisdom is the actual agent of that creation: "The Lord by wisdom hath founded the earth" (Prov 3:19). The person who finds Wisdom is happy, for "she is more precious than rubies: and all the things thou canst desire are not to be compared unto her" (Prov 3:15). Wisdom is a woman prophet, speaking in her own power, in her own way: "Wisdom crieth without; she uttereth her voice in the streets: she crieth in the chief place of concourse, in the openings of the gates: in the city she uttereth her words, saying . . . Turn you at my reproof: behold I will pour out my spirit unto you, I will make known my words unto you" (Prov 1:20-23). Elsewhere in the Old Testament female imagery is employed to personify God as a compassionate mother (Is 49:15), a midwife (Ps 22:9-10), and a woman in labor (Is 42:14). In Baruch Jerusalem is "the mother of the nation" (Bar 4:5-29), and in Lamentations Jerusalem has "become a widow" because "her children are gone unto captivity before the enemy" (Lam 1:1,5).

The New Testament continues much of this imagery. Jerusalem, according to Paul, "is the mother of us all" (Gal 4:26). In Revelation, an apocalyptic book immersed in symbolism, Jerusalem is also personified as a woman "having the glory of God: and her light was like unto a stone most precious" (Rev 21:11). Moreover, Jerusalem is "the holy city, new Jerusalem, coming down from God out of Heaven, prepared as a bride adorned for her husband" (Rev 21:2). The bride-bridegroom analogy is also in John's gospel (Jn 3:29). The heart of Revelation, however, is chapters 12 to 14, which personify the church as a woman: "And there appeared a great wonder in heaven: a woman clothed with the sun, and the moon under her feet, and upon her head a crown of twelve stars" (Rev 12:1). The fact that the church is personified as a woman in both New Testament and Old is essential to any study of women within Christianity, because the relationship between Christ and the church is at the center of Christianity.

The first Christians were quick to elaborate upon and expand scriptural female imagery. Their writings were filled with such scriptural metaphors and reflections. Polycarp wrote that "faith which has been given to you, and which, being followed by hope, and preceded by love towards God, and Christ, and our neighbor, 'is mother to us all.'"[33] Justin Martyr employed the same metaphor,[34] as did Irenaeus in *Against Heresies*. In the same passage in which Irenaeus reflected upon Jerusalem as mother, he also reflected upon the image of Jerusalem as a bride, found in Revelations 21:2.[35] Tertullian in *Against Marcion* employed the image of mother Jerusalem,[36] as did Origen in *De principiis*[37] and Hippolytus in *Refutation of All Heresies*.[38]

The image of the church as mother is of particular importance because of the role the church plays in the salvific plan, as just noted. We find it in the literature as early as the end of the second century, and by the fourth century it was quite common. The first known reference is in a letter written ca. 177 that described the persecutions of Christians in Lyons and Vienne and alluded to the church as "the virgin mother who was receiving her stillborn children back alive."[39] Hippolytus argued that the source of the personification was scripture itself.[40] According to Hippolytus, Revelation makes the identification of the church as mother quite unmistakable: "By the 'woman clothed with the sun,' he meant most manifestly the Church." Moreover, the church is a mother with a most significant motherly task. Since her child "is to rule all the nations," the mother church "becomes the instructor of all the nations."[41] For Irenaeus, the church nourishes all "into life from the mother's breasts," because "where the church is, there is the Spirit of God."[42] Cyprian used maternal imagery in many of his treatises[43] and stressed that to be denied knowledge of the church as mother is as serious as to be denied knowledge of God as Father,[44] for one "can no longer have God for his Father who has not the church for his mother."[45]

Tertullian conferred more dignity to the personification by designating the church "Lady Mother the Church,"[46] and he presented her in an even stronger position of authority and dominance than Cyprian: "[I]n the Son and the Father the Mother is recognized, since upon her the terms 'Father' and 'Son' depend for their meaning."[47] We have already seen that Tertullian reflected upon Paul's personification of Jerusalem as mother in Galatians;[48] he also called the church "the true Mother of all the living"[49] (as well as calling Wisdom "Mother Wisdom").[50] Methodius Olympus used many images when referring to the church, but the major symbols permeating the whole of his *Banquet of the Ten Virgins* were female. The church is "our mother the church," the "bride of the Word," "the spouse," and "sister."[51] Methodius also used the metaphor graphically, as in his description of the church giving "birth to a male where the Church swells and travails in birth until Christ is formed in us."[52]

Woman in the person of Eve also was used frequently to personify sin and vice, but aside from Tertullian and his infamous metaphor comparing all women to Eve, "who opened the door to the devil,"[53] it is not a dominant image during the period. We come across such statements as Venatius Honorius's "those whom guilty Eve had before infected," but most are qualified, as was his. Before he finished his sentence, he included reference to the image of woman under the New Law; those infected persons were now restored by Christ and "fed with abundant milk at the bosom of the Church."[54] Origen employed the Old Testament imagery of the harlot to symbolize a wayward people, but in the same homily he also noted that "the soul can be called female."[55] Elsewhere he preached that "the appellations of Bride and Bridegroom denote either the Church in her relation to Christ, or the soul in her union with God the Word."[56] In yet another homily he argued that although at first we are tempted to think of virtue as a wife, "when we reach perfection so that we are capable also of teaching others, let us then no longer enclose virtue within our bosom as a wife, but as a sister . . . [as] the divine word says: 'Say that wisdom is your sister.'"[57] Origen used a variety of female images in a positive manner: Sara "represents *arete*, which is the virtue of the soul"; the death of Sara was "the consummation of virtue"; and divine learning was "his wife."[58] Surprisingly, in his lengthy commentary on Genesis, he completely ignored the second creation story in which Eve is portrayed as sinner and temptress. Given the opportunity to elaborate at length upon the evils of Eve and all women as types of Eve, Origen decided not to.

2

Women in Early Christian Communities

BECAUSE HISTORIANS ARE SO HEAVILY DEPENDENT on written documentation, and because it is difficult to ascertain how representative or influential a work is, there is always the possibility that too much weight is placed on a specific written work. To avoid giving unwarranted significance to early Christian writings of individual theologians regarding woman's spiritual nature, we will now explore whether these writings corresponded to the lives of the early Christians.

Scripture is, not surprisingly, one of the best sources we have for information concerning the lives of ordinary Christians. The New Testament is not overly concerned with identifying the early Christians by name, male or female, and among those who are identified, few are women. Consequently, the question of how many women ministered is hard to answer, but we do know the names of some. The story of Jesus's close relationship with Mary and Martha is told at length in both John and Luke: "They made him supper; and Martha served," and later Mary "anointed the feet of Jesus, and wiped his feet with her hair" (Jn 12:2-3). Mary, wife of Cleophas, Mary Magdalene, and Mary, the mother of Jesus, "stood by the cross of Jesus" (Jn 19:25). Mary Magdalene was the first to go to Jesus's sepulcher and the first the risen Jesus spoke to (Jn 20:18). Mary Magdalene, Joanna, and Susanna "ministered unto him" when Jesus came through their village preaching (Luke 8:1-3).

Acts 12:12 introduces us to "Mary, mother of John" in whose house "many gathered together praying," to Tabitha of Joppa who "was full of good works and almsdeeds" (Acts 9:36), and to the merchant Lydia of Thyatira, who opened up her home to Paul and his companions (Acts 16:15). Prisca, mentioned in 2 Timothy 4:19; Acts 18:2 and 18:26; Romans 16:3; and 1 Corinthians 16:19, and her companion-husband Aquila were Paul's "helpers in Christ Jesus" and sailed with him to Syria on a missionary journey. They also completed the instruction of Apollos begun by Paul (Acts 18:24-26). Phoebe was "our sister" and "a servant of the church" at Cenchrea, about whom Paul instructed the Roman church to "receive her in the Lord, as becometh said and that ye assist her in whatsoever business she hath need of you: for she hath been a succourer of many, and of myself also" (Rom 16:1-2). Besides Phoebe and Prisca, Paul commended and saluted Mary, Tryphosa, Persis, Junia, and Olympas, all women who "laboured much in the Lord" (Rom 16:12). Eudias and Syntyche "laboured with [Paul] in the Lord" (Phil 4:2-3).

There is, then, abundant evidence that women participated actively in Jesus's ministry, in the first communities, and in early Christian missionary work. In some areas of ministry it is hard to discern exactly what the practices of the first Christians were. Paul tells the Corinthians to "let your women keep silence in the churches: for it is not permitted unto them to speak; but they are commanded to be under obedience, as also saith the law. And if they will learn anything, let them ask their husbands at home: for it is a shame for women to speak in the church" (1 Cor 14:34-35). We have seen, however, that "aged women" were "teachers of good things" (Tit 2:3), that Aquila and Prisca completed the instructions of Apollos (Acts 18:26), and that Philip's daughters were prophets (Acts 21:9). Obviously theory and practice did not always coincide.

In two areas we have no difficulty in discerning early Christian practice: There are no women among the Twelve and no women priests (presbyteroi). So little is known about presbyters during the first century that it is hard to assess what this means. Before the structural organization began its journey toward rigid institutionalization in the fourth century, church offices and officers were rarely referred to. In the earliest texts, individual members were mentioned by name, not title, and then only infrequently. When the church grew and organization became more important, titles replaced names and then categories replaced titles.[1] Only when we get to the last stage of organization were the responsibilities, position, and status of the presbyters clearly defined. James Burtchaell maintains that prior to this ossification, "men and women who carried no titles . . . were the ones to whom believers most notably deferred. The people who bore most powerfully in their persons the force of divine conviction . . . did God's work. They spoke with authority."[2] We cannot, therefore, persuasively argue that the absence of women presbyters in the first communities indicates that women were denied spiritual equality. Many turned to women for spiritual guidance, and surely they would not have done so if women were considered spiritually inferior.

A possible reason for women's absence among the presbyters lies in the intermediary nature of the presbyter's role. The Old Testament priest offered up the first fruits of the temporal, physical world to the God of the eternal, spiritual world. The priest's function therefore extended into both worlds. However equal women were in the spiritual realm, they were not equal in the physical world. Once the church became more encumbered in this world, women's inequality in earthly matters eventually began to limit severely their opportunities to participate in ministry because, like the Old Testament priest, the Christian priest functioned in both worlds. A woman was equal in only one of those worlds.

While the average Christian woman did not aspire to the priesthood, she did expect full membership in the community, and this was readily available to early Christian women, as discussed. The inclusive nature of the Christian community was communicated to future generations most effectively through a metaphor: the Body of Christ. The metaphor is scriptural, based on Paul's passage in 1 Corinthians 12, and is found in one of the earliest Christian documents, Clement of Rome's *Letter to the Corinthians.* Clement employed the image to help the Corinthians, then involved in a schism, realize the comprehensive nature of their membership in the church and the consequent need for unity. "Let us take our body. The head without the feet is nothing, and so also the feet without the head are nothing. The smallest members of our body are necessary and useful to the whole body. But all conspire together and unite in a single obedience, so that the whole body may be saved."[3] This sense of all belonging equally to the community and of all being equally saved is not contradicted in any extant document, whether it be an epistle addressed to an audience, a theological reflection, or an account of events or lives. In many ways, it is simply a restatement of Christianity's definition of humanity. If all humans are made in the image and likeness of God, then all humans are equally members of God's church. There is no exception. Children and servants, male and female, are included in this definition.[4]

In numerous passages in early Christian literature the Body of Christ is "likened [to] the unity of our body throughout its manifold and divers members," as Tertullian argued, in order to prove that "there is but one Lord of the human body."[5] According to Origen, knowledge of humanity's union in one body was essential knowledge for salvation, "for it is one single body that awaits its justification, one body that is promised a future resurrection."[6] Salvation, then, is communal, and women are full members of the community. "[T]he living church," we read in the *Second Epistle of Clement,* "is the 'body of Christ.' For the Scripture says: 'God made man male and female;' the male is Christ and the female is the church."[7] This passage is perhaps more difficult, for it seems to infer woman's inferiority within the Body of Christ. The male was identified with Christ, the highest dignity that can be bestowed; any personification of woman after this could surely only be inferior. If, however, we put the statement in the wider context of early Christian theology, this is not the proper conclusion. The female is the church and the church is the Body of Christ. Only a soul or only a body was "something else" other than a human, as Irenaeus said.[8] The female is thus also Christ just as the male is also the Body of Christ.

Besides the church being female, it is also, Origen reminded us, "the whole assembly of the saints . . . a corporate personality."[9] The belief in the necessity of communal salvation was already common by the second century; we find it in *The Shepherd of Hermas*, written in the first half of the second century, and in the letters of Ignatius of Antioch.[10] Clement of Alexandria believed that all people enjoyed the same fellowship with Christ, that there was only "one universal salvation of humanity," and that all could expect "the same equality before the righteous and loving God," for "all who have abandoned the desires of the flesh are equal and spiritual before the Lord."[11] Lactantius made sure everyone knew who was included in the term *humanity* before he proceeded to analyze "what was the reason for making the human race." Stoics almost arrived at the correct answer when they said that creation was for the sake of men, but Lactantius scornly pointed out the flaw: "They err not a little on this very point, that they do not say for the sake of man, but of men. The term 'man,' one, singular, embraces the whole human race."[12] In the third century Cyprian wrote a treatise, *On the Unity of the Church*, that argued that schisms arose only when Christians forgot the inclusive, communal nature of the church—"this sacrament of unity," as he called it. "The church also is one, which is spread abroad far and wide into a multitude. . . . [S]he is one mother, plentiful in the results of fruitfulness: from her womb we are born, by her milk we are nourished, by her spirit we are animated."[13] In another treatise, *On the Lord's Prayer*, Cyprian applied this principle to prayer. Prayer is "public and common; and when we pray, we pray not for one, but for the whole people, because we the whole people are one." If someone still questioned women's inclusion, Cyprian eliminated any doubt by reminding his readers that after Christ's ascension the apostles and disciples gathered together "in prayer, with the women, and Mary."[14] Moreover, Cyprian argued that women's prayers were the best model to imitate.[15]

Further evidence of the church's inclusive nature and the community's belief in the spiritual equality of women is found in the testimonies of families to their dead. Early Christian epitaphs on tombs show that in death—the ultimate test of a Christian's belief—women were indistinguishable from men. "Euskia," one inscription reads, "the blameless one, who lived a life of goodness and purity for twenty-five years, died on the feast of our lady Lucia, for whom no praise is adequate. She was a perfect Christian, well pleasing to her husband, and endued with much grace."[16] Most inscriptions were shorter and seemingly oblivious to the sex of the dead, such as "May thy soul be in the midst of the Saints" or "She was received by God and by the Saints."[17] It was also common for the family of the dead to ask a particular saint to intercede on behalf of their beloved, and here again they were not preoccupied with sex. The family of one woman inscribed "May Saint Lawrence receive her soul,"[18] while two other families commended the souls of male relatives to Saint Basilla.[19] The community of saints included both men and women.

The little we know of early Christian practices supports this conclusion. Prayer is an excellent reservoir of evidence, for surely a greater number of Christians were exposed to the theological formulations in formal prayer than those in treatises written by theologians.[20] A prayer said by an individual, by the entire assembly, or by the leader of the assembly in an individual's name has an impact on a person that cannot be duplicated by more formal theological works. The theology helps inform the prayer, but the prayer itself has the more direct and immediate effect. It is, therefore, incumbent on any study of Christianity's attitudes toward women to examine the prayer of the church for any light it can shed on women's history.

The very first thing the apostles did after Jesus left them and ascended into heaven was to return to the upper room in Jerusalem to continue "with one accord in prayer and supplication, with the women, and Mary, the mother of Jesus, and with his brethren" (Acts 1:14). Prayer constituted, therefore, the first official act of the nascent church. Women were not only present for this act, they were mentioned before the men, and one of the women was individually named, whereas no man was. This passage encompassed the two fundamental principles concerning women and prayer that were upheld in early Christianity. Women participated fully in the prayer life of the church, and the prayer was thus offered "with one accord." No evidence indicates anything to the contrary. Women's prayer was not inferior. It was part of the whole community's prayer that rose up "with one accord." This unity was considered such an essential element of prayer that when Luke relates the story of Pentecost, he begins by telling us "when the day of Pentecost was fully come, they were all with one accord in one place" (Acts 2:1). After the first Pentecost sermon, 3,000 new converts joined the church in "fellowship, in breaking of bread, and in prayer" (Acts 2:42) and continued "daily with one accord" (Acts 2:46). Yet again Luke repeated the two elements before he introduced the classic description of the first community: "And when they [men and women] heard that, they lifted up their voice to God with one accord. . . ."(Acts 4:24).[21] He also emphasized that the composition of the community doing this praying remained the same as it grew: "And believers were the more added to the Lord, multitudes both of men and women" (Acts 5:14).

Some of the first prayers of Christians are recorded in the New Testament, and they are predominantly prayers of petition, intercession, thanksgiving, and praise.[22] The Lord's Prayer had a place of honor among the first Christians; the *Didache* mandated that everyone pray the Lord's Prayer three times a day,[23] and it probably was recited at eucharistic liturgies early on.[24] Tertullian wrote a commentary on it, in which he identified its main components: the rendering of honor, a testimony of faith, the offering of obedience, the remembrance of hope, a petition for life, the confession of sins, and solicitude regarding temptation. It is, from any possible perspective, a universal prayer for all. The only term that could be questioned is the male designation for God as Father. Yet Tertullian anticipated any objection by explaining right from the beginning why humans address God as Father. "Our Lord very frequently spoke to us of God the Father; in fact, He even taught us to call none on earth 'father,' but only the one we have in heaven. . . . Moreover, when we say 'Father,' we also add a title to God's name."[25] Next, in a passage already referred to, Tertullian explained how the validity of the title Mother presupposed the name Father. "In the Father, the Son is also addressed. For Christ said, 'I and the Father are one.' Nor is the Mother Church passed over without mention, for in the Son and the Father the Mother is recognized, since upon her the terms 'Father' and 'Son' depend for their meaning. With this one form, then, or word, we honor God with His own. . . ."[26]

Cyprian likewise wrote a commentary on the Lord's Prayer, and here we find two significant passages that bear on the subject of women and prayer. Cyprian opened and closed his treatise by offering up women and their prayers as models for all Christians to imitate. He first presented Hannah.

> And this Hannah in the First Book of Kings, who was a type of the church, maintains and observes, in that she prayed to God not with clamorous petition, but silently and modestly, within the recesses of her heart. She spoke with hidden prayer, but with manifest faith. She

spoke not with her voice, but with her heart, because she knew that thus God hears; and she effectually obtained what she sought because she asked it with belief. Divine Scripture asserts this, when it says, "She spake in her heart, and her lips moved, and her voice was not heard; and God did hear her."[27]

After he reflected upon prayer itself, he concluded by once more commending his readers to follow the example of another woman. This time he offered them the perseverance and steadfastness of Anna who "without intermission" prayed and watched and fasted "night and day." In fact, he believed her prayer was so noteworthy that it is she whom Christians should tell Gentiles and Jews to turn to for enlightenment.[28]

The New Testament contains many other prayers recited by the apostles, the first Christians, and even Jesus himself. Most of them appear to be spontaneous reactions to a particular situation. The prayer recited by the apostles as they chose Judas's replacement (Acts 1:24), for example, arose out of a need for guidance, and the prayer of the community after Peter's and John's release (Acts 4:24-31) originated in the communities frightened that they might not be strong enough to continue their witness. The epistles of Paul contain numerous prayers; since many epistles were intended to be read publicly to the assembly, as stated in Colossians 4:16 and 1 Thessalonians 5:27, we know some of the prayers that were part of the spiritual life of the first Christians. We also know short prayer phrases such as "Maranatha" (Our Lord cometh), "Amen" (let it be so), and "eucharisteo" (I give thanks) were commonplace, as were doxologies like that in Revelation 11:17: "We give thee thanks, O Lord God Almighty, which art, and wast, and art to come; because thou has taken to thee thy great power, and hast reigned." In each instance the prayer approached God humbly and contained no prerequisite on the part of the petitioner. One of the earliest recorded prayers outside of scripture is found in *First Epistle of Clement*, and it too is filled with praise, thanksgiving, petition, and awe for God, as in the early prayer recorded in *The Didache*.[29] The early creeds, on the other hand, are immersed in the mysteries of the faith. Scriptural creeds (1 Cor 8:6; 1 Cor 15:3-5; Rom 1:3-4, 4:24-25, 8:34; Phil 2:6-11; 1 Tim 2:5-15; 1 Tim 3:16; 1 Pet 3:18-22) concentrate on Jesus's person, mission, and lordship. The most complete baptismal interrogation is contained in Hippolytus's *Apostolic Tradition*, and it allows us to see the requirements, priorities, and standards demanded of both men and women.

Dost thou believe in Christ Jesus, the Son of God who was born of the Holy Spirit and the Virgin Mary, who was crucified in the days of

Pontius Pilate and died and rose the third day living from the dead and ascended into the heavens, and sat down at the right hand of the Father, and will come to judge the living and the dead?

I believe.

Dost thou believe in the Holy Spirit in the Holy Church, and the Resurrection of the flesh?

I believe.[30]

The Eucharistic prayers of the first Christians also allow us to view what they considered the essence of their faith. Probably the earliest is found in *The Didache*. While taking the cup, the assembly gave thanks to the Father for making Jesus known to them. While taking the bread, they gave thanks for the life and knowledge gained through knowing Jesus. They paused to implore the Father to "let thy church be gathered together from the ends of the earth" and then continued with their prayers of thanksgiving. They thanked the Father for the knowledge, faith, and immortality that came from knowing Jesus; they thanked Him for the spiritual drink and eternal life they receive through Jesus; and, finally, they thanked Him for all things that proceeded from His might. They closed with another plea to remember the church, keep it from evil, and make it perfect in love.[31]

The prayers of thanksgiving were joined by pleas for church unity. In Justin Martyr's discussion of the Eucharist, the concern with church unity was quite evident. After relating the words and actions of the rite, Justin commented that they all would "remind each other of these things" and "always keep together." On Sundays, the day chosen for "the common assembly," everyone "who lives in cities or in the country gather together to one place" for another Eucharist. First they would listen to the scriptural readings and an instruction and then they "rise together and pray." After the distribution of the bread and wine, they took up a collection for members of the community in need.[32]

The Eucharist was the center of Christian spirituality from the very beginning, and not the least important element of the liturgy was its demand that all Christians participate in community. It was this community that formed the inclusive Body of Christ, which we have seen was a metaphor that specifically included women. As Christianity spread among different classes and geographical areas, the Eucharist increasingly became pivotal in Christianity's task of merging all peoples into one. The liturgy was the time and the place where all divisions—social, geographical, and sexual—were transcended in the unity of Christ. Unless these differences were transcended successfully, the early Christians believed they would not survive. Hence they insisted on the unity of all, which, in turn, was posited on the equality of all peoples made in the image and likeness of God.

Liturgical prayer, then, was characterized by direct, simple language in an inclusive, universal voice. The early Christians' deepest convictions are contained in these prayers, and one of the most obvious convictions is that all people, without distinction, approach God in the same way, humbly, as sinners. Men as well as women readily admitted to that status.

Widowed women comprised the only group of Christians who had a unique role in the prayer life of the church. Widows had been accorded a position of special consideration in the Old Testament; they were protected and cared for by the larger community.[33] In Acts we see the first Christians continuing this Hebrew tradition. As the Christian community began to grow, they realized that the widows were not being taken care of properly and decided to appoint seven men to do so (Acts 6:1-5). Paul writes at length about them in 1 Timothy, and here we see them not only as objects of concern (Christians with widowed relatives are to "relieve them") but as a distinct group who have special duties and status within the community (1 Tim 5:3-16). Their primary charge is to "continueth in supplications and prayers night and day" (1 Tim 5:5). Polycarp tells the Philadelphians to "teach the widows to be prudent . . . and to pray without ceasing for all."[34] In the *Constitutions of the Holy Apostles* we are reminded of Paul's stipulation that "women are not avowed to teach in the church but only to pray." The author encourages the widow to do this in an extraordinary way: "Let the widow therefore own herself to be the 'altar of God.'"[35] The same sentiments are found in the *Didascalia*: "A widow should not concern herself with anything but praying for her benefactor and for the entire church."[36] In later centuries the duties of widows expanded greatly and may have included a semiclerical status in the East; in these early centuries the charge given to the first groups of widows that distinguished them as a separate and special entity was to pray. Widows were the only group of Christians that we know of so charged.

All Christians, however, were charged with bearing witness to their faith. The obligation is rooted in the Old Testament and emphasized extensively in the New Testament. All of Israel bears witness to Yahweh: "You yourselves are my witnesses—it is Yahweh who speaks—my servants whom I have chosen that men may know and believe me and understand that it is I" (Is 43:9-10). Nations must see Israel's very existence as testimony to the goodness of Yahweh. The prophets are witnesses to Israel and to all nations of Yahweh's message.

The obligation of God's chosen people to bear witness is transmitted to the New Israel by John the Baptist: "There was a man sent from God, whose name was John. The same came for a witness, to bear witness to the light, that all men through him might believe" (Jn 1:6-7). When Jews asked him to identify himself, John did so by claiming he was a witness in the tradition of the prophets: "I am the voice of one crying in the wilderness, Make straight the way of the Lord, as said the prophet Esaias" (Jn 1:23). Jesus's admiration for John's witness and the central role witness plays in the salvation history is emphasized by Jesus in his defense against the accusation that he made himself equal to Yahweh. "If I bear witness of myself, my witness is not true. There is another that beareth witness of me; and I know that the witness which he witnesseth of me is true. Ye sent unto John and he bare witness unto the truth. . . . But I have greater witness than that of John: for the work which the Father have given me to finish, the same works that I do, bear witness of me, that the Father hath sent me. And the Father himself, which hath sent me, hath borne witness of me" (Jn 5:31-37).

To be absolutely sure the apostles understood the importance of witness, Jesus made it his last spoken command to them: "And ye shall be witnesses unto me both in Jerusalem, and in all Judaea, and in Samaria, and unto the uttermost part of the earth" (Acts 1:8). The apostles were obedient followers, for in Acts they refer to themselves repeatedly as witnesses, and they are described by others as witnesses more than any other designation.[37]

The first Christians accepted this obligation readily and believed that it was because of their witness that "great grace was upon them all" (Acts 4:33). They also realized early on that besides grace, witness often brought suffering. This is reflected in history of the noun *martus*, witness, and the verb *marturein*, to witness. It underwent a diachronistic semantic change during the century after the Resurrection.[38] By the end of the first century we find *marturein* in the *Epistle of Clement to the Corinthians* to describe the deaths of Peter and Paul as martyrdom—to suffer while giving witness.[39] In *The Martyrdom of Polycarp*, written sometime in the latter part of the second century, *martus* completed its change and now meant a dying witness.[40] Christian literature from this point on used the word *martus* to describe one who suffers death in order to bear witness. *Martus* is now martyr.

It is helpful to understand the development of the word *martyr* before we look into the phenomenon of martyrdom for evidence concerning how women were viewed in spiritual terms. If we start with the original Old Testament mandate for all Israel to bear witness to Yahweh, we know all meant all—men, women, and children. And we know that the first Christians took Jesus's mandate to bear witness to the ends of the earth quite literally; it was the chief motivation and justification for their missionary work.[41] The Old Testament definition of humanity included women, Jesus's redemptive act included women, and the Christian obligation to bear witness included women. If women's spiritual equality made them eligible for the gift of salvation, it also made them subject to the same obligations as men, and the sources bear this out. Women as well as men bore witness to Jesus's message in all phases of its manifestation: as testifiers, as suffering witnesses, and as martyrs.

Fortunately, once *martus* became martyr, sources multiply, and consequently so does our ability to view women. The acts of the early martyrs, as these sources are commonly called, have been duly analyzed in modern times for their historical value.[42] Some have been found to be too void of basic facts to be considered historical, but most are valid historical portrayals. Historical or unhistorical, both are important because of the influence exerted through the acts. "To share," the act of *The Martyrdom of Pionius* reminded the community, "in the remembrances of the saints . . . gives strength to those who are striving to imitate the better things."[43] The stories kept Christians focused on their goal and reinforced their priorities in life like little else could do. "Nothing could be more amazing than the fearless courage of these saints," wrote Eusebius. "You would see a youngster not yet twenty standing without fetters, spreading out his arms in the form of a cross, and with a mind unafraid and unshakable occupying himself in the most unhurried prayers to the Almighty, not budging in the least," while wild animals, hot irons, and swords torturously put him to death. Christians who actually saw these atrocities experienced "the ever-present divine power of Him to whom they testified,"[44] which in turn gave them the courage to testify, *marturein*, even unto death. The deaths "were proof of God's favour and achieved the spiritual strengthening of men [*hominis*] as well," and the acts commemorating the deaths were set forth in writing precisely that "honour might be rendered to God and comfort to men."[45] We do not know how many Christians were persecuted in the ante-Nicene church, but secular documents support Christian sources in supposing that the number was significant. Eusebius reported how some "women were tied by one foot and hoisted high in the air;" others had each leg fastened to two different tree boughs bent forward, after which the torturers "let the boughs fly back to their normal position; thus they managed to tear apart the limbs of their victims in a moment." It was thus "in this way they carried on, not for a few days or weeks, but year after year. Sometimes ten or more, sometimes over twenty were put to death, at other times at least thirty, and at yet others not far short of sixty; and there were occasions when on a single day a hundred men as well as women and little children were killed, condemned to a succession of ever-changing punishments."[46]

Many were martyred within arenas after official court pronouncements of condemnation; some of the acts, like those of the women Agapê, Irenê, Chionê, Agathonice, and Charito, and perhaps Crispina, are based on these court records. Other martyrs were massacred wholesale, like "a little Christian town in Phrygia," which was encircled and burned to the ground. "And why? Because all the inhabitants of the town without exception," Eusebius reported, "declared themselves Christian and absolutely refused to obey the command to commit idolatry."[47]

It is hard to read the acts without being struck by the spiritual equality that permeates the narratives. Women had the same obligation to bear witness as men; women spoke of themselves as men's spiritual equals; female martyrs were as equally revered by the Christian community as male martyrs; and women as well as men could and did emerge as leaders among the persecuted because the criterion was spiritual purity, not gender. On occasion we do identify elements of inequality surrounding the physical nature of women, but not the spiritual nature. Teachers, presbyters, and bishops are placed ahead of women in most martyr lists, but this may be due more to class prejudice than perceived spiritual inequality. In the eyes of the law, Christian women were subject to the same demands as Christian men of the same class,[48] although their tortures on the way to death were sometimes of a more sexual nature. Irenê was guilty not only of being a Christian but also hiding "so many tablets, books, parchments, codices, and pages of the writings of the former Christians,"[49] so she was sentenced for life to be placed "naked in the brothel."[50] Sabrina's interrogators told her after she laughed at them, "You are going to suffer something you do not like. Women who refuse to sacrifice are put into a brothel."[51]

Tortured women occasionally evoked more sympathy from the crowd and from interrogators. Eutychia's inquisitor "urge[d] Eutychia to cease this madness and to return to sound reason,"[52] so she and her unborn baby could be spared execution. Spectators and persecutors may have had different expectations in their dealings with women from what the reality was. Blandina's perseverance in the face of such repeated, prolonged, and gruesome tortures left the crowd in awe: "The pagans themselves admitted that no woman had ever suffered so much in their experience."[53] Sometimes captors' expectations led to swifter punishment. Ammonarion, Mecuna, Dionysia, and an unnamed woman were seized in a persecution at Alexandria and refused to submit: "The governor was ashamed to go on torturing without result and to be defeated by women, so they died by the sword without being put to any further test by torture."[54] Eutychia was imprisoned instead of being executed immediately, because she was seven months' pregnant.[55] When Agathonice removed her clothes prior to entering the arena, "the crowd saw how beautiful she was [and] they grieved in mourning for her."[56] In the end, though, the result was the same. Christians, male or female, who persisted in their witness became martyrs to the faith.

The story of Blandina reveals perhaps more than any other narrative the emphasis the early Christians put on a person's spiritual nature and on women's spiritual equality. During a persecution in Gaul, the prefect "publicly ordered a full-scale investigation of all Christians." The result was mass arrests and imprisonments. As the Christians "underwent torments beyond all description" while awaiting execution, they formed a tight-knit community. They looked to Sanctus, "a noble athlete . . . a pillar and ground of the community there, and on Blandina," a woman and a slave. What makes this upheaval of secular standards even more dramatic is that "Blandina's earthly mistress . . . was herself among the martyrs." Blandina's spiritual leadership among the imprisoned "proved that the things that men think cheap, ugly, and contemptuous are deemed worthy of glory before God."[57] It was Blandina's example that "aroused intense enthusiasm in those who were undergoing their ordeal," for they saw in Blandina as she hung on a post, hands stretched out in the form of a cross, "him who was crucified for them." With this visual image before them they once more believed that through their witness they would "have eternal fellowship in the living God." It was Blandina, a woman and a slave, "tiny, weak, and insignificant as she was" in the eyes of the world, who provided "inspiration to her brothers" as they faced their tortures.[58] The tormentors recognized Blandina's strength and initiated an intense campaign to break her. The crowd grew angrier and angrier at her and her perseverance. She was brought into the arena everyday to watch the torture of her fellow Christians and forced to swear to the pagan gods. A boy of fifteen, Ponticus, was also singled out by the officials, and together Blandina and Ponticus were subjected "to every atrocity and led . . . through every torture" to make them abandon their witness. The crowd soon "realized that she was urging him on and strengthening him," and so he was executed. Blandina was the only Christian left "on the last day of the gladiatorial games." After one final scourging, branding, and animal baiting, she was "tossed into a net and exposed to a bull" and died.[59]

In the act of Saint Crispina we have a portrait of a different kind. Crispina was a lady of Toura of obvious high social standing. The act relates her interrogation by the proconsul Anullinus. The conflict between pagan and Christian ways was played out on a theological plane rather than in an arena. Anullinus verbally attacked the "folly of [Crispina's] mind," and Crispina offered statements of faith to defend it. As they bantered back and forth it became apparent to Anullinus that his reasons were not persuading Crispina, and, in frustration, he tried to see if physical humiliation would weaken her will. His command, "Let her be completely disfigured by having her hair cut and her head shaved with a razor till she is bald,"[60] did not help him attain his desired goal. Crispina persisted in the dialogue and drew the combat back to the theological plane as her disdain for the pagan gods became more pronounced. "I should be very happy to lose my head for the sake of my God," Crispina proclaimed. "For I refuse to sacrifice to these ridiculous deaf and dumb statues."[61] Frustrated, Anullinus refused to "suffer this impious Christian woman any further," had the minutes of her trial read from the record, and "ordered her to be executed with the sword."[62]

Similarly, in the *Martyrdom of Saints Agapê, Irenê, and Chionê at Saloniki* and their companions Agatha, Cassia, Philippa, and Eutychia, the narrative that is passed on to generations is focused on the reasoned defense all the women offered to their captives, not their physical tortures (although their sentences were mentioned). All were already strong, determined, and tested women by the time they were captured, for during the persecution of Maximian they "abandoned their native city, their family, property, and possessions . . . and took refuge on a high mountain."[63] At their trial the prefect Dulcitus was impressed by the persistence they exhibited "for such a long time, in spite of strong warnings and so many decrees, sanctioned by stern threats"[64] to remain Christian. Perhaps their fortitude aroused admiration, for after the first hearing he condemned only Agapê and Chionê to death. Agatha, Irenê, Cassia, and Philippa were imprisoned temporarily because of their youth; Eutychia was imprisoned because of her youth and her pregnancy. After the two older women "were consumed in the flames," Irenê was called again before Dulcitus and questioned at length about all the Christian reading material she possessed. Here we are given a glimpse into Irenê's perception of her own spiritual nature. When asked who advised her "to retain those parchments and writings," she said, "It was God Almighty." Dulcitus persisted and demanded to know whether any of her family or friends knew about her possessions. Again she adamantly denied that anyone did. It is quite clear that Irenê believed her spiritual life to be beyond the control of any person, male or female. She was spiritually free, and the books that the women read every night and day nourished them and kept them spiritually free.[65] She was answerable only to God. If she was socially, legally, and physically dependent on men, she was spiritually independent. Dulcitus then took another tack and inquired about the women's flight into the mountains the year before. Here the answer is even more surprising. The seven women plotted and carried out their escape by themselves. For a year they survived by themselves, living off the land, contrary to every expectation, until the first persecution stopped. Dulcitus was beyond amazement.

"Was your father aware of this?" asked the prefect.

Irenê answered: "I swear by almighty God, he was not aware; he knew nothing at all about it.

"Were any of your neighbors aware of this?" asked the prefect.

Irenê answered: "Go and question our neighbors, and inquire about the area to see whether anyone knew where we were."[66]

The women's source of strength was their self-perception. Ultimately, only the spiritual world mattered, and, ultimately, they had to answer only to God. Thus they could and did bypass all familiar, legal, and social restraints, and acted only in accord with the demands of their spiritual nature. If they had considered their spiritual natures to be inferior to that of men's, presumably they would have not acted without male hierarchical approval. They also believed their spiritual being to be superior to all other aspects of their life. When asked by Dulcitus why she disobeyed "the command of our lords the emperors and Caesars," Cassia answered quite to the point: "I wish to save my soul."[67]

Of all the acts of the martyrs, male or female, none has been more popular or influential than *The Martyrdom of Saints Perpetua and Felicitas.* The tale itself became a model for all later acts,[68] and Perpetua became one of the most admired and well-known martyrs of all times. The act was read publicly in the African church to the whole community, and during Augustine's time it was sometimes regarded with the same reverence given Scripture.[69] The popularity of Perpetua and Felicitas was not limited solely to the African church; by the end of the fourth century their feasts were commemorated in the Philocalen calendar at Rome and the Syriac calendar at Antioch. Arguably, Perpetua and Felicitas were the most universally honored saints in all calendars and martyrologies during Late Antiquity. Of all the Christians martyred during nearly four centuries of persecution, why did two women foster so much devotion and attention?

The story of their martyrdom is gripping, all the more so since Perpetua wrote her own story. In 203 five friends were arrested at Carthage during persecutions initiated by Septimius Severus; two of them were women, Perpetua and the slave Felicitas. At the time of her arrest Perpetua was twenty-two, had just given birth, and was not yet a baptized Christian. Their incarceration prior to their hearing was mild, and she received a visit from her father, who was intent upon dissuading her from becoming a Christian. When she resolutely refused, "he moved towards me as though he would pluck my eyes out," and then he departed. She was baptized a few days later and "gave thanks to the Lord that I was separated from my father." Perpetua was grateful for his absence, because she was obviously very close to her family ("I was in pain because I saw them suffering out of pity for me") and, in particular, to her father. "I have favored you above all your brothers," he reminded her as he tried once again to persuade her to abandon Christianity after the group was moved to a prison. Perpetua knew he "spoke out of love for me" and that "he alone of all my kin would be unhappy to see me suffer," yet her spiritual ties were stronger than her familial ties.[70]

The companions finally were called to the forum for a hearing, and here her father tried for a third time to dissuade her. His attempt ended in angering the governor, who then ordered the father "thrown to the ground and beaten with a rod." Perpetua was forced to look on as her father was humiliated in "his pathetic old age," and she felt "just as if I myself had been beaten." The hearing continued, and the sentence was passed: They were all "condemned to the beasts."[71] Not one to give up, her father came to Perpetua a fourth and final time, immediately preceding the gladiatorial games. The scene was repeated, with the same result. However sorry Perpetua was for his anguish over her imminent death, she remained resolute.

Perpetua's dual roles as mother and daughter made her decision extraordinarily painful. Her love and concern for her newborn son permeated her narrative. She wrote that she was "terrified" when they were moved to the unsanitary, stifling prison because "to crown all, I was tortured with worry for my baby there." The prison held many other Christians, though, besides the five companions, and two of those were deacons who "bribed soldiers to allow us to go to a better part of the prison" so Perpetua could nurse her baby. Her fear drove her to give the baby to her mother and brother to care for, but she was miserable without him. Somehow she got permission to take the baby back in prison, and "at once I recovered my health, relieved as I was of my worry and anxiety over the child. My prison had suddenly become a palace, so that I wanted to be there rather than anywhere else."[72] Sometime before the hearing Perpetua gave her son to the care of her family again, because when her father arrived at the hearing he brought the baby. After she refused to recant and received her death sentence, her first thoughts focused on her son and her desire to have him with her during her final days. Her father, still angry at her decision, refused to give him back to her. Her heartache was made more bearable, however, because the baby, who "had got used to being nursed at the breast," at this very time weaned himself and "had no further desire for the breast." Satisfied that she had been able to complete her maternal task of nourishment, she rejoiced "and so I was relieved of my anxiety for my child."[73]

Besides giving a detailed account of the emotional cost of her decision to abandon her earthly obligations as daughter and mother, Perpetua provided an account of four visions she has while awaiting execution. The first vision came before the sentencing. Her brother suggested to her that she ask for a vision so she could find out whether she was going to be condemned or freed. "Faithfully I promised that I would, for I knew that I could speak with the Lord, whose great blessings I had come to experience."[74] She was correct; she received her answer: They were all to die. Her second vision was of a brother, Dinocrates, who had died of cancer at age seven. In her vision she saw him suffering. "I was confident that I could help him . . . and I prayed for my brother day and night."[75] A third vision revealed her request granted; Dinocrates' suffering ceased.

Her fourth vision occurred the "day before we were to fight with the beast"[76] and served to calm her fears and to strengthen her confidence in victory. She was brought into the arena, but she was confused because there were no beasts to fight. Instead, an intimidating Egyptian appeared and readied to do battle with her: "My clothes were stripped off and suddenly I was a man." Yet another man appeared of "marvelous stature," taller than the walls of the amphitheater itself. He carried "a green branch on which there were golden apples," and announced to the crowd that Perpetua would receive the branch if she defeated the Egyptian. After Perpetua "kept striking him in the face" and "began to pummel him," the Egyptian "fell flat on his face" and Perpetua "stepped on his head." She began her triumphant walk toward the Porta Sanavivaria (Gate of Life) and "then I awoke. I realized that it was not with wild animals that I would fight but with the Devil, but I knew that I would win the victory."[77] With this last entry on the eve of the contests Perpetua ends her account.[78]

Perpetua commissioned an anonymous author to continue her story. It is this author who tells us the story of Felicitas and the death of all the martyrs. Felicitas gave birth to a girl two days before the fight. When one of the guards taunted her because she found the delivery so difficult and then claimed she would never be able to withstand the tortures of the beasts, she stoutly answered, "'What I am suffering now, I suffer by myself. But then another will be inside who will suffer for me, just as I shall be suffering for him.'"[79] On the designated day the prisoners were marched into the arena. When the women were stripped naked to fight a mad heifer, "even the crowd was horrified when they saw that one was a delicate young girl and the other was a woman fresh from childbirth with the milk still dripping from her breasts." The first encounter with the heifer left Perpetua and Felicitas alive, but after a respite when Perpetua gathered all the Christians around her to encourage them to "all stand fast in the faith and love one another,"[80] they were called back into the center of the arena and put to death by sword. "Perpetua, however, had to taste yet more pain. She screamed as she was struck on the bone; then she took the trembling hand of the young gladiator and guided it to her throat. It was as though so great a woman, feared as she was by the unclean spirit, could not be dispatched unless she herself were willing."[81]

So ended the magnificent tale of Christianity's most popular martyrs. Whereas Perpetua's narrative about her earthly life indicated the superior position given the spiritual life, her narrative of the visions indicated both her and her companions' belief in the spiritual equality of men and women. Perpetua, "the beloved of God," the "wife of Christ,"[82] was the recognized spiritual leader of the martyrs. Only when she needed help meeting the physical needs of her baby did she turn to men to help her. In all other instances she was in charge of her destiny. She represented the martyrs in negotiations with the persecutors. She shamed the persecutors into allowing the Christians to keep their physical dignity ("'Why can you not even allow us to refresh ourselves properly?'" Perpetua demanded of the tribune. "So it was that he gave the order that they were to be more humanely treated.")[83] and, more important, their spiritual dignity (when forced to put on pagan robes, "Perpetua strenuously resisted this to the end. . . . 'We agreed to pledge our lives provided that we would do no such thing.'" The tribune relented).[84] Spiritual leadership in any religious group is rooted in the group's recognition of a person's spiritual worth. Perpetua's brother had no doubt about this: "Dear sister, you are greatly privileged." Perpetua had no doubt about it: "I knew that I could speak with the Lord."[85] She knew through experience that she had direct access to God, and the community of Christians accepted this as fact. When Perpetua returned dazed and not able to recollect the events surrounding her first bout in the arena, the rest of the Christians assumed it was because "so absorbed had she been in ecstasy in the Spirit."[86] No one doubted that such an intense, intimate relationship between God and a woman was possible. Nor did Perpetua doubt that a woman could intercede spiritually on behalf of a man; she prayed for Dinocrates, and his suffering stopped. Her final vision, the most complex, was also Perpetua's most unequivocal statement about women's spiritual equality. To beat the Egyptian physically in her vision she must physically become a man. But when she awoke from her sleep, she "realized that it was not with wild animals [the physical enemy] that I would fight [in the arena] but with the Devil [a spiritual enemy]." With the realization that the real battle was a spiritual one, she knew she "would win the victory"; she knew her spiritual worth. She need not turn into a man spiritually. She was not spiritually inferior in any way and could easily defeat the devil.[87]

3

Fourth-Century Theologians

THE THEOLOGIANS OF THE CRUCIAL FOURTH CENTURY did not alter the received scriptural definition of humanity in any radical way; rather they continued to elaborate on the insights articulated during the first three centuries. Gregory of Nyssa, an original thinker in so many areas, did not attempt to be creative in matters of Christian anthropology. Instead, he contemplated the same key scriptural verses that were central in the formation of Christianity's first definition of humanity and simply made them more accessible and persuasive. *On the Making of Man* was the chief vehicle for his anthropology, and within that treatise Genesis 1:26 was the chief source for his conclusions. "In what then does the greatness of man [anthropos] consist, according to the doctrine of the church? Not in his likeness to the created world, but in his being in the image of the nature of the Creator."[1]

The exact, precise nature of this image "perhaps only the very Truth knows,"[2] but if we "take up once more the Holy Scripture itself" we "may perhaps find some guidance." After the statement of humanity's image and likeness to God, "it adds this saying: 'And God created man [anthropos]; in the image of God created He him; male and female created He them.'"[3] The likeness does not reside in the color of the eye or the eyebrow, "but instead of these, [in] the purity, freedom from passion, blessedness, alienation from all evil, and all those attributes of the like kind."[4] More important, "the Godhead is mind and word," and "you see in yourself word and understanding, an imitation of the very Mind and Word." Since "God is love," love too is an essential characteristic of humanity's nature, for "if this be absent, the whole stamp of the likeness" is diminished.[5] "The greatness of man consist," therefore, not in being a microcosm of the world, as some of Gregory's contemporaries held, but in "being in the image of the nature of the Creator."[6] By reflecting further upon these passages, Gregory concluded the following:

> I think that by these words Holy Scripture conveys to us a great and
> lofty doctrine; and the doctrine is this. While two natures—the Divine
> and incorporeal nature, and the irrational life of brutes—are separated
> from each other as extremes, human nature is the mean between them:
> for in the compound nature of man we may behold a part of each of
> the natures I have mentioned,—of the Divine, the rational and intelli-
> gent element, which does not admit the distinction of male and female;
> of the irrational, our bodily form and structure, divided into male and
> female: for each of these elements is certainly to be found in all that
> partakes of human life.[7]

Gregory believed that this revelation has much to teach us. It tells us that
there is in every man and woman "the principle of all excellence, all virtue
and wisdom, and every higher thing we conceive."[8] It also meant that "we
are free from necessity, and not in bondage to any natural power, but have
decision in our own power as we please."[9] And, Gregory stated twice, the
passage specifically applied to all humans who "equally bear in themselves
the Divine image."[10] The word *man, [anthropos]*, referred to "all mankind,"[11]
male and female as a whole, the fullness of all humans, past, present, and
future. "The name given to the man created is not the particular, but the
general name: thus we are led by the employment of the general name of
our nature to some such view as this—that in Divine foreknowledge and
power all humanity is included in the first creation."[12]

For Gregory, the mystery of humanity was revealed in Genesis 1:26-
27. He rarely referred to Genesis 2:7 and never considered the text crucial
to a definition of humanity. Humans were made in the image and likeness
of God. Humanity's goal was to "re-form" itself into its original form in the
Garden, a spiritualized body of that image. This was definitely not a denial
of the body, for Gregory considered the unity of spirit and body absolutely
essential to its relationship to the Divine, nor was it a denial of the sexual
nature of humans. Gregory's anthropology did, however, place less importance on the sexual division of humanity, because his focus was on the nature
of humanity prior to the Fall. Sexual division was present prior to the Fall,
but it "was added to His work last"[13] because sex was not functional in the
Garden as a means of procreation, nor was "the desire that tends to procreation."[14] Only after the Fall did these things come. God "by exercise of His
foreknowledge" did not have to wait till after the Fall to see "the failure of
their will" to keep the good course, hence He "formed for our nature that
contrivance for increase," meaning sexual reproduction, "which befits those
who had fallen into sin."[15] In short, God is undivided because He is perfect;

humanity is divided because it is imperfect. The resurrected, perfected body after Judgment Day will be the pre-Fall, predivided body.

The male and the female aspect of humanity played a minor role in Gregory's anthropology. While today's psychologists may have innumerable problems with such an interpretation of sexuality in a definition of humanity, historians must judge it on different terms. What is significant to our study here is that Gregory's anthropology placed men and women on a spiritually level playing field. By deemphasizing whether a person was male or female and emphasizing instead their commonality as humans made in the image of God, the basis for discrimination was greatly reduced. Here women were not inferior to men, because women as well as men were "the image of that nature which is immortal, pure, and everlasting."[16] Contemporary social, legal, or economic discrimination of women could not be justified by Gregory's anthropology, but, on the other hand, neither were they explicitly attacked. They were simply left unexamined and unchallenged.

While *On the Making of Man* contains the fullest expression of Gregory's anthropology, he referred often to his understanding of humanity's nature in his other writings. *On the Soul and the Resurrection* is a treatise premised on his definition. It is of particular interest to us because Gregory wrote this treatise in the form of a dialogue between his sister Macrina and himself. The theological discussion of the nature of the soul was a thinly veiled Christianization of Plato's *Phaedo* and came from the mouth of Macrina. The occasion for the discourse was a visit Gregory made to Macrina after the death of their brother, the renowned Basil. This family was unique in Christianity for the number of influential and brilliant members it included. Macrina the Elder was the grandmother, Emmelia the mother, and Basil, Macrina, Peter, and Gregory of Nyssa the children; all are revered as saints. When we examine the dynamics of the family we find Macrina, "the Teacher," as Gregory called her, at the spiritual and emotional center. Gregory wrote that it was Macrina who turned Basil around when he "returned after his long period of education . . . puffed up beyond measure." She promptly "took him in hand" and redirected his attention and energies to the spiritual life. Next Macrina "persuaded her mother to give up her ordinary life"[17] and "to adopt [Macrina's] own standard of humility."[18] After Peter was born Macrina "reared him herself and educated him on a lofty system of training, practicing him from infancy in holy studies," and thus Peter was "always looking to his sister as the model of all good."[19] When the death of another brother (Naucratus) devastated her mother, Macrina "becoming a prop for her mother's weakness, raised her up from the abyss of grief," in spite of the "natural affection" Macrina herself felt for this "favorite brother" she had lost.[20] Gregory likewise depended on Macrina for comfort at the death of Basil, and "so I journeyed to her," Gregory wrote, "yearning for an interchange of sympathy over the loss of her brother."[21] *On the Soul and the Resurrection* is Gregory's summary of this visit. He again insisted that the treatise contained Macrina's theological interpretations in his *The Life of St. Macrina.*

> When in the course of conversation mention was made of the great Basil, my soul saddened and my face fell dejectedly. But so far was she from sharing in my affection that, treating the mention of the saint as an occasion for yet loftier philosophy, she discussed various subjects, inquiring into human affairs and revealing in her conversation the divine purpose concealed in disasters. Besides this, she discussed the future life, as if inspired by the Holy Spirit, so that it almost seemed as if my soul were lifted by the help of her words away from mortal nature and placed within the heavenly sanctuary. . . . [S]he discoursed to us on the nature of the soul and explained the reason of life in the flesh, and why man was made, and how he was mortal, and the origin of death and the nature of the journey from death to life again. In all of which she told her tale clearly and consecutively as if inspired by the power of the Holy Spirit.[22]

These statements of Gregory have long been dismissed because of the obvious Platonic molding of the treatise. The presence of Platonic influence, however, does not eliminate the possibility of Macrina's influence.[23] At best, *On the Soul and Resurrection* contains the understanding a fourth-century woman had of Christianity's definition of humanity, filtered through a male theologian. At least, we have a treatise containing what a male theologian considered acceptable for a woman to believe about human nature.

Gregory's anxiety revealed itself in his doubts about whether the soul outlives the death of the body. "The soul itself," Macrina replied, "is a competent instructress," who tells us she "is an essence created, and living, and intellectual."[24] The soul's power is so awe-inspiring that it is tempting to conclude "that the Deity and the Mind of man are identical."[25] Macrina herself continually emphasized the dignity of the soul but stopped short of what she considered a blasphemous conclusion. "Rather," she told Gregory, "as the Scripture tells you, say that the one is *like* the other. For that which is 'made in the image' of the Deity necessarily possesses a likeness to its prototype in every respect; it resembles it in being intellec- tual, immaterial, unconnected with any notion of weight, and in eluding any measurement of its dimensions."[26] However great this resemblance is, it is at all times an image, for "it would be no longer an 'image' if it were altogether identical with that other; but where we have *A* in that uncreated prototype, we have *a* in the image." Our greatness lies in the fact that "those ineffable qualities of Deity shine forth within the narrow limits of our nature."[27] Our creation in God's image also means we possess free will, which in turn means the soul can choose "whatever it may wish to be,"[28] including becoming "wholly and thoroughly carnal in thought."[29] To avoid that predicament we must, "whether by forethought here, or by purgation hereafter," free our soul "from any emotional connection" with the brute creation, and then "there will be nothing to impede its contemplation of the Beautiful . . . the Deity."[30]

Throughout the treatise Macrina has nothing to say about the sexual differentiation of humans. The focal point of her faith is God as creator and His creation of the soul of humans in His image. "The speculative, critical, world-surveying faculty of the soul is its peculiar property by virtue of its very nature, and that thereby the soul preserves within itself the image of the divine grace";[31] the creation of the body is not in God's image and, therefore, is of no concern to her. At no point does she indicate that a female body—or a male body, for that matter—diminishes or increases the soul's image and likeness of God. She includes her own soul in the discussion of the nature of the soul and repeatedly insists that the whole of "humanity is, in a way, like God."[32] The anthropology spoken by Macrina in *On the Soul and the Resurrection* is the same we have seen articulated by Gregory in *On the Making of Man*, probably written in the same year, 380, and together they provide a thorough discussion of the topic.

Other theologians from the immediate post-Nicean world are not as easy to interpret as Gregory of Nyssa. None expressed an anthropology as fully developed as he. All of them had opinions about women, and most discussed basic beliefs about humanity at some point in their writings. Their overwhelming reference point was Genesis 1:26. Athanasius, the most important theologian in the first half of the fourth century, wrote that God made "the human race after His own image, and constituted man able to see and know realities by means of this assimilation to Himself," and that the "purity of soul is sufficient of itself to reflect God."[33] Leo the Great argued that God "gave much to humanity at our origin, when He made us according to His image."[34] According to Hilary of Poitiers, "through the knowledge of God a human being becomes the perfect image of God. Through godliness a human being gains immortality, and through immortality a human being shall live forever as the image of his Creator."[35]

Many theologians sent mixed messages. Their written works contained some passages that acknowledged women's spiritual equality and some that implied such inequality in related matters that the sincerity of their belief in spiritual equality is called into question. Other theologians enjoyed friendships and relationships with women that belie the harsh statements found in their writings. Jerome and John Chrysostom are two such theologians. John Chrysostom, writing to a young monk tempted to marry, warns that a woman's "bodily beauty is only a white-washed tombstone, for inside it is full of filth,"[36] but in his own life, Olympias was one of his dearest, most trusted friends, and their friendship was based on their spiritual affinity. "I am cheered, light-hearted, and not in a light way proud on account of your greatness of soul, and the repeated victories you have won," John wrote to her. "And this, not only for your own sake, but also for that large and populous city [Constantinople] where you are like a tower, a haven, and a wall of defense, speaking with the eloquence of example and through your suffering instructing both sexes."[37] We even see John extend his understanding of friendship to include elements beyond a spiritual relationship. When he was sent in exile during a political conflict, John and Olympias's friendship was tested by the physical separation, and John lamented thus: "To those who love each other, it is not enough to be linked at soul-level. This does not comfort them, but they need physical presence."[38]

Jerome is likewise enigmatic. The virtual disgust for things pertaining to a woman's physical being that he enunciates in some of his letters makes it difficult at first to consider him capable of holding any positive attitudes toward women, but his opinion of women's spiritual nature was indeed positive. Those whom Jerome admired most were women, and he admired them for their spiritual capabilities. "Who can recall without a sigh the earnestness of her prayers, the brilliancy of her conversation, the tenacity of her memory, and the quickness of her intellect," Jerome wrote at the death of Blaesilla, his dearest friend Paula's daughter. "As I think of her my eyes fill with tears, sobs impede my voice, and such is my emotion that my tongue cleaves to the roof of my mouth."[39] About a third of his large collection of letters are addressed to women with whom he shared friendships. To Marcella, he confides his discoveries "—to speak quite frankly to a friend—"[40] and to Eustochium, a gracious thank-you letter for "doves, bracelets, and a letter."[41] It was Paula, however, to whom he felt the deepest bond of friendship, and during the last twenty years of her life, she and Jerome lived the monastic life side by side in two monasteries she founded in Bethlehem. Jerome's letter commemorating Paula's death is among his longest and rivals his commemoration of Blaesilla in eloquence. It is impossible to read any of these letters and not identify a friendship build on true spiritual equality.

These examples are significant, for, as Rosemary Rader argues, "true friendship, by definition, presumes a sense of equality."[42] Early Christian communities were exceptional, in that heterosexual friendships flourished within them "to a degree not possible in Jewish or Greco-Roman communities."[43] These friendships flourished among all classes. Besides the friendship of famous individuals preserved in early Christian literature, we also know that the formation of male-female friendships were quite common in the prisons for the persecuted. Here their common belief in their mutual spiritual destinies helped forge friendship that would see the martyrs to their end, as the acts of the Christian martyrs attest to again and again. The friendships formed among the martyrs of Lyons and in Perpetua and Felicitas's group is evident throughout the narratives of their deaths. Rader argues that celibacy was the key to those friendships, and certainly that would be compatible with the theology reviewed here. In the spiritual realm women were equal to men. A vow of celibacy freed them to contend only with their spiritual and equal nature. Friendships based on acknowledged spiritual equality was possible.

There is no doubt, however, that despite the argument that male theologians perhaps did not live what they preached, their negative appraisals of women were read and repeated. Whether there were more negative comments than positive ones is difficult if not impossible to assess. Gregory Nazianzen is extreme when drawing logical conclusions from women's spiritual equality; if they are spiritually equal to men, then why do governments and laws make them unequal? "There is only one Creator of man and of woman, one dust from which both have come, one image [of God], one law, one death, one resurrection," so Gregory will not approve of human laws that make men and women unequal, such as the one absolving husbands from infidelity but condemning women. "I do not accept this legislation; I do not approve this custom," he writes. "The law was made by men, and for that reason it is directed against women."[44] Theodoretos of Cyrrhos comes close to agreeing with Gregory Nazianzen but stops short of extending the logic of his argument—"God prescribes the same laws to men and to women, since their difference resides in the structure of the body, and not in the soul"—into the legal realm. Instead, he is content to note its application in the liturgical world: "[T]he law which permits [men] to take part in the divine mysteries does not forbid [women] and even orders them, like the men, to be initiated to the divine mysteries and to take part in them."[45]

Ambrose presents us with an anthropology and theology of womanhood containing both positive and negative themes that is somewhat typical of the post-Nicean church fathers. "Our soul, therefore, is made to the image of God," Ambrose begins, but the flesh "cannot be made to the image of God."[46] In his treatise *Hexameron* Ambrose argues that "in Genesis the word 'soul' is used for man" and that "the soul is called *homo* in Latin and *anthropos* in Greek, the former being derived from 'humanity' and the latter from a word associated with the lively faculty of 'seeing.'"[47] He therefore implicitly acknowledges that woman is made in the image of God, but in another treatise, *Paradise*, he also associates woman with the body, which is mortal and not in the image of God. Here he states that "the woman stands for our senses and the man, for our minds."[48] Since Satan presents himself in the garden as "a type of the pleasures of the body," Eve is condemned before Adam.[49] Eve's guilt is mitigated by her admission of wrongdoing, and thus she receives "a milder and more salutary sentence" than Adam.[50]

As in most of his thought, Augustine's anthropology is complex, at times contradictory, and always influential. It is his influence that makes his opinions about women crucial to our investigation. Many of the early, lesser-known Christian writers, particularly those whose works did not circulate widely, have been of interest to us here as providing examples of opinions current in that period, not as ones whose thoughts shaped future opinions. With Augustine we have ample evidence to indicate that his usefulness to us and his greatness lie in the influence he exerted over centuries of Christian thought. We must judge his work not as typical of his day but as atypical, as is all work of genius. This is not to say he started anew or reinvented Christianity. His work is firmly rooted in Scripture, and he is thoroughly versed in the writings of all other Christian writers. His interpretation of women's spiritual nature is at the same time traditional and innovative, positive and negative.

Probably the biggest problem in trying to assess Augustine's opinions on women is that they underwent development as his theology matured. The fact that he was such a prolific writer does not make it easier for the historian; with so many passages on the subject, identifying consistencies, inconsistencies, and stages of development sometimes can be daunting. Interpreters of Augustine throughout the centuries have reached very different conclusions about his thought, despite always using his own words to support their theses. We should begin, then, by noting that some scholars have accused Augustine, given the influence he had enjoyed throughout Christianity, of being primarily responsible for Christian misogyny.[51] Others have come to his defense, exonerating him completely,[52] while still others have stood somewhere in between.[53] We will not attempt to label Augustine one way or the other but rather to draw attention to his positive perceptions without denying his negative opinions.

Augustine's anthropology is scattered throughout much of his writing, not the least being *Confessions* and *City of God*, his two greatest and most-read masterpieces. More formal analyses of humanity are found in his books dealing with Genesis, such as *On Genesis against the Manichaeans, One Unfinished Book on the Literal Meaning of Genesis*, and *On the Literal Meaning of Genesis*; his tracts *On Holy Virginity, On the Good of Marriage*, and *The Trinity*, as well as his *Retractions* are also helpful in determining his stance on women. We must remember to place everything Augustine wrote about women in the context of his time. The fourth century was beset with controversies concerning creation and anthropology. On the one hand were Pelagius and Jovinian, and on the other hand were the Manichaeans. Pelagius called many aspects of Genesis into question and, in particular, challenged Augustine's teaching on the need for grace to remain chaste. Jovinian disputed the Christian elevation of virginity, and the Manichaeans preached about the evils of sex. It is no surprise to find that Augustine's first arguments were constructed to refute one of these unorthodox groups, the Manichaeans.[54] He was not too comfortable with his argument, though, and a few years later he modified his stance slightly; in his last years he approached the scriptural passages on creation differently yet again. He treated them symbolically, while at the same time he acknowledged them to be historically accurate.

As his interpretation changed, so his appreciation for women's spiritual nature grew. He recognized women as the possessors in full of the image and likeness of God, as stated in Genesis 1:26, and when discussing Genesis 1:26-27 in *The Trinity* he emphasized the spiritual equality of woman. "For [Paul] says that human nature itself, which is complete in both sexes, has been made to the image of God, and he does not exclude the woman from being understood as the image of God." Apparently, some part of Augustine was not comfortable with unlimited equality, so he argued that woman's equality does not extend beyond the spiritual. Only "with her husband" is she the image of God, "but when she is assigned as a help-mate, a function that pertains to her alone, then she is not the image of God."[55] Like so many theologians before him, when Augustine turned to Genesis 2:18-24, woman slipped from the platform of equality into a position of subordination. In Genesis 1 Eve is *homo*, and as such equal to Adam; in Genesis 2 she is *femina*, and as such subordinate to Adam.

The question of image became even more complicated when Augustine tried to reconcile Genesis 1:26 with Genesis 2:18 and Paul's contradictory statement in 1 Corinthians 11:7.

> We should then take the expression "God created man" to refer to his spirit; whereas the statement "God formed man," would apply to his

body. But they do not realize that there could have been no distinction of male and female except in relation to the body. There is, of course, the subtle theory that the mind of man, being a form of rational life and precisely the part in which he is made to the image of God, is partly occupied with the contemplation of eternal truth and partly with the administration of temporal things, and thus it is made, in a sense, masculine and feminine, the masculine part as the planner, the feminine as the one that obeys. But it is not in this double function that the image of God is found, but rather in that part which is devoted to the contemplation of immutable truth.[56]

"The image of God," Augustine tells us, "does not remain except in that part of the mind of man in which it clings to the contemplation and consideration of eternal reason, which, as is evident, not only men but also women possess." Given this truth, "who is it, then, that would exclude women from the fellowship" in Christ?[57] In other works, however, Augustine argued a woman's subordination is natural, because man is "the more honorable sex," and "the weaker mind should serve the stronger."[58] Even in his autobiographical *Confessions* Augustine took time to give thanks for woman's subordination, for "in her mind and her rational intelligence she has a nature the equal of man's, but in sex she is physically subject to him in the same way as our natural impulses need to be subjected to the reasoning power of the mind."[59] A similar statement is found in *The Literal Meaning of Genesis*, where Augustine repeated three times in one passage that even though woman's physical body would lead one to think she was not made in the image of God, her rational mind proved she was man's equal and made in God's image.[60]

Like Ambrose, Augustine emphasized God's purpose in creating woman: She is man's helper. The primary help man needs from woman is in producing offspring. All other needs could be met just as well by another man. "For what food is to the health of the body, coition is to the health of the race,"[61] and for procreation man needs woman. Furthermore, nothing else God creates is as similar to man as woman, so the two will find compatibility in living the married life together. Marriage was a good for Augustine (he commented in *Retractions* that he wrote *On Marriage and Concupiscence* to "defend the good of marriage to prevent the belief that marriage is vitiated by 'the concupiscence of the flesh.'"),[62] so the relationship between husband and wife must likewise be good. The woman's role as man's helper did not mean that a husband was free to mistreat his wife. "Saint Paul says: Serve each other in love. He would never say 'Dominate each other.'"[63]

These are some of the passages that future generations were exposed to and often used for reference and authority. In the case of Augustine, however, his writings on personal relationships with individual women are almost as important in assessing any impact he had on Christianity's understanding of women's spiritual nature as are his formal theological treatises. Augustine, thanks to his superb, gripping autobiography, is not merely a theologian; he is a fellow Christian with whom the reader feels a personal relationship after being allowed into the deepest and most intimate recesses of his being. Because we know Augustine at levels we rarely if ever experience with any historical person, his personal witness has a unique power. How he treated women in his life and how he wrote about real women in *Confessions* may have had more historical impact than his abstract writings about women in general.

In *Confessions* Augustine placed two women center stage: Monica, his mother, and his nameless concubine. After Augustine, we probably know more about Monica than any other character in his autobiography; one could argue that one cannot know Augustine without Monica. She was the anchor, the love, the chief relationship in his life, and Augustine's descriptions of her and their love are among the most touching passages in his narrative. Augustine wrote much about her. "Her good upbringing had been due not so much to the attentiveness of her mother as to the care of an aged servant" who was treated "as an honored member of their Christian household."[64] At the proper age Monica was married to Patricius, Augustine's father (about whom Augustine has very little to say, except in relation to Monica).[65] After Augustine's birth his mother and his nurses gave him "the comfort of woman's milk . . . because they loved me in the way that you had ordained;"[66] admiration for female servants and the role they played in child rearing was common to both Monica and Augustine. Monica worried about him in motherly ways during his adolescence. When Augustine was sixteen, his father "saw signs of active virility coming to life" in Augustine at the public baths and began to "relish the thought of having grandchildren." Monica's reaction was not one of happiness but worry as "she began to dread that I might follow in the crooked path."[67]

They remained very close as Augustine entered into adulthood, and at one point he found motherly love perhaps a "too jealous love." When Augustine decided to leave Carthage and move to Rome, "She wept bitterly to see me go and followed me to the water's edge, clinging to me with all her strength in the hope that I would either come home or take her with me." Telling her the wind was not proper yet for sailing, Augustine got her to spend the night in a shrine not far from the ship. Then "during the night, secretly, I sailed away," Augustine related. He excused Monica's behavior, though, and attributed it to two factors. First, "as mothers do, and far more than most, she loved to have me with her," and, second, she did not know that his trip to Rome eventually would answer her most ardent desire for him—conversion to Christianity.[68]

It is in this realm of the spiritual that Augustine and Monica developed their adult relationship. We never hear the slightest hint that Augustine's appreciation of this "chaste, devout, and prudent woman"[69] was diminished because of her sex. Throughout his work we see Augustine offer her, beyond the respect due her as mother, the respect due a virtuous Christian. As Augustine began his journey toward conversion, his appreciation for Monica's spiritual capacity and her asceticism increased even more. He became very aware "how much greater was the anxiety she suffered for my spiritual birth than the physical pain she had endured in bringing me into the world."[70] After a short stay in Rome, Augustine took a position in Milan and came into contact with Ambrose, whose preaching brought Augustine even closer to Christianity. Monica moved to Milan once her son got settled, and she too developed a friendship with Ambrose. Augustine reported that Ambrose "too had warmed to her for her truly pious way of life, her zeal in good works, and her regular church going" and that often "he would break out in praise of her."[71]

There is no doubt in Augustine's mind that he found his God in Christianity "because my mother, your faithful servant, wept to you for me, shedding more tears for my spiritual death than other mother shed for the bodily death of a son."[72] Their relationship intensified after Augustine's conversion and entered a new phase as their spiritual life deepened simultaneously. In one of the rarest passages in mystical literature, Augustine described at length a particular experience they shared, when "my mother and I were alone" one afternoon, gazing out a window overlooking their garden. They wondered what heaven would be like.

> Our conversation led us to the conclusion that no bodily pleasure, however great it might be and whatever earthly light might shed lustre upon it, was worthy of comparison, or even of mention, beside the happiness of the life of the saints. As the flame of love burned stronger in us and raised us higher towards the eternal God, our thoughts ranged over the whole compass of material things in their various degrees, up to the heavens themselves, from which the sun and the moon and the stars shine down upon the earth. Higher still we climbed, thinking and speaking all the while in wonder at all that you have made. At length we came to our own souls and passed beyond them to that place of

everlasting plenty. . . . And while we spoke of the eternal Wisdom, longing for it and straining for it with all the strength of our hearts, for one fleeting instant we reached out and touched it. Then with a sigh, leaving our spiritual harvest bound to it, we returned to the sound of our own speech, in which each word has a beginning and an ending— far, far different from your Word, our Lord. . . .[73]

It would be hard to imagine a greater testimony to the spiritual equality of man and woman. The man whom many have judged to be the greatest, most influential theologian in Christianity tells us in this passage that he and a woman "touched the eternal Wisdom" together. Being "entranced and absorbed"[74] by God is the quintessential personal experience, yet each was also intensely aware that the other shared the same experience. They had so long ago acknowledged their spiritual equality that they register no surprise nor do they question the mutuality of the experience. Social, generational, familial, and gender relationships are transcended, and all that is left are two naked, equal creatures enveloped in their Creator.

Augustine tells us about another woman in his life, his mistress of ten years. When he first introduced us to her it was coldly and abruptly. He had "no special reason" for living with her, except to satisfy his "restless passions."[75] Yet when he described his break with her as he prepared to marry another (which he never did), we see a whole other side of the relationship. "The woman with whom I had been living was torn from my side as an obstacle to my marriage," Augustine lamented, in a manner that allows us to see how deep the wound was, "and this was a blow which crushed my heart to bleeding, because I loved her dearly." The love was mutual, and even after all the years between the event and the narration Augustine's admiration of the woman still shone through clearly. "She went back to Africa, vowing never to give herself to any other man," while Augustine, in his weakness "was too unhappy"[76] to follow suit. Instead, he took another mistress to while away the time until the anticipated marriage was to take place. He wrote disparagingly about his uncontrolled sexual urges and about his consequential actions with women, but he did not talk disparagingly about the women.

There is a denominator common to all these theologians. No matter how enthusiastically or begrudgingly they accept the spiritual equality of women in their theological works, they all treat the individual women in their lives as spiritual equals. The examples go on and on. Gregory Nazianzen's respect, admiration, and awe for the women in his life is found throughout his works. At his father's funeral oration, Gregory spent as much time extolling the virtues of Nonna, his mother, as of Gregory, his father and a bishop. "She is a woman who," Gregory began, "has acknowledged but one kind of beauty, that of the soul, and the preservation, or the restoration as far as possible, of the Divine image."[77] It was Nonna who, upset because her husband was not a Christian, "fell before God day and night, entreating for the salvation" of her husband Gregory, "influencing him in many ways, by means of reproach, admonitions, attentions, estrangements, and, above all by her own character with its fervor for piety"[78] until he converted. Even more noteworthy, Gregory believed his father's success as a bishop "was the result of his wife's prayers and guidance, and it was from her that he learned his ideal of a good shepherd's life."[79] In his sister Gorgonia he saw a perfect model of a Christian spouse. Gorgonia "was able to avoid the disadvantages of [the worldly life], and to select and combine all that is best in both [the worldly life and the spiritual life] . . . proving that neither of them absolutely binds us to, or separates us from, God or the world." She willingly "entered upon a carnal union" but did not become "therefore separated from the Spirit." Instead of experiencing a conflict between her two allegiances, Gorgonia "won over her husband to her side, and made of him a good fellow-servant, instead of an unreasonable master."[80] Ambrose wrote to his sister Marcellina as to his equal in all matters, even political. Basil the Great wrote to canonesses as his theological and intellectual equals,[81] Gregory of Nyssa considered Macrina so pure that it seemed "as if some angel had taken human form,"[82] Paulinus of Nola gushed in admiration for Melanie the Elder, "famous amongst the holy women of God," who was Rufinus of Aqueleia's partner in every sense of the word.[83] Melanie the Elder and Rufinus together established monasteries, dispensed alms, and brought heretics back into the church.[84]

Knowledge of the relationships these theologians had with women is pertinent for reasons other than providing us with insight into the lives of the men. It is significant for the attention it brings to an unanswered question. If the authors' negative or ambivalent statements about women did not result in their own negative or ambivalent behavior or attitudes toward women, on what basis can we assume that readers' behavior and attitudes were influenced negatively? Do we know if these statements even had any effect on what women thought about themselves? In a homily on the martyr Julitta, Basil had her say, "'We are of the same stuff as men. Like them, we are created according to the image of God. The female sex is made receptive to virtue by the Creator, just as the male is. How? Are we not related to men in all things?'"[85] We have little reason to believe this was a direct quote from Julitta, but it was certainly what Basil wanted her to say. As argued before, at best what we have is a statement reflecting a woman's self-image and, at least, a statement summarizing what a man believed a woman's self-image was. Perhaps we have been overemphasizing the importance of formal theological statements. The statements are of historical significance as influential molders of attitudes only if readers or listeners altered their own behavior to align themselves with those statements. If the vast majority of women thought of themselves as spiritually equal to men before God, and if the vast majority of men acted in agreement, the relevance of these statements may be less than previously supposed. If we cannot find behavior that corresponds to the negative written assessments of women's spiritual nature found during these centuries of church institutionalization, then we must assume some other force was responsible for equalitarian attitudes toward women. Perhaps the less-sensational statements of equalitarian spirituality of the first three centuries remained dominant, or at least remained audible enough for many women and men to adopt them as their standards. Our answer must be found in the lives of the women themselves, which we will examine next.

4

Fourth-Century Women

IN THE FOURTH CENTURY the number of sources pertaining to Christian women increase significantly, particularly those about individual women. With few exceptions we still do not have much written by women themselves,[1] but we do have numerous vitae, some recorded sayings of women, and many letters written to women with which it is possible to reconstruct a great deal of their lives. Besides documents directly related to women, with the institutional growth of the church in this century we also have more sources on church practices, regulations, and devotions. Thus we are in a rather good position to see what Christians, both male and female, thought about Christian women.

One of the most highly debated questions of the day, in the secular realm as well as the religious, involved sex.[2] We have already noted the presence of theological controversies in the first centuries of Christianity concerning the place of sexual activity in the lives of Christians. Fundamental to all Christian discussion of sexual activity was the definition of humanity. The spiritual nature of humanity was made in the image and likeness of God. This spiritual nature could rise to the height of perfection by gaining complete control over the physical nature, and people tried to achieve this goal through asceticism, in particular through celibacy. Soon celibacy became the most identifying virtue of both male and female ascetics.

With the magisterial work of Peter Brown on Western society's concept of the body, we have been given excellent access to the mentality that encouraged asceticism and the reason why Christians believed it was a way to achieve perfection of their spiritual nature.[3] In light of his work, interpretations of women's celibacy as the result of the desire of male theologians to neuter women biologically, or as the result of women's desires to become asexual and to spiritualize their inferior bodies must be reevaluated.[4] As persuasive as these interpretations may at first appear, they are all built on an anachronistic reading of the texts, a lack of appreciation for historical context, and a failure to appreciate what the facts of these women's lives tell us. The issue confronted by early Christians was not of power between male and female, or of the repressions of an individual act as an end in itself, or even of a repulsion from the physical. It was, Brown argues, an issue of free will and control over one's own destiny. Sex in late antiquity was not seen as the private, personal act it is today. It was, above all else, considered a social act; "virginity was a state that was expected to be terminated by a social act."[5] When a person surrendered his or her virginity, he or she was succumbing to the demands of society to stand in solidarity with that society and to perpetuate the human race. Coitus was the necessary act that "implied solidarity in a willingness to be conscripted into society." To withhold one's virginity was to stand outside the solidarity of society; it was a deliberate choice not to join the normal structures and roles of society. To put it in modern parlance, virgins claimed that their bodies were theirs to control and to do with as they pleased. The body, Brown argues, became in this way "a tangible *locus* on which the freedom of the will could be exercised, in choices that intimately affected the conventional fabric of society." Other Christians were very much aware of these radical implications, which they perceived to be to their benefit, and thus supported the state of virginity wholeheartedly. In effect virgins were voiding the sexual social contract that held the larger society together. Doing so ultimately freed members to gather themselves in new communities, Christian groups no longer held together by kinship but united by one common factor: freedom of choice. This is why many early Christians metaphorically called virginity the angelic life. Angels formed a harmonious society apart from human society, and by choosing virginity the Christian was freely choosing to enter into solidarity with this other society—a society of spiritually equal people. This fact provides a deeper understanding of the exhortations to withstand the temptations of the flesh, found in so many discussions of virginity. The encouragement was offered not simply to help bolster a virgin's determination to deny him- or herself sexual activity but "to brace the person against the force of social convention that threatened to sweep the individual, with the violence of a landslip, into his or her 'natural' social role as a married person, sexually active in order to produce children."[6]

Christians also encouraged virginity, Brown continues, because of their need for mediation between the divine and the human. He quotes Gregory of Nyssa's phrase that "virginity has become the linking-force that assures the intimacy of human beings with God."[7] Why Christians chose virginity, "an intensely physical state of the body," as a point of mediation was not so much because such a body could be treated as a "temple of the Holy Spirit"[8] but because virginity was so "profoundly asocial—it did not belong to society as naturally defined."[9] In the end, Brown concludes, virginity is really about "the nature of human solidarity . . . about what the individual did and did not need to share with fellow humans."[10] As such, it necessarily "led to significant modification of long-established views of the human person,"[11] and, we might add, to modification of expectations of behavior, particularly the behavior of women.

Carolyn Walker Bynum's work forms a provocative complement to Brown's interpretation,[12] especially as it pertains to our focus here. Bynum reminds us that Christianity is not a dualistic religion and that throughout its history it has vigorously "defended the idea that body is crucial to self in the most strident and extensive, the most philosophically and theologically confused (and rich) form."[13] The concept of the person in Christianity is not one of a soul trapped inside a body, despite what many critics in the past have charged, and Christian asceticism is not a manifestation of a person's hostility toward the somatic. Neither was woman's asceticism a result of some internalized misogyny,[14] nor a form of self-mutilation to escape the femaleness of their person. It was, Bynum says in agreement with Brown, a "rejection of a world in which they had little control over their bodies and their destinies."[15] For both Brown and Bynum, then, asceticism and its chief manifestation, the adoption of virginity, are about free will and control over one's destiny. It is time now to test these interpretations and see if they hold true for the women of the post-Nicean world. If indeed they do, then we must conclude that society's encouragement of women's participation in the virginal life was a very positive indication that women were considered to possess the same spiritual potential and to be as spiritually important to their community as men.

We know that by the beginning of the fourth century practice of virginity was well established among Christians. The Council of Elvira in Spain, ca. 300, addressed questions about the regulation of virgins, indicating their widespread presence even in the westernmost part of the Mediterranean. In the beginning virgins lived at home and pursued their goal individually, but there were many problems inherent to such a situation. Living at home meant involvement in relationships that bound one in solidarity to that home. Even in the fifth century writers were still telling stories about how difficult it was to live an ascetic, virginal life at home because familial affections diverted one's attention from asceticism's focus: self, not family. When relating the story of a female virgin in Alexandria who was blinded to "God's way" because of her desire to care for a niece, Palladius reflected upon the underlying problem. "Now it is possible," Palladius reasoned, "for a person to be moved by a pious intention and to give help to his relative, should they be needy, without being contemptuous of his own soul. Whenever one subjects his whole soul to solicitude for a relative, he falls under the law which counts his soul as superfluous."[16]

When the ascetic life became more widespread in the fourth century and the institutionalization of the life began, the same principle was advocated. Asceticism meant cutting off all ties with family, indeed, with the whole of society: The ascetic broke away from the solidarity of society with a supreme act of the will and freely joined other like-minded ascetics. Although home asceticism continued to be practiced, increasingly ascetics gravitated to a soon-crowded desert. Women ascetics were not as numerous in the movement as men, but the sources provide every indication that they were as revered. When abba Piteroum, "the famous anchorite," swelled with pride over his ascetic accomplishments, an angel quickly put his feats in their proper perspective by telling him about "someone more pious than yourself," a woman living in a community of virgins at Tabennisi.[17] Piteroum traveled to Tabennisi and insisted on seeing all the women therein. Because of his great age and reputation, they acquiesced. When they all assembled, though, Piteroum did not see the holy one he sought. The women then told him there was one more woman still working in the kitchen, one who was "touched," that is, mentally impaired. He commanded them to bring her forth, which they did forcibly. When the woman entered the room, both she and Piteroum fell down before each other and implored the other's blessing. "All the women were amazed at this and said: 'Father, take no insults. She is touched.' Piteroum then addressed all the women: 'You are the ones who are touched! This woman is spiritual mother'—so they called them spiritually—'to both you and me and I pray that I may be deemed as worthy as she on the Day of Judgment.'"[18]

The spiritual mother, or amma, was revered for the same reasons the abba was revered. Asceticism gave both men and women a reason and the freedom to choose an unconventional course of action, and the Christian community rewarded such behavior with resounding approval. Palladius was greatly impressed with the "high degree of virtue" exhibited by the "very severe and austere life" of the husband and wife Verus and Bosporia,[19] but in no matter did he admire them more than when they completely flaunted the conventions of the day by "practic[ing] charity to such an extent that they even cheated their own children, if we look at the future with worldly eyes."[20] Time and again asceticism gave women a reason to refuse marriage arrangements and to dispose of their wealth as they pleased. In the town of Ancyra "lived many others virgins, probably two thousand or more. They practiced chastity and were remarkable women indeed." The most revered of these women was Magna. She was forcibly married to a man, but she "kept putting him off, as many say, so that she remained intact." He died soon after their marriage, and she vowed never to remarry but to live "a most ascetic and chaste life." She proceeded to dispense with her fortune, giving it to hospitals and the poor.[21] Palladius also tells us about Veneria, the wife of a count, who distributed her wealth so wisely that she "was released from the disappointments which accompany wealth." He also wrote about Theodora, the wife of a tribune, the sisters Hosia and Adolia, and Basianillia, the wife of a general,[22] all of whom distributed their wealth to live the ascetic life. Palladius was quite clear about why he was recording these acts in his history: "I must also commemorate in this book the courageous women to whom God granted struggles equal to those of men, so that no one could plead as an excuse that women are too weak to practice virtue successfully."[23]

After a generation or two of desert living, the limits of living the ascetic life in such conditions were recognized, and the ascetics developed yet another form to facilitate their goals. The name given this form is monasticism. It preserved the goals of home asceticism and desert living, but it made some significant alterations. The ascetic no longer lived at home, tied to familial relationships and roles, nor lived in isolation from all other humans. Instead, ascetics formed a new community based not on kinship but on freedom of choice. Palladius's *Lausaic History* provides one of the most reliable sources we have about the early stages of monasticism and is most helpful in the analysis of both the position of women ascetics in early monasticism and the larger Christian society's opinion of these women. In his opening sentence Palladius tells us, "In this book is recorded the wonderfully virtuous and ascetic life of the holy fathers, monks, and anchorites of the desert." His purpose for recording this was "for the emulation and imitation" of those who wished to lead a holy life. His third sentence is of interest to us, for here he wrote about women in a much more admiring tone than he did about men. "It is written also to commemorate women far advanced in years and illustrious God-inspired mothers who have performed feats of virtuous asceticism in strong and perfect intention, as exemplars and models for those women who wish to wear the crown of self-abnegation and chastity."[24]

Besides commemorating their feats, Palladius also described for us the women's monastery at Tabennisi, commonly designated as the first known monastery for women.[25] Pachomius, originally a hermit living in the Thebaid desert, established the first known male cenobitic monastery after an angel told him to "go out and call the young monks together and dwell with them. Rule them by the model which I am now giving you."[26] Pachomius's rule attracted many followers, and before long his monastery became "the mother of all the other monasteries, having thirteen hundred men."[27] Pachomius also wrote a rule for his sister Mary and her monastery "of some four hundred women" at Tabennisi.[28] The monastery for men and the one for women "had the same sort of management and the same way of life, except for the cloak." They were physically close to each other, on opposite sides of a river, and they were spiritually close to each other, sharing their highest aspirations: "When a virgin died, the others laid her out for burial, and they carried her body and placed it on the bank of the river. The brethren would cross on a ferry boat and carrying palm leaves and olive branches bring the body over and bury it in the common cemetery."[29] Given the extraordinary stress Christians of the time placed on the resurrection of the body,[30] burial in a common cemetery is indeed significant. More obvious but as significant is their living the same type of ascetic life. In life and in death men and women approached God side by side.

We have, from this point onward, numerous examples to illustrate the effect asceticism had on women's physical and social lives, how women perceived asceticism, and how society perceived women ascetics. Ambrose related a story about the noble woman who while "being urged to a marriage by her parents and kinsfolk, took refuge at the holy altar." Ambrose's comment is telling: "Whither could a virgin better flee, than thither where the Virgin Sacrifice is offered?"[31] Indeed, celibacy was an excellent refuge for a woman, for while the larger society scorned the choice and the chooser, Christianity exalted both. Marcella, the first known Roman woman "publicly to call herself a nun,"[32] chose to remain celibate after the early death of her husband. When the powerful consular Cerealis sought her hand in marriage, he offered to give her his entire fortune if she consented. The pressure from her mother who "went out of her way to secure for the young widow so exalted a protector" to agree was great, and Marcella's refusal was accepted only after she persuasively argued that the issue was not money or security but celibacy. "'[H]ad I a wish to marry,'" Marcella stated, according to Jerome, "'and not rather to dedicate myself to perpetual chastity, I should look for a husband and not for an inheritance.'"[33] After her refusal of Cerealis and all he had to offer, others realized that they could not change her decision, and the offers of marriage stopped. The "slander-loving community"[34] of Rome, Marcella's world, of course made her decision a target of calumny, especially after her profession of the monastic life "—so strange and ignominious and degrading did it then seem—" to the Roman world, but Christians praised and imitated her. Soon Marcella was "gradually train[ing]" such "pupils" as Sophronia and Eustochium, "that paragon of virgins."[35]

Marcella lived an ascetic life quietly and "in holy tranquillity" until "a tornado of heresy which threw everything into confusion" made her reconsider her low profile. She decided to become the leader within the Christian community in opposition to this "new heresy [which] was drawing to itself not only priests and monks but also many of the laity."[36] Jerome was a main target of the heretics, and we can see the appreciation he had for Marcella's support in every line of his narrative. He wanted to make it perfectly clear that the dispute was settled chiefly because of her initiative.

> She it was who originated the condemnation of the heretics. She it was who furnished witnesses first taught by them and then carried away by their heretical teaching. She it was who showed how large a number they had deceived and who brought up against them the impious books *On First Principles,* books which were passing from hand to hand after being "improved" by the hand of the scorpion. She it was lastly who called on the heretics in letter after letter to appear in their own defense. They did not indeed venture to come, for they were so conscience-stricken that they let the case go against them by default rather than face their accusers and be convicted by them. This glorious victory originated with Marcella, she was the source and cause of this great blessing.[37]

In case anyone thinks that his praise of Marcella was exaggerated because he personally benefited from her activity, he reminded us that there are many similar incidents he could write about, but he mentions only these few so as "not to tire out the reader by a wearisome recapitulation" or give anyone reason to think he was "giving vent to my own rancour" against the heretics.[38]

Marcella's involvement in theological controversy was not that surprising, given her lifelong engagement in intellectual activity. Jerome offered this comparison for her level of theological competence: "This much only will I say, that whatever in me was the fruit of long study and as such made by constant meditation a part of my nature, this she tasted, this she learned and made her own. Consequently after my departure from Rome, in case of a dispute arising as to the testimony of scripture on any subject, recourse was had to her to settle it."[39] Nor was Marcella's theological competence unique among female ascetics; nearly all those whom we know of were actively involved in intellectual pursuits. Melanie the Elder, a prominent member of Marcella's Roman circle, "was most erudite and fond of literature, and she turned night into day going through every writing of the ancient commentators—three million lines of Origen and two and a half million lines of Gregory, Stephen, Pierius, Basil, and other worthy men." With dogged determination and willpower she got them to yield their treasures. "And she did not read them once only and in an offhand way, but she worked on them, dredging through each work seven or eight times."[40] Olympias likewise realized the ascetic life meant the abandonment of some things and the attainment of others. Only after "she disposed of all her goods" did she become occupied "in no small contests on the behalf of truth" and "instruct many women."[41]

Macrina, we have already noted, was called the Teacher by Gregory of Nyssa. She was well versed in Scripture and in Hellenistic philosophy.[42] Paula and her two daughters, Eustochium and Blaesilla, were highly educated and scholars in their own right. Blaesilla was literate in Greek, Latin, and Hebrew, and "even rivalled the great Origen in those acquirements which won for him the admiration of Greece,"[43] while Eustochium reached "the same accomplishment" level as her mother. Paula herself was a chief source of intellectual stimulation for Jerome, who confessed that he was in awe of her command of the Hebrew language.[44] It was Paula's critical eye that found Jerome's 383 translation of the Psalter "corrupted through the fault of copyists" and urged him to issue a revision; this revision, called the Gallican Psalter, became the standard translation for the next millennium.[45] The bulk of the Old Testament Vulgate was addressed to Paula and Eustochium, for reasons he made clear in his preface to the Book of Esther: "Paula and Eustochium, you so learned in Hebrew literature and so skillful to judge the merit of a translation, look over this one, and see if I have added to or taken from the original, or whether I have not, like an exact and sincere interpreter, turned this history into Latin, just as we read it together in Hebrew."[46] He also translated Job, the Books of Solomon, and Origen's commentaries on St. Luke for Paula and Eustochium, and he addressed his commentaries on Galatians, Isiah, Titus, Philemon, Ephesians, Ezekiel, Nahum, Micah, Zephaniah, and Haggai to them. Fabiola's zeal and eagerness to study Scripture "did not bring with it any feeling of satiety," and she had little tolerance for ignorance. When Jerome did not know the answer to a question she asked, "she began to press me harder still," Jerome wrote, "expostulating with me as though it were a thing unallowable that I should be ignorant" of the matter. She cajoled against him until she was able "to exhort from me a promise that I would devote a special work to this subject for her use."[47]

Women's freedom to pursue intellectual activities was not the only trait that flowed from the tradition of spiritual equality in Christianity. Within the Christian community repercussions of the tradition were multiple; they even affected many areas of a woman's physical and social life. All female ascetics made a definite, conscious, and free decision to disregard the sexual expectations of society. All consequently underwent a loss of status within the larger society and an increase in status within their new society, Christianity. This elevated status gave them actual, not merely symbolic, control over their bodies, possessions, and destinies; thus by freely choosing celibacy they gained freedom to make other choices. It also put them in a position that others saw as ideal for mediation between the human and the divine. Finally, their choice increased their awareness of the body's crucial role in their salvation and of the nondualistic nature of a person. Fundamental to each of these new realities was Christianity's tradition of spiritual equality for women. Without this presupposition Christian society would have had no reason to deviate from secular society's norms. Let us continue to examine historical illustrations of these claims.

Melanie the Elder's decision to ignore the sexual demands of her world resulted in a traumatic confrontation preserved in writing by Palladius and Paulinus of Nola. Widowed at twenty-two with a young son to care for, she made plans to sail from Rome to the East in order to live the ascetic life there, but "she told no one, for she would have been stopped."[48] She placed her son under the guardianship of the prefect of the city, and then proceeded to set off for Alexandria. Her plans were almost foiled when "the devil attempted, through the utmost pressure of her noble relatives, whom he equipped to detain her, to block her design and prevent her from going. . . . She gladly threw off the bonds of human love with the ropes of the ship, as all wept. She joined unwearied battle with the waves of the sea" and sailed away.[49]

Melanie the Younger's adoption of the ascetic life was in a setting as dramatic as her grandmother's, Melanie the Elder, but the former's choice is quite consciously and explicitly intended as a way of freeing her from sex and childbearing. Married at fourteen to a seventeen-year-old Pinian, she had an almost instant dislike for sex. "With much piteous wailing" Melanie offered to practically become Pinian's slave and to hand over all her possessions to him "if only you will leave my body free." Pinian refused her offer, but made this counteroffer: "If and when by the ordinance of God we have two children to inherit our possessions, then both of us together shall renounce the world."[50] After the first baby was born she pleaded with him again and again to allow her "to keep bodily chastity," but he still wanted a second child. Melanie conceived and this time gave birth prematurely to a boy who died shortly thereafter. The birth and death of the child left her "exceedingly troubled," and she began "giving up on life." Pinian in turn became desperate at the thought of losing her all together, and at this point Melanie struck one final time: "If you want me to continue living, give your word before God that we will spend the rest of our lives in chastity. . . ."[51] Pinian agreed.

Melaine the Younger still had to face the disapproval of her family. When the parents would not consent to the couple abandoning "their frivolous and worldly mode of life," Melanie and Pinian "refused to eat unless their parents would agree."[52] Their hunger strike lasted until Melanie's father lay on his deathbed. In his last hours he begged forgiveness and granted the two of them "the power to gratify your desire for God as you please." His grant was not purely altruistic; he wanted something definite in return, something only those living the ascetic, angelic life could grant: mediation. "May you only intercede on my behalf with God, the ruler of all." Upon hearing his words "they felt free from fear" and immediately left Rome, and severed all ties to begin "training in the practice" of asceticism, "just as it is written, 'Hear, daughter, and see; turn your ear and forget your people and your father's house, and the king will desire your beauty.'"[53]

Olympias faced opposition from the emperor Theodosius himself in her attempt to free herself from marriage. Married young, Olympias was a widow probably before the marriage was consummated. Since she was orphaned, extremely wealthy, and related to the emperor, Theodosius became personally involved in plans to have her remarried. While marriage negotiations, which Olympias vigorously resisted, were going on, she also was "falsely accused before the emperor Theodosius of having dispensed her goods in a disorderly fashion."[54] Theodosius, "when he had heard the testimony against the pious Olympias," placed her under a guardianship until she was thirty. The guardian, however, conspired with her intended spouse to "oppress her to such a degree" so she would agree to "meekly bear the option of marriage."[55] The plan backfired when the oppression only led Olympias to more intense ascetic behavior. "The emperor, upon his return from the battle against Maximus, gave the order that she could exercise control over her own possessions, since he had heard of the intensity of her ascetic discipline." Upon gaining complete control over her actions, she immediately "distributed all of her unlimited and immense wealth and assisted everyone, simply and without distinction."[56]

It is nigh impossible to deny the explicit connection between women's asceticism and the control over their destinies that even contemporaries recognized. For asceticism to be asceticism, it had to be freely chosen. Women, exactly like men, had to exercise their free will and personally determine what they wanted to do with their bodies if they truly desired to be ascetics. Christian society was willing to grant women control not only over their bodies but over many worldly things—possessions, relationships, everyday existence, and even location—if they were willing to embrace the ascetic life, so highly and necessary for the good of the whole did Christians regard the pursuit of spiritual perfection. "So close is the tie" between husband and wife, Jerome comments, "that they have no power over their own bodies,"[57] but for women the marriage tie also meant that they had no power over many aspects of their lives. Celibate women were not so bound, and if they either had no living parents or broke their ties with them, they could have the power to direct their own lives. Asceticism gave them the ability to sever limiting ties; nay, it *demanded* that they do so. The emotional toll of severing ties could be very high, as we see in the oceanside scene of Paula's departure from her children as she readied to sail to the East: "Little Lexotius piteously stretched forth his hands from the shore. Rufina, a grown-up girl, by her tears silently besought her mother to stay until she was married." Crushed with longing, Paula's "frame was wrung with anguish, and her limbs seemed as though they were torn asunder as she struggled with her grief." But Paula was determined to pursue the ascetic life, and so she "forgot that she was a mother, that she might prove herself the handmaiden of Christ." No matter how difficult, no matter how "unnatural as is this separation," the ties had to be broken.[58]

The effect of the loosening of ties and the resultant control women assumed over their lives is seen most easily in the matter of possessions. Many of the most renowned ascetics of the period gained part of their fame by founding monasteries and by caring for the poor. Both activities took money. Without the women's control over their own fortunes, they would not have been able to accomplish what they did. Upon adopting the ascetic life Fabiola "broke up and sold all that she could lay hands on of her property (it was large and suitable to her rank), and turning it into money she laid out this for the benefit of the poor. She was the first person to found a hospital," according to Jerome, and was so generous to monasteries that there was not one "which was not supported by Fabiola's wealth."[59] She did not have to ask her husband's permission, because she did not have one.

Olympias's distribution of her own money was restricted until the emperor acknowledged her exemplary asceticism. Once acknowledged, Olympias was given primary control over her money.[60] Melanie the Younger fought hard for the right to control her fortune once she and Pinian embraced the ascetic life, even to the point of appealing to Empress Serena for help when Pinian's brother incited their slaves to rebel if they were not given to him. All the empress needed was to meet Melanie and come face to face with her asceticism to be persuaded. "Come, see the woman who four years ago we beheld vigorous in all her worldly rank, who has now grown old in heavenly wisdom," Serena called to her servants when Melanie visited the empress. Melanie "does not fear weakness of the flesh nor voluntary poverty, nor any other things," Serena continued. "She has rather even bridled nature itself and delivered herself to death daily, demonstrating to everyone by her very deeds that before God, woman is not surpassed by man in anything that pertains to virtue, if her decision is strong." Serena got Emperor Honorius to issue a decree that all their possessions should be sold as Melanie desired and that "their money deriving from them should be remitted to Melanie and Pinian."[61] Paula originally gained the attention of Roman society because of her extravagant almsgiving after the death of her husband and her adoption of the ascetic life. "So lavish was her charity that she robbed her children,"[62] her relatives complained, but the Christian community looked upon her distribution of wealth, even to the detriment of her children's welfare, as an admirable trait. "Jesus is witness that Paula has left not a single penny" to her children at her death. "Could there be a more splendid instance of self-renunciation?" queried Jerome.[63]

Melanie the Elder was no exception; "So much wealth did she spend in holy zeal" that it is impossible to give a full accounting. It was "from her own treasury" that "she made donations to churches, monasteries, guests and prisons,"[64] and it was she who decided where and to whom each donation was going. In Melanie the Elder's life, it is also easy to see how asceticism gave women control over relationships as well as possessions. Melanie the Elder made acquaintance with "a Greek named Apronianus," married to her cousin. She not only "instructed and made [him] a Christian" but "even prevailed upon him to exert self-control concerning his own wife." Within her immediate family she was the controlling force. "She even taught her son's wife Albina" and her grandson Publicola[65] the ways of the ascetic life, and protected all members of her family who had embraced that life from the criticisms of "the members of the Senate and their wives, who would have stood in the way of their renunciation." As the end of her life neared "she sold everything which remained, and with the money she received she went [back] to Jerusalem. Then she distributed her wealth within forty days and fell asleep in fine old age, in the deepest meekness. She left a monastery at Jerusalem, too, and funds for it."[66] Here we see a female ascetic determining and controlling her money, her relationships, and her location.

Macrina's central and controlling role in her family has already been discussed. She was Peter's "father, teacher, tutor, mother, [and] giver of all good advice";[67] she was "her mother's guide and led her on to this philosophic and spiritual manner of life"; and she was the glory of the family, according to Gregory.[68] Asella's dramatic staged adoption of asceticism was as much a statement about her relationship to her family and the world as anything else. Her first act was to take her gold necklace and sell it without her parents' permission. "Then putting on a dark dress such as her mother had never been willing that she should wear, she concluded her pious enterprise by consecrating herself forthwith to the Lord. She thus showed her relatives that they need hope to wring no further concessions from one who, by her very dress, had condemned the world."[69] Marcella utilized her position as the first professed monastic Roman woman to establish a teacher-pupil relationship with many illustrious women in Rome.[70] Her palace on the Aventine Hill was a convent of sorts, where these women followed a strict life of asceticism and looked to Marcella as their mistress and friend. When highly placed bishops and theologians such as Oceanus, Paumachus, Epiphanus, and Jerome went to Rome from the East for a council in 382, they sought out Marcella's friendship and frequented her palace, so reputable and pivotal was she in the Roman community.

The pursuit of spiritual perfection also brought women a certain freedom of movement that would otherwise be lacking in their lives. One manifestation of this freedom is seen in the pilgrimages many women made. Melanie the Elder sailed from Rome in 372 to embark upon the ascetic life. She eventually founded monasteries to fulfill this purpose, but before so doing she went on a pilgrimage to the desert to learn the ways of asceticism from the masters. First she traveled in the Nitrian desert valley, about sixty miles south of Alexandria, and met "Pambo, Arsisius, Sarapion the Great, Paphnutius of Scete, Isidore the Confessor, and Dioscorus, bishop of Hermopolis. And she spent up to half a year with them, making the rounds of the desert and seeking out all the holy men." When many of these men were banished, Melanie "followed them and served them from her own private treasury."[71] Paula made an extensive pilgrimage to monastic sites throughout the East prior to settling in Bethlehem. After sailing from Italy she visited ascetics and holy places along the way until she reached the Holy Land, which filled her with awe as she journeyed throughout the territory. She made a pilgrimage to the Nitrian desert as well. There she "was met by the holy and venerable Bishop Isidorus the Confessor, and by innumerable crowds of monks." She visited an overwhelming number of these desert fathers—"whose cell did she not enter?"—so freely and was accepted so openly and equally as one of them, that "forgetful of her sex" the monks "all invited her" to come and "dwell with her maidens among so many thousands of monks." It was only "a greater longing for the holy places" that made her decide against settling in the desert where she was so openly declared to be spiritually equal to the male inhabitants and for establishing her monasteries in Bethlehem.[72]

The most famous women pilgrim is Egeria. A native from a far western province of the Roman empire (the bishop of Edessa congratulated her for making such a long journey of faith "right from the other end of the earth"),[73] Egeria was a member, perhaps the superior, of a group of women religious who sent her on this journey between 381 and 389. Little else is known about her background, but her values, character, and personality shine through in the journal she kept for the members of her community. Egeria also described in her journal the various liturgical services she encountered. It is therefore an invaluable source for ancient pilgrimages and liturgy, all the more important because it is from a woman's perspective. It also provides us with evidence of the freedom a female pilgrim had to travel as she pleased and of how such women were perceived by others. We can conclude without controversy that they were viewed no differently from male pilgrims.

For most of the pilgrimage Egeria traveled with guided groups, and she was enthusiastically welcomed at every stage of the journey. Everyplace she visited the holy men inhabiting the surrounding monasteries "were far kinder than I deserved, greeting me warmly, and having conversations."[74] It is clear that women were among those being visited as well as among the visitors: In a city in Isauria Egeria stayed for two days, "visiting all the holy monks and apotactites, the men as well as the women."[75] The bishop of Edessa, impressed by the distance Egeria had come, went out of his way to make her pilgrimage worthwhile and urged her to "please let us show you all the places Christians should visit here."[76] The personal tour ended with the bishop giving Egeria an accurate manuscript of the *Letter of Abgar,* which Egeria's community also had but in a manuscript "not so complete."[77] Another bishop, one from Charra, also gave Egeria a personal tour of the site where Abraham's house stood and of Jacob's well, where monks lived nearby. "I went round with the bishop and visited the holy monks in their cells; I gave thanks to God, and to them too, since they were so kind and welcoming when I entered them cells, and entertained me with the kind of conversation which befits monks."[78]

In every phase of the lengthy pilgrimage Egeria was fully accepted by fellow male pilgrims, male tour guides, bishops in dioceses she stayed in, and monks they visited. The pilgrimage experience was obviously structured for both women and men: "There is a tremendous number of cells for men and women" around the pilgrimage sites for the pilgrims to spend the night. Egeria as a solitary woman ascetic pilgrim was not an oddity either. She met other women as she traveled around the Holy Land and once ran into "one of my dearest friends, a holy deaconess called Marthana" who was a superior of a women's community. "I had come to know her in Jerusalem when she was up there on pilgrimage," Egeria confided. "I simply cannot tell you how pleased we were to see each other again."[79] Everything about Egeria's pilgrimage and all we can surmise through her personal comments indicate that a woman experienced quite an impressive degree of freedom, control, and equality while on pilgrimage.

Women were able to gain access to such experience because, as we have said, Christian society considered the presence of an ascetic a blessing. Not only was their example important as a model to imitate, but their ability to rise above the natural was comforting. The perfect ascetics were more than human, but not divine. They were, in the eyes of their fellow Christians, a helpful bridge between the natural and the supernatural, because, as Gregory of Nyssa said, virginity "remains in heaven" even while "it nevertheless stretches out hands" for human salvation.[80] As Melanie the Younger's father said when facing death, he very much wanted his daughter to become an ascetic because he needed someone close to God to intercede for him at Judgment. Most Christians did not have to wait until death was imminent to acknowledge their desire for mediators between themselves and God. Christians on the whole agreed with the sentiments expressed by Pseudo-Athanasius: "In every house of Christians it is needful that there be a virgin, for the salvation of the whole house is this one virgin. And when wrath cometh upon the whole city, it shall not come upon the house wherein the virgin is."[81]

The life of Piamoun offers an example of an entire village's elevation of a woman into a powerful and appreciated intercessor. Piamoun was an industrious, chaste ascetic who possessed the gift of prophecy. When a disturbance broke out between her village and another over the distribution of water, she foresaw an attack being planned by the neighboring village on her own. She "sent for the elders" and told them to meet with the other villagers and resolve their differences "lest you all die along with the populace." Frightened though the elders were, none of them was brave enough to undertake the needed negotiations, so they begged Piamoun to go. She would not agree to do so, but instead went home and spent the night deep in prayer, imploring God to save the town. The next morning the neighboring villagers marched off to attack, but when they got about three miles away from Piamoun's village they were miraculously unable to move any farther. "It was made known to them that this hindrance was due to her intercession. So they went to the village, suing for peace, making it clear that this was 'because of God and the prayers of Piamoun, for they stopped us.'"[82]

Mediation between God and society did not necessarily have to be even this visible or specific. The mere presence of Macrina in all her spiritual splendor was perceived as the reason why God relieved the people of the more devastating effects of a famine: "That the corn for relief of need, though constantly distributed, suffered no perceptible diminution" could be attributable only to Macrina's intercession with God on their behalf.[83]

The woman ascetic was also a mediator on an individual basis and often fulfilled the role of spiritual guide and intercessor between God and men. We have discussed at length Monica's role in Augustine's and her husband Patricius's conversions and Melanie the Younger's role in her husband's embrace of the ascetic life. Her influence over Pinian continued throughout their lives. She was his spiritual counselor and decided all matters, spiritual and material, for them both. As they started on their ascetic training Pinian had a difficult time giving up the dress of his noble class. Melanie broached the matter with him, urging him to "be persuaded by me as your spiritual mother and sister, and give up the Cilician clothes." Pinian recognized Melanie's authoritative voice and "straightway he obeyed her excellent advice, judging this to be advantageous for the salvation of them both."[84] Melanie the Elder was the spiritual guide of Evagrius Ponticus, the great theologian of monasticism, and was responsible for his physical and spiritual health. After Evagrius had abandoned his commitment to the ascetic life, he was struck with an illness that would not respond to treatment. Melanie got him to confess his desertion and then interceded on his behalf once he renewed his commitment. Her prayer was heard, and Evagrius "was well again in a matter of days."[85]

As for women ascetics' attitudes toward their bodies, they did not seem to differ from that of men's. Both considered the body crucial to the salvation of the individual because through the body the innermost regions of the soul could be reached and transformed most easily. "For it is said," amma Syncletica taught, "'I am affected and in pain.' By this share of wretchedness you will be made perfect."[86] Only through bodily tribulations can the soul be tested and strengthened. "Just as the trees, if they have not stood before the winter's storms cannot bear fruit, so it is with us," amma Theodora said. "This present age is a storm and it is only through many trials and temptations that we can obtain an inheritance in the kingdom of heaven."[87] *Accidie*, faintheartedness, was one of the most dreaded vices for the desert ascetics precisely because of the inseparability of the body and soul. "Once evil comes and weighs down your soul through *accidie*," Theodora warned, it simultaneously "attacks your body through sickness, debility, weakening of the knees, and all the members. It dissipates the strength of soul and body, so that one believes one is ill and no longer able to pray."[88] Unless one was aware of this inseparable relationship and took appropriate steps to guard against problems within either the body or the soul, all would be lost. "The soul is then like a ship when great waves break over it, and at the same time it sinks because the hold is too full," Syncletica explained. "We are just like that: we lose as much by the exterior faults we commit as by the thoughts inside us."[89] We do not find in the sayings of women ascetics or in their lives evidence that they disdained their bodies or that they internalized a dualistic or a misogynist attitude toward the female body similar to the one men had toward women's bodies. Instead we find a keen awareness of the beneficial role the body can play in the attainment of salvation. As Asella knew, if one were to attain salvation it must be "with a sound body and a still sounder soul."[90]

Besides avoiding sexual activity, these women subjected their bodies to many rigorous practices, because they believed as amma Theodora believed: "Give the body discipline and you will see that the body is for him who made it."[91] The sincere ascetic was always to avoid indulging in bodily comfort. When Melanie the Elder saw her son resting on a leather cushion while they were traveling from Jerusalem to Egypt, "she scoffed at his weakness" and advised him to imitate her. "I am sixty years old," she said, and "I have not yet made concessions to my bodily desires, nor have I used a couch for resting, nor have I ever made a journey on a litter."[92]

Asceticism was to be moderate, for if extreme, there would be reason to believe it was inspired by the devil. Syncletica taught that the key to distinguishing between holy and demonic asceticism was "clearly through its quality of balance," for "in truth lack of proportion always corrupts."[93] We find this principle adhered to by Marcella, who "practiced fasting, but in moderation. She abstained from eating flesh, and she knew rather the scent of wine than its taste; touching it only for her stomach's sake and for her other infirmities."[94] Asella was said to be consistent and moderate in all her asceticism: "Her pale face indicates continence but does not betoken ostentation. Her speech is silent and her silence is speech. Her pace is neither too fast, nor too slow. Her demeanor is always the same."[95] Melanie the Younger and Pinian began their practice of asceticism slowly "because of their pampered youth." Carefully they considered the appropriateness of moderation. "If we take upon ourselves an ascetic discipline that is beyond our strength, we will not be able to bear it because of the softness of our way of life. Our body [sic] will not be able to bear it, will weaken completely, and later we will be likely to surrender ourselves to sensuality."[96] Macrina set about "weaning [her mother] from all accustomed luxuries" but certainly not from necessities. Instead she proposed her mother "to live on a footing of equality with the staff of maids, so as to share with them in the same food, the same kind of bed, and in all the necessaries of life, without any regard to differences of rank."[97] Lea underwent many ascetic disciplines, but never to the extreme; "she avoided ostentation that she might not have her reward in this world" by allowing "her asceticism [to] bring her too much attention to herself."[98]

Female ascetics also are seen attending to the bodily needs of others, even as they disciplined their own bodies. Fabiola was well known for her fasts and her disregard for bodily appearance and comfort, but she was better known for her work with "the unfortunate victims of sickness and want," whom she often fed "with her own hand, and moisten[ed] the scarce breathing lips of the dying with sips of liquid."[99] Olympias took a personal interest in the public bread supply[100] and built a home for the sick and an orphanage. Paula built a guest house in Bethlehem for pilgrims, and Melanie the Elder supported guests and prisoners. These women did not make distinctions between caring for male bodies and female bodies. Fabiola "showed the same liberality towards the clergy and monks and virgins" and "often too did wash away the matter discharged from wounds which others, even though men, could not bear to look at."[101] Whereas men ascetics made a point of avoiding contact with women[102] in fear of arousing sexual passions, we have no evidence that women ascetics shared these qualms. Palladius tells us about an "old woman [who] had such a high degree of self-control that when I had entered and taken a seat, she came and sat with me and placed her hands on my shoulders in a burst of frankness."[103] When Athananius was accused of crimes during the Arian controversy, he fled to the home of a "so pretty and young" woman, and "she hid the most holy man for six years, until the death of Constantus. She washed his feet and cared for all his bodily needs and his personal affairs."[104]

As we come to an end of our examination of post-Nicean women ascetics and assess the overall results, we find that the sources do indeed support Brown's and Bynum's theses. Asceticism was a socially liberating and spiritually elevating movement, particularly for women, since women had fewer areas in which they could exercise their free will, raise their status, and control their destinies. What is key to our study here is that Christians allowed and encouraged women to engage in a spiritual exercise that often resulted in bodily and social emancipation. They allowed this because they perceived women to be as able to achieve salvation as any man. They not only permitted women to pursue an ascetic life but rewarded them for it, and quite highly too. The holy woman ascetic was equal to (and in some cases, superior to) the holy man in every single way, and the proof of this equality rests in the degree of holiness women attained. And while Brown's and Bynum's work turns our attention in a healthy way to the social, economic, and physical realities involved in asceticism, we as historians always must remember that, while women ascetics were affected by and often aware of these realities, it was never their focus. They were spiritually motivated to engage in behavior that would help attain a spiritual goal. It is for this reason that Christian society embraced women ascetics; it was a society bound together by spiritual motivations to attain a spiritual goal. Given Christianity's definition of humanity, there was no reason to restrict women's participation in asceticism or, for that matter, to use it to neuter women. The soul was saved through the body, be it male or female. Bynum has concluded that early Christian discussions of the bodily resurrection were not displaced discussions of gender or sex but were exactly what their proponents said they were, discussions of death. Likewise, early Christianity's ascetic practices were not about gender or sex. They were exactly what their proponents said they were, exercises in holiness. A woman became an ascetic not to become a man but to become a saint.

It is important to remember that almost all the sources we have dealt with in this chapter were written by men. While this factor can be disturbing in many historical tasks, it is actually helpful to us here, for it reveals what men—the most prominent intellectual male leaders of the day—thought about these women and their deeds. It is an even more interesting factor when one realizes that many of these men who wrote derogatorily about women in the abstract wrote very positively, warmly, and admiringly about individual, real women. Again, it gives the historian pause when trying to assign weight to the formal treatises of the period.

5

Devotional Life and Mary in Late Antiquity

THE AVERAGE CHRISTIAN in the post-Nicean church did not write theological treatises, practice asceticism, or join a monastic community. The common Christian did, however, participate in liturgical services, partake in pietistic devotions, honor saints, and offer private and communal prayers, just as he or she did in the pre-Nicean church. When we examine the post-Nicean spiritual world, we find new objects of devotion and a few innovations in religious services, and on the subject of women we find the continuation of a tradition of spiritual equality.

By the fourth century we also have a bit more information than previously about prayer practices, thanks to incidental remarks in theologians' writings and some from monastic writings. Women were as involved and committed to individual and communal prayer as men, and in Augustine's autobiography we are given much information about the prayer life of one woman, Monica, his mother. Augustine wrote that Monica "never let a day go by unless she had brought an offering to your altar, and never failed to come to your church twice every day, each morning and night, not to listen to empty tales and old wives' gossip, but so that she might hear the preaching of your word and you might listen to her prayers."[1] While in Africa it was Monica's custom "to take meal-cakes and bread and wine to the shrines of the saints on their memorial days"; this she did "to perform an act of piety, not to seek pleasure for herself." When she moved to Milan, Ambrose, the bishop there, forbade this custom, so "instead of her basket full of the fruits of the earth she learned to bring to the shrines of the martyrs a heart full of prayers far purer than any of these gifts. In this way she was able to give what she could to the poor and the Communion of the Lord's Body was celebrated at the shrines of the saints."[2] Augustine was sure that Monica's prayers were effective, for God was "there to hear her prayer." He never even hints that her prayers would have been dealt with differently from a man's: "It could not be," Augustine proclaimed to God, "that you would have deceived her in the visions you sent her and the answers you gave to her prayers."[3]

Augustine also provided us with insight into the nature of Monica's prayer. She had supreme confidence in the worth of her prayer; when caught in a storm at sea, "it was she who put heart into the crew" and "promised then that they would make the land in safety, because you had given her this promise in a vision."[4] When Augustine told her he had finally abandoned Manicheanism "she did not leap for joy as though this news was unexpected"; she had prayed for it. Even though she always believed her prayer would be answered, this did not mean she prayed any less humbly. Repeatedly Augustine emphasized these dual characteristics of Monica's prayer, total supplication and utmost confidence: "For in her prayers to you she wept for me as though I were dead, but she also knew that you would recall me to life."[5] Monica's prayers were from the depth of her soul and were continual. As her prayers began to bear fruit, she did not lessen her efforts but prayed "all the more fervently" and "hurried all the more eagerly to church."[6] She was confident enough about her relationship with God that she did not hesitate to request direct communication from Him through visions. When Augustine was trying to decide about his anticipated marriage, "at my request and by her own desire she daily beseeched [God] with heartfelt prayers to send her some revelation in a vision" about what he should do. The communication did not come this time, but apparently Monica often prayed for such messages and often received them, because "she always said that by some sense, which she could not describe in words, she was able to distinguish between your revelations and her own natural dreams."[7]

Gregory of Nyssa gives us one of the earliest examples of a woman's deathbed prayer[8] when he recorded Macrina's last prayer. Given the crisis that produced these utterances, we may assume the prayer made a special imprint on his mind and that his subsequent record of them is relatively accurate. The first part of the prayer is filled with expected petitions and thoughts about "the end of this life [and] the beginning to us of true life,"[9] but the second part is revealing.

> O God eternal, to Whom I have been attached from my mother's womb, Whom my soul has loved with all its strength, to Whom I have dedicated both my flesh and my soul from my youth up until now— do Thou give me an angel of light to conduct me to the place of refreshment, where is the water of rest, in the bosom of the holy Fathers. Thou that didst break the flaming sword and didst restore to

Paradise the man that was crucified with Thee and implored Thy mercies, remember me, too, in Thy Kingdom; because I, too, was crucified with Thee, having nailed my flesh to the cross for fear of Thee, and of Thy judgments that have I been afraid. Let not the terrible chasm separate me from Thy elect. Nor let the Slanderer stand against me in the way; nor let my sin be found before Thy eyes, if in anything I have sinned in word or deed or thought, led astray by the weakness of our nature. O Thou Who hast power on earth to forgive sins, forgive me, that I may be refreshed and may be found before Thee when I put off my body, without defilement on my soul. But may my soul be received into Thy hands spotless and undefiled, as an offering before Thee.[10]

Macrina was acutely aware that as a person she was composed of body and soul and that salvation came to both body and soul. Hence she reminded God that she always had given Him both her body and her soul. There is no indication that she deemed women spiritually inferior and, therefore, needful of special consideration. Nor is there any hesitancy or any apologies for her body being only the body of a woman. If anything, she was reminding God about the special uniqueness of a woman's body when she referred to her dedication to God from her mother's womb. It is also the only reference to women's distinctiveness. Nothing else in this prayer would limit its authorship to a woman. It is the prayer of one who firmly rejects dualism and has a keen appreciation for the value of the body. Her salvation comes through both body and soul. Her willingness to subject her body to pain and torture through identification with Jesus's crucifixion is why she believes her soul will be received in heaven. Macrina was particularly attached to devotions to the crucifixion, believing that "the symbol of the Holy Cross" was given to us to "save our life."[11] When she finished her last prayer "she sealed her eyes and mouth and heart with the cross";[12] earlier in her life the sign of the cross was instrumental in her cure from a breast tumor. Her mother urged her to see a doctor about it, but instead Macrina prayed all night. She applied a mud pack made from her tears to her breast and then asked her mother to cross it. "When the mother put her hand within her bosom, to make the sign of the cross on the part, the sign worked and the tumor disappeared."[13]

When the deaconess Lampadia started preparing Macrina's body for burial, she found another sign of the latter's devotion to the Cross. " 'See,' she said, looking at [Gregory], 'what sort of an ornament has hung on the saint's neck!' " When Gregory approached, "she loosened the fastener behind, then stretched out her hand and showed us the representation of a cross of iron and a ring of the same material, both of which were fastened by a slender thread and rested continually on the heart."[14] From the surprise of Lampadia and the details Gregory went at length to provide, we can conclude that our modern-day custom of wearing necklace crosses was unexpected at that time. What is more significant than the origin of cross jewelry is Macrina's full identification with the most physical aspect of Jesus's life, his crucifixion. Jesus's male body, strung out on the cross, was unembarrassingly embraced by a woman intensely aware of her own body and the role it played in her salvation. Instead of Macrina's female body driving a wedge between her and Jesus, it brought her closer to Jesus in all his humanity.[15] We have, in other words, no evidence that women agreed with or were internalizing any negative statements about their physical inferiority before God. Rather we have indications that women used their physicality to draw closer to God.

These conclusions are reinforced in another woman's dying prayer. In Melanie the Younger's biography, Gerontius recorded a prayer she recited on her last visit to the martyrion. Melanie knew she was dying, with only a matter of days left, and she prayed accordingly.

> God, the Lord of the holy martyrs, who knows all things before they come to pass, you know what I chose from the beginning, that I love you with all my heart, and from fear of you, my bone has been glued to my flesh. For I have given my soul and body to you, who formed me in my mother's womb, and you have taken my right hand to guide me in your counsel. But being human, I have sinned against you many times both in word and in deed, against you who alone are pure and without sin. Therefore accept my prayer, which I offer to you with these tears, through the intercession of your holy athletes, and purify me, your servant, so that in my coming to you, the steps of my soul may be unfettered and the evil demons of this air not hold me back, but that I may go to you spotless, guided by your holy angels. May I be deemed worthy of your heavenly bridal chamber, when I have heard your blessed voice by which you will say to those who please you, "Come, the blessed of my Father, inherit the kingdom prepared for you from the creation of the world." For to you belongs inexpressible compassion and abundant piety; you will save all those who hope in you.[16]

The similarities between the two prayers are obvious. Both prayers referred to mothers' wombs. Both women emphasized that they dedicated their whole person, body and soul, to God. Both referred to their fear of the

Lord. Both acknowledged their sinfulness, in word and in deed. Most significantly, both emphasized that this sinfulness was rooted in the inherent weakness of human nature; neither attributed it to their weak *female* nature. Both expressed complete confidence in their salvation, and both believed that their souls would enter God's presence spotless. Neither prayer was the least bit apologetic for her female nature or worried that it might not be found to be acceptable. Both prayers contained evidence that the women have internalized a belief in their spiritual worth in the eyes of God.

The similarities are so striking that one must ask if these are formula prayers for the dying. Conclusions based on these two prayers alone can be only tentative. Formulaic or not, the prayers still contain the characteristics we have pointed out, and whether they originated directly from the women or were patterned prayers written by male hagiographers, they were prayers that Christians, both men and women, accepted and revered as appropriate for women. If they were the real prayers of dying women, the male hagiographers highlighted them as excellent summations of what these women believed—and those hagiographers in turn believed that these prayers reinforced the sanctity of their subjects.

Egeria recorded no special prayer in her journal, but we have a very full description of the occasions and the content of her prayer life as a pilgrim. Her years as a pilgrim were filled with informal private and communal prayers as well as liturgical prayer. At the first site she visited, Mount Sinai, the pilgrims established a prayer routine that they maintained throughout: "And it was always our practice when we managed to reach one of the places we wanted to see to have first a prayer, than a reading from the book, then to say an appropriate psalm and another prayer. By God's grace we always followed this practice whenever we were able to reach a place we wanted to see."[17] Privately, though, Egeria would add her own prayers, because "I know I should never cease to give thanks to God, but I thank him specially for this wonderful experience he has given me, beyond anything I could expect or deserve."[18] Occasionally the prayer service at a holy place was longer, as, for example, when they reached the summit of Mount Sinai. Here "the whole passage had been read to us from the Book of Moses (on the very spot!) [and] we made the Offering in the usual way and received Communion."[19] They always "prayed very earnestly" at these sites, and Egeria confessed that no matter what the circumstances, "whenever we arrived, I always wanted the Bible passage to be read to us."[20] When they reached the plain of Jordan where Moses imparted his last blessing, they added "not only the song, but also the blessings [Moses] pronounced over the children of Israel."[21] What is most notable in the journal is how careful Egeria was to include the prayer ritual the pilgrims followed in each holy place. The journal is replete with such phrases as "as usual we had there a prayer, a reading from the Book of Moses, and one psalm."[22] Even though she wrote "as usual," she still believed it necessary to state the fact explicitly in each visit's description. On some of these pilgrimages Egeria was the only woman. Only infrequently did she refer to her fellow pilgrims, but once she wrote after she decided to visit the tomb of Job, "I set off from Jerusalem with some holy men who were kind enough to keep me company on the journey."[23] On this pilgrimage the same prayer routine was followed, and Egeria and her prayers were welcomed by "the holy presbyter and clergy of the place"[24] on an equal basis with the men.

Egeria also felt obligated to describe in detail "the daily services they have in holy places." Before dawn the neighboring men and women ascetics "and also some lay men and women" started congregating in the Anastasis (the main church in Jerusalem) to "join in singing the refrains to the hymns, psalms, and antiphons" until daybreak.[25] After dawn they all recited the Morning Hymns, this time with the bishop. This was repeated at midday and three o'clock; at four o'clock they had a more elaborate service, Lucernare, highlighted by the lighting of lamps, singing, and a "Prayer for All." On the vigil for Sunday "as many as can get in, as if it was Easter," gathered at the Anastasis to celebrate. Again, Egeria singled out only one prayer for mention, this time "the Commemoration of All." At the end of the service "the bishop retires to his house," but "some lay men and women like to stay on there till daybreak." At daybreak on Sunday "the people assemble in the Great Church built by Constantine" and proceeded to "do what is everywhere the custom on the Lord's Day."[26] Every aspect of Egeria's description indicates an inclusive service for all Christians.

The only distinction in treatment Egeria noted was one between the faithful and the catechumen, those studying for baptism at Easter. After submitting their names, they were brought up to the bishop's chair on the second day of Lent, "men coming with their fathers and women with their mothers." The bishop asked a series of questions about their suitability for baptism; "He asks the men and the women the same questions." When accepted, "all those to be baptized, the men and the women, sit around in a circle. There is a place where the fathers and mothers stand" to listen to the bishop preach and teach the basics of Christianity. This teaching lasted for three hours a day for seven weeks. In the eighth week, the Holy Week, "the candidates go up to the bishop, men with their fathers and women with their mothers and repeat the Creed to him." Finally they were baptized on Easter.

Throughout the entire description Egeria went to pains to emphasize that women and men were treated the same way.[27]

The prayers that were recited at these public worship services have been preserved only in bits and pieces. During the fourth and fifth centuries the Psalter dominated these prayer services, and one of the innovations of this period was the transformation of the church's psalmody. Augustine described the early chant of the psalms as one when a single reader used "such slight inflexions of the voice, that he seemed to say the psalms rather than to sing them."[28] With the increase in size of the congregation, often such a solitary voice could not be heard. At this point the antiphonal chanting of choirs began. Typically the congregation would be divided in two, and each would chant alternate verses of a psalm. Basil described the procedure for us. After reminding his audience that "we have orders of men and women" who "chant hymns to our God continuously," he wrote:

> Among us the people come early after nightfall to the house of prayer, and in labor and affliction and continual tears confess to God. Finally, rising up from their prayers, they begin the chanting of psalms. And now, divided into two parts, they chant antiphonally, becoming master of the text of the Scriptural passages, and at the same time directing their attention and the recollectedness of their hearts. Then, again, leaving it to one to intone the melody, the rest chant in response; thus, having spent the night in a variety of psalmody and intervening prayers, when day at length begins to dawn, all in common, as with one voice and one heart, offer up the psalm of confession to the Lord, each one making His own the words of repentance.[29]

The emphasis Basil placed on the inclusive, communal nature of the psalmody cannot be missed.

During this period hymns also began to gain importance. Many were written by Ambrose and were not concerned with gender. Ones commonly sung with the Psalter often had themes to tie them to the hour or the day they were sung. Hymns contain the same general themes as prayers: praise, thanksgiving, and petition. They are all offered with a communal voice. To martyrs Ambrose sang: "With joyous voices let us sing the blood shed for Christ, the victories of the martyrs. . . . We now beseech Thee, O Redeemer, that Thou unite forever Thy suppliant servants in the fellowship of the martyrs."[30] His hymn about virgins resounded thus: "O Jesus, Crown of Virgins, Thou whom that Mother conceived, who alone as a Virgin did bear a Child; graciously accept these our prayers. . . . Wherever Thou go, the Virgins follow, and with voices of praise, singing, they hasten after Thee and cause sweet hymns to resound."[31] Of the hymns examined, this one probably contains the most references to gender, given the fact that the word *virgin* by this time referred to a female celibate. Except for the doxology with its praise of the Father and Son, masculine imagery was not common. Hymns that dealt with sin, repentance, or the call to conversion did not refer to Eve or even use human imagery but relied on images related to darkness and the like. One hymn by Prudentius, for example, pleaded thus: "Do Thou, O Christ, drive away sleep, break the bonds of night; free us from the sins of former days and infuse new light in us."[32] Similarly, in another popular hymn Prudentius wrote: "O night, and darkness, and clouds, confused and disordered state of the world, depart! Light enters, the sky grows bright, Christ is at hand."[33] If Tertullian's and Origen's negative metaphors of women and sin were known (and we can assume that Ambrose and Prudentius were familiar with their writings), they were not employed by authors of hymns. Early Christian hymnody was not a vehicle for disseminating these metaphors.

Many of the people who attended these long and continual prayer services were *monazontes*, lay men and women who dedicated themselves, usually through a vow, to a religious life. At this time there were two alternatives for an intense religious life, one could live at home or live in a monastic community. By the end of the fourth century, monastic communities were increasingly popular alternatives. As religious life became more communal and institutionalized, so too did its prayer life.

Melanie the Younger's biography provided us with a description of how monastic women participated in the prayer life of the church. The first thing Melanie did was instruct the women on the proper attitude necessary for worship. The women must "stay vigilant during the night office, to oppose evil thoughts with sobriety, and not to let their attention wander." All their energy must be geared "to focus[ing] their minds on singing the Psalms." They "should perform our liturgy with much fear and trembling" and, in particular, "sing Psalms in all fear and trembling." For the night office Melanie "awakened the sisters for a service of praise." They also chanted at Terce, Sext, and None. "'As for evening prayers,' she said, 'we ought to undertake them with zeal'" because "'we have passed the course of day in peace.'" Melanie also urged the women "'to be especially zealous on Sundays and the other important feast days to give themselves to uninterrupted psalmody.'"[34] In other words, women's monastic prayer life resembled men's monastic prayer life in content, form, and time.

We do not have as much information about Paula's monasteries as Melanie the Younger's, but we have enough to realize that, again, women's prayer life was indistinguishable from men's. She organized "numerous virgins whom she had gathered out of different provinces, some of whom are of noble birth while others belonged to the middle or lower classes" into three companies that worked and ate separately but that "met together for psalm-singing and prayer." They chanted the Alleluia, and "at dawn, at the third, sixth, and ninth hours, at evening, and at midnight they recited the Psalter each in turn. No sister was allowed to be ignorant of the psalms, and all had every day to learn a certain portion of the holy scriptures." They attended Sunday eucharistic services at the nearest church as full members of the congregation.[35]

Augustine wrote a letter to his sister's community, at her request, in which he addressed the principles he deemed essential to monastic life. The letter is often dubbed *Regula sororum*, but actually it probably never was used as a community rule. The letter is, however, of value to us as insight into what Augustine's opinion of women's prayer life should be. "When you pray to God in psalms and hymns, meditate in your heart on what you utter with your voice, and do not sing anything that is not noted to be sung."[36] The women always should "be instant in prayer at the hours and times appointed." Individual, private prayer is as important as formal, communal prayer, so the oratory should be open "so that if some of the Sisters have time and wish to pray even outside the appointed hours, those who wish to do something else there may not be a hindrance to them."[37] Nothing in the letter indicates different demands or expectations from those practiced by Augustine himself when he lived in a community at Tagaste.[38]

We know that Macrina's monastery observed the Office, for in her last moments she participated in Lucernare and the lighting of the evening lamps. With her last bit of strength "she opened the orb of her eyes and looked towards the light, clearly wanting to repeat the thanksgiving sung at the Lighting of the Lamps."[39] After her death, while Gregory and Lampadia readied Macrina's body, the rest of the women were "singing psalms mingled with the lamentations." News of Macrina's death spread quickly through the neighborhood, and a "multitude of men and women" soon filled the monastery as "the all-night vigil for her, accompanied by hymn singing" continued. Gregory was disturbed by the chaotic nature of the spontaneous prayer service, so he took charge: "I divided the visitors according to sex, and put the crowds of women with the band of virgins, while the men folk I put in the ranks of the monks. I arranged that psalms should be sung by both sexes in rhythmical and harmonious fashion, as in chorus singing, so that all the voices blend suitably."[40] Male and female alternating choirs were apparently very familiar to Gregory.

The more one reviews the sources concerning singing, the more obvious it becomes that singing was a great leveling experience and was used to unite the congregation in a very real "harmonious fashion," as Gregory said. Augustine discussed a situation in Milan that illuminates masterfully the role hymns and psalmody played in forging a sense of community among all Christians. When Ambrose was pitted against Justina, empress-regent for the boy Valentinian, the Christians in Milan lent their full support to Ambrose and were "ready to die with their bishop" if Justina's anger so demanded. Monica, not Augustine, played "a leading part in that anxious time of vigilance" (Augustine "was not yet fired by the warmth" of Christianity). Still, "these were stirring times" for Augustine and the whole city, which was "in a state of alarm and excitement. It was then that the practice of singing hymns and psalms was introduced, in keeping with the usage of the Eastern churches, to revive the flagging spirits of the people during their long and cheerless watch." Augustine more than once admitted to having "wept all the more when I heard your hymns and holy songs."[41] The "sweet singing of your church" was a moving, unifying, personal yet communal experience for all Christians, for as Augustine confessed, "the music surged in my ears, truth seeped into my heart, and my feelings of devotion overflowed."[42] Once one had found Christ, the singing must continue, for all "travelers do this in order to keep up their spirits," Augustine reminded his parishioners. "Do you also sing on the way, I beseech you, by the very road on which you walk, sing on this road."[43]

Augustine's appreciation for music was not merely pietistic; it was also inextricably bound to his understanding of the theological doctrine of the Mystical Body. "The members of Christ, many though they be, are bound to one another by the ties of charity and peace under the one Head, who is our Saviour Himself, and form one man," Augustine preached to the people. Singing was a unique, concrete manifestation of this abstract doctrine. "Often their voice is heard in the Psalms as the voice of one man; the cry of one is as the cry of all, for all are one in One." These thoughts are common throughout his sermons. We have an obligation to worship God both individually and collectively, and one without the other is not sufficient. "And because we are many, the Scripture says that we praise God all together [collaudamus]; and because we are one, it says that we each praise Him [laudamus]."[44] Even when the individual sings, he or she never really sings alone: "Let him rise up, this one chanter; let this man sing from the heart of each of us, and let each one of us be in this man. When each of you sings a verse, it is still this one man that sings, since you are all one in Christ."[45]

This unity of all Christians is not superficial or extraneous; for the post-Nicean church it is at the heart of Christianity. We saw the foundations laid in the ante-Nicean church. Theologians of the post-Nicean church continued to build upon that foundation until a very strong theology of community was in place. Augustine was the prime articulator of the theology, and his works are replete with references to and Pauline images of the Mystical Body and of the unity of Christians. Augustine was not alone, however; most theologians included elements of the doctrine in their works.[46] It is hard to imagine that somehow churchmen were professing belief in this doctrine of unity, preaching it, promoting it, and eloquently defending it, all while excluding half the members of the church from its domain. Certainly we have no written proof nor know of any practices that indicate such exclusion. I believe this doctrine is key to understanding the spiritual position of women in the church. At a time when clericalism was being institutionalized, we must remember that the Pauline doctrine of the Mystical Body, so explicitly inclusive and unitive, was developed and promoted. God, the people were constantly being reminded by preachers like Augustine, "has fashioned and modeled our hearts, modeled them one by one, giving us each a heart, but without destroying their unity," and if any one of these individual hearts denies that one of "the faithful who are baptized in Christ have put on Christ," then "they offer insult to their Head if they say they are not holy; for then His members would not be holy."[47] Marking one member of the body as inferior affects the entire body, for "if one member suffers, all the members suffer with it."[48] In case there is still doubt about the implications of treating a member of the church as an inferior, Augustine spelled it out with precision: "If thou lovest only a part, thou art divided; if thou art divided, thou art not in the body; if thou art not in the body, thou art not under the Head." Christ, the Head, "loves His body," and so must Christians. "If someone wished to kiss thy cheek, but insisted at the same time on trampling thy feet, . . . wouldst thou not interrupt his expressions of respect and cry out: 'What are thou doing, man? Thou art trampling upon me!'"[49] These were the messages preached to men and to women as they gathered together to worship their Christian God.

Before we put Egeria's journal to rest, we must examine her description of a feast "observed here with special magnificence" on the fortieth day after Epiphany and held "with the same solemnity as at the feast of Easter." It is a feast to commemorate "the passage from the Gospel about Joseph and Mary taking the Lord to the Temple, and about Simeon and the prophetess Anna."[50] Egeria was referring to the feast of the Purification. It originated in the East and was celebrated forty days after January 6, the Eastern feast of

Christmas. Those areas that celebrated Christmas on December 25 (principally in the West by 336) eventually had an analogous commemoration of February 2. In its earliest days, the commemoration was a joint one for the Circumcision and the Purification, but by the mid-fourth century they were celebrated separately. Simultaneous with the separation came a change in emphasis within the commemoration of the Purification. It became more a feast about Mary, whereas previously it focused more on Jesus. Within the next two centuries feast days, commemorations, devotions, and overall attention to Mary increased dramatically. The reasons for the rise in devotion to Mary are complex and the subject of much speculation. We shall try to avoid the extremes of the controversies surrounding Marian devotions and concentrate on the content of these devotions. Only after the facts are presented can readers judge their impact, if any, on Christians' attitudes toward women's spiritual worth.

Direct scriptural reference to Mary is sparse, except in Luke, who provides the most explicit information about Mary in his first two chapters. Here we have the Annunciation (Lk 1:26-38), the Visitation (Lk 1:39-56), the Nativity (Lk 2:1-20), the Purification (Lk 2:22-40), and the Finding in the Temple (Lk 2:43-50). Elsewhere we have the wedding feast at Cana (Jn 2:1-11); the scene at the foot of the cross (Jn 19:25-27); Jesus's genealogy (Mt 1:16); the Nativity, Epiphany, and flight into Egypt stories of Matthew (Mt 1:18-2:21); Pentecost (Acts 1:14); an inconsequential reference in Mark (MBA 3:31-35); and one indirect reference in Paul (Gal 4:4). These references, while not abundant, are significant and are at the core of later devotions. The Magnificat is simultaneously the first Christian hymn, the first Marian hymn, and the longest speech of Mary recorded in Scripture. Its central theme is Mary's gratitude to God for raising her to such high estates and her awareness that "all generations shall call me blessed" (Lk 1:48).

Ante-Nicean theologians had little to say about Mary or about these scriptural references. Ignatius of Antioch's *Letter to the Ephesians* (ca.110) contains the first known mention of Mary as the source for Jesus's humanity: "There is one physician who is possessed both of flesh and spirit; both made and not made . . . both of Mary and of God."[51] Justin Martyr mentioned her next, ca. 155, this time when discussing the mystery of Jesus's conception at length,[52] and contrasted her to Eve.[53] In the latter discussion we have the seed of a fruitful vine planted; Mary as the new Eve was a popular portrait throughout the next centuries. Irenaeus, the first to articulate a developed Mariology, included the New Eve theme in *Against Heresies*.[54] Tertullian continued Irenaeus's Eve-Mary comparison but presented a more imperfect image of Mary while doing so.[55] He also called into question Mary's perpetual virginity,[56] while Clement of Alexandria affirmed it.[57] Origen presented a little bit of all the above. He talked at length about Mary's virginity[58] but added nothing new to the discussion. Origen is most remembered in Mariology as the first to use the phrase *Theotokos*, Bearer of God, or Mother of God.[59]

As can be seen, these theologians discussed Mary only minimally. Yet a popular tradition coexisted with early church writings, one articulated in noncanonical and apocryphal literature and demonstrated in the devotions of the people. Much of what was written about Mary in these works was soon forgotten, but a commemoration of a few pertinent events contained in these stories found their way into the pietistic life of the people.

The earliest known invocation of Mary as protector and Theotokos is dated to the third century: "Under your mercy we take refuge, Theotokos, do not reject our supplications in necessity, but deliver us from danger."[60] Gregory Nazianzen wrote about a woman praying to Mary for help, and Sozomen told about the greatness of Gregory Nazianzen's church, where "the power of God was there manifest," and that this power "was accredited to Mary, the Mother of God, the holy virgin, for she does manifest herself in this way."[61] Gregory of Nyssa was the only theologian in this period to refer to any of the apocryphal stories about Mary.[62]

Devotion to Mary is abundantly evident in the writings of Ephrem the Syrian, the first major writer to specifically promote her veneration. His most important writings on Marian devotion are contained in a collection of hymns he composed for liturgical celebrations during the Christmas cycle, called *The Hymns of the Nativity*. Their importance for us here lies in their influence and function. "His hymns," Kathleen McVey summarizes in her translations of the collection, "incorporated early into the liturgy, have remained central in both the East and the West Syrian liturgical traditions. From this paramount position they have exerted a formative influence on all aspects of ecclesiastical life . . . [and] played a significant role in the development of both Byzantine hymnography and Western medieval religious drama."[63] In other words, innumerable people were exposed to them, sung them, and presumably believed them.[64]

Ephrem called his collection lullabyes, because some of them were composed as songs that Mary sung to Jesus.[65] "I shall not be jealous, my Son, that you are both with me and with everyone," begins the sixteenth hymn. "'The Babe that I carry has carried me,' said Mary," are the opening lines of the seventeenth.[66] Much is scripturally based, as is this paraphrase of the Magnificat: "Mary was aglow. She, too, sang: 'Who has granted to this barren one to conceive and give birth to the One (Who is also) many, to the small

(Who is also) great."[67] Most of the hymns, however, were poetic theological statements about the Incarnation and the role that Mary played in it. Again and again Ephrem emphasized the indispensable, mysterious, and paradoxical role of Mary: "Our Lord, no one knows how to address Your mother," hymn 11 sings, "but if your mother is incomprehensible, who is capable of (comprehending) you?"[68] She was an apparent contradiction, for she gave birth through "conception within her without sexual union."[69] Even to Mary the paradox and mystery were overwhelming; "You are within me, and You are outside of me, O Mystifier of His Mother."[70] As the hymns contemplate the mystery the paradox becomes even deeper: "She gave Him milk from what He made exist. She gave Him food from what He had created."[71] Jesus likewise was a paradox: "A wonder is your mother; the Lord entered her and became a servant; He entered able to speak and He became silent in her; He entered her thundering and His voice grew silent. . . . The womb of Your mother overthrew the orders."[72]

At the heart of the mystery and paradox is the irreplaceable Mary; "Who will sing a lullabye to the child of her womb as Mary (did)?"[73] The hymns praise Mary as a second Eve, who will today "rejoice in Sheol" because the Son Mary conceived "will crush the head of the serpent that wounded her."[74] Mary was a second Sarah, who "sang lullabyes to Isaac."[75] Most of all, she was praised because Mary, "who without vows and without prayer, in her virginity conceived and brought forth the Lord of all."[76] This meant that Mary was most deserving of the title *blessed*, since "Indeed you were able to say how much and how and where the Great One, Who became small, dwelt in you."[77] All was incomprehensible—"Mary's lap astonishes me that it sufficed for You, my Lord"[78]—unless one acknowledged that it was "by power from Him Mary's womb became able to bear the One Who bears all."[79]

When these lines are envisioned as sung in a sacred setting within a communal liturgy, then the full importance of these hymns emerges. The strong imagery, the forceful theological arguments, and the beauty of the poetry all combined to make a tremendous impact on the congregation. In contrast to formal theological literature, people take songs home with them almost effortlessly. As we have already mentioned, hymns also affect people emotionally and evoke different levels of responses than would treatises. We need not diminish the importance of theological works of the period in order to appreciate the influence and significance Ephrem's hymns had on Christians' perception of women's spiritual dignity. He dealt with one woman, Mary, not all women, yet this one woman was "able to bear the One Who bears all."[80] In this sense Mary represented not only all women, but all men as well.

In the fourth and fifth centuries hymns and the devotions they summarized began to gain official attention, particularly after the church started assigning specific days to commemorate saints. During these centuries Mary emerged individualized and venerated. Consequently she was less intertwined with Jesus. The Purification, we have already noted, separated from the Circumcision by the middle of the fourth century. The origins of the feast of the Assumption are less clear. Some scholars believe the feast predated the Council of Ephesus (431) and was celebrated in the East as the Commemoration of Mary, usually on the Sunday before Christmas.[81] Evidence available from mid-fourth-century Jerusalem, however, indicates that while Mary's death was being discussed, further theological development was necessary before a firm belief crystallized.

The writings of Epiphanius of Salamis, leader of a monastic community near Jerusalem, allow us to see the transition and development as it is occurring. He wrote at length about contemporary popular discussions concerning the death of Mary. He saw validity on both sides of the question: "Whether she died or not." There is no definitive statement in Scripture, "no indication whether she died or did not die, whether she was buried or not buried." Until something more convincing appeared, Epiphanius declared that "for my part, I venture on no pronouncement, but keep my own counsel and remain silent," because "Scripture surpasses the mind of man and has left the matter an open question."[82] Epiphanius also referred to a heresy concerning Mary's sexual relationship with Joseph after Jesus's birth and to one concerning the worship of Mary as a goddess.[83] The latter heresy was adhered to by "certain women" (called Collyridians) who annually "put out bread and offer it in Mary's name."[84] Apparently enough people were attracted to such groups that Epiphanius believed it necessary to refute the premise: "For which scripture ever taught such a thing? . . . For [Mary] is a chosen vessel, but a woman, and in no way different in nature, highly honored though she is in her will and her senses."[85] Furthermore, "if he does not want angels to be worshipped, how much more does he not want this for her born of Ann?"[86] Two facts are noteworthy here. First, Epiphanius's comments and reactions indicate the presence of a strong, unwritten tradition among the people of devotion to Mary, and second, the first written testimony we have to this devotion immediately established their proper content. For such devotion to be acceptable it must be distinctly different from worship due God; it must not be worship at all.[87]

Such debates may have continued for some time, but in the fifth century a doctrinal dispute positioned the debate in the limelight, and one of the results was the furthering of popular devotions to Mary. The conflict involved the imperial family, the bishop of Constantinople, the city's populace, and an ecumenical council. At the center of the controversy were two women, Mary and Empress Pulcheria.

In 395 Emperor Arcadius took the throne in the eastern half of the Roman Empire, and during his reign church and state became increasingly unified. According to Sozomen, John Chrysostom's "mandate from the emperor enjoining his immediate departure"[88] was the result of his opposition to a statue of Arcadius's wife, Eudoxia, being "placed upon a column of porphyry on a high platform" outside the church, amid the celebration of the people. "John charged that these proceedings reflected dishonor on the church." Eudoxia was enraged at John "openly disclaiming against her in the church,"[89] and the two remained at odds until her death. When Arcadius died in 408 he left three young girls and one son, but from the beginning the oldest of the girls, Pulcheria, took control and became "the protector of [Theodsius II, the boy] and of his government." At fourteen "she first devoted her virginity to God, and instructed her sisters in the same course of life" in a public ceremony with "God, the priests, and all the subjects of the Roman empire as witnesses." After so establishing herself and isolating herself from outside influence—"she permitted no man to enter her palace"—she began ruling the empire, which she did "excellently and with great orderliness." Fluent in Greek and Latin, she directed the business of the empire, but always "in the name of her brother." She likewise took control of his education, reserving for herself his education in manners and princely behavior, and, most important, his religious education. Pulcheria's own religious life was beyond reproach, according to Sozomen. "With how much fear she worshipped God, it would take long for anyone to say; and how many houses of prayer she built magnificently, and how many hostelries and monastic communities she established, the arrangement for the expenses for their perpetual support, and the provision for the inmates." Sozomen anticipated the skeptical reader, so he challenged the doubter to verify his portrait of Pulcheria through other means: "If anyone pleases to examine the truth from the business itself, and not be convinced by my words, he will learn that they are not falsely described by me."[90]

From all accounts, Pulcheria was a power to be reckoned with, in both the political and the ecclesiastical spheres. Even after Theodosius II matured and married, Pulcheria remained in the center of power. During the late 420s the preaching of Proclus gained attention. By 428 his preaching on Mary became a matter of particular attention to the newly appointed bishop, Nestorius, who disagreed with Proclus's emphasis on Mary as Theotokos. Nestorius's chief associate Anastasius, for whom Nestorius "had the highest esteem," preached in rebuttal to Proclus, "Let no one call Mary Theotokos: for Mary was but a woman; and it is impossible that God should be born of a woman. These words," Socrates records, "created a great sensation, and troubled many both of the clergy and laity." Nestorius, "eager to establish Anastasius' proposition," immediately defended the sermon by delivering "several public discourses on the subject, in which he assumed a controversial attitude, and totally rejected the epithet Theotokos."[91] Nestorius allowed that Mary was Christokos, mother of Christ, "but it is one thing to say that the God who is the Word of the Father was cojoined to him who was born from Mary . . . but quite another that the Deity needed a birth involving months [of pregnancy]."[92]

By late spring 429 Cyril, patriarch of Alexandria, entered into the fray and identified the issue as Christological rather than strictly Mariological. Mary was Theotokos because "Godhead and Manhood completed for us the one Lord and Christ and Son by their unutterable and unspeakable concurrence into unity."[93] Cyril passed on his information about Nestorius's interpretation to Pope Celestine, who in turn called a synod in Rome in August 430. The synod condemned Nestorius and gave him ten days to recant. When the recantation was not forthcoming, and when other bishops and theologians were drawn into the matter, Theodosius II notified the bishops in November of that year that a council would be held in June to pass judgment on Nestorius's position. When the council met at Ephesus, Nestorius's chief supporter, John of Antioch, was late in arriving, so Cyril was able to condemn Nestorius without real opposition on the first day. The reaction of the city's populous that night is a reminder of how real these supposedly abstract theological debates were to Christians; there was a massive torchlit procession in celebration of the victory of Mary Theotokos.[94]

Behind the scenes another significant battle was being fought, this one between Nestorius and Pulcheria. Pulcheria had closely identified herself with ecclesiastical practices: Her imperial robe was used as an altar covering; her picture hung above the altar; she and her group of virgins dominated Vespers at the episcopal church; and the Virginity Festival, celebrated in Constantinople during the 420s, was closely associated with Pulcheria and her group.[95] Nestorius opposed her dominance in church affairs from the start. He quickly stopped using her robe, took down her picture, prohibited her from attending Vespers, and then attacked the Virgin Mary with whom Pulcheria had so closely identified herself. As tension between the two mounted, Nestorius barred her from entering the sanctuary to receive Communion on Easter and refused to "compare a woman [Pulcheria] corrupted of men to the bride of Christ."[96]

This context formed the background for the sermon by Proclus that initiated the Nestorian controversy. A close ally of the empress, Proclus defended Pulcheria as much as Mary when he preached at the Virginity Festival in 428. The feast, Proclus proclaimed, "has the purpose of purity, and is the perfect boast of the society of women, and the glory of the female sex, because of the occurrence of the Mother and the Virgin." All of creation should "leap about," and "the human race exult in joy, because women are honored."[97] According to Vasiliki Limberis, from this point on, "Pulcheria made the battle against Nestorius her personal vendetta."[98]

The story of Pulcheria, Nestorius, and Mary as Theotokos is basically a narrative in church-state relations and in imperial politics, but that does not mean that there were no implications for women's history. As a result of Pulcheria's personal devotion to Mary (and obviously because of her wealth and position), three churches dedicated to Mary were built, and Marian relics—her shroud, her cincture, and St. Luke's icon of her—were housed within the city walls. Pulcheria's close ties with the people of Constantinople led to the public adoption of many of her private devotions to Mary. Finally, Pulcheria's activity and devotion prepared the way for the statement by the Council of Ephesus that forever defined the church's belief in Mary's role in salvific history as Theotokos. Thus a woman played a major role in the spread of devotion to another woman.

After Ephesus devotion to Mary increased. It became a permanent, public, and official aspect of orthodox Christianity. The number of churches dedicated to Mary multiplied, as did the number of sermons on Mary, well into the next few centuries.[99] Apocryphal stories continued to become attached to doctrine and devotions, but it was not a wholesale adoption, and discretion was urged upon all. "We are wholly unable to follow the fictitious statements which are found in the fabulous lives of the Virgin, and which resemble the writings of the Greek poets, who in their works on theology relate mere myths about their gods; neither will we invent lives of her in order to gratify her," wrote an anonymous Coptic devotee to Mary.[100] In the West Leo the Great avoided the myths and reiterated the doctrinal emphasis of Ephesus in a famous letter to Flavian, bishop of Constantinople: "[The Son was] truly conceived of the Holy Spirit within the womb of His Virgin Mother, who bore Him while preserving her virginity just as, preserving her virginity, she conceived Him." While "this birth in time in no way minimized His divine and eternal birth," Mary's participation, "singularly wonderful and wonderfully singular," brought forth the One who is able "to pay the debt of our fallen state."[101] At the Council of Chalcedon (451) this letter became a part of official conciliar statements.[102]

The Eastern church continued to be more attached to Marian devotions than the Western during the fifth and sixth centuries. Marian poetry
in particular thrived. Jacob of Sarung continued in Ephrem's tradition, and
his poems were used extensively in liturgy, his *Ode on the Blessed Virgin Mary*
being the most popular; it articulated a highly developed Mariology. In
Akathistos, one of "the most widely known and popular [hymns] with the
laity" and "the oldest continuously performed" hymn in Eastern Orthodoxy,[103] Mary herself is praised extensively, not just what God's actions
accomplished within her. "Hail! to you, who opened the gates of paradise,"
the hymn resounds, "who has shown Christ as the loving Lord . . . who
redeemed us from the pagan religion . . . who has rescued us from the mire
of transgression."[104] This hymn presents a more engaging portrait of Mary
than most other hymns to date. It is a portrait of an active, initiating Mary:
"Hail! that you astound as thunder your foes. Hail! That you shed light of
great brilliancy. Hail! that you spring forth the multi-streamed river."[105]
Mary is also seen here as having intellectual prowess: "Hail! to you, . . . who
extricates us from the depths of ignorance. Hail! to you who illuminates
many in knowledge."[106]

In the West, Venantius Fortunatus has been identified as the author of
two popular early Marian hymns, *Ave maris stellis* (Hail thou star of ocean) and
Quem terra, pontus, sidera (The God whom earth and sea and sky), but they may
be of later origin. The reoccurring theme in the latter is the blessedness of
Mary and "the Virgin's Womb, filled with the grace of heaven."[107] The Marian
feasts of the Purification, Assumption, Annunciation, and Nativity gradually
spread to the West about a century after each was established in the East; by
the end of the seventh century the feasts were universally observed.

What effect, if any, these Marian devotions had on Christians' perceptions of women's spiritual dignity is, as usual, hard to ascertain. Did the
rise of Marian devotions in the post-Nicean world elevate Christians' appreciation of women's spiritual dignity or women's opinions of their own
spiritual worth? It is hard to imagine that the church's official lauding of
Mary did not reassure men and women that women fully participated in and
were included in salvific history, any more than it is plausible to argue that
reading the misogynist statements of a Tertullian was not unsettling. Beyond
what common sense and experience tell us, we have little else to declare with
certainty. With the Council of Ephesus Marian devotions became firmly
rooted in conciliar tradition and, as such, became part of revelation in the
eyes of the Roman church. The fact that much of the devotion to Mary was
nonscriptural is a stumbling block to most Protestants, but it was not so for
the Christians of the post-Nicean church. The fact that Marian devotions

resemble goddess cults is problematic to some modern scholars, but as Jaroslav Pelikan argues in his study on Mary's impact on culture, Christianity "had in Mary a way of simultaneously affirming and yet correcting what those goddesses symbolized." He also claims that there are "some extremely valuable resources" historians have neglected that suggest that "the silent millions among Medieval women" identified with Mary, "with her humility, yes, but also with her defiance and with her victory."[108] We also must remember that the church was always careful—in theory if not in practice—to make a clear distinction between the worship *(latria)* due God, the veneration *(dulia)* given to saints, and the higher veneration *(hyperdulia)* given to Mary. These developments can perhaps best be summarized by simply stating that devotion to Mary grew within a community that possessed a nonmisogynist, inclusive definition of humanity's spiritual nature and was compatible with that tradition.

6

Early Medieval Saints East and West

BY THE SIXTH CENTURY so many political and social changes had occurred within the civilizations of the Mediterranean that historians have long distinguished them temporally and spatially. They call the era medieval rather than ancient, and the areas the East and the West. Christianity thrived in the new period in both areas, but as a result of the increasingly distinct cultures developing in the East and the West, differences in the way Christianity was observed become more obvious. During the sixth through eleventh centuries, or the Early Middle Ages, there was still much in common. We will continue to discuss pertinent developments in the East during this period, but after the schism of 1054 attention will be devoted solely to the West as Christian culture divided more sharply into East and West. Moreover, due to the radical nature of the political and social changes that occurred in the West during these centuries, the types of sources available to us also change and present today's historians with a whole new set of challenges. As the West was busy merging its classical, Germanic, and Christian cultures, less energy was available to channel into speculative activities. The preoccupation with the concrete rather than the abstract has its benefits for us, though, because it means that while there were few intellectual discussions in the West about women, there were many more descriptions of individual women and society's attitude toward them. The phenomenon of the Christian saint begins here with its accompanying hagiography. We have seen how difficult it sometimes is to appraise the impact an abstract treatise has on society's opinion of women and to determine whether it truly reflects or influences actual group behavior, or merely represents the speculative wishes of one individual (who may not even follow his own dictates in his personal life). While there are some difficulties inherent in analyzing early medieval hagiography, Christian society's beliefs about the spiritual nature of women is contained therein and is accessible to us. This chapter examines written sources on the actual lives of early medieval women in order to consider their behavior and Christian society's assessment of that behavior.

Often overshadowed by Greek and Latin contributions, the Syrian Orient played a dominant role in the shaping of early Christian culture, and it continued to do so during this period. We already have discussed Syrian development of feminine symbols in ecclesiology and theology. The School of Persians, established at Nisibair and forced to move to Edessa in 363, was unique in its day. It prefigured elements found in medieval seminaries and universities, taught in the vernacular (Syriac is a dialect of Aramaic, Jesus's spoken language), and nurtured the teachings of its greatest scholar, Ephrem the Syrian, whose witness to Mary in hymnology has been examined. Ephrem was the greatest Christian poet of the fourth century,[1] and with his hymns early Marian devotion peaked in the Syrian Orient.[2] Besides insight into attitudes toward Mary, Syrian literature provides us with a series of legendary and historical vitae of women renowned in the Early Middle Ages. Most of the vitae were based on personal recollections or eyewitness accounts and thus contain a core historical reality. Even the vitae that were exceptions to this rule probably were based on a kernel of historical fact.[3] All except perhaps the vita of Fibronia were written by men, so they were also reflections of men's beliefs about women's spiritual worth. What we find is a very positive perception of women's spiritual nature. The women were presented as models of virtue and inspirations to all Christians. The stories were immensely popular during the Middle Ages, in both East and West, particularly those of Mary, the niece of Abraham, and Pelagia the Penitent, and manuscripts are found in every medieval language. Both Eastern and Western liturgical calendars honor these women with commemorations.[4]

John of Ephesus is a primary source for Syrian hagiography. In the 560s he wrote *Lives of the Eastern Saints,* a collection of fifty-eight vitae of ascetic men and women whom he personally was acquainted with and admired for their piety. His twelfth vita was the first to deal with women, and he offered us a lengthy justification for his inclusion of women. "Since we learn from the divine Paul who said, 'In Christ Jesus there is neither male nor female' it seemed to us that we should introduce the story of those who are by nature females, since mention of them in no way lessens this series of stories about holy men. Furthermore, their course of life was not lower than the exalted path upon which every one of these holy men has journeyed, and even their way of life was great and surpasses telling."[5]

The first two women he wrote about were sisters, the elderly Mary and a younger sister Euphemia, a widow who "took up a regulated life of devotion and wore the garb of a religious, while learning the psalms and teaching them to her daughter, who had been thoroughly instructed since her early youth in psalmody, the Scriptures, and writing."[6] The older sister spent "most of the time" sitting "amongst the poor" and "in front of Golgotha with her eyes raised up."[7] After three years of praying thus, her reputation for holiness spread. This frightened her for she "dreaded being honored by people, lest she lose the fruits of her ascetic labor; and when she saw this happening, she fled immediately." She decided to travel from place to place "for the rest of her life" and to return to Golgotha only once each year to "offer worship in the place of God's suffering."[8]

Euphemia mimicked Mary's prayerful and ascetic life in most aspects, but added to it a life of service to the poor and suffering. She maintained a sparse household for herself and her daughter "to whom she had given religious instruction since she was quite small."[9] She supported a "small business she and her daughter ran."[10] If any bread not bought by the work of her own hands "happened" to enter her house, she and her daughter refused to eat it. She worked for the town's nobility and divided her pay in half, one part for their household and the other "for the relief of the poor and the sick and those in prison." She spent hours seeking out the destitute. In John's narrative it is obvious that her behavior went beyond ordinary charitable activities. "Indeed she went around all the squares of the city; wherever she found someone ill or crippled or blind, or an old person unable to walk, she would sit down beside each in turn, asking, 'What would you like today dear? Would you just like me to buy you some green vegetables?'"[11] So intent was she on relieving any who suffered that even if the needy tried to avoid her, it was impossible "to escape without her visiting once or twice daily, since she was capable of dashing about all day." She always made sure she brought spiritual as well as physical comfort, urging the sick to imitate "Lazarus, who by persevering with patience and not complaining inherited the kingdom of Heaven." In this way "she was called Tabitha throughout the city" because she reminded all of the good Tabitha of Jappa honored in Acts 9:36.[12]

The events following the Council of Chalcedon provide evidence that the vast majority of laity shared John's high opinion of the women's spiritual worth. Opposition to the Council led to bitter disputes, with Euphemia in the midst of them. Opposition leaders claimed she and her daughter were too popular and beloved; they were "upsetting this city—why, the citizens revere and honor them more than the bishops!"[13] Euphemia was imprisoned after refusing to receive Communion from opposition clergy. The people would not tolerate such treatment of Euphemia, a woman whose power rested on the laity's perception of her spiritual dignity. Consequently, "all the city was begging for her release" and soon worked itself into "a state of uproar concerning her."[14] The officials released her and instead banished her and her daughter from the city.

In the story of Susan, John again found it necessary to justify including the vita of a woman within his collection, and again quoted Galatians 3:28: "In Christianity Jesus, there is neither male nor female, nor slave nor free." This time he added an argument contrasting human weakness with divine strength, a favorite analogy in discussions of women's spiritual worth. God's strength was most obvious in weakness, so it manifested itself "not only in men who are powerful in appearance and mighty and forceful, but also in weak, feeble, frail women." God's strength "fortifies and gives them courage until they too bear the struggle with undaunted strength."[15] Susan, John confessed, "holy and manly in Christ, so astonished me by her appearance, words, and strength in God that she seemed to me not at all out of place in this series of stories of holy men, with whom she strains to enter to same narrow gate, as indeed she already has done."[16]

Susan was born of noble parents and ran away while still a mere child to make a pilgrimage to Jerusalem. Next she tried to join a monastery but initially was rejected because of her youth. When the nuns realized she was a foreigner, they took pity and admitted her. Life inside the monastery was not easy. Many picked on her because she was still so young, but eventually perception of her spiritual dignity won them over. For ten years she lived in peace, until the Chalcedonian disputes disrupted the community. Church officials gave the women the option of submitting to Chalcedonian faith or leaving the monastery. Susan chose to leave. She and some other women moved to the desert to live the eremitic life. Three years later the women's reputation led eleven men to seek them out and establish a community alongside theirs. "Report of her strength was heard everywhere," and eventually "news of her perfection" incited John to go meet her in person. He was not disappointed. After Susan "related to us many things," John was "left in great wonder of her words" and ended his visit "marveling at the practice of the holy woman."[17]

John singled out only three other women for lengthy discussion: Caesaria, Sosiana, and Mary the Anchorite. What is most interesting is that each of the women he discussed attained sanctity through a different path, which indicates his recognition of women's spiritual diversity. Caesaria the Patrician was a powerful, wealthy woman married within her social class. She longed for the ascetic life, and eventually, either by consent of her husband or after his death, she embraced "asceticism beyond measure."[18]

When John met her he immediately began "advising her to give up high things and embrace moderate things, lest being unable to endure she might either lose her strength or fall into severe illness and be forced from necessity to give it all up."[19] John was wrong. She was able to endure and asked for yet more hardships. When she decided to pursue the life of an anchorite, John repeated the same doubts, saying that such a life would be "beyond her capacity and strength and condition."[20] Distressed that he would not agree (John had taken on the role of what later ages would call a confessor-spiritual director), she instead founded two monasteries, one for men and one for women, and became a recluse in the women's. Her chamberwoman Sosiana shared most of Caesaria's spiritual aspirations by a private vow. While her husband lived they abstained from "holding carnal intercourse with one another" and instead filled their lives with "fasting and prayers, and genuflection and recitation of service and watching by night."[21] After her husband's death and Caesaria's entrance into monasticism, Sosiana disbanded her household and donated everything to the church. Mary the Anchorite, inspired by a holy man she had met in her youth, decided, against family opposition, to live the monastic life, "and from that time she took that holy old man as her model in all things."[22]

Other Syrian sources show a similar diversity. A letter written in 524 by the bishop of Beth Arshom related the gruesome details of a notorious incident during the persecution of Christians in the sixth century by Jewish invaders. "Laymen and women" were corraled into a church that they filled "from wall to wall." The invaders then "piled up wood all around the outside of the church and set alight to it, thus burning the church along with everyone inside it."[23] The letter also presents individual portraits of some of the women martyrs of Najran, such as the peculiar servant Mahya, "a disagreeable woman, impudent and abusive, disliked by everyone because of her disagreeable ways."[24] When all her family, owners, and companion were put to death, she became determined to suffer martyrdom also. The problem was that because of her disagreeable personality and bullying ways, she knew the persecutors would think it too much trouble to capture and kill her. To counteract this Mahya took to the streets, calling upon all to come with her to confront the enemy. She even offered to stop abusing everyone if they would come. "Look at me; there is no one as wicked as me; follow me, so that I don't have to go alone—otherwise the Jews will run away from me as usual, and will not put me to death."[25]

No one accompanied her, but eventually she was admitted into the king's presence, despite his advisors warning against this "very Satan of the Christians." After daring the king to "get up and butcher me too," he "ordered her to be stripped naked." At this point she proudly proclaimed: "It is to your shame, and to the shame of all your fellow Jews that you have done this; I am not ashamed myself, for I have done this many times of my own will; I have been naked in the presence of men without feeling ashamed, for I am woman—such as was created by God."[26] Her speech helped her attain her goal, for the king then gave orders to have one of her legs tied to a donkey and the other to an ox and to be thus dragged around the town three times. After that she was hung upside down until evening as a target for arrows and stones.

Another portrait preserved by Simeon is one of the wealthy, beautiful martyr Ruhm, known throughout the area "because of all her acts of kindness to everyone."[27] She possessed a more likable personality, but in her own way was just as intent and aggressive as Mahya in pursuing her end when the choice between martyrdom and heresy was given her. Ruhm embraced martyrdom with the same determination and energy as Mahya. She too "ran out into the street into the middle of town" to proclaim her decision to accept death, although Ruhm decided to address her remarks mainly to the "women of Najran, Christians, Jews and Pagan."[28] She asked not that they accompany her to death but that they listen to her explanations and pray for her. "Blessed are you, my fellow women, if you listen to my words; blessed are you, fellow women, if you recognized this truth, for whose sake I am going to die—both I and my daughters. Blessed are you, my fellow women, if you love Christ."[29] Ruhm had much to lose by her choice. "I possess gold and silver, male and female servants, and my own income; I lack nothing," she reminded the town's women, "and I tell you, this very day I am the possessor of 40,000 denarii, sealed up and stored in my treasury, separate from my husband's. I have jewelry, pearls, and jacynths"[30] as well as physical beauty. But to Ruhm these things only "provide testimony that I have not preferred them" to the joys of Christ. "Of my own free will I leave everything behind, in order to go and receive a substitute for it from my Lord."[31]

When Ruhm finished her speech "a wail went up from all the women of the town." This further infuriated the king to the extent that he "wanted to put [his messengers] to death for having allowed her to speak at such length." Ruhm was undeterred and proceeded to meet her death, "her face uncovered without feeling any shame, and holding her daughters by the hand, all dressed up as for a wedding feast."[32] When one of the daughters (now properly identified as a granddaughter) spit at the king during their interrogation, he angrily ordered the children killed and their blood be "actually poured into her grandmother's mouth."[33] Ruhm's execution followed immediately.

These sources provide us with much to ponder. The women's spiritual feats and virtues were as admired as any man's, and the recording of their vitae ensured that they were perceived as models to be imitated by both men and women. Even in the stories of the women martyrs we encounter behavioral models for all Christians. The women's courage, public proclamations, acceptance of their bodies, lack of shame in exposure, and use of free will were all exalted. The portraits by John of Ephesus often emphasized the domestic virtues of the women, particularly in the case of Euphemia, but the stronger focus was on their prayer life and on the revered status this prayer life gave them in the community. They were powerful witnesses to be heard and imitated.

Perhaps the most personal witness we have of the spiritual importance of these women in Christian communities is found in the writings of Martyrios, a seventh-century East Syrian monk. In his *Book of Perfection* Martyrios took time out from his discussion of men to tell us about a highly influential woman in his own life. He too found it necessary to use the Pauline strength-in-weakness theme to justify his focus on women, and in his justification we can sense his frustration when facing theory versus reality: "But why should I just talk about men? Let us examine the weak nature of the frail female sex to see whether the beauty of the virtuous life is not also revealed to us in the godlike women who trampled on sin and Satan. I myself am ashamed to gaze on their valiant deeds when I consider the laxity of us men; but it is right that this beauty should be made public—to our greater confusion and to the glory of these women."[34]

Martyrios chose to "let the example of just one of all these women [Shirin] suffice" to prove his point. Shirin was already around eighty years old when Martyrios met her in his childhood, but young as he was, he was able to perceive her spiritual perfection. "Only someone who had actually seen her can fully know how serene and gentle she was, how pure, and full of simplicity, how she brimmed over with compassionate love for everyone and how deeply joyous she was to receive strangers and to see their comfort."[35] Martyrios was not alone in his admiration; "the very sight of her moved everyone to wonder." He stated that Shirin's reputation for holiness was so vast that monks and abbots "from afar would give her greeting, entreating her to pray for them." When she traveled about these abbots "would minister to her needs like eager disciples, holding her in great respect." Their respect was so extensive that "all of the monastic abbots of the time—men of perfection whose glories we have told of earlier— considered her a blessed spiritual mother."[36] Martyrios considered this fact important enough to repeat, with added emphasis, so the reader can truly appreciate the greatness of this woman. "Monks and other strangers" considered "her as a holy spiritual mother," and "women in particular frequented her company," including Martyrios's mother. As Martyrios reminisced we see how deeply two women, Shirin and his mother, influenced his own spiritual life: "Set on fire by the very sight of her, my mother was consumed by a zeal for her way of life, which she wanted to imitate as far as she had the strength to do so. And ever since I was a child she would exhort me to choose to live a life that conformed with Shirin's." To reinforce Shirin's model behavior on Martyrios, his mother would "bring me to see this blessed woman regularly, since she lived in our village; in this way she would draw the holy women's blessings upon myself and instill in my heart all the greater ardor for the life of perfection as a result of seeing and hearing her. This ardor grew stronger every day, until my desire that originated from that source as it were consumed my youthful days."[37] Few more personal testimonies to the power of a saintly woman's influence on a man's spiritual life exist from this period.

The ideal of sanctity contained in early medieval Western women's hagiography differed in some respects from that in Eastern hagiography. The difference most likely is attributable to the Germanization that Christianity was undergoing in the West as the two cultures merged. As James Russell comments, Christian missionaries knew that any attempt to alter the Germanic value system radically would have ended in failure, so instead they "sought to redefine the Germanic values of strength, courage, and loyalty in such a manner that would reduce their incompatibility with Christian values, while at the same time 'inculturating' Christian values."[38] One effective and easily available way to achieve this goal was through personal witness. Radegund, one of the most popular German saints, had enough strength of character to leave her husband, Clothar, after he killed her brother, enough courage to stand firm in the face of rioting Franks as she ordered their temple burned down, and enough loyalty to her country to work diligently for peace among the nobles. Radegund's personal witness was a testimony to Christian values.

Personal witness was communicated more effectively to the Germans than written testimony. Throughout the early medieval period they looked to the holy person to learn about Christianity perhaps more than other societies did. Because of the strong pedagogical element in Western hagiography, vitae of German women are quite valuable to us here. First, the vitae reveal rather directly Christianity's opinion about women's spiritual worth; second, they teach us that women's witness was as essential as men's; and third, since the lives of women were used to teach others the truths of

Christianity, we know that society considered women's spiritual lives of great importance.

It is not surprising, therefore, to find the theme of witness common to early medieval Western vitae of women. The person's ability to bear effective witness to the truths of Christianity was of primary importance to the Germans. They were more impressed with the concrete than the abstract, as missionaries quickly learned when they preached to Germans for the first time.[39] Personal witness communicated more than written theology, and thus they looked to the life of the holy person to learn about the doctrines of Christianity. The vita of Bertilla, abbess of Chelles, was read to the many communities in the refectory and on feast days, and opens with a clear statement on the value of witness: "The brighter the religious life of holy virgins shines in merit, the more it is celebrated by word of mouth and praised in the tongues of all people. For as long as it presents an example of good behavior to others, it should move every voice to praise."[40]

The witness of women dominates all the vitae. Austreberta, abbess of Pavilly, bore such effective witness that many "who lived in the neighborhood, seeing her example and teaching, not only came to offer sons and daughters to God but many hurried to the monasteries themselves" to imitate her virtuous life.[41] Balthild, queen of Neustria, "left a holy example of humility and patience" and "showed that everything should be done as a result of consultation" with other nuns; this was her golden rule of piety, which she left "as a model to her companions."[42] Waldetrude, abbess of Mons, "gave an example to all of uncommon behavior";[43] while the hagiographer of Gertrude, abbess "over the men and women who lived as Christ's servants under her authority," confessed that he was writing her vita so her example "may illuminate the darkness in our hearts."[44] The gender of the person witnessing was irrelevant in the hagiographer's eyes; only the truth being witnessed to was of consequence. Hence hagiographers did not qualify their statements about women's witness by claiming that it only influenced other women. To the contrary, the writers were quite insistent that the women's witness had impact "over the men and women," on all "who lived in the neighborhood," or simply stated, "to all."[45]

The largest group of extant vitae we have are of the Merovingians. Radegund was by far the most beloved and revered of the Merovingian women. Substantial sources exist from which we can reconstruct her life, thus providing us with one of the most complete portraits of any early medieval person. Our good fortune continues, for the authors are of proven merit and were in positions to offer different perspectives of Radegund's life: Gregory of Tours, Venantius Fortunatus, and Baudonivia. We even have letters attributed to

Radegund, particularly the poetic *Thuringian War*.[46] Fortunatus begins Radegund's vita with the same Pauline formula that prefaced the vitae of Eastern
women saints: "Our Redeemer is so richly and abundantly generous that He
wins mighty victories through the female sex and, despite their frail physique,
He confers glory and greatness on women through strength of mind. By faith,
Christ makes them strong who were born weak so that, when those who
appeared to be imbeciles are crowned with their merits by Him who made
them, they garner praise for their Creator who hid heavenly treasure in earthen
vessels. For Christ the king dwells with his riches in their bowels."[47]

That being said, Fortunatus proceeds to heap praise on Radegund,
"that holiest of women,"[48] in superlative terms. Captured at age seven by
King Clothar during a war with her Thuringian family, she was brought up
at a royal villa in Athies where she "was taught letters and other things
suitable to her sex";[49] later letters reveal a rather well-educated women.[50]
Upon reaching a marriageable age, she became the bride of Clothar and was
"made his queen at Soissons." She accepted—even embraced—her role as
queen while at the same time "she avoided the trappings of royalty" by
practicing charity at every opportunity. She was a model of royal benefi-
cence and always "gave away a tithe of all that came to her before accepting
any for herself." She sought out hermits and the needy, believing "that
whatever she did not give to paupers was truly lost," because it "was their
own in reality." Radegund willingly accepted being "noble sprout sprung
from royal stock" because she believed that if "she played the part of the
wife" and queen to Clothar, ultimately she would be able "to serve Christ
more devoutly acting as a model laywoman."[51] Indeed, "the more secular
power was bestowed on her," the more she became "Christ's partner."[52]

She judged her situation altered, however, when Clothar had her
brother "killed unjustly by the hands of wicked men."[53] Radegund left
Clothar immediately and sought out Médard, bishop of Noyon, to beg him
to consecrate her to God and clothe her "in the robe of a monacha [nun]."
The king's men were dispatched to stop the consecration and even went so
far as to attempt "to drag him brutally through the basilica from the altar to
keep him from veiling the king's spouse." When Médard was understandably
intimidated, Radegund took matters into her own hands and, "sizing up the
situation, entered the sacristy, put on a monastic garb and proceeded straight
to the altar," and confronted Médard with her iron-clad determination. "If
you shrink from consecrating me," she boldly warned him, "and fear man
more than God, Pastor, He will require His sheep's soul from your hand."
Médard swiftly heeded her words and consecrated her. Radegund then
"divested herself of the noble costume" she wore as queen and placed it and

her gems and jewelry on the altar.[54] Clothar eventually reconciled with his wife and even agreed to build a monastery for her at Poitiers. A community took up residence there around 561. Radegund entered not as its head but rather "subordinated herself to the legally constituted abbess, reserv[ing] no authority of her own."[55] Still, she was the spiritual center of the monastery and frequently preached to the women—"her flock,"[56] as she called them.

Both Fortunatus and Baudonivia tell us much about Radegund's everyday life after she entered the monastery, and the picture they paint became commonplace in later descriptions of female monastic saints. In "an oratory dedicated in the name of the blessed Mary," Radegund "prepared herself for God's service," daily giving herself over to "ceaseless prayers and vigils, and devotion to reading."[57] Even "when she seemed to cease meditating or preaching on the psalms," she had one of the other women read them to her.[58] Radegund was insistent upon being the servant of the servants, the lowest of the low, and so frequently got up "while all the monachas were deep in sleep" to clean their shoes and the like. She took her turn doing the chores of the community, "never too disgusted to carry off what others shuddered to look upon." This included chores like "cleaning the privies" and removing "the stinking dung."[59] She gave freely to the poor from her fortune, providing a daily meal "to her enrolled paupers," and twice a week "she prepared a bath" for them. She scrubbed them herself and clothed them with new garments "if she noticed that anyone's clothes were shoddy."[60] Her sanctity, in other words, manifested itself in the spirit and thoroughness in which she mastered her domestic chores.

Miracles were a major avenue through which Radegund's spiritual dignity was made manifest, and one of Baudonivia's stated goals is "to publish a few of her many miracles," which she insists are true. "God be my witness," Baudonivia proclaims, "I swear that I am relating what I have heard and attesting to what I have seen."[61] The miracles Radegund performed were of a benign nature: The seas were calmed while her envoys were traveling back from Constantinople and thus "returned her servants to life from the jaws of death"; people were cured of toothaches, fevers, and smallpox; her raised right hand making the sign of the cross made "the whole multitude of demons" flee from the walls of a monastery; pesky birds took flight at her order. More dramatic miracles occurred after her death. Sight was restored to a blind person, a woman was exorcised of her demons, and a housemaid who "rashly dared to presume to seat herself in [Radegund's] high seat" burned "for three days and three nights" until Radegund answered her prayers and "quenched the blazing fire."[62] To her contemporaries these miracles proved Radegund's spiritual worth. As Gregory of Tours wrote after

Radegund's funeral, "I would not have stopped weeping if I did not realize that the blessed Radegund had departed from her convent in body but not in power."[63]

From the quality, quantity, and contents of the sources, clearly Radegund was one of the most beloved saints of her period, male or female. The traits that her contemporaries most admired, however, were not unique to her. Perhaps no one else lived them to such impressionable perfection, but other women did invoke the same kind of respect from their contemporaries as Radegund did, if not the same degree. Clothild, another sainted queen, possessed similar virtues. She engaged in almsgiving, fasts, physical penances, and the foundation of monasteries. She embraced her queenship as a means to further her spiritual life and devoted much of her energy to the conversion of her husband and to the suppression of heretical Arian Christianity in the realm.

Balthild was an Anglo-Saxon captured in raid by slavers who eventually ended up marrying Clovis II, king of Neustria and Burgundy. We are told how she "ministered to priests and poor alike, feeding the needy, clothing the naked, and taking care to order the burial of the dead."[64] After her husband's death she acted as regent for her son for a while, and while political historians debate the value of her reign,[65] the author of her vita tells us of her religious accomplishments during the regency, namely the prohibition of simony and the outlawing of infanticide.[66] She also had the monastery at Chelles built and determined to enter it in retirement. When that time came, like Radegund, she entered as "a servant and lowliest bondswoman" and took on "the dirtiest cleaning jobs for the sisters in the kitchen, personally cleaning up the dung in the latrine," all done "in perfect joy of spirit."[67] Again like Radegund, she did not completely abandon her former role as queen but rather used her political power to advise the abbess on how the monastery might continue to enjoy the good fame with which it began. Unlike Radegund's hagiographers, Balthild's did not emphasize any domestic virtues in the perception of her sanctity. God's power was still manifest through Balthild in the same manner, though, with numerous miracles that cured the faithful through "her holy intercession from whatever plague or illness." The hagiographer compared Balthild with three other sainted queens—Clothild, Ultragotha, and Radegund—before ending the vita and reminding us not to "think her merits inferior to those who came before her for we know she surpassed them in zealous striving for what is holy."[68]

Many other women dominated their world because of their spiritual dignity. True, most of them were more easily identified because they already were distinct from the masses by their noble birth, but before they are dismissed because of this factor, we must remember that only a very small number of biographical narratives were written about any early medieval people of any class. These women had to have achieved something deemed essential by contemporaries for them to have distinguished themselves from other nobles, other women, and other people. In each instance these narratives communicate what that "something" was. Due to the manifestation of spiritual virtues in such a visible, concrete manner, their contemporaries thought them excellent examples for other to follow. Christian society believed in the ability of humans to attain spiritual perfection, and these women were held up of models who achieved that goal. Positions of secular power gave them a visibility peasants did not have, but if all these women had was secular power, the vitae would not have been written.

Gregory of Tours wrote about a few such women. He wrote at length about a nonnoble married woman, Monegundis, with two daughters, who became very influential in his diocese. He too feels the need to remind his readers why women are models of spiritual perfection when they cannot be in secular matters: "[God] gives us as models not only men, but also the lesser sex, who fight not feebly, but with a virile strength; He brings into His celestial kingdom not only men, who fight as they should, but also women who exert themselves in the struggle with success."[69] Monegundis's long fasts and her ability to have Christ "work such things through her" as restoring sight and sound led to her being "glorified among her relations." Afraid that she might become vain because of this attention, she "left her husband, her family, her whole house, and went full of faith, to the basilica of the holy bishop Martin [of Tours]." When she gained too much attention there for her spiritual gifts, "her husband, having heard of the reputation of the saint, assembled his friends and neighbors and came after her and brought her back with him." Undeterred, Monegundis simply "gave herself over to continual prayer and fasting" until she could once more return to St. Martin's basilica. Soon she was able to do so; upon arriving, "she gathered together a small number of nuns in that place, and stayed there, persevering in faith and in prayer."[70]

To contemporary Christians, Monegundis's miracles proved that God worked through and with women. Monegundis herself "protested that she was unworthy" to cure a poisoned boy even though he and his parents were sure God worked through her, but "she nevertheless gave in" and performed the miracle. When a blind women, also confident that Monegundis was a spiritually powerful woman, insisted that she cure her, Monegundis protested in frustration, "What is between you and me, men of God *[homines Dei]*? Does not St. Martin live here who each day shines with the work of his miracles?

Go to him and pray that he may deign to visit you. For I am only a sinner; what can I do?" The woman did not share Monegundis's hesitation; she was sure God's power was within Monegundis because "God daily accomplishes remarkable deeds through those who fear his name. That," the woman added with confidence, "is why I came to you as a suppliant."[71]

Gregory frequently used miracles in his narrative to prove the spiritual power of the person he was discussing. He told about a tombstone near Paris with the inscription "Here lies Criscentia, a girl dedicated to God," but no one could "remember of what her merit had been and what she had done in this world." When a man's tremors were calmed after contact with the tomb, people started suspecting "that the virgin could have influence with the divine majesty." A few more miracles followed, and "after the reception of this proof" the people acknowledged "the power of the virgin."[72] Gregory related a similar incident that occurred at the gravesite of a young woman in the church of St. Venerandus. After constant storms, a section of the vaulting fell on her coffin and exposed her "as intact as if she had been recently taken from this world." No one made any effort to cover her or repair the coffin for a year, until the wife of the count at Clermont lost her sight and sought a cure. In a vision the woman was told "find a clean stone and quickly cover the sarcophagus of the girl." When she did as instructed, her sight was fully restored, "hence there is no doubt that this girl who could offer such benefits to an ill woman possessed outstanding merit."[73] Gregory makes no mention of class or social status in this episode, for class was not a factor in his mind. The women's power came from God who worked through them, not from any condition of the women's birth. As he explained in the case of Monegundis, it was because of her spiritual perfection that "God repeatedly deigned to reveal miracles through her."[74] One woman was so holy she "was honored with a funeral in heaven."[75]

With the increased presence and importance of monasteries in the Early Middle Ages, the demand to record the lives of popular abbesses also increased as society agreed on the benefit of having holy women as models. Abbess Gertrude's hagiographer argued that it would "help those who seek the road to the heavenly fatherland . . . if I strive to record in writing or preaching some small part of the lives and conduct of holy men and women, virgins of Christ, for the advancement and edification of my neighbors."[76] Abbess Aldegund's hagiographer provided us with a theological justification for his writing:

> We assist at the feasts of holy virgins revolving in a cycle of anniver-
> saries celebrated by Christ's conscientious prelates, while the cloudy

courses of this world pass on, and the waxing and waning of our years runs out. . . . Therefore, examples of virtues of God's chosen should be related so that those who hear what good people have achieved may be joyful, enlightened, and set afire from this good memory, whence they may aspire to the joy of the eternal fatherland. Thus, to deserve help from their intercession we celebrate these votive offices every year.[77]

A more concise argument is found in the opening lines of Abbess Bertilla's vita: "The brighter the religious life of holy virgins shines in merit, the more it is celebrated by word of mouth and praised in the tongues of all people."[78] The motive for writing a vita for Abbess Austreberta is the same, "so that the publicity might bring that bright gem to a wider audience."[79] Regardless of how the motive is expressed, implicit and common to the vitae of these Merovingian women are an admiration for the spiritual heights they attained and a belief that others could benefit from knowing about them. The women are held up as examples of spiritual perfection for all Christians to revere and imitate.

The same sentiments are present in other areas throughout the West. In the prologue of the earliest vita of Brigit of Kildare, Cogitosus confessed his hesitancy in recording her deeds because the "subject matter is quite beyond my limited powers." He proceeded only because the goal was indeed worthwhile: "It is hoped that these [deeds] bring to the public eye the greatness and the worth of the virgin radiant with good virtues."[80] Despite its questionable value as a source for her history, Cogitosus's vita is a rich source for the historian interested in the customs, expectations, attitudes, and concerns of the day. An obvious but often overlooked aspect of the vita is the centrality of a woman's role in the formation of a relatively young church. The Celtic church was barely two centuries old when Cogitosus wrote his edifying and catechical work. Brigit was used as a model of Christian virtue for all to follow. Considering that there are only three other Irish vitae from this period, two about Patrick and one about Columba, and that Brigit's vita is the earliest of the four, this is indeed significant. Throughout the history of the Celtic church she has been considered "one of the two pillars with pre-eminent Patrick," in the words of one of the oldest Celtic hymns *"Brigit be' bithmaith."*[81] The vita enjoyed a long manuscript tradition, and Kildare was a celebrated pilgrimage site for the many who revered her example.

It is also interesting to note the degree of power that Brigit is portrayed as wielding in her society. Cogitosus stated this fact even before he began the body of his vita, telling us that "countless people of both sexes drawn by the name of her good deeds flocked to her from every province through the whole of Ireland and pledged their vows to her." To accommodate the masses, she built a double monastery[82] at Mag Liffe, which became "the head of almost all the Irish Churches with supremacy over all the monasteries of the Irish and its *paruchia* [jurisdiction] extends over the whole land of Ireland, reaching from sea to sea." The claim was much debated by Cogitosus's contemporaries from Armagh, where Patrick's church was, and which does eventually become the primatial see, but of significance here is the fact that Kildare rested its claim on the authority of a woman, Brigit. Cogitosus continued, writing about how "as she vigilantly watched over the churches attached to her in many provinces," she realized she needed a resident bishop to "govern the church with her" so "her churches might lack nothing as regards to priestly orders." She recruited a hermit named Conleth to become bishop, and thus he and "the most blessed chief abbess of the virgins governed their primatial church by means of a mutually happy alliance."[83] The extent to which her rule was observed cannot be ascertained due to lack of sources, but the fact that generations of Christians reading the vita believed she did rule and still exalted her as a model par excellence to follow is, again, to be noted. As her spiritual superiority was made manifest by God when "even brute animals and beasts were unable to resist her words and her will,"[84] so too was her spiritual purity evident when God exercised his power through the rule of Brigit, "whom God foreknew and predestined according to his own image."[85]

In later vitae, this emphasis on Brigit's spiritual authority over all Christians, men and women, is accentuated even more. Instead of Cogitosus's generalizations we are given more specific incidences when men obeyed her. When an episcopal council met in Tailitue, a woman accused one of the bishops there of fathering her baby, which the bishop denied. When the council could not determine who was telling the truth, they, "having heard of the wonderful works of Saint Brigit, said, 'this matter can be settled by her.'" Even Patrick is said to implore her: "My most beloved daughter, holy Brigit, do us the honor of revealing the truth."[86] The episode was repeated in a third vita even more emphatically. The bishops believed Brigit's power was without limits, "for there is nothing in heaven or earth which she might request of Christ, which would be refused her,"[87] and hence even Patrick bowed to her authority.[88] Kings were in awe of her power. When she sought the release of a prisoner of a king in Mag Cliatch, he "freely gave her the prisoner" once he experienced her ability to make his foster family play harps at her bidding.[89] Clergy "came to her from a distance" as well as virgins, bishops, and kings,[90] and "she was welcomed with great honor and jubilation by the whole people."[91]

Brigit demonstrated concern for injustices, the unfortunate, and the needs of her community of women in many passages in the vitae. When a peasant was imprisoned for mistakingly breaking a precious cup, Brigit prayed to God to restore the vessel so "the wretched man was set free"; when she passed a tired couple exhausted from carrying heavy loads in the sun, she took "compassion on them and gave them her chariot horses to carry the loads"; when her community suffered from a bread shortage, she went "to look for corn and to go to the bishop Abar in Mag Géisille to ask him for grain";[92] and so on. Brigit was, in summary, a woman who had reached such spiritual perfection in her life that all willingly recognized the authority her spiritual dignity gave her, rendered her obedience, and followed her example; they "all glorified her as a type of Mary."[93] And while only Patrick and Columba were perceived as being her spiritual equals, other women did succeed in following Brigit's example faithfully enough to earn the admiration and respect of the Irish in their own right. Moninne (sometimes called Darerca) and Ita were two such women. Both were founders of important women's monasteries. Ita attained particular fame by virtue of her school for boys. So many future bishops spent their years under Ita's tutelage that she is often called the foster mother of the saints of Ireland.[94] Considering the limited amount of attention given to education in the early medieval West, Ita's involvement is quite noteworthy.

Other religious women were also aware of the spiritual benefits of education, as we can discern in the correspondence of Boniface. An Anglo-Saxon born in Wessex, Boniface became a missionary among the Germans late in life. He maintained close friendships and frequent correspondence with many Anglo-Saxon women who supported his efforts in every way they could. One way was to supply Boniface with needed books. The gratitude he felt toward Abbess Eadburga, a woman with whom he "has long since been bound by the ties of spiritual propinquity," is evident in his thanking her "because she has consoled with spiritual light by the gift of sacred books an exile in Germany."[95] When he found himself in need of more books he wrote to Eadburga for them, and his closing remarks indicated that she had done such book-manufacturing frequently: "Do then, dearest sister, with this petition of mine as you have always done with my requests, so that here also your works may shine forth in golden letters for the glory of our heavenly Father."[96]

It was not only material things that women gave and missionaries asked for; the women's spiritual support was so much in demand. Boniface always asked Bugga[97] and Eadburga to pray for him and "for those heathen who have been given into our charge."[98] The plea of three missionaries to Abbess Cuniburt and her community makes clear how much they were depending on the women's spiritual support for the success of their mission. The missionaries argued that if "you will be pleased to keep us in communion with your holy congregation and with the support of your prayers," conversions will follow. Their plea was followed by the following unsolicited declaration: "We also wish it known to your care and your wisdom that if any one of us should happen to visit Britain we should not prefer the obedience and government of any man to subjection under your good-will; for we place the greatest confidence of our hearts in you."[99]

It is with Leoba, Boniface's partner in life and death—it was "his wish that after his death her bones should be placed next to his in the tomb, so that they who had served God during their lifetime with equal sincerity and zeal should await together the day of resurrection"[100]—that we gain full appreciation for the understanding powerful men like Boniface had of the spiritual nature of women. As his deathbed wish reveals, he clearly believed Leoba and he to be equal in the eyes of God. Theirs was a true partnership of equals. Physical or social questions of female subordination did not enter into their relationship because it was rooted in the spiritual, and their actions were judged in spiritual terms. Leoba "had no desire to gain earthly possessions but only those of heaven," and people admired her accordingly. "The fragrance of her holiness and wisdom drew to her the affections of all," including Pippin, King of the Franks, and Charlemagne; she had a close friendship with Charlemagne's wife, Queen Hiltigard. She shied away from the court even though her spiritual qualities had made her presence there much desired "because of her wide knowledge of scripture and her prudence in counsel." The elite of her day recognized her spiritual gifts and embraced her without exception: "The princes loved her, the nobles received her, the bishops welcomed her with joy."[101]

A letter that Leoba wrote to Boniface provides a unique glimpse into the inner soul of this impressive woman. At the time of the correspondence Leoba was a member of a women's monastic community, where her mother had placed her in at a young age "to be taught the sacred sciences." While she would do whatever was asked of her, "she spent more time in reading and listening to Sacred Scripture than she gave to manual labour."[102] This thirst for knowledge lead her to write to Boniface around 732. She was distantly related to him, and she claims this as the pretense for her bold introduction of herself to him. The real motivation for her letter becomes evident about midway through the note: "I beg you also to be so kind as to correct the unskilled style of this letter and to send me, by way of example, a few kind works which I greatly long to hear. I have composed the following verses according to the rules of poetic art," she adds, now that she has his attention, "not trusting to my own presumption, but trying only to exercise my little talents and needing your assistance."[103] Boniface was obviously impressed by this determined, aggressive, ambitious woman who actively pursued her own education. We see that Leoba was aware of both her talents and her limitations. She is confident enough to approach the reputable renown with her accomplishments yet humble enough to realize she has much to learn.

Her appreciation for learning through example is also found in her letter, and Rudolf repeats this often in her vita: Leoba always reserved time "to give spiritual instruction to her disciples" and did so by "point[ing] out both by word and example how to reach the heights of perfection."[104] The letter also reveals initiative, a much-admired trait in an age when much was to be done. It is not surprising to the historian, then, to see Boniface respond so positively to his new correspondent. When he decided that his newly converted territory could benefit from the establishment of monasteries therein, he wrote Tetta, abbess of Leoba's community at Wimborne, "asking her to send Leoba to accompany him on this journey and to take part in this embassy." Leoba did so, and the lasting success of the Anglo-Saxon missionary attempts in Germany are due in no small part to her contributions, a fact that Boniface willingly acknowledged. She directed her new monastery at Bischofsheim with such skill that the women there "made such progress in her teaching that many of them afterwards became superior of others, so that there was hardly a convent of nuns in that part which had not one of her disciples as abbess."[105]

The foundation and perfection of these monasteries became her life's work, and she continually "visited the various convents of nuns, and, like a mistress of novices, stimulated them to vie with one another in reaching perfection." To the end of her days "her deepest concern was the work she had set on foot" with these convents.[106] She continued to strive throughout her life "by constant reflection to attain a perfect knowledge of divine things so that through the combination of her reading with her quick intelligence, by natural gifts and hard work she became extremely learned" and mastered all "the writings of the church Fathers, the decrees of the Councils, and the whole of ecclesiastical law."[107]

Many of the virtues for which Leoba was extolled in her vita are those that helped her attain and maintain her authority and respect within the monastic world. Rudolf wrote that she "observed great moderation in all her acts and arrangements and always kept the practical end in view." She was very much "aware of the necessity for concentration of mind in prayer and study," so she always preached moderation in both and never allowed any of the nuns "to stay up late, for she said that lack of sleep dulled the mind, especially study." She spent much of her day reading, and "discontinued it only for prayer or for the refreshment of her body with food or sleep: the Scriptures were never out of her hands."[108] For Rudolf, Leoba's wisdom and holiness were her chief identifying characteristics and the source of her power; this is a recurring theme throughout the vita, along with the impact of her word and example on others. It was Leoba's "reputation for learning and holiness" that led Boniface to ask her to assist him in the field, and when she said yes, he was overjoyed "because he knew that by her holiness and wisdom she would confer many benefits by word and example."[109] She knew that "she had been appointed to govern others because of her holiness and wisdom" yet "both in her speech and behavior" she acted as if "she was the least of them all."[110]

Leoba did not take her charge lightly and obviously truly believed that her words and actions would directly help bring her salvation and indirectly, because of the power of her edifying witness, bring salvation to others. In a letter to Boniface, Abbesses Canguth and Bugga articulate the sentiments Leoba's life reflects: "We are worried, not only by the thought of our own souls, but what is still more difficult and more important, by the thought of the souls of all who are entrusted to us, male and female, of diverse ages and dispositions whom we have to serve and finally to render an account before the supreme judgment seat of Christ. . . ."[111] It is this sense of social responsibility that we see demonstrated in Leoba's witness, and it is at the core of her holiness and wisdom. The domestic virtues that are extolled so highly and with such emphasis in many of the vitae of the Merovingian women are all absent in Leoba's vita; none of the miracles such as those found in Brigit's vitae are present either. What we do find in Leoba's vita is a deep admiration for the spiritual heights she attained and a firm belief that her example could and did influence people for the better.

7

Early Medieval Monasticism and Church Life

MOST OF THE WOMEN discussed in previous chapters were members of a monastic community. That we have the most information about women religious is to be expected. Literacy within monastic institutions was higher than anywhere else during the Early Middle Ages, and thus one would not have to search far or for long to find a willing hagiographer. Fortunately for us, not only are sources on women religious most abundant, but they are also the most helpful in pursuing our goal. They allow us to see how individual women were perceived by their society and to assess whether their position in society was the exception or the rule.

Although we have discussed the lives of many women monastics, we have not yet examined monasticism itself for insight into society's perception of women. An examination of the institution during the Early Middle Ages promises to be especially fruitful, for during this period it formalized the office of abbess in its rules,[1] and it gave birth to a unique phenomenon in the West, the double monastery, an institution in which a woman ruled both men and women. The fact that such an arrangement was not only possible but actual indicates just how strong the tradition of spiritual equality was within Christianity. When removed from the conditions of legal and social inequality in the secular realm, women enjoyed the benefits of spiritual equality within the spiritual realm.

At the basis of monasticism was the desire to live an intense Christian life within a community setting. Christians learned early on that while asceticism was an essential element in any pursuit of such a life, it needed to be moderated. Examples have been discussed in earlier chapters. Within a generation of the first desert ascetics, rules to regulate practices were being written by individuals and accepted by groups. Although Pachomius's rules, one written for his community and one for his sister's community,[2] are the first rules we know of by name, in all probability a women's rule predated his own, for we are told that Anthony placed his sister in the community of virgins before he began his life in the desert.[3] As the number of communities increased, so did the number of rules, but most rules have been lost to posterity. Enough are extant, however, to give us a fair indication of how women were perceived within monasticism. Those authored by men are all the more useful to us because they are a testimony to men's spiritual expectations of women.[4]

According to Caesarius of Arles, the activity that nuns engaged in was of the highest order. Even though he founded the monastery of St. John the Baptist in 512 for his sister Caesaria and her community, he deemed his work as bishop and founder to be less pleasing to God than the work of women inside the monastery. "Hence I ask you," he implored the women in the introduction to the rule he wrote for them, that even though "I have labored in the constructing of a monastery for you, I beg by your holy prayers to have me made a companion to your journey; so that when you happily enter the kingdom with the holy and wise virgins . . . I remain not outside with the foolish." The prayers and the dedication of the women were what mattered, not their sex. Monks and nuns desired the same thing, to be "worthy of the eternal."[5] The need for a distinct rule for women did not arise because their goal differed from men but only because some women's customs "differ from the customs of monks."[6] By virtue of that goal and the holiness that both men and women attained while pursuing it, monastics were in a spiritually exalted position in the Christian community. They were the mediators who could help people, even bishops like Caesarius, enter the kingdom of heaven with them.

Leander of Seville, in his manual for his sister Florentina and her fellow nuns, states the theological reasonings for these conclusions: "For you are the first fruits of the body of the Church. You, then, out of the whole mass of Christ's body, are oblations accepted by God and consecrated on the altars."[7] He then tells Florentina his personal thoughts about the matter. He wants her to "realize that your brother's most fervent desire is that you should be with Christ," but he also acknowledges that "I do not have within myself what I wish you to achieve." Consequently, he relied heavily on her for his spiritual well-being.

> You are my shelter in Christ; you, dearest sister, are my security; you are my most sacred offering, through which I doubt not that I shall be purified of the uncleanness of my sins. . . . With His left hand, in which

is honor and glory, under your head, with His right arm, in which is
length of life, He will embrace you. Held thus in the Bridgegroom's
embraces, you may ask and obtain pardon for me. Your love in Christ
shall be my indulgence, and however little hope of forgiveness I have,
if the sister whom I love shall be married to Christ, and, if it is that
terrible and dreadful judgment when there is a weighing of deeds, acts,
and omissions, and I, woe is me, am forced to give an account of my
own services, you will be my comfort and my solace, then, the punishment that is due me for my errors may possibly be relieved by the
intercession of your chastity.[8]

It is a theme that Leander repeats again and again throughout his work.[9]

While the purpose of women's monasticism is the same as men's, by
the Early Middle Ages it was becoming increasingly obvious that rules
written with men in mind did not always satisfy women's communal and
physical needs. Abbess Gauthstruda asked Donatus of Besançon to examine
the popular men's monastic rules of the day and pick out regulations that
would be relevant and "proper for the care of the female sex." Gauthstruda
knew that "the rules for preaching fathers" were not always suitable for her
community "since they were written for men and not for women." In order
to satisfy the women Donatus included rules "a few which . . . were suggested
by your holy colleagues" in his handbook because only the women themselves were aware of their own circumstances and needs.[10] Caesarius already
had stated a similar motive and scenario for writing his rule: "And, because
many things in monasteries of women seem to differ from the customs of
monks, we have chosen a few things from among many, according to which
the elder religious can live under rule with the younger, and strive to carry
out spiritually what they see to be especially adapted for their sex."[11]

The adjustments made were, in the end, only slight and not substantive. The chief reason for the commonality is the dependence of all monastic
rules on patristic writings.[12] Caesarius proudly proclaimed twice in his rule
that it is based on "the prescriptions of the ancient Fathers."[13] The rules also
borrow freely from one another, without attribution. The result was an
institutional portrait more monolithic than diverse. The goal of each rule
was to create an atmosphere conducive to salvation; the rules accomplished
this by promoting a spirituality consistent with Scripture, by regulations that
would safeguard a person's ability to live an intensely spiritual life, and with
an emphasis on the virtues particularly helpful in attaining that end. Each of
these three elements—spirituality, the regulations, and the virtues—varied
in specifics, but all were always present. They were embodied in women's

rules as well as men's. All rules start with the assumption that the aspiring novice to the monastic life was capable of achieving that goal. The fact that an overwhelming majority of nuns did live successfully under rules originally intended for men for centuries and centuries is testimony to the genderless nature of the institution. Our primary conclusion after a comparison of male and female monastic rules is that the men who wrote and endorsed these rules[14] did not perceive any substantive differences in the spiritual goals and spiritual natures of the women they were writing for. They considered women equal (hence sometimes women collaborated with the men while composing the rules) to male religious and, as we saw with Leander, even superior to men who "do not have within [themselves]"[15] to be monastics. Braulio of Saragossa even went so far as to equate the spiritual accomplishments of an abbess with that of a bishop.[16] After all, Leander stated in his rule, "both sexes are the work of God."[17]

This fundamental principle led to the structuring of the institutions in a way that distinguished monasticism from all other institutions of the day. Women were in charge of women's monasteries. This fact is such commonplace knowledge that its uniqueness often escapes us. The first and the last issue discussed in Donatus of Besançon's rule was the office of abbess, "the mother of the monastery who will be first in dignity among the congregation."[18] According to Caesarius, the abbess was "superior in rank" and was to "be obeyed without murmuring."[19] Her authority was so central to the success of the monastery that Caesarius even believed she should not be bound by obedience to the bishop residing over the monastery's diocese. "If at any time any abbess," Caesarius encouraged the women, "should desire to be subject to and to be within the household of the bishop of this city, under the inspiration of God, with our permission, resist on this occasion with reverence and with dignity, and on no account permit it to be done." To that end Caesarius obtained "a letter of the most holy Pope of the city of Rome"[20] to exempt the women's monastery from episcopal authority.

Here is another one of the few times when the implications of women's spiritual equality spilled over into the secular world and challenged the monopoly men had on the exercise of power. The basis of the power of the office of abbess was firmly rooted within the spiritual community, but since that community had to maintain ties with the larger community outside its walls, the abbess's power also extended outside the walls. The abbess had first and foremost "to be solicitous for the salvation of souls" within the community, but because these souls had bodies, she also had "to think continually of the need for bodily nourishment" and about "the temporalities of the monastery." This in turn meant the abbess must be able "to entertain visitors and [to] reply to letters from the faithful"[21] and in general be able "to converse wisely with those who come to her, and with edification and humility."[22] Early medieval Christians accepted the presence of the abbess's authority within one of their most respected institutions without question because it was rooted in women's spiritual equality—which they accepted without question.

Probably nowhere was the power of the abbess more evident than in Anglo-Saxon England. Women's communities came rather late to England, the first southern ones established in the 630s at Folkestone and at Lyminge and northern ones a bit later. The union between nobility and monasticism was also extremely strong there; Queen Ethelburga and Eanswith, daughter of the Eadbald, king of Kent, were the respective founders of the two above-mentioned southern monasteries. Perhaps because Christianity and monasticism were relatively late in reaching England, Anglo-Saxon women were known to travel to the continent to join a community. Bede tells us this was why King Eadbald's granddaughter joined a Frankish community: Earcongota "served God in a convent in Frankish territory founded by the noble Abbess Fara at a place called Brie: for as yet there were few monasteries built in English territory, and many who wished to enter conventual life went from Britain to the Frankish realm or Gaul for that purpose." Noble women went "to be betrothed to their heavenly Bridegroom, especially to the houses of Brie, Chelles, and Andelys."[23]

Before the end of the seventh century, however, Anglo-Saxon monasteries for women had spread significantly[24] and a golden age of English abbesses was in full bloom. The most beloved of these abbesses was Hilda, who originally had planned to follow her sister Hereswitha to the Frankish monastery at Chelles around the year 647. Before she could leave "she was recalled home by Bishop Aidan and was granted one hide of land on the north bank of the River Wear" to found a monastery for herself and some companions. She soon moved on to another monastery, this one at Hartlepool, founded a few years previously by Heiu, "a devout servant of Christ, said to have been the first woman in the province of the Northumbrians to take vows and be clothed as a nun." Heiu had left the monastery and the abbessacy was vacant, so Hilda was appointed in her place. Working with Bishop Aidan "and other devout men who knew her and admired her innate wisdom and love of God's service," she soon had a model monastery. This led her to "organize a monastery at a place known as Streanaeshalch" [Whitby], and soon she established there "the same regular life as in her former monastery." Hilda "taught the observance of righteousness, mercy, purity, and other virtues, but especially of peace and charity" to the women.

She insisted that the women live according to "the example of the primitive church, no one there was rich, no one was needy, for everything was held in common." The women lived up to the standards so admirably that Hilda's reputation spread far and wide "not only [among] ordinary folk, but kings and princes used to come and ask her advice in their difficulties and take it." Even people "living at a distance" found the "inspiring story of her industry and goodness" edifying and used her as "an example of holy life" to imitate.[25] What she is most remembered for is her role in the great Synod of Whitby in 664. Called to resolve "church matters" on which the Celtic and Anglo-Saxon churches disagreed,[26] the synod had profound influence on the future of Christianity in England. The fact that the synod, attended by all the leading churchmen of the isles, was held at a monastery ruled by a woman is a tribute to Hilda's importance among her contemporaries.

What is more significant is that Whitby was not a women's monastery; it was a double monastery. While describing Hilda's intellectual and educational achievements, Bede tells us that "those under her direction were required to make a thorough study of the Scriptures and occupy themselves in good works, to such good effect" that five of her students became bishops.[27] Obviously, then, hers was a double monastery. Although Whitby is probably the best-known double monastery, it was not the first. Affiliated monasteries and double monsteries existed from the very beginning of monasticism.[28] In chapter 4 we discussed the monasteries of Pachomius and Mary; the men's and the women's monasteries "had the same sort of management and same way of life and were located across a river from each other.[29] Gregory of Nyssa and Basil the Great's sister Macrina presided over a double monastery in the latter half of the fourth century; another brother, Peter, presided over the men's monastery across the river from the women's house that Macrina presided over. Double monasteries may have existed in sixth-century Ireland; Cogitosus describes Brigit's monastery at Kildare as having "three chapels," one for the celebrant, one for "priests and the faithful of the male sex," and a third for "the nuns and congregation of women."[30] St. Martin's and Sts. Mary and John's were founded in sixth-century Gaul by Bishop Syagrius and his sister Brunechild; they received the same papal privileges and were always closely associated. Eugendus ruled a monastery of monks and nuns at Autun, as did Martin of Vertou at Durin, near Nantes. There was a known double monastery at Metz at the end of the sixth century.[31]

Only during the seventh century, however, did the double monastery become widespread and very influential. The first swell of enthusiasm for double monasteries was in Merovingian Gaul. Fara (or Burgundofara) founded the double monastery at Brie in 617; the renowned double monastery at Remiremont was founded around the same time. Jouarre, the double monastery where Hilda of Whitby's sister was a member, was founded in 634. Women from Jouarre went to the double monasteries of Chelles, Soissons, and Nivelle as abbesses; Rheims, Marchienned, Maubeuge, Chasteaulieu, Hasnon, Vienne, Troyes, Tuffe, Avenay, and Andelys are some of the better-known double monasteries. In the vita of Salaberga, abbess of a double monastery at Laon, the hagiographer tells us that "bands of monks and holy maidens began to spring up through all the provinces of Gaul. They thronged not only through the fields, farms and villages and castles but even in the lonely wilderness. Monasteries began to blossom just from the rules of the blessed Benedict and Columbanus where only a few had appeared in the area before that time."[32] The hagiographer's comment is borne out by the facts, which also show that most of these were double monasteries where the abbess ruled not only the women but also the men. In Gaul the only notable exceptions where men ruled were Jumièges and Bèze.[33]

The double monastery enjoyed the same level of popularity among Anglo-Saxon women when it arrived on English shores a generation after Brie was founded. As we have already seen in Bede's account, the Whitby double monastery was patterned after "the same regular life as in [Hilda's] former monastery"[34] at Hartlepool; scholars thus assume that Hartlepool was a double monastery. The double monastery of Coldingham, ruled by Ebba, was founded around the same time, and from there a member of the community named Etheldreda was "made Abbess in the district called Ely, where she built a convent and became the virgin mother of many virgins vowed to God." Under her successor Sexburga, Ely became a double monastery of note. Sexburga was also the founder of a double monastery at Sheppey; her daughter Werburga was abbess of several monasteries in Mersia.[35] Throughout the latter half of the seventh century, double monasteries continued to be founded and to thrive. Bede writes at length about the saintly abbess Ethelburga and the community of men and women she ruled over in Barking Abbey where they resided together in life and in death, for we are told that when Hildilid succeeded Ethelburga as abbess "she decided that the bones of Christ's servants buried there, both men and women, should be exhumed and transferred to a single tomb within the church of the blessed Mother of God."[36] Another famous double monastery, Wimbourne, we have discussed already; it was where Leoba began her monastic life.

Walburga also heeded Boniface's call for missionaries to Germany. In 748 she and forty other women left Wimbourne to join Boniface in his endeavors. In 752 the double monastery of Heidenheim was founded, where Walburga was abbess of both male and female houses after the death of her brother Winnibald. One of the women there, Huneberc, wrote "a brief account of the early life of the venerable Willibald,"[37] Walburga's other brother, thus providing evidence that the Anglo-Saxon women maintained their interest in intellectual pursuits from their Wimbourne days.[38] Whether Leoba's monastery at Bischofsheim was a double monastery is not certain, nor are we sure whether a monastery at Milz was double. Gregory the Great wrote about double monasteries in Sardinia, but we know of none in Italy.[39]

In Spain family monasteries, where parents and children resided in separate quarters within one abbey, were indistinguishable from double monasteries and were popular enough by the early seventh century to have the Council of Seville address problems that arose due to a lack of strong structure.[40] Anyone, "whether free or slaves, rich or poor, married or single, foolish or wise, unskilled or trained, young or old, whatever they are"[41] could become a member of good standing if they "in no wise deviate from the true path."[42] Within this context women seemingly fared rather well. Spanish double and family monasteries remained popular throughout the early medieval period; some scholars put the number of Spanish double monasteries at two hundred.[43] Contrary to northern houses, most of them were ruled by abbots rather than abbesses, although Mary Bateson does cite a few exceptions.[44]

The double monastery, along with the rest of society, suffered severely during the invasions and chaotic times of the late eighth and the ninth centuries. It also suffered from a conciliar condemnation. The Second Council of Nicea in 787 decreed "that from henceforth no double monastery shall be erected; because this has become an offense and cause of complaint to many. In the case of those persons who with the members of their family propose to leave the world and follow the monastic life, let the men go into a monastery for men, and the women into a monastery for women, for this is well-pleasing to God. The double monasteries which are already in existence, shall observe the rule of our holy Father Basil."[45] This decree may or may not have had an impact on the institution; it is hard to evaluate because in the areas where double monasteries thrived, no extant documents refer to it. The double monastery did suffer a severe decline, however, in the century following the decree, but so did all institutions, religious and secular.

When monasticism reasserted itself in the tenth century, it was within a new set of historical conditions, conditions that did not foster the double monastery. In Frankish society "double monasteries did not disappear, but the community of monks was transformed into a community of canons" who were much less likely to share a sense of communal endeavor with the women than monks were, according to Suzanne Wemple.[46] Frankish women's communities were gradually transformed by the end of the ninth century into Benedictine communities or into canonesses with a few canons assigned to minister to them. In England all monastic activity came to an abrupt end during the Danish invasions. Many renowned double monasteries of the seventh and eighth centuries did not survive; the women of Whitby, Barking, and Ely were all massacred by the invaders, and their buildings were destroyed by 870. Alfred the Great supported a monastic revival when he came into power at the end of the ninth century: He built a women's monastery at Shaftesbury, and his wife, Elswitha, built one at Nunnaminister in Winchester. During the course of the tenth century English monasticism did recover somewhat, to a large degree due to the contributions and activities of various aristocratic women.[47] Still, by the time of the Norman invasion in 1066 there were only a handful of women's monasteries in England and no double monasteries.[48] Many of the famous double monasteries destroyed during the invasions were reestablished as male monasteries.[49]

The idea of the double monstery did survive, though, to be revived in the High Middle Ages. The Order of Fontevrault and the Gilbertine Order both originally had double monasteries and were quite influential during the twelve century. The most famous and successful double monasteries in the late medieval period were those of the Order of the Holy Savior (the Bridgettines), founded by Birgitta of Sweden in the late fourteenth century. We can conclude, then, that the principle at the foundation of the double monastery, that a women's spiritual authority over men is consistent with her spiritual equality, was not disowned or even discredited in later ages, even if new double monasteries were not established then. By the time Birgitta of Sweden was establishing her houses in the late fourteenth century, most women were attracted to entirely new forms of religious life, best personified by the beguines of the Low Countries, and were not drawn in large numbers to more traditional forms of monasticism. During the early medieval period, "traditional" monasticism was still new, and the fact that the double monastery was born and flourished during its early years is testimony to the egalitarian opinion of women that the institution embraced.

This is not to deny that society sometimes tried to restrict or limit monastic women and their monasteries. Monastic women often felt the restriction of conciliar or governmental regulations. The Carolingians in particular tried to put monasticism under their controlling thumb in the name of reform. The Council of Verneuil in 755 attempted to eliminate home asceticism by ordering all tonsured men and veiled women to place themselves under obedience to a rule (that is, join a monastery) or to a bishop (become a canon or canoness).[50] Legislation also was passed to force small, unregulated female communities to join together into one large community.[51] The reforms of Benedict of Aniane led to Carolingian legislation and the decrees of the Council of Chalôns in 813, the Council of Aix in 816, and the synod at Aachen in 817. The goal was uniform observation of the Benedictine Rule in all male and female monasteries. Whereas Abbess Hilda hosted the Synod of Whitby, no abbesses are known to have even participated in the Carolingian synods. The Synod of Frankfurt in 794 made it the king's business to depose unworthy abbesses.[52] Around 796 the Council of Friuli prohibited Frankish women from going on pilgrimages. The Council of Paris in 829 restricted the tasks a religious woman could perform, but its decrees are perhaps more interesting for the information they give about the quasi-sacerdotal tasks women were performing that necessitated the prohibition: "It is against divine law and canonical instruction for women to intrude on the other side of holy altars, to touch impudently the consecrated vessels, administer for priests sacerdotal vestments, and, which is even worse, more indecent and more inappropriate, to distribute the body and blood of the Lord to the people. . . . It is certainly amazing that women, whose sex by no means makes them competent, despite the laws, were able to gain license to do things that are prohibited even to secular men."[53]

Many other similar pieces of legislation were passed during the age of invasions; there was a movement, mostly futile, to enclose all nuns within their monasteries. As we can see, the decrees certainly did attempt to restrict and limit women's choices and movement, but none of them challenged the tradition of women's spiritual parity. The decrees addressed only the physical aspects of women religious but left intact their spiritual aspects. In fact, the episcopal capitularies of the period emphasize that when dealing with the pastoral care of individuals, women in leadership positions are to be guided by the same principles as men: "Let bishops, abbots and abbesses who are in charge of others strive with the greatest devotion to surpass those subject to them in diligence and let them not oppress their subjects with a harsh rule or tyranny, but they should watch over the flock entrusted to them with sincere love, with mercy and charity, and by examples of good works."[54] These capitularies reiterated and legislated the same sentiments we heard early Christian theologians articulate, that "everyone ought to reflect on the sublimity and nobility of the human condition which is made in the image of God" and that this image manifests itself in the human ability "to reason and to distinguish between good and bad." All Christians, "whether of nobility or low class, whether men or women or children," are spiritually equal and attain salvation the same way.[55]

We have seen how the principle of spiritual equality functioned within women's monasticism, how it consequently produced the leadership role of abbess reserved exclusively for women, and how it created an institution where women's authority at times extended over men. As a generation of scholars have proven, the influence of monasticism and the power of its witness far exceeded what the numbers alone would indicate; nevertheless, we must turn our attention away from this elite and toward the vast majority of women who lived outside the monastery. We must continue to examine the Christianity that the laity came into contact with for attitudes and beliefs about women.

Chief among the obligations of the laity was attendance at weekly liturgies, and these changed little in substance, form, or tone from what we saw previously. The most notable addition was the official inclusion of commemorations of the saints within the liturgical calendar. These commemorations were included first in the canon of the mass itself. Although the shape of worship became fixed early on, the prayers apparently were not. *The Apostolic Tradition of Hippolytus* (ca. 215) is the earliest example we have of liturgical prayers, but there is no evidence to lead us to believe they were anything more than local or regional prayers. In 348 the church of Jerusalem was including references to prophets, apostles, and local martyrs in liturgical prayers.[56] At the end of the century the Synod of Hippo (393) and the Synods of Carthage (397 and 407) offered guidelines for liturgical prayers and started requiring approval of prayers by the hierarchy.[57] Unfortunately, none of the prayers of the African church survived, nor have any from the early church in Gaul.

The earliest liturgical prayers to survive in the Roman church also developed without leaving a documented trail. We have to wait until the seventh century before we find reliable sources, and then we see that the prayers are fixed; they then remain basically unchanged until modern times. The Leonine sacramentary, preserved in an incomplete seventh-century manuscript, was likely composed in the first half of the sixth century. An eighth-century manuscript that may date back to the end of the fifth century preserved a complete copy of the Gelasian sacramentary. This and the Gregorian sacramentary, possibly from Gregory the Great's time, are informative in our quest, because both contain complete formularies for saints' feasts[58] as well as the fixed canon. Here we find two sources where individual saints were called upon by name. The first list of saints mentioned in the *Communicantes* was headed by a woman, Mary, followed by the original church hierarchy, the twelve apostles, and then twelve martyrs, listed in hierarchical order—popes, clergy, and laymen. The *Nobis quoque peccatoribus,* the first known ending of the canon, was similar in its structural approach, this time with two groups of seven each, but here one of the groups was entirely female: Felicitas and Perpetua, two African martyrs; Agatha and Lucy, two Sicilian martyrs; Agnes and Cecelia, two Roman martyrs; and Anastasia, a martyr of Sirmium.[59] In commemorations of the hierarchy women did not have a place, but in communal commemorations they were recognized along with men.

The development of a sanctoral cycle was a slow but uncomplicated process. Originally all saints were martyrs; by the fifth century, Prudentius tells us, masses were being celebrated on the anniversary of the martyrs' deaths.[60] In the vita of Melanie the Younger, written in 452 or 453, we are told she "spent the whole night kneeling in her chapel, keeping vigil" for the feast of Saint Lawrence. At dawn she went "to the church of the martyr," prayed for a while, and then "returned from the martyr's shrine."[61] Sidonius Apollinarius provided an even more vivid account of sanctoral celebrations in the fifth century: "We went to the tomb of S. Justus before daylight, to keep his anniversary. The crowd was enormous so that the basilica and the crypt and the porches together could not contain it. First, the vigils were celebrated,"[62] followed by the chanting of psalms, a break, and then solemn mass. Meanwhile, the Council of Carthage of 419, one of the seven ecumenical councils, passed a canon that brought to everyone's attention the beautiful acta of the martyrs discussed earlier. Canon 46 reads: "The passions of the martyrs may be read when their anniversary days are celebrated." This was first stated in canon 36 of the Synod of Hippo twenty-six years earlier: "The passions of the martyrs are to be read on their commemoration."[63]

The anniversaries of martyrs were kept locally and were observed in the cemeteries where martyrs were interred; two chief cemeteries of the Roman Christians were named for two first-century women martyrs, Domitilla and Prisca. In Rome careful records were kept of martyrs' feast days and the cemetery where each was commemorated, but by the sixth century accessibility to the cemeteries diminished. Liturgies began to be celebrated at churches named for the martyr rather than at his or her burial place. Some of the earliest and most important churches were named for women. Constantine's daughter Constantia had a basilica built over the tomb of Agnes at about the same time that veneration of Cecilia resulted in the construction of a church dedicated to her in Trastevere; in the early fifth century Boniface I (d. 422) built a church on Cecilia's grave. Many important Roman titular churches[64] were named for women: Saints Prisca, Pudentiana, Anastasis,

Praxedes, Balbina, Potenziana, Cecilia, Susanna, Agatha, and, of course, Mary all had churches dedicated in their honor. In the wake of the Marian pronouncements of the Council of Ephesus, the basilica of St. Maria Maggiore (the first Roman church dedicated to Mary) was consecrated and became one of the seven principal stational churches of Rome.[65] Numerous other Marian churches also filled Rome: Maria Rotonda, Maria del Popolo, Maria in Trastevere, Maria in Via Lata, Maria in Aracoeli, Maria Liberatrice, and Maria sopra Minerva. By the eighth century it was common to name churches after saints and to transfer some of their bones—relics—from their original resting place to the new church.[66]

Simultaneous with the naming of churches was the commemoration of saints in the church calendar. The earliest calendars to survive in the Roman church listed the martyrs and where their cult was observed. Most were quite short; the oldest calendar contained only twenty-four commemorations. Common to most of the calendars were Agnes, Perpetua, Felicitas, Basilla, Felicity, Prisca, Cecilia, and Lucy. By the end of the seventh century Roman calendars included four feasts of Mary: the Purification, the Annunciation, the Assumption, and her Nativity.

We know that these practices were not peculiar to Rome, for Bede and Aldhelm testified to church naming and the observance of Marian feasts in the Anglo-Saxon church. "With her own birth the Virgin Mary consecrated this very day, on which the dedication of [Abbess] Bugga's church gleans brightly," Aldhelm wrote in his *Carmina Ecclesiastica*, restoring "the joys in our mind when the feast of St. Mary returns at its accustomed time."[67] Bede preserved a homily for the feast of the Purification and a hymn commemorating Mary's nativity. He included the Purification, the Annunciation, the Assumption, and the Nativity in his martyrology, and described at length the people's observation of these Marian feasts.

> [I]n the same month of the feast day of St. Mary all the people together with their priests and ministers with devout hymns went in procession through the churches and suitable places in the city, and all carried in their hands burning wax candles given by the pope. With the growth of that good custom, he instructed that they do it also on the other feasts of the same Blessed Mother and Perpetual Virgin, not by any means for the five-yearly expiation of the earthly empire, but in perennial memory of the heavenly kingdom.[68]

During the course of the early medieval period such processions and recitations of litanies became increasingly popular. The first fully developed litany we know of is in the fourth-century *Apostolic Constitutions,* and it was basically a communal prayer of petition in the form of a dialogue within the eucharistic liturgy. Soon litanies found their way into areas other than liturgy and processions; by the end of the period they were essential elements in numerous public and private devotions.[69] Litanies were chanted at church dedications and at monks' professions, and they were included in the Divine Office and the Office for the Visitation of the Sick and Dying. The laity recited them when using personal prayer books, and they were part of some penitential practices, particularly the Act of Contrition. The penitential of Vigila of Alvelda (ca. 800) exacted a penance of ten days for anyone who "violates the fast of Lent or of the litanies," that is, anyone who did not observe the liturgical practices of the Rogation Days, which included recitation of litanies.[70] Litanies also were recited during the episcopal procession on Holy Saturday. Scholars agree that litanies were a common facet in worship in Eastern churches as well from the fourth century on.[71]

The list of individual saints included in all these litanies was not standardized beyond the fact that they all began with a petition to Mary.[72] After that usually came nonhuman figures (angels), biblical figures (apostles and prophets), and members of the hierarchy (popes). The remaining list of saints fluctuated greatly from litany to litany. The earliest surviving copy of a Western litany comes from the eighth century, although textual criticism indicates many Western litanies were patterned on earlier ones. By the ninth century litanies frequently were included in processions and in private devotions throughout England, France, and Germany.[73] By the end of the early medieval period, then, litanies to the saints were common, popular, and used in a variety of settings. The saints in these litanies were people who had achieved such a degree of spiritual perfection that if they would, in the words of the litanies' refrain, *ora pro nobis,* pray for the faithful, the faithful would be saved. Saints in these litanies were not only powerful; they were models of holiness to be imitated. Women were included in every one of the litanies examined. Their numbers were not equal to men, but that would have been an irrelevant and unobserved statistic to medieval people looking for direction and an example to follow in their quest for salvation. The presence of even one woman may have been enough because her presence admitted to the possibility of women achieving spiritual perfection. Regardless, in most litanies women saints were plentiful. In one ninth-century litany from Rheims, one that Michael Lapidge claims served as the model for all subsequent Anglo-Saxon litanies in the next century,[74] thirty-seven women were listed,[75] with, of course, Mary being the first saint invoked. The eleventh-century Gallican Psalter written at Exeter invoked sixty-seven women, with Mary being the first saint listed, a tenth-century Gallican Psalter invoked thirty-three, as did a ninth-century sacramentary called the Leafric Missal, which invoked Mary three times. In an eighth- or ninth-century fragmentary prayer book from Mercia, twenty-one women were prayed to, while only eighteen men were mentioned.[76]

The women listed came from a wide range of social backgrounds and roles. Most were early martyrs who dominated so much of Christian spirituality during the first millennium: Perpetua, Felicitas, Agnes, Cecilia, Lucy, and the like. Women who played major roles in the development of monasticism were honored, and these included mothers, queens, wives, virgins, the rich, and the poor. There were local saints in the litanies as well as saints universally recognized throughout the West. There was, in short, a model for everyone. The fact that litanies were also sung and prayed so extensively in private devotions makes it hard to assess the impact these female models had on women and on men, but it must have been significant, given the emphasis Scripture places on witness and the power of example.[77]

In the early tenth-century customaries of Cluny, we see that recitation of litanies was part of their daily devotions.[78] Another development that occurred within monasticism related to the honoring of women saints, the adoption of an office of the Blessed Virgin. Commonly called the Little Office, it reached its fullest form and highest degree of popularity in a later age,[79] but its origins are in the private devotions of the ninth and tenth century. We find reference to it in the vitae of the tenth century; by the following century Peter Damian was recommending its daily recitation to all "whose spirit burns a little more fervently with the love of God,"[80] and Urban II was ordering its recitation by clergy on Saturdays for the success of the Crusades.[81] It followed closely the shape and formulas of the Divine Office and was void of any apocryphal material. There also developed by the ninth century an abbreviated office for All Saints.[82] In the Divine Office some vigils of the saints included hagiographical material.[83] This was yet another way by which the spritual equality of women saints remained in the consciousness of Christian society.

Singing gained prominence during the early medieval period. We have already noted the spread of litanies in public worship and private devotions. The structure of the litany demanded the community's involvement (although individual recitation was always acceptable), for it was intended as a singing dialogue between the celebrant, deacon, or cantor and the people. What we have discussed concerning singing in previous periods continues to hold true here, although prayful singing underwent dramatic increases. Responsorial psalmody increased in popularity and could be found in almost all services: Liturgy, rituals, vigils, offices, processions, and domestic gatherings were all occasions for community singing. By the eighth century this interest led to the formation of choir schools throughout the East and the West.[84] The hymns of Venantius Fortunatus in particular gained prominence. In one of his most beloved hymns, *Pange, lingua*, Venantius Fortunatus revealed his understanding of original sin, and it was to Adam that he looked: "Grieving because of the infidelity of the first-created man, when by eating the fatal fruit he rushed headlong to death, the Creator himself even chose the tree that would render the harm of the (former) tree."[85] Not singling out Eve, he devoted a whole stanza to Mary's loving care of the Infant Jesus. The hymns of Rabanus Maurus were included in the office of many saints and angels. His *Placara, Christi, servulis* included two stanzas in tribute to "you purple-robed martyrs" (men and women) and "chaste choir of virgins (women)," as does his *Salutis aeternae dator*.[86] Numerous hymns were dedicated to singing the praise of martyrs.[87]

Perhaps the most popular and beloved hymn of the whole era was *Ave, maris stella*, an anonymous hymn found in a ninth-century manuscript but probably written in the eighth.[88] The imagery of Mary here as loving mother and helper inspired much popular devotion to her during the High Middle Ages. The dominant image was of a woman who was a caring, approachable "happy gate of heaven" who would "break the chains of sinners, give light to the blind, drive away our evils, ask for all good things." Mary was the one to turn to for comfort and direction because she was the ultimate model to imitate: "O incomparable Virgin, meek above all others, make us, freed from sin, meek and chaste."[89] Also during this period Paul the Deacon translated *Theophilus* into Latin. Here Mary was portrayed as the powerful mediator who saved Theophilus from a contract he made with the devil.[90] This popular Greek legend became a mainstay in Western culture and the basis of the *Faust* literature.

The strains of this Marian imagery found an echo in the sermons of Ambrose Autpert, author of the first known Latin sermons exclusively on Mary.[91] He too pictured Mary as the author of *Ave, maris stella* did, as a very humble mother. "O happy kisses pressed on the lips of the infant," Autpert wrote, "when as your true son he played with you as his mother." This wonderfully human mother is also our mother, for "if Christ is the brother of believers, why should she, who has given birth to Christ, not be the mother of believers?"[92] Hilda Graef argues that this new emphasis on Mary's human motherhood "is mainly due to the emergence of the Germanic peoples in the West, with their more emotional approach," noticeable different from previous Greek and Roman approaches.[93] Such bald assertions may be imprecisely defined or hard to defend with specific facts, given the scarcity of material available on early medieval Germanic society, but surely the increasing number of differences between ancient and early medieval Marian portrayals is due in some degree to the process of Germanization that was going on in the West at this time. What Graef instinctively identified a generation ago is currently being examined intensely, and the results to date indicate that we need to appreciate even more the impact of the Germans and the Celts on all aspects of Christianity, including on our focus here, the perception of women.[94]

The effect German, in particular Celtic, culture had on attitudes within Christianity toward sin has long been recognized. It is much more difficult to discern whether these societies also had an effect on attitudes toward women's relationship to sin and their inherent spiritual worth. The abundant penitential literature and the canonical decrees produced during the era provide us with ample sources to examine, but to date little work has been done on the spiritual image of women contained within. An inordinate amount of attention recently has been directed toward the treatment of sex in the medieval period, but this is due more to our preoccupation with sex than with theirs. One gets a sense from the sources that the people of the period regarded sex as rather commonplace and unavoidable; as Charles Wood so aptly observes, "it would be difficult to think of any other age in which the facts of life came closer to being no more than just that."[95] In a random sampling of four hundred canonical texts, James Brundage has found that about ten percent of them were concerned with sexual topics.[96] The early penitentials (that is, the handbooks written to aid the confessors in the fair assignment of penances to penitents) deal with sexual offenses and complications in marital relationships much more extensively, but it is clear that much of this focus was due to the effect unregulated sex had on the family, economics, and public order. This is seen in the following typical canon from an Irish synod: "If anyone gives his daughter in honorable marriage, and she loves another, and [the father] yields to his daughter and receives the marriage payment, both shall be shut out of the church."[97] The Anglo-Saxon penitential of Theodore included similar attempts to regulate possible chaotic situations: "If [a wife] has been taken into captivity her husband shall wait five years [to remarry]; so also shall the woman do if such things have happened to the man. If, therefore, a man has taken another wife, he shall receive the former wife when she returns from captivity and put away the later one; so also shall she do, as we have said above, if such things have happened to her husband."[98]

In matters of sexual sin the man was seen as the responsible transgressor, not the woman as temptress; "If anyone desires a woman and cannot commit the act, that is, if the woman does not admit him, let him do penance half a year on bread and water, and for a whole year let him refrain from wine and meat and the communion of the altar." This principle is applied to adulterous situations as well: "If any layman has desired to commit adultery or fornication with a married woman, and has lusted after his neighbor's wife, and not committed the act, that is, has not been able to, because the woman did not admit him, yet he was ready to fornicate, let him confess his guilt to the priest, and so let him do penance for forty days on bread and water."[99]

The penitential discussed a variety of possible situations, and in none of them was the woman portrayed as temptress. "If any of the laity has committed fortification with women who are free from wedlock, that is, with widows or virgins, if with a widow, let him do penance for one year, if with a virgin, for two years, provided that he pays her relatives the price of her disgrace."[100] Even if the case involves coitus after a husband and wife have separated by the husband's entrance into the priesthood, the fault was still the man's: "If any cleric or deacon, or a man in any orders, who in the world was a layman with sons and daughters, after his profession has again known his mate, and again begotten a child of her, let him know he has committed adultery, and has sinned no less that if he had been a cleric from his youth, and had sinned with a strange girl. . . ."[101] That the penances listed were always harsher when the fornication resulted in a child reinforces the interpretation that the penitentials were concerned with regulating sex for social order and not with reinforcing gender spiritual superiority.

In most matters the penitentials attempted to curb, discipline, and direct social behavior in the absence of strong civil law rather than to transform or radically alter behavior. The spiritual equality of women we have seen in the vitae and in the monasteries often was lost in the penitentials because they were more concerned with the order in this world. They accepted without question the social and physical inequality of women in the world, and focused "more heavily upon reparation for past offenses than upon reformation of future behavior."[102] It is true, though, to say that given their acceptance of the social and physical inequality of women, the penitentials frequently went out of their way to make sure women were treated acceptably in matters of marriage and sex. Hence the penitential of Theodore reminded fathers that "a girl of seventeen years has the power of her own body"[103] and that therefore "after that age a father may not bestow his daughter in marriage against her will."[104] In the marital conflicts of Carolingian kings, bishops were often champions of the women involved, premised on the belief that an adult woman had a free will, and thus she, like a man, must give her consent for a marriage to

be valid. "What the father wishes, the maiden shall do, since the head of
the woman is the man [*vir*]," echoes canon 27 of the Second Synod of St.
Patrick. "But the will of the maiden is to be inquired after by the father,
since God left man [*hominem*] in the hand of his own counsel."[105] While
there was often, but not always, a difference in the penance meted out to
men and to women (the penitential of Adamnon explicitly stated that "men
and women are equally liable for large and small dues"),[106] they were both
held to the same standards of behavior: "If any cleric or woman who
practices magic misleads anyone by the magic, it is a monstrous sin, but a
sin that can be expiated by penance."[107] The important factor was repentance, and as long as this was present the community should be satisfied:
"If anyone having committed a fault comes to a priest for confession of his
own free will, we command that he or she be not condemned by any-
body."[108] Both genders also were given the same leniency in their road to
repentance: "If any man or woman is nigh unto death, although he or she
has been a sinner and pleads for the communion of Christ we say that it
is not to be denied to him or her if one promises to take the vow, and let
him or her do well and be received by Him."[109] Ultimately, the spiritual
equality of men and women was communicated strongly but in the
negative: Both were sinners who could be forgiven if they repented.

8

The High Middle Ages: Hermits and Scholars

AFTER MANY CENTURIES OF DORMANCY, theology awakened in the new schools of the West during the eleventh century and came fully alive in the twelfth and thirteenth centuries. Among the first to be involved in this awakening were a group of scholars who, often at the height of their career, chose to leave the schools and join a nascent movement. In the tenth and early eleventh century the movement was eremitic; in its maturity during the late eleventh and twelve century it took the form of the *vita apostolica* (apostolic life) and eventually was institutionalized in the thirteenth century by mendicant orders.

The earliest documentation we have of the movement is from Italy in the late ninth century; it reached north of the Alps a century later.[1] Once Romuald[2] began to preach about it at the turn of the millennium, the eremitic movement gained momentum. In Italy disciples became as numerous as the hermits in the Thebaid desert at the beginning of the third-century monastic movement, according to David Knowles.[3] The disciples wanted even more asceticism than contemporary monasticism could offer, a life described by Stephen of Muret's hagiographer as "more remote from all the temporal cares of the world, so much the richer in heavenly goods."[4] Romuald roamed throughout Italy during the last decades of the tenth century, inspiring many to join him in the search for a simpler, more austere monastic life. In 1012 he established the semieremitic monastery of Camaldoli, which, in turn, inspired the foundation of many other hermitages. The biographer of Romuald, Peter Damian, famed schoolmaster from Ravenna, eventually became more important to the movement than Romuald, for his writings spread the movement even farther throughout the West.[5] Bruno of Cologne left his position as chancellor of the school at Rheims in 1080 to embark upon the eremitic life in the region of Grenoble. Shortly after, he founded the Carthusian Order at the Grande

Chartreuse for those who followed his example.[6] Robert of Arbrissel, a pupil of Anselm of Laon and a teacher himself at Angers, withdrew to the wilderness of the Craon forests to live the solitary life. Disciples soon flocked to him and within four years he founded a monastery at LaRoe for them, then another at Fontevrault and the religious order known by that name.[7] Stephen of Muret, educated in Italy, left the academic world to establish the Grandmontines; Gilbert of Sempringham, founder of the Gilbertine Order, was trained to the level of magister in France, possibly at Laon; Stephen Harding, a student at Dorset and then Paris, was a cofounder of the Cistercians; and Bernard of Tiron, a renowned student of grammar and dialectics, founded a monastery at Tiron.[8] The vita of Vitalis of Savigny tells us that Vitalis, Robert of Abrissel, and Bernard of Tiron "with other most bright and knowledgeable people formed a group in the forementioned territory"[9] of northern France and that Vitalis eventually established a monastery at Savigny. Gaufridi Grossi tells us in Bernard of Tiron's vita that, as in Italy, "there were solitaries living all over in various abodes in the deserted region adjoining Gaul and Britain which at that time was filled like a second Egypt, with a multitude of hermits."[10]

The movement is of interest to us here because it provides us with a group of men to examine, arguably those among the best and the brightest and certainly of proven leadership, who were exposed to medieval theology as it developed in the new schools and who then left the world of ideas to construct a new life structured on the principles of that theology. Of the scholars and founders mentioned, only Peter Damian left us an appreciable body of writing after his immersion into eremiticism; the rest we must view chiefly from their rules and their orders, although there are a few documents here and there.

Peter Damian is also the most difficult to grasp, indeed probably the most difficult of all eleventh-century writers. The difficulty rests not in the complexity of his thought but in its contradictory nature. His diatribes against intellectual pursuits, for example, are often quoted, yet they are not often understood in their proper context. Although he dramatically declared in his famous treatise, Liber "Dominus vobiscum," that "I reject Plato," Pythagoras, Euclid, and Nicomachus and that he dismissed "all the rhetors with their embellishments and reflexions without distinction, and all the dialecticians," he really did not.[11] To the contrary, he used these tools himself to write some of the most influential treatises of the century.[12] If one reads Dominus vobiscum in its entirety, one sees that Damian's true intention was to convince the reader to prioritize intellectual pursuits. Christ who is all Truth must be pursued at all times. Secular knowledge was not opposed to Christ the Truth but actually could help one arrive at Truth. Never, however, was the means to become the end. In other words, Damian used rhetorical embellishments, which paradoxically included the condemnation of rhetoric, to persuade his readers of the validity of his argument. His approach so impressed his contemporaries that it became a formative influence in the development of the medieval *ars dictandi* and a stylistic model for rhetorical denunciation.[13]

All of this is a necessary tangent to impress upon the reader the complexity of many medieval thinkers and the difficulty inherent in analyzing their thoughts about women. Most would assume that, given Damian's often-quoted diatribes against sexual immorality in his *Liber Gomorrhianus*,[14] he would be the last person to look for elements of the tradition of spiritual equality. What becomes apparent upon closer examination, however, is that it was the unrestrained, public misuse of sex that he railed against, not sex itself, and certainly not women. Sin was always personal to Damian, and it was the person, not the temptation, who was responsible for sin. When he confessed his own experiences with lust he scapegoated no one or no thing, not even noting the object or person that excited him: "At times lustful desire is kindled and flares up within me, agitates my whole being, causing my genitalia to grow hard." Passion, be it anger or lust, is a fact of life. If Damian controlled it within himself, if "at these disturbances I never lift a finger to help them, nor provide fuel for these raging fires," then surely "the fires of lust will burn themselves out for lack of fuel." The answer is within the control of each individual: "Let everyone do to me what he will; I must look for patience within myself."[15] With such an approach toward sin, there is little room for woman as seducer or gateway to the devil.

The chief reason why Damian dwelt so much on sexual misbehavior was rooted in quite another concern. As the Western church struggled to become as independent, mature institution, ecclesiastical leaders like Damian realized that the reform movement would fail if the church did not produce a leadership that was exemplary and worthy of the laity's respect. Hence Damian's main target in his diatribes were the sexual sins of those in authority, because of the nature of Christian leadership. "Since all ecclesiastical orders are accumulated in one awesome structure in you alone, you surely defile all of them as you pollute yourself," he insisted."[16]

Here we come face to face with the chief tenet of Damian's theology and life: the Mystical Body of Christ. It is within this doctrine that Damian's understanding of women was rooted, and it was the guiding principle that shaped his interactions with women throughout his clerical career. The fullest expression of the doctrine is found in the treatise, *Dominus vobiscum*. It is a masterpiece of literature, persuasion, and theology, and one of the richest expressions of the medieval understanding of human nature and community. Giovanni Miccoli has rightfully called it "one of the most important ecclesiological works among all the theological literature of the Middle Ages";[17] it should be considered likewise in women's literature.

To Damian, the starting point in understanding one's self was in acknowledging the unity of each solitary individual with every other individual. This was possible because "the church of Christ is so joined together by the bond of love that in many it is one, and in each it is mystically complete. Thus we at once observe that the whole church is rightly called the one and only bride of Christ, and we believe each individual soul, by the mystery of baptism, to be the Whole Church." This theme was repeated again and again with even more insistence. The individual who believed in Christ was united with all other believers in Christ and could never be separated from the whole. This whole, the church, "even though she seems to be divided into parts with respect to her physical circumstances," cannot be divided because "the integrity of her inmost unity can in no way be broken up." It was indeed "fused into one by the fire of the Holy Spirit," the same Spirit "who dwells in each and at the same time fills all," making our solitude "at once plural and our community singular." Try as we might, we cannot alter this truth. As difficult as it may be to grasp rationally, faith demands acquiescence. Regardless of appearance, no matter how "physically distinct" we appear to ourselves, "we cannot be separated from one another in spirit if we remain in Him."[18]

Damian was quite conscious of the implications this doctrine has on the question of women. He addressed it directly, leaving us with no lingering doubts. "And so it is that in celebrating Mass, when we say: 'Remember, Lord, your servants and handmaids,' that immediately we add, 'for whom we offer, or who themselves offer to you, this sacrifice of praise.' From these prayers it is obvious that this sacrifice of praise is offered by all the faithful, not only by men but also by women, even though it appears to be offered only by the priest in particular. . . . [For] the sacrifice placed on the altar by the priest is offered in common by all the family of God."[19]

After making sure all understand quite explicitly that the church included all men and all women, even pressing all to "search diligently through the open fields of Holy Scripture" to discover for themselves "that the Church is often represented by one man or one woman," Damian emphasized the equality of all in the eyes of the church. "By the mystery of intimate unity" that binds all believers together, "the Church is there spiritually present" for every single woman and man "participating in the same faith and fraternal love." What Damian was talking about here is an indivisible community in which men and women can be members and can have equal access to the privileges and rewards of the community. "This necessary communion of the faithful of Christ was so certainly a fact that [the church fathers] set this communion in the creed of the Catholic faith and commanded us to repeat it often as something belonging to the basic concepts of the Christian faith." Male or female, as members of the communion of saints you "are admitted into one eternal life."[20]

Damian did not shy away from these beliefs but brought them to their logical conclusion whenever the opportunity arose. When discussing the creation of man and woman, he began by noting that God made one man, not many, and one woman from the rib of the only man. At first this appears puzzling, since the creation of all other species involved several kinds of each. Damian's explanation was concise: God was content "to make only one man" from whom "He decided to generate the female sex to demonstrate the value of love and to join them in the bond of mutual love, so that in keeping with their very origin, they who are demonstrably from one and the same body should never go their separate ways. And to this point Paul says, 'There is one body and one spirit, just as you are called to the one hope that belongs to your call.'" Again the themes of unity and equality dominate Damian's understanding of woman's creation and the subsequent introduction of marriage. Because of human weakness the flame of love grew weak "as the race was extended," and so "to restore the flickering fire of mutual love, the contract of marriage was thereupon introduced."[21]

Damian went even further in a letter to Duchess Beatrice of Tuscany, written to congratulate her on her and her husband Godrey's decision to embrace marital continence. When Godfrey first told Damian about it, Damian was led to believe that Beatrice "did not gladly go along." When he found out that she was in eager agreement with the arrangement, Damian "shouted with joy. Now you are free," he wrote to her, "of that ancient curse in which it was said to the first woman, 'You will be in the power of your husband and he shall be your master.'" He continued, reminding her of Sarah's decision to live chastely with Abraham. After Sarah made her decision, "God said to Abraham, 'Pay attention to everything that Sarah will say to you.' Notice that as a result of her chastity, she to whom Abraham had previously given orders he was now commanded to obey, so that now he was to listen to her in everything, whereas formerly he had controlled her as her master."[22] Damian was quite definite about the source of Eve's submission and Sarah's authority: It was Eve's abandonment of spiritual perfection—exemplified by celibacy—and Sarah's embrace of it. Once the goals of the spiritual world were adopted, Godfrey was no longer Beatrice's master but her spiritual equal.

Damian's excessive rhetoric and highly charged language has contributed greatly to modern scholars' penchant for both misinterpreting and
ignoring him. This is most unfortunate, for dismissal of his written works
has led to historians undervaluing Damian's influence on the culture of the
day. Moreover, without Damian in center stage our understanding of the
history of the eleventh century is most deficient. He was instrumental in
the origin and success of the eremitic movement, the monastic reform
movement, the clerical reform of the church, the church's move for
independence from secular lordship, the intellectual awakening of the
West, the growth of schools, the new canonical orders, the enforcement
of celibacy among Western clergy, and the *vita apostolica*. No other figure,
not even Pope Gregory VII, left a more indelible mark on that society than
Damian. His perception of women and their spiritual dignity within the
Mystical Body of Christ is most noteworthy because everything he did
and said was most noteworthy.

What about the rest of the eremitical movement: What were the
leaders' beliefs concerning women? The eremitic life by its very nature is
sparsely documented. We have few references[23] about hermits until after
they become organized into religious orders; when the vitae of the founders
of these groups were written, many authors noted the size and composition
of the crowds following them in the early days. Robert of Arbrissel's
hagiographer Baldric wrote that the hermits who looked to Robert for
leadership included "many of both sex."[24] When Robert established the
group in Fontevrault, Baldric noted that "women, poor and noble, widows
and virgins, old and young, prostitutes and despisers of men" were members,
as were different classes of men.[25] We know that by the latter part of the
eleventh century there were enough women living in the wilderness of
northern France for people in other countries to know about them, for
around 1080 Eve of Wilton and an unnamed woman left the royal abbey of
Wilton in England to join the men and women hermits across the channel.[26]

As the twelfth century approached, documentation increased, and
now we can benefit from recent regional studies. Not only were women
hermits fully accepted by society and the hierarchy in England, but there
they dominated the movement.[27] Ireland had a hermit tradition that predated the eleventh-century continental eremitic movement; thirteen, possibly fourteen women hermits are recognized as saints. Some of them, like
Burian (seventh century), Domnica (eighth century), and Modwena (ninth
century), migrated to England, thus fertilizing English soil for later reception. Two Irish hermits, Maxentias and Germanie, settled in France, which
also had a strong, visible, female eremitic tradition during the Early Middle

Ages. Three Merovingian saints—Monegondes, Bertilie, and Bertha—retired to the solitary life toward the end of their days. The most famous Italian woman hermit was probably Gregory the Great's mother, Silvia, although there were many more. In the Early Middle Ages, few regions could not boast of some saintly woman hermit. Germany, Switzerland, the Low Countries, and even Moorish Spain all commemorated at least a few female hermits as saints.[28] The eremitic life is most austere, and abundant evidence exists from the time of the first desert hermits onward that women were always among the select few able to lead such a life. More significantly, Christianity always has considered the eremitic life to be the most intense religious life one could choose. Accordingly it has always given hermits its utmost respect and admiration. When the eremitic movement blossomed during the High Middle Ages, women were among its members and were among those subsequently respected and admired. Indeed, some of the most influential women of the period lived in solitude for at least some part of their lives: Eve of Wilton, Christina of Markyate, the renowned Hildegard of Bingen and her aunt Jutta, Rose of Viterbo, and Juliana of Mont-Cornillon are just a few examples.

By the twelfth century much of the original eremitic movement was being channeled into institutional forms. The group surrounding Bruno of Cologne formed the elite Carthusian Order, universally revered as the most rigorous and worthy of respect of all religious orders. Always extremely selective about its membership, around 1140 it accepted women from a Provençal monastery into its monastic family. In the forests near Coucy, France, male and female hermits gathered around Norbert of Xanten, settling in a double monastery called Prémontrè in 1121. Gilbert of Sempringham originally intended to found a religious order for men, but "when he found no men willing to lead such strict lives for God's sake, Gilbert thought it right to make over everything he owned to the use of such girls as, being truly poor in spirit, could obtain the kingdom of heaven for themselves and for others." Seven young women from Sempringham were already living an ascetic life in the village; they agreed to adopt Gilbert's rule, and he agreed to provide for the women's material needs. In due time the women were enclosed "to live a solitary life under the wall on the northern side of the church of St. Andrew the Apostle in the village of Sempringham."[29]

By the mid twelfth century the eremitic movement was spent. Its legacy was carried on into the thirteenth and fourteenth centuries by anchoritism and the new monastic orders. Of the monastic orders born of the eremitic movement, only Fontevrault remained hospitable to women; Penny Schine Gold argues that this can be attributed to the institutionalization of women into the essence of the order from the very beginning and to the fact that the order's rule explicitly expressed that.[30] The other orders failed to do so, with resulting disorganization and then discontent with female members.

The anchoritic life inherited much from eremitism, but it differed in its permanency of location and by its total dependence on the local community to support and protect the individual. Typically, an anchorite (often called a recluse) would be permanently enclosed in a cell adjoining a parish church. Because the person was so dependent on the community for existence, an elaborate set of applications, commitments, permissions, licenses, and rites soon surrounded the enclosure of an anchorite. The willingness of the community to go to such extremes to support one individual's mode of existence is indisputable evidence of how highly the anchorite was revered and of how desirable the presence of an anchorite was to that community. Whereas women lacked support from the male branch of the order during the thirteenth century in many new religious orders, no equivalent rift arose between the anchorites and their communities. Women anchorites were as appreciated by men anchorites and the larger community as men were. In fact, women anchorites were often in the majority. Ann Warren's study of English anchorites informs us that not only were women markedly more numerous there (in the thirteenth century she identifies 123 women and only thirty-seven men as English anchorites) but that they came from the laity and from every social class.[31] The life undoubtedly granted women willing to endure it superior spiritual status within the community.

The anchorite literature born of this movement is not plentiful, but it is distinctive. Even casual reading discloses the high standards of behavior demanded of the recluses by the supporting community. In a letter to his unnamed anchorite sister, Aelred of Rievaulx devotes about a third of his time discussing the external demands of the life and the rest on interior demands. It was not written for his sister's formation, for she had been living the life for years by that time, but "for the young girls who, on your advice, are eager to embrace a life like yours."[32] The letter emphasized silence before all else, for "therein lies great peace and abundant fruit." Idleness also must be avoided, for it is "the enemy of the soul," and the day must be filled with "hours of manual labor, reading, and prayer." Part of her prayer should be "the office in honor of our Lady," followed by "the commemoration of the saints." Manual labor should fill the predawn hours, and while awaiting Terce and None "she should divide her time" among reading, devotions, and manual labor. After Vespers "she should quietly read a little of the *Lives of the Fathers*, of their rules, or of their miracles." Fasting and vigils must be assiduously observed during Lent "insofar as her whole life is the expression of [Lent]."[33] The life of penance was not to be the penance of Martha's activity but of Mary's single-minded dedication. Like Mary, the anchorite's life was of sitting and listening at Jesus's feet. "Let Martha carry out her part, although it is admitted to be good, Mary's is declared better."[34]

What is most interesting in this rule is the presence of the local community in the background. Silence was important because it formed a barrier between the recluse and the supportive but sometimes intruding community. By so ardently desiring to participate in the anchorite's life, they put that life in jeopardy. "How seldom nowadays will you find a recluse alone," Aelred commented. "At her window will be seated some garrulous old gossip pouring idle tales into her ears," which ultimately deprived the anchorite of the peace needed to live the life successfully. Aelred talked about limiting "the legitimate claims of almsgiving and hospitality" and about never allowing "children access to your cell," clearly indicating how frequently the anchorite was forced into such demanding situations; he particularly advised against "assuming the obligation of hospitality, even towards her sisters in religion."[35]

In another section of the letter Aelred offered a defense of the life and reasons for the community's indebtedness to the women.

> What good then will you be able to do to your neighbor? Nothing is more valuable, a certain holy man has said [Gregory the Great], than good will. Let this be your offering. What is more useful than prayer? Let this be your largesse. What is more humane that pity? Let this be your alms. So embrace the whole world with the arms of your love and in that act at once consider and congratulate the good, contemplate and mourn over the wicked. In that act look upon the afflicted and the oppressed and feel compassion for them. In that act call to mind the wretchedness of the poor, the groans of the orphans, the abandonment of widows, the gloom of the sorrowful, the needs of travelers, the prayers of virgins, the perils of those at sea, the temptation of monks, the responsibilities of prelates, the labors of those waging war. In your love take them all to your heart, weep over them, offer your prayers for them. Such alms are more pleasing to God, more acceptable to Christ, more becoming your profession, more fruitful to those who receive them.[36]

Many of Aelred's themes were common to all anchorite literature. The best-known work of the genre, *Ancrene Wisse*, written at the turn of the thirteenth century, echoed his portrayal of the life. Silence was a most valuable asset to the recluse: "Our precious St. Mary, who ought to be an example for all women, was of so few words that nowhere in Holy Writ do we find that she spoke, except for four times; but because of this rarity of speech, her words were heavy and full of power. . . . Take a lesson from this and learn it ardently, that sparse speech has much strength." Hence the anchorite should "always keep silence at meals," keep total silence every Friday, "in the Advent and Ember weeks, Wednesday and Friday; in Lent, three days, and all Holy week until noon, except on Easter eve," and never "talk with anyone through the church window." By doing this the anchorite avoids the plight of Eve, who "held a long discussion with the serpent, told him the whole lesson about the apple that God had taught her and Adam; and so the enemy understood her weakness right away through her words, and found a way into her for her destruction."[37] In imitation of Mary the anchorite must live a life of contemplation, in "stillness and rest from all the world's noise, so that nothing may prevent her from hearing God's voice."[38]

The life also must be one of penance: "All you ever endure is penance, and hard penance, my dear sisters; all the good you ever do, all you suffer, is martyrdom for you in the most severe of orders, for night and day you are up on God's cross."[39] Here the anchorite's model was none other than Jesus himself. Just as narrowness and bitterness "belong to the anchoress," so did they belong to Jesus, "for the womb is a narrow dwelling, where our Lord was a recluse; and this word 'Mary' as I have often said, means 'bitterness.' If you then suffer bitterness in a narrow place, you are his fellows, recluse as he was in Mary's womb. Are you imprisoned within four wide walls?—and he in a narrow cradle, nailed to the cross, enclosed tight in a stone tomb. Mary's womb and this tomb were his anchorhouses."[40]

It is in the following passage of *Ancrene Wisse*, however, that we behold the full extent of society's opinion of these women.

> The bird of night under the eaves [Ps 101:7] symbolizes recluses, who dwell under the eaves of a church because they understand that they should be of so holy a life that the whole of Holy Church, that is, Christian people, can lean upon them and trust them, while they hold her up with their holiness of life and their blessed prayers. This is why an anchoress is called an anchoress, and is enclosed under a church like an anchor under the side of a ship, to hold that ship so that waves and storms do not overturn it. In the same way all Holy Church, which is called a ship, must anchor on the anchoress, in order that she may so hold it that the devil's blasts, which are temptations, do not overturn it. Every anchoress has made this agreement, both through the title of

anchoress and the fact that she dwells under the church, to shore her up if she shows signs of falling.[41]

In the vita of Christina of Markyate we get a glimpse of how some women actually lived what men theorized about in rules. How much the anchoritic life was one of penance is vividly captured in the description of Christina's living arrangements when she began sharing Roger's hermitage with him. Because she was still being sought by her scorned husband, "they acted with circumspection" and searched for living quarters for her "so concealed that to anyone looking from the outside" could not see her. Roger found an angled space in his cell no bigger than "a span and a half" (thirteen and a half inches) in which she entered. Roger then covered "this prison" with so heavy a log "that it could not be put in its place or taken away by the recluse."

> And so, thus confined, the handmaid of Christ sat in a hard stone until Roger's death, that is, four years and more, concealed even from those who dwelt together with Roger. O what trials she had to bear of cold and heat, hunger, and thirst, daily fasting! The confined space would not allow her to wear even the necessary clothing when she was cold. The airless little enclosure became stifling when she was hot. Through long fasting, her bowels became contracted and dried up. But what was more unbearable than all this was that she could not go out until the evening to satisfy the demands of nature. Even when she was in dire need, she could not open the door for herself, and Roger usually did not come until late.[42]

Part of the importance of the anchorite and of anchorite literature is the sphere of public space that the two permeated. It is improbable that the thoughts of a scholar like Abelard concerning women's spiritual dignity were known among the scattered Christian communities of thirteenth-century Europe;[43] it is highly probable that the presence of anchorites was known within these same villages. Everyone knew these women, supported their vocation actively or passively, and believed them to be capable of great spiritual achievement. Christina of Markyate's hagiographer tells us how "her growing reputation" drew a "number of maidens"[44] to join her in her eremitic life; her reputation for holiness also led to "frequent visits from the heads of celebrated monasteries in distant parts of England and from across the sea, who wished to take her away with them and by her presence add importance and prestige to their places."[45] Hagiographic literature had a greater opportunity to influence society directly, for Christians were exposed to it more than to the works of the scholastics. Works like the passions of *Margaret* and *Juliana* probably were written originally as vitae in the Early Middle Ages[46] and rendered in new form during the High Middle Ages, to be performed in the vernacular before an illiterate community in a public square on feast days. The broad audience appeal often is included in introductory comments, such as those in *Juliana:* "I want to tell you a story. You have heard it many times, but were unable to understand it, hence my desire to relate to you. Latin is difficult for you, . . . but you understand the vernacular."[47] The author of *Margaret*[48] addressed "all you who have ears and hearing, widows along with the wedded! And maidens especially listen very carefully,"[49] while the author of *Juliana* confided that he specifically undertook this work so "all the unlearned who cannot understand the Latin language, [can] listen, and hear the life of a maiden, which is translated from Latin into the English laguage."[50]

In the work of *Margaret* we also catch a glimpse of the conflict the author and presumably the audience experienced as they rejoiced in the spiritual feats of this woman. The exalted spiritual dignity of women was always in sharp contrast with the expectations of society in other realms, and we hear this frustration expressed by the demon intent upon corrupting Margaret. When he was defeated "he began to cry out and howl, 'Margaret, maiden, what'll become of me?'" Any defeat was humiliating, but the demon's real problem was that he could not accept that his defeat was "through a girl! And this is even worse for me, that the whole of the race you come from are in our bonds, and you've broken out of them." In the face of a woman's spiritual strength, "we're weak and worth nothing at all, when a girl defeats our great pride like this."[51] The demon continued his diatribe, explaining to Margaret "why we afflict and hate maidens the most." It was because Jesus "was born of a maiden, and through the power of maidenhood humanity was reborn, and all we owned taken away and robbed from us."[52] Regardless of the paradox—or because of it—the spiritual superiority of the woman remained intact. A woman's ability to intercede for the community was undeniable. Those attending church services on Margaret's feast day would hear these closing remarks proclaimed loudly in her name:

> I beg and beseech you, who are my riches and joy, that whoever writes
> a book of my life, acquires a copy of it, or owns it and has it very often
> at hand, or whoever reads it or eagerly asks a reader for it, let all their
> sins be forgiven at once, Ruler of Heaven. Whoever makes a chapel or
> church in my name, or endows one with a light or lamp, Lord, grant

them and give them the light of heaven. In the house where a woman is in labor-pain with a child, as soon as she calls to mind your name and my pain, Lord, quickly help her, Lord, and hear her prayer; and in that house let no malformed child be born, neither lame nor hump-backed, neither deaf nor mute, nor afflicted by devils. And whoever mentions my name with their mouth, lovely Lord, release them from death at the last Judgment.[53]

Exploration of the intellectual world for opinions of women's spiritual status is challenging because of the increase in sources during the High Middle Ages, the conflicting opinions among scholars, the inner contradictions within some works, and the contrast between some scholastics' works and their lives. Still, we can continue to identify strands of a positive tradition, intertwined though they sometimes are with a negative one.

Anselm, traditionally noted as the first of the great schoolmen, reiterated the early Christian anthropology of spiritual equality in the new logic of the day. In his *Monologium,* a philosophical and theological treatise on the existence of God, he univocally stated that "undoubtedly all human souls are of the same nature."[54] Moreover, "there is no doubt that the human soul is a rational creature," that "it must have been created for this end, that it might love the supreme Being,"[55] and that "no being is unjustly deprived by the supremely great and supremely good Creator of that good for which it was created."[56] In the abstract, then, Anselm allowed for no distinctions among humans and established full equality in their nature and in their end. Despite their full spiritual equality at creation, to Anselm woman, in the person of Eve, is the "cause of our condemnation" and of "man's sin." Regardless, women need "not despair of attaining the inheritance of the blessed," for their spiritual end remains the same. In fact, it was again a woman, this time in the person of Mary, who restored to both men and women the means to salvation. It was altogether "proper that from woman also so great a blessing should arise" because "so dire an evil arose from women."[57]

When discussing in *Cur Deus Homo* whence Jesus received his human nature, Anselm argued that it was only logical that he received it from Mary alone: "If it was a virgin which brought all evil upon the human race, it is much more appropriate that a virgin should be the occasion of all good."[58] Mary was given a very exalted position in Anselm's thought, at the expense of Eve. Woman correspondingly occupied both the lowest and the highest positions in salvific history. It is a paradox that Anselm did not belabor, but he did promote devotion to Mary and her role in redemption with vigor; the popularity and theological content of his three Marian prayers make him a major contributor to medieval Mariology. Through Mary "the elements are renewed, the netherworld is healed, the demons are trodden under foot, humanity is saved and angels are restored." Anselm even constructed a parallel Mariological argument to his famed ontological argument: "Every nature is created by God and God is born from Mary. God has created all things, and Mary has given birth to God. God, who has made all things has made himself from Mary, and thus he has re-created all he created. . . . Therefore, God is the Father of all created things, and Mary is the Mother of all re-created things." Elsewhere in his prayers he stated that "Our God has become our brother through Mary" and that "both salvation and damnation depend on the will of the good Brother and the merciful Mother."[59] We have here Anselm's foundation for belief in Mary's coredemptor role.

In his discussion of the Trinity, Anselm contemplated "whether it is more fitting to call them Father and Son than mother and daughter, since in them there is no distinction of sex"; the question itself acknowledges the spiritual equality of man and woman. Anselm bowed to the biological wisdom of his day to answer the question, maintaining that while even in nature "as among certain kinds of birds" the female is sometimes "larger and stronger" than the male, "at any rate, it is more consistent to call the supreme Spirit father than mother, for this reason, that the first and principal cause of offspring is always in the father."[60] Interest in such a query is significant, for it signals the beginning of a widespread devotion among medieval clergy to the maternal Jesus. The Jesus-as-Mother theme was somewhat popular among Cistercian writers and attained its clearest expression in the theology of the mystic Julian of Norwich.

Abelard's opinion of women, while not radical, was certainly less traditional than Anselm's and did break new ground in some areas. Abelard, like Anselm, believed Eve had greater responsibility for the fall and that women were capable of turning "the curse of Eve into the blessing of Mary."[61] He also believed that woman's creation from man's side indicated physical equality before the fall; woman's culpability for the fall resulted in her physical subordination.[62] Reference to women's physical frailty was frequent. In his rule for women's monasteries Abelard reminded the nuns, for instance, that "solitude is indeed all the more necessary for your woman's frailty, inasmuch as for our part we are less attacked by the conflicts of carnal temptations and less likely to stray towards bodily things through the senses."[63] Abelard was hardly a champion of woman's dignity, yet he did expound on the Pauline paradox, as quoted by Heloise: "'Power comes to its full strength in weakness' (2 Cor 12:9)." Because women were weaker and more culpable, "their virtue is more pleasing and more perfect to God."[64]

Jesus himself bestowed more intimacies and favors on women than on men. Mary his Mother bore him, Elizabeth prophesized his divinity, Martha served him, Mary anointed his feet, the three Marys stood by the Cross, and Mary Magdalene was the first to see the resurrected Christ; in fact, "the greatest miracles of resurrection were shown only, or mostly, to women, and were performed for them or on them."[65]

In the examination of Jesus's attitude toward women, Abelard abandoned his emphasis on the physical frailty of woman and the sin of Eve and instead stressed women's spiritual parity. "Who is so unique and singular in dignity as Christ, in whom, the Apostle says, there is 'neither male nor female'? In the body of Christ, which is the Church, difference of sex, therefore, confers no dignity. For Christ looks not to the condition of sex, but to the quality of merits."[66] The *vita apostolica* movement of his day, with its demand to imitate Christ in all things, may have indirectly influenced his turning to Christ's example for direction; Mary Martin McLaughlin has labeled Abelard's attitude "evangelical feminism."[67] While his thoughts on women's spiritual nature are scattered throughout his works, they are consistent, and they find their fullest expression in the letters to Heloise. In reply to her request to "prescribe some Rule for us and write it down, a Rule which shall be suitable for women,"[68] Abelard answered that "women are not to be distinguished from men in those things that pertain to God or to any excellence in religion,"[69] and then turned to the classic description of the *vita apostolica* in Acts 4:32-35 to defend his stance. Moreover, Scripture provided him with ample examples for illustration: Miriam and Anna sang the first hymns, Deborah and Judith participated in services, and the daughters of Aaron belonged to the hereditary priesthood of Levi.[70] Abelard was not satisfied with simply proving women's spiritual equality; he believed women "even rise above men."[71] Here again Scripture provided his proof. Mary replaced Eve before Christ replaced Adam, and Anna and Elizabeth were models of Christian holiness before the apostles or John the Baptist.

Although Heloise is not considered a scholastic, her views on these issues are valuable as a gauge in evaluating Abelard's. Not surprisingly, they replicate his views in most aspects. Given how little time they spent together before entering monastic life and the scarcity of correspondence afterward, one would have to look to the academic environment of the day for a common influence; often we forget that Heloise was as immersed in that culture as Abelard. She, like Abelard, considered Eve as evil, "the first woman in the beginning who lured man from Paradise, and she who had been created by the Lord as his helpmate became the instrument of his total downfall."[72] She certainly agreed with Abelard's emphasis on the frailty of the female sex; her letters were heavily sprinkled with references to "the weaker sex whose frailty and infirmity is generally known." When arguing for a new rule specifically for women, this was her basic thesis. She wanted a rule that lowers the physical demands for women "since those whom nature created unequal cannot properly be made equal in labor."[73] There does appear to be a nuance in Heloise's argument that is lacking in Abelard's. She wanted fewer demands made on women's inherently weaker physical nature so more time could be devoted to strengthening women's inherently equal spiritual nature. To Heloise, "it is clear that virtues alone win merit in the eyes of God, and that those who are equal in virtue however different in works, deserve equally of him."[74] Twice Heloise openly states that this path is the way for women to become equals to men: "It should be sufficient for our infirmity, and, indeed, a high tribute to it, if we live continently and without possessions, wholly occupied by service to God, and in doing so equal the leaders of the Church themselves in our way of life or religious laymen or even those who are called Canons Regular and profess especially to follow the apostolic life."[75]

As interesting as Abelard and Heloise's opinions are as windows to opinions held by twelfth-century people, we must not mistakenly presume that they influenced all future generations of Christians. As mentioned, Nikolaus Häring has convincingly shown that although immensely popular in his own day and in ours, Abelard's works did not survive long in the medieval world, with many extant manuscripts defective and fragmentary. Häring even goes so far as to claim that "if St. Bernard had not kept his memory alive, the Middle Ages would have been ignorant of the fact that a *magister Petrus Abelardus* ever existed."[76]

One scholastic who did not share such a fate was Peter Lombard, although his situation is perhaps reversed. He was both representative of and influential in the Middle Ages, and yet often is ignored today. His influence was immense in the new schools of the medieval world, mainly because his *Four Books of Sentences*, a synthesis of Christian theology, was what we would call today the standard text in theology for centuries.

In *Sentences* and in commentaries Lombard did not hesitate to diverge from or contradict previous opinions, if he believed it warranted. One of his boldest challenges was to Paul himself over the issue of women. Lombard was not content to ignore the inherent contradictions between Paul's strictures concerning the public silence of women[77] and his enthusiastic acceptance of women's ministry. In his commentary on Paul's command to "Let your women keep silence in the churches: for it is not permitted unto them to speak; but let them be in subjection" (1 Cor 14:34), Lombard argued that the Pauline prohibition was aimed at solving a local problem in Corinth and was not intended to be a universal prohibition. Indeed, "all the rest of the people are called to the faith by their example."[78] This is especially evident when the issue of deacons is examined. Paul uttered no prohibitions against ordaining women deacons and even commended "our sister Phoebe, a deaconess *[diakonos]* of the church at Cenchreae," (Rom 16:1) to the Romans. According to Lombard, this contradicted Paul's blanket relegation of women to the domestic sphere.

By applying such criticism to scripture itself, Lombard hoped to alleviate the contradictions about women that offended his sense of logical consistency. In his criticism of Paul's statements about women in 1 Timothy 2, he was even bolder. Here Paul proclaims, "But I suffer not a woman to teach, not to usurp authority over the man, but to be in silence, for Adam was first formed, then Eve" (1 Tim 2:12-13). Women's subjection, particularly childbirth, was a punishment, according to Paul, for the first sin, because "Adam was not deceived, but the woman being deceived was in the transgression" (1 Tim 2:14). Lombard dismissed this as ludicrous. "If salvation comes not from the works of baptism but from bearing children," then how are "virgins and widows" saved? Women are saved "not by the results of concupiscence but by kindness towards friends and by not offending God."[79] Finally, in a commentary on 1 Corinthians, Lombard attacked Paul's misogamist views on the basis that they were premised on the belief in an imminent second coming.[80] In *Sentences* he presented his own theology of marriage, and it soon became the dominant theory of medieval society.[81] To understand its origin and its impact we must first review its presuppositions, as found in Lombard's discussion of the creation of man and woman.

Lombard rooted his theology in the belief that the souls of humans, both male or female, "are made in the image and of God," that "this image of God passes from one man *[homine]* to all men *[homines]*," and therefore "is present in woman as well as man."[82] What is common to man's soul is common to woman's. The creation of man and woman's bodies, while different in manner, did not indicate inequality. Instead, Lombard emphasized what each creature had in common, creation as fully grown adults. The fact that Eve was formed from Adam's side indicated only the intense love that binds husband and wife and the common paternity of all humans. Like many before him, Lombard interpreted Eve's creation from Adam's side and "not his head, so that man would be seen to dominate, nor from his feet, indicating servitude" in order "to show that she was created in loving partnership."[83]

Given this understanding of woman's creation and nature, it is not surprising to find Lombard championing the theory of consensual marriage.

During the eleventh and twelfth centuries some debate was heard among theologians over the essence of marriage, and various theories vied for acceptance. At times the debate was heated; Peter Damian's sarcastic remarks reveal just how pointed it could get: "If they maintain that marriage rests on intercourse, then how is it that the holy canons forbid people to be joined in marriage without public weddings? Do they want the man to mount his wife in public? . . . If indeed marriage is made by coitus, then every time a man makes love to his wife no doubt they get married all over again."[84] Gratian acknowledges the importance of consent but believed consummation was the essential element in marriage formation. Certain Bolognese canon lawyers such as Paucapalea, Rolandus, and Rufinus, tried to qualify this consummation theory slightly, but without much success.

With Peter Lombard we have the defeat of Gratian's theory and the victory of the consensual theory.[85] In *Sentences* he argued that the essence of marriage "is the marital union of a male and female involving living together in undivided partnership,"[86] not the sexual act. Marriage was more than the uniting of two physical bodies—two unequal physical bodies: "Marriage is also a sign of the spiritual union and affection of souls, by which husbands and wives ought to be united."[87] Society still overwhelmingly considered the female body inferior. Intentionally or not, the consensual theory decreased the importance in marriage of that part of woman that was considered inferior, the body, and elevated the significance of her soul, that part perceived as equal, "for as between husband and wife there is a union in the harmony of their spirits." Casting marriage in these terms had great ecclesiastical and social implications. If marriage is primarily "a sacred sign" representing "the union of Christ and the Church," then the church had a say over marital arrangements.[88] Already during the Early Middle Ages the church often had been the only resource of women forced into marriage. Pope Nicholas I, writing on the marital problems of Carolingian King Lothar, said he would not accept Queen Theutberga's forced statement requesting divorce "for if this is permitted, every husband whose wife has been acquitted by law, if he hates her, will be able to break her with many afflictions, and force from her what is not legitimately offered."[89] The consensual theory also fit more easily into the concept of a sacrament that theologians such as Peter Lombard were busy developing.[90] The now-sacramental nature of marriage with its stipulation of intention, and a court system willing and able to annul marriages formed without free consent, meant that patriarchical, familial control of marriage was breached, in theory at least. Canon lawyers went so far as to endorse secret marriages, and church courts upheld them, despite many an irate family.[91] Forced marriages increasingly became a thing of the past,[92] and women gradually—very gradually—gained significant, real marital freedom as a result of their spiritual parity.

The influence of Peter Lombard is readily seen in Thomas Aquinas's remarks about woman's spiritual nature. Much of what Thomas had to say about the creation of woman is found in his *Commentary on the Sentences* of Peter and then later enhanced in his *Summa Theologica*. In many key points Thomas followed in Peter's footsteps, adding Aristotle and his own thoughts along the way. In his tedious, slow way Thomas established that the soul "is the first principle of life," that "this principle by which we primarily understand, whether it be called the intellect or the intellectual soul, is the form of the body," that "forasmuch as man *[homo]* is rational is it necessary that man have a free will," and the "the soul, as a part of human nature, has its natural perfection only as united to the body."[93] The first man and the first woman came "into existence outside the ordinary course of nature," man from slime and woman from a rib of man.[94] Thomas's answer to why woman was made from man's rib was derived from Peter Lombard's *Sentences*. It was "first, to signify the social union of man and woman," for she was not man's master, "so she was not made from his head." Neither was she his slave, "so she was not made from his feet." Second, it was for the sacramental symbolism, "for from the side of Christ" blood and water flowed "on which the Church was established."[95] In response to the more loaded question of whether woman possessed the fullness of God's image, Thomas argued thus: "Therefore we must understand that when Scripture had said, 'to the image of God He created them,' it added, 'male and female He created them,' not to imply that the image of God came through the distinction of sex, but that the image of God belongs to both sexes, since it is in the mind, wherein there is no sexual distinction. Wherefore the Apostle (Col 3:10) after saying, 'According to the image of Him that created him,' added, 'Where there is neither male nor female.'"[96] Since, "as Augustine says, 'Where an image exists, there forthwith is likeness,'" Thomas concluded "that likeness is essential to an image" and that women, therefore, possessed the same "end or term" as men insofar as they were both made to the image and likeness of God.[97] In short, women's spiritual equality is beyond question.

Marriage for Thomas was not a union of inferior and superior. It was rather "an equiparant relation,"[98] "an inseparable union of souls by which husband and wife are pledged by a bond of mutual affection that cannot be sundered."[99] At the center of his theology of marriage was the consensual theory triumphant. Without consent there was no marriage, for "one person does not receive power over that which is at the free disposal of another without the latter's consent."[100] Thomas clearly saw the social implications of the free-will consent requirement for marriage and dealt with it directly: "Whether one can be compelled by one's father's command to marry?" Thomas not only answered with a resounding "no" but also reminded us that even "a betrothal contracted by parents" would be void "without their children's consent."[101] Compulsory consent invalidated marriage, because "matrimony signifies the union of Christ with the Church, which union is according to the liberty of love." Consent, therefore, must be totally, "completely voluntary, because it has to be perpetual; and consequently it is invalidated by violence of a mixed nature."[102]

Because marriage was placed firmly in the church's domain, the writings of canon lawyers as well as theologians offer us plenty of opportunities to assess the schoolmen's opinions about marriage. As a group, canonists introduced a new awareness and concern for the personal and social implications of marriage, particularly as it pertained to sex and women.[103] The effects on women of this new awareness were varied. Because discussions of sex were increasingly premised on Aristotelian biological views of woman, including the "scientific" view of the female as the incomplete male,[104] debate about sex reinforced opinions of woman's physical inferiority. "As regards individual nature, woman is defective and misbegotten, for the active force in the male seed tends to the production of a perfect likeness in the masculine sex; while the production of woman comes from a defect in the active force or from some material indisposition," Thomas stated emphatically, even though he also acknowledged that "as regards human nature in general, woman is not misbegotten."[105] Woman's physical condition often was incorporated into theological debates, some serious, some exercises in hypothetical situations: Could Christ have been born a woman? Is male sex a requirement for ordination? Did Mary menstruate?[106] One must remember, however, the specific context in which these discussions were taking place and by whom. Preoccupation with sex and woman's physicality arose during the eleventh-century Gregorian Reform with its mandate for clerical continence, and it continued to flourish during those years in which clerical celibacy was being enforced. That clergy in the schools should be preoccupied with questions of sex, women, and the female physical nature is not surprising, nor is it surprising that so many discussions mirrored the world's negative stereotype about them. They were, after all, trying to build a world in which continence was manageable. What better way than to make the object of their desire less desirable?

What is surprising, given the environment in which these questions were asked and given the fact that the answers were responded to by the very clergy most concerned about continence, is that the tradition of spiritual equality was not attacked. Instead, the tradition was maintained and expanded into the social realm in regard to marriage. The consensual theory of marriage, formally encoded by the end of the twelfth century in the papal teachings of Alexander III's decretal *Veniens ad nos,* required the free-will consent of two people. "Consent means a joining of souls," the decretalist Tancred said,[107] and souls are indistinguishable by sex.

Of all the discussions the scholastics had concerning women, the debate on marriage had the greatest impact on the immediate world beyond the walls of academia. The esoteric debates on such nonreal matters as whether there was sex in paradise, whether childbearing was painful before the fall, and the like often were not dialogues with society but rather monologues within the schools. In the case of marriage, however, we can see how society and the schools influenced and reflected each other.[108] We can also see how the opinions of the hermits and scholars echoed in the devotions and culture of society at large, an area we will examine next.

9

The New Spirituality and Medieval Culture

AT THE CLOSE OF THE ELEVENTH CENTURY there was another movement afoot in Western culture, closely related in origin to the scholastic movements yet quite different in its manifestation. Not all men and women growing up in the environment of the great intellectual awakening of the eleventh century and desirous of the *vita apostolica* became hermits or scholars. Many entered cenobitic communities and made their mark in history by developing a new spirituality, more affective and emotional than the rational spirituality of scholasticism. For some the spirituality led to mysticism, a movement that reached its fullest expression with women in the late medieval period.

For others the new spirituality led to mendicancy. As with the eremitic and the scholastic movements, proponents of one movement were often members of another, meaning that they were not exclusionary movements but often overlapped. Indeed, with historical distance we see that their common matrix in the *vita apostolica* of the eleventh century and in "an increasing sense," as Bynum says, "of humankind's creation 'in the image and likeness of God'"[1] made them more related than they themselves probably were aware. Where and with whom we want to place the first visible signs of a new spirituality is arbitrary, but most accounts start with Anselm of Bec. Despite the fact that his *Proslogium* is best known for his ontological argument, it is not a philosophical treatise as much as it is a prayful mediation in which Anselm revealed how thoroughly his spirituality was based on his understanding of his humanness. While contemplating "the unapproachable light in which Thou dwellest," for example, Anselm described his soul's frustration as it searched for its God in quite physical terms: "For it looks, and does not see thy beauty. It hearkens, and does not hear thy harmony. It smells, and does not perceive thy fragrance. It tastes, and does not recognize thy sweetness. It touches, and does not feel thy pleasantness."[2] His appeal to the senses was always balanced by an appeal to the rational, however; a few sentences prior to these statements he challenged the reader to accept as logically conclusive that "O Lord, thou art not only that than which a greater cannot be conceived, but thou art a being greater than can be conceived,"[3] and a few sentences afterward he questioned whether wisdom and truth were "parts of thee, or is each one of these rather the whole, which thou art?"[4] Anselm presented, in other words, a spirituality that used the emotions to bring wisdom to the mind and ultimately to the soul: "And now, my soul, arouse and lift up all thy understanding and conceive, so far as thou canst, of what character and how great is [God] . . . [for] if the created life is good, how good is the creative life!"[5] Anselm's reverence and devotion for Mary and the saints, and his exploration of the humanity of Jesus, followed logically from this focus.

The Cistercians were the most visible heirs to Anselm's spirituality, particularly Bernard of Clairvaux. Drawn to the new monastery at Citeaux, Bernard entered it in 1112 and soon was the dominating force of the community and the chief spokesman for the new spirituality. That spirituality altered Anselm's balance between emotions and rational knowledge by demoting knowledge, especially the rational knowledge sought in the new schools. Love of God was at the center of Bernard's spirituality, an emotional love that culminates in mysticism. Bernard had no qualms about appealing to the emotional and the sensual, because they, better than logic, could unleash the power of love within and bring true wisdom. "You have it within your power," Bernard wrote to the former countess Ermengarde in a letter that well illustrated his approach to human relationships, "not yet indeed to know me, but at any rate to guess something of what I feel."[6] When it came to the human-divine relationship he was even clearer and more insistent about the low status of knowledge. "You deceive yourself, my son," Bernard warned Thomas of St. Omer, "if you think you can learn from the masters of the world what is a gift of God and can be obtained only by those who follow Christ and scorn the world. This is a knowledge imparted, not by books, but by grace, not by the letter but by the Spirit; not by mere book learning but by the practice of the commandments of God." If Thomas really wanted true knowledge, then "how much better for you to learn Jesus, Jesus crucified."[7]

The positioning of love as superior to rational knowledge had wide-reaching, even radical, implications. It becomes the foundation of the late medieval mystical movement, a movement that treated men and women equally, since God's choice determined membership, not worldly characteristics: "What you have been able to do by the grace of God is yours, what you have been given by your birth is the gift of your ancestors."[8] To those who believed in the superiority of love over rational knowledge, the mystic was more esteemed than the scholar. This prioritizing is one of the facts often overlooked when historians assess the significance of theological treatises in the formation of social attitudes and behaviors. Illiterate medieval society may have been more immediately influenced by the mystic living in the neighborhood than by the theologian writing behind academic walls.[9] This is not to diminish the unquestionable significance of intellectuals and their more indirect influence; it is simply to remind us that medieval society acknowledged mysticism as a valid avenue for attaining truth, the very same goal of scholasticism, that it was very visible in a great many of their communities, and that women were as capable of mysticism as men. In fact, as Bynum points out, "in the thirteenth century women were more likely than men to be mystics, to gain reputations based on their mystical abilities, and . . . were primarily responsible for encouraging and propagating some of the most distinctive aspects of late medieval piety."[10]

Because their premises were the same, the spirituality of many medieval women and of the Cistercians had much in common. They both used highly charged, emotion-laden language to evoke pietistic responses, both relied on the personal, and both fostered a mysticism in which the soul was transformed into the likeness of God. Sometimes we even find all these combined in a single passage, as in Bernard's *On Loving God*,[11] or in a vision received by Hadewijch, an obscure but impressive Beguine mystic, on the feast of Mary's Nativity, when "I saw in the spirit a queen come in" with three maidens. "The queen approached me dreadfully fast and set her foot on my throat, and cried with a more terrible voice and said: 'Do you know who I am?' And I said, 'Yes, indeed! Long enough have you caused me woe and pain. You are my soul's faculty of Reason, and these are the officials of my own household.'" The first maiden was Holy Fear, "who has examined my perfection in all that belongs to the life of Love." The second maiden was discernment, whose job it was to "distinguish Love's will, kingdom and good pleasure from yours. The third maiden was Wisdom, through whom I have acknowledged your power and your works when you let yourself be led by Love." Once Hadewijch acknowledged the necessary presence of the three maidens, "then Reason became subject to me, and I left her. But Love came and embraced me; and I came out of the spirit and remained lying until late in the day, inebriated with unspeakable wonders."[12]

Given the fact that women were universally perceived to be physically inferior, one would suppose that a spirituality that emphasizes physical aspects of human nature would by medieval standards be antifeminist. Somehow it avoided this near-inevitable conclusion and was instead most generous in the position it allocated to women in the scheme of creation. The new spirituality embraced women and was embraced by them in ways that scholastic theology did and was not. The feminization of religious language, the greatly increased use of female imagery, and the popularity and multiplication of Marian devotions all contributed to the creation of an atmosphere in which women and the feminine were visible, plentiful, and respected. When Bynum warns us to remember that "there is little evidence that the popularity of feminine and maternal imagery in the High Middle Ages reflects an increased respect for actual women by men,"[13] we also must remember the opposite. We have little evidence that it did not. More significantly, we do have evidence, much evidence, that aspects of the new spirituality, like female imagery (for example, the maternal Jesus), did contribute to the creation of a milieu in which women—actual women— flourished in their Christian worlds. The number of women saints[14]—that is, women whom the whole of Western society agreed[15] were worthy of imitation, models of intercession, and united with God—increased significantly in the centuries following the spread of the new spirituality. The number of women who wrote or dictated their spiritual experiences increased likewise, thus placing women firmly in the midst of the medieval literary tradition and providing us for the first time with ample sources to examine for women's own perceptions of their spiritual nature.

When we examine the writings and the vitae of women living in cenobitic or mendicant communities or of women mystics, we are struck by women's acceptance of their spiritual equality. Hildegard of Bingen's theology of love is unsustainable without a theology of spiritual equality. While it is unique in its eloquence, it is consistent with other women's theologies of love, particularly those of Angela of Foligno and Hadewijch. While meditating on the creation of Adam and Eve, Hildegard expressed it thus:

> When God created Adam, Adam experienced a sense of great love in the sleep that God instilled in him. And God gave a form to that love of the man, and so woman is the man's love. . . . When Adam gazed at Eve, he was entirely filled with wisdom, for he saw the mother of the children to come. And when she gazed at Adam, it was as if she were gazing into heaven, or as the human soul strives upwards, longing for heavenly things—for her hope was fixed in him. And so there will be and must be one and the same love in man and woman, and no other.[16]

What is even more striking is the note of unhesitating self-assurance of their spiritual worth with which these women wrote or were written about. Angela of Foligno, after describing her mystical union with Christ in which she "felt that Christ was within me, embracing my soul with the very arm with which he was crucified," told her scribe later that "I was so completely certain that God was at work in me that even if everyone in the world were to say that I ought to doubt this, I would not believe them."[17] Hadewijch was so sure of God's special love for her that occasionally she was overwhelmed: "When I think of what God wills with me, and what he has done for me in preference to others, it is a wonder how I remain alive, unless because of the great Love who can do all things. But it is certainly a great marvel to me when I think that God prefers me to all creatures I ever saw."[18] In Margaret of Ypres's vita, it was her hagiographer Thomas de Cantimpré who appeared overwhelmingly assured of Margaret's sanctity. "Who could unfold the power and extent of her prayer?" Thomas commented while describing her prayer. "I do not believe anyone could do this easily, least of all myself."[19] Every pietistic behavior of hers was spoken of with a reverential awe. "Who could ever show forth in words the fire of love for Christ in which she burned?" Thomas asked. "Who ever heard or saw such things?" was his comment after detailing her penitential practices at age seven, and after summarizing her fasting practices at age nine, he exacerbatingly queries, "What are you doing, O woman, powerful in everything." In frustration when faced with her spiritual victories, Thomas completed his reflection by rhetorically asking his male readers to compare their record with hers: "And what of you, O strong and bearded man?"[20]

From whence came the certainty of women's spiritual dignity? The sources vary as much as the women themselves. Often assurances came from within their visions. Hadewijch received many such assurances. "One Easter Sunday," for example, Hadewijch related, "I had gone to God; and he embraced me in my interior senses" and "brought me before the Countenance of the Holy Spirit," from whom she "received all understanding" about herself and her spiritual destiny. "When you fully bring me yourself, as pure humanity in myself, through all the ways of perfect Love, you shall have fruition of me as the Love who I am. And then you will be love, as I am Love."[21] In her poetry Hadewijch articulated her certainty thus: "Through Love I can fully conquer my misery and exile; I know victory will be mine."[22] Not that Hadewijch had to wait for a vision of this knowledge, for she had "understood that, since my childhood, God had drawn me to himself alone, far from all the other beings whom he welcomes to himself in other manners." Part of her certitude came from deep within herself and her understanding of that self, as we hear in this confident, almost brazen, and yet quite revealing statement: "For I am a free human creature, and also pure as to one part, and I can desire freely with my will, and I can will as highly as I wish, and seize and receive from God all that he is, without objection or anger on his part—what no saint can do."[23]

While Hadewijch's confidence was extreme in the power of its articulation, it was not an exception, but the rule. Margaret of Ebner was likewise reassured by her divine voices. "On All Saints' Day I came into choir," Margaret reported. "These words were also spoken to me: 'Rejoice that your Lord and God is so near to your soul. . . . Suffer me for the sake of my love, and I will reward you with myself and will fulfill all your desires with myself and will give you what no eye has seen nor ear heard and what has never been given to any human heart—I will give you my Holy Divinity for eternal joy."[24] Similar general statements verifying the divine origin of the visions and promising eternal reward can be found in almost all of the literature. Sometimes the claim of divine origin is more specific than others, perhaps to give even more certitude to the women. Hildegard of Bingen wrote without hesitation in a letter to a community of canonesses: "These words do not come from a human being but from the Living Light. Let one who hears see and believe where these words come from."[25] Angela of Foligno, on the other hand, seemed to need more assurance than Margaret and Hildegard. Angela "had asked the Blessed Virgin that at the coming feast she obtain a grace from her Son through which I would know that I had not been deceived by the words which had been spoken to me. . . . I had even been told in that discourse that I would be given the grace that I would never do anything without God's permission."[26]

Still, confidence like Hadewijch's is uncommon, insofar as she displays no need to have her spirituality verified by sources other than her visions. Most women looked to a variety of sources for reinforcement. Despite Hildegard's stalwart certitude of her spiritual standing as God's chosen mouthpiece in her letter to the canonesses, elsewhere she laid bare her ambivalence about her divine inspiration. "Now, father," she wrote to Bernard of Clairvaux, "I seek consolation from you, that I may be assured." Two years prior she had had a vision, and her problem now was her "great anxiety about this vision with respect to how much I should speak about what I have seen and heard."[27] Another time she worried about her inspiration while writing her masterpiece *Scivias,* so she submitted it to Pope Eugenius for judgment even before it was finished. Her ambivalence was particularly evident in that letter. She began firmly and with certainty—"I have written those things to you which God saw fit to teach me in a true vision, by mystic inspiration"—but her conviction was shaken when faced with criticism: "In their instability, many people, those wise in worldly things, disparage these writings of mine, criticizing me, a poor creature formed from a rib, ignorant of philosophical matters." Consequently, Hildegard needed to be assured that the pope would "not spurn these mysteries of God" that she wrote about.[28]

Mechtild of Magdeburg reacted likewise in the face of criticism and needed further reinforcement. Hers came again from God. When she "was warned about [her] book and told by many that it should not be preserved but rather thrown to the flames," God told her to "doubt not thyself."[29] Even though she believed she was unworthy to be God's instrument, she also insisted that "this book has come lovingly from God and is not drawn from human senses."[30]

Surely the reaction of fellow Christians must have reinforced these women's sense of spiritual worth. Juliana of Mont-Cornillon's spiritual dignity so impressed those in her world that her anonymous hagiographer wrote that "the bishop of Liege, who cherished Juliana for her exceptional holiness, ordered that a new oratory should be built for her." Before long "many religious people and dignitaries flocked there to commend themselves to Juliana's prayers, edified by what they saw in her and heard from her lips." The hagiographer then added enthusiastically, "Who that was wise and wished to grow in spirit would not go to see and read the immaculate law of the Lord? I do not mean the law inscribed in books, but the law written in Juliana's attitude and conduct. Everything in her was disciplined, everything was a mark of virtue, an image of perfection."[31] Letters to Hildegard frequently communicated the people's acknowledgment of her spiritual value. One community of nuns wished to be received into the community Hildegard was abbess of because "the Lord, who foreknew you and made you His elect, has illuminated you and filled you with the spirit of prophecy in our time. Christ has gladdened us especially in this: that He not only foresaw and predestined you, a woman, for this purpose, but also His grace has illuminated many through your teaching." Being told by Gertrude von Stahleck that "there is no one like you nor anyone so beloved in Christ"[32] surely quieted doubts Hildegard might have harbored about her spiritual nature in the eyes of God.

The testimony of well-established holy people was also reassuring, like the deathbed praise of Marie d'Oignies for Lutgard of Aywières: "'Under heaven the world has no more faithful or more efficacious intercessor in prayers for the liberation of souls from purgatory and for sinners than the lady Lutgard.'"[33] Even a stranger's testimony helped Lutgard's fears concerning the validity of her spiritual endeavors. One day she was called to the parlor to greet a "man, unknown to everyone," who said as she entered, "'The

Almighty commands you to do these things: beginning from this moment you are to live secure concerning the rest because the Lord is well pleased in you.' Saying these things the young man immediately disappeared."[34] Mechtild of Hackeborn needed the spirit of a deceased Dominican friend to appear to her to calm her fears. "Pray for me that we may not be deceived by the devil in the gift which is given to us," Mechtild pleaded. "Clothe yourself in the armor of faith and believe firmly and steadfastly that the gift comes from God," the friend replied.[35] Likewise, Diana d'Andalo's letter from Jordan of Saxony must have bolstered her convictions: "As a little encouragement to you, I will mention briefly something which I dreamed about you recently." He then summarizes the dream in which Diana said "The Lord spoke to me like this: 'I and Diana, I and Diana, I and Diana.'" Jordan concluded by telling her "You can imagine that I find this most consoling."[36]

Often the women told of visions in which God would offer physical evidence to them in order to convince them of their spiritual worth. Lutgard's vita included a description of a vision in which "she saw Jesus the Prince of our salvation with His wounds blood-red as if recently opened, standing before the face of the Father and supplicating the Father for sinners. Turning towards Lutgard, He said, 'Do you not see how I am offering myself up totally to the Father for My sinners? Therefore do I wish that you offer yourself up totally for my sinners.'" Lutgard obviously needed constant reinforcement, for "the Lord Jesus said this same thing to her almost everyday."[37]

Often reinforcement came from other women. Eve, the recluse of St. Martin-on-the-Mount, had "been touched by Christ's inspiration" to live in a hermitage since her childhood, but "nevertheless she was frightened by the loftiness of her purpose." Her friend, Juliana of Mont-Cornillon, "banished vain fear from her heart with powerful words, and by her exhortation succeeded in giving her courage to fulfill her purpose."[38] Catherine, the patron of Lutgard's monastery, told her to "have confidence, daughter, because the Almighty will always increase grace in you until, at the highest peak of life, you will acquire the most powerful merit among the virgins."[39] Clare of Assisi encouraged Agnes of Prague throughout her correspondence with her: "What you do, may you [always] do and never abandon . . . go forward securely, joyfully, and swiftly, on the path of prudent happiness, believing nothing, agreeing with nothing which would dissuade you from this resolution."[40]

In summation, we can state that the new spirituality of the High Middle Ages was quite compatible with the tradition of women's spiritual equality. Even more than men, women realized that the new spirituality was also compatible with mysticism, and thus it should come as no surprise to see women playing an influential role in the medieval mystical movement. Although much of the literature that emanated from the movement has been neglected over the centuries, the scholarly investigation of the medieval period during our own age and the birth of women's studies during the past few decades have been responsible for the rediscovery of these works and for a keener appreciation of their value. We now have a more accurate understanding of the medieval centuries and subsequently are more cognizant of the positions women held during the period and why. Christianity's tradition of women's spiritual equality played a major role in medieval women's influence on the cultural creations of their time.

Certainly the most stupendous of medieval creations was the cathedral, and here the presence of women was expressed in many ways. The vast majority of the sculpted figures were male, but female figures were well represented too, sometimes as women and sometimes as personifications. Eve and Mary were the most common figures and probably were found in every cathedral built during the period. Most of the portrayals of Eve are predictable, such as that at Fontevrault, where Adam and Eve walk together out of the Garden, with eyes cast downward. Some show Adam and Eve as equal partners in guilt, as at Reims. At Strasbourg we even see a reversal of the biblical account, with a confident, worldly Adam offering the apple to a gullible Eve.

The representations of Mary covered every phase of her biblical and legendary life. In the early cathedrals Mary was always accompanied by her son Jesus. Increasingly Mary-centered scenes were created, the Visitation and Annunciation being the most prevalent. By the end of the twelfth century Mary began to be portrayed as a queen; the earliest known sculpted representation of the Resurrection and Coronation of Mary is found on the lintel and tympanum of Senlis, begun ca. 1185. The Senlis doorway subsequently became a model for many cathedrals, notably those at Mantes and Chartres.[41] The right bay of the Royal Portal at Chartres is entirely dedicated to Mary. The lower lintel portrays the Annunciation, Visitation, Nativity, and the Annunciation to the shepherds. The second lintel contains the Presentation, while on the tympanum is the enthroned Mary with her son, modeled on Senlis; she is surrounded by the seven liberal arts and the scholars who excelled in each. On the north porch Mary was given the central bay, with her Death, Assumption, and Coronation represented. By the thirteenth century apocryphal episodes were gaining popularity, especially legends that revealed Mary as emotional and human, as in the trumeau figures of the north porch of Chartres where the apostles surround a reclining Mary. One apostle holds her heart, while Christ embraces her soul.

A similar scene is preserved on the Assumption window at Chartres. In short, the representation of Mary in sculpture echoed the sentiments found in the new spirituality.

The location of these sculptures is, of course, telling. In almost all of the major Gothic cathedrals sculpted images of Mary are centrally located. The Coronation of the Virgin is on the central portal of the north transept at Chartres, the queen of Gothic cathedrals. Reims' central portal holds the Annunciation, the Visitation with Elizabeth, and the Presentation at the Temple. The right-hand portal at Amiens portrays the Coronation and Mary's Death and Assumption, while the trumeau and jambs hold scenes from the Annunciation and Visitation; the Madonna on the trumeau of the north transept in Notre Dame is an exquisite example of the high Gothic form.

Biblical women were next in popularity after Mary, as, for example, Elizabeth and Veronica (at Worcester Cathedral), Anna and the Canaanite women (at Moissac), the Three Marys (at the abbey of Santa Domingo de Silos), Judith (at Vezelay), Esther (at Chartres), Martha and Mary (at St. Gilles), and the Queen of Sheba (at Amiens). Also popular were local saints (abbesses Etheldreda at Ely and Werburgh at Chester) and legendary saints (Mary the Egyptian at the Abbey of Alspach). The laity also were represented, particularly donors (Uta at Naumburg), but more often in sculptured scenes of everyday life. At Vezelay we see a shepherdess and a mother combing her child's hair, at Strasbourg a blacksmith's wife, and at Chartres a woman employed in the wool trade. At Notre Dame one unknown holy woman gazes in full rapture at the Lord at the Last Judgment as she affectionately holds her husband's hand and draws his attention to the Lord while he turns as if going in the opposite direction.

Depictions of women are even more plentiful on stained glass windows. Rose windows, often called the ultimate jewels of the cathedrals, appeared around 1200 in France and spread rapidly throughout the country during the next fifty years. Although found in a few other Western countries, they are essentially a French phenomenon. To psychologist Carl G. Jung, rose windows are mandalas or archetypes that present the viewer with "a pattern of order" in which "confusion is held together by the protective circle",[42] in the center of most north rose windows is Mary, representing "the sum of all the past, the culmination and quintessence of the Old Testament."[43] Probably the most admired rose window of all, the Rose of France, is the north window at Chartres, which is dedicated entirely to Mary. Immediately beneath it are the St. Anne lancet and the spandrels containing the double heraldry of Queen Blanche of Castile, probably the window's donor. Another donor, Eleanor of Aquitaine, is herself depicted on the great east window of the cathedral of Poitiers. Matilda, countess of Nevers, donated an upper window of the inner choir aisle in the Bourges Cathedral, and in the lower corner she kneels with window in hand, offering it to the archbishop of Bourges. Female personification, especially of Philosophy as queen of the liberal arts and of the remaining liberal arts (at Laon, north rose window) was not uncommon.

Women also were represented in the stained glass windows of the smaller churches. In England depictions of St. Catherine were common-place, as were those of Mary Magdalene. Portrayals of generic women also were frequently seen: Tewkesbury Abbey captures the piety of a kneeling woman on its east window, St. Mary the Virgin Church in Oxfordshire depicts a devote gentlewoman on its north window, and While-Notley Church in Essex has a learned woman holding a book.[44] Women, in short, were inescapable, visible, and sometimes even dominant in the great cathe-drals and parish churches of the Gothic period. In their sculpture, in their stained glass, and in the transcendent beauty of these female figures, the cathedrals and churches embraced the spiritual equality of women and made it aesthetically manifest for all to contemplate. If we agree with Otto von Simpson that medieval society perceived the church as "mystically and liturgically, an image of heaven,"[45] then we likewise may argue that medieval society believed a woman, Mary, reigned in heaven and was wholly accept-ing of a woman in that position.

It is with the dedication of the magnificent cathedrals, the embodi-ment of the era's highest ideals, that we come face to face with the centrality of Mary in the minds and hearts of all medieval people. It cut across all boundaries, class, gender, and geography. To the peasant, to the clergy, to the new merchant class, and to the ruling class who attended services in these sacred buildings, they were in Mary's house, or palace, as Henry Adams called them many years ago in his highly influential essay on Mary's importance in the medieval period, *Mont-Saint-Michel and Chartres*. "The palaces of earthly queens were hovels," wrote Adams, "compared with these palaces of the Queen of Heaven at Chartres, Paris, Laon, Noyon, Rheims, Amiens, Rouen, Bayeux, Coutances—a list that might be stretched into a volume."[46] Besides the cathedrals themselves being dedicated to Mary, many great churches contained separate chapels dedicated to her. In England these became known as Lady chapels and often were attached unto the cathedral after construction of the original building was complete; the Lady chapel at Ely is an extraordinary example of such.

Dedications to Mary were not reserved just to cathedrals; Mary was the most common patron of parish churches. In an age where every organization had a patron, few people were left untouched by her patronage. If they somehow managed to avoid Mary through patronage, it is doubtful that they could escape allotting her a good portion of their devotional activity, for Marian devotions multiplied rapidly during the High Middle Ages. The Little Office that we saw recommended for universal use by Peter Damian and mandated by Urban II for clerical recital on Saturdays contained the Hail Mary, thus inadvertently popularizing that prayer. Meanwhile, another devotion was developing, the recitation of psalms with 150 verse antiphons. Soon the Hail Mary from the Little Office was being substituted for psalms in this greeting Psalter and the antiphons omitted. Through a series of alterations the rosary eventually emerged. William of Malmesbury was the first to mention a woman, Lady Godiva of Coventry, using prayer beads.[47]

From the All Saints' Day litany grew a litany devoted solely to Mary, the content of which reveals just how many titles she had accumulated by the High Middle Ages. Many of them had their origin in the growing Western interest in the Passion, which in turn was encouraged by the increased traffic to the Holy Lands in the age of Crusades. The Mater Dolorosa cult arose in Italy in the eleventh century and benefited from contact with the Holy Land. Much of the new art created in Italy in the latter years of the Crusades reflected a dual preoccupation with the Passion and with Mary; the Pieta, the Crucifixion with the Three Marys, and the Deposition all became favorite subjects. The *Stabat Mater dolorosa*, one of the best-loved Latin hymns in Christianity, was written during this time. "The sorrowful Mother stood weeping by the Cross while on it hung her Son," the hymn laments. "Who is the person who would not weep if he saw the Mother of Christ in such distress?" The singer is united with Mary as the hymn implores, "I long to stand with you beside the cross and unite myself to you in grief."[48] Growing devotions to a very human Mary did not supplant the regal Mary but lived compatibly alongside her, as witnessed by another medieval masterpiece, the *Salve, Regina:* "Hail, holy Queen, Mother of mercy, our life, our sweetness, and our hope."[49] The revered *Angelus* had its beginning in the thirteenth century with the Franciscans. In 1269 their general chapter urged all Franciscans to promote the practice of reciting the Hail Mary when the churches bells were rung three times in the evening. With Pope John XXII's endorsement in 1327, the practice, by then more elaborate, spread throughout the West.[50] The spread of these Marian devotions was accomplished with the aid of the new mendicant orders and without any real dissent within the church. Only one feast was disputed, that of the Immaculate Conception. Bernard of Clairvaux, an unoriginal but enthusiastic advocate of Mary (his sermons are probably the most influential of all Marian homilies), complained about attempts to establish the feast, but it kept spreading. Peter Lombard and Thomas Aquinas both attempted to squelch the debate over the theological veracity of the Immaculate Conception before it caused further division but to no avail. In the Late Middle Ages the debate over the Immaculate Conception was sharply drawn, when the Dominicans and the Franciscans made it a major issue dividing their orders.

The art of the High Middle Ages was not, of course, restricted to architecture, sculpture, and stained glass. Painting, especially in Italy, was beginning its journey into the Renaissance, and even at this earliest stage we find women portrayed in all their spiritual dignity. One of the first subjects to inspire artists' imaginations was Clare of Assisi. Within two years of her death she was officially canonized, added to the church calendar and litany to the saints, and had a vita written by Thomas of Celano; within four years construction of a church in her honor, the Church of Santa Chiara in Assisi, was begun, and the paintings therein followed shortly.[51]

While Clare is forever linked with Francis in the modern mind, the art depicting her nevertheless is distinct from that depicting him and, in fact, distinct from previous images of holy women. Just as the new spirituality placed more emphasis on the affective and the human, so too did thirteenth-century Italian art. The famed monumental panel, the Santa Chiara dossal (ca. 1281-1285), presents not a virgin bride holding a traditional and symbolic lily but a determined, stern, and very real woman whose life triumphs are represented in the eight pictorial narratives surrounding her. The episodes chosen depict the many stages Clare had to pass through before she received both heavenly and earthly recognition of her spiritual perfection. The narrative pictorial, highly reflective of the literary narrative of Thomas of Celano's vita,[52] starts on Palm Sunday, the day when "Clare, radiant in festive splendor among the crowds of women," as Thomas wrote, "out of modesty" did not move forward to receive palms; the bishop, therefore, went down from the altar to her "and laid the palm in her hand." The second episode immortalizes that same night as Clare "abandoned home, city, and kinsfolk, and hastened to Saint Mary of the Porziuncola" where the friars "received the virgin Clare with lighted torches," while the third scene continues the ceremony as "her tresses were shorn at the hands of the Friars."[53] In the fourth representation we see how Clare's family "ran to the place" where she had made her commitment and "resorted to physical force, crafty counsels and flattering promises, in their attempt to dissuade

Clare from such a sorry choice."[54] This episode brings us to the top of the left side of the dossal; on the right side the familiar struggle of women for spiritual independence is continued in a scene depicting Agnes, Clare's "sister of tender age," trying to "give herself wholly to the service of the Lord." Her family was "infuriated with rage," and twelve men went to the convent to retrieve Agnes. When she refused "one of the knights in an outburst of anger rushed upon her and, sparing neither blows nor kicks, attempted to drag her away by her hair, while the others pressed forward and lifted her up in their arms." Thanks to Clare's prayful intercession, when "Sir Monaldus, Agnes' uncle, beside himself with rage, tried to deal her a fatal blow . . . a terrible pain suddenly seized" his arm as he raised it, and eventually the men surrendered Agnes to Clare's care.[55] An insert in the picture has Agnes receiving a tonsure from St. Francis.

In a study of the dossal, Jeryldene Wood argues that what is being represented here is Clare's renunciation of the noble class into which she was born. Francis renounced only his family's material assets; Clare's sacrifice included the renunciation of her social status. The portrayal of the family while they forcibly tried to interfere with Clare's spiritual decision, "so unworthy of her noble race," as her vita records, "and so contrary to all family tradition,"[56] is one of aristocrats whose lineage is being endangered and security threatened by the denial of their ability to make the marriage alliances they desired.[57] In her vita and in the art representing her vocational choice, then, Clare's ability to make her own spiritual decisions and the precedence of spiritual choices over all other choices—to control her own destiny—was acknowledged and admired by the larger society. "It was not long before the fame of the sanctity of the virgin Clare spread to nearby regions," Thomas tells us. All sorts of people "hastened after her example"; married women, virgins, "the noble and illustrious," mothers and daughters, husbands and wives, and even young men "spurred on by the heroic example of the weaker sex," all came to partake "of this angelic life which shone forth through Clare."[58]

That these aspects of Clare's life were emphasized in the art that adorned her church in Assisi is indeed significant. Assisi enjoyed a flourishing pilgrimage trade, and the spiritual dignity of a woman, so engagingly captured on the dossal, was widely viewed. Dossals had just made their appearance in the art world when Clare's was commissioned. The earliest extant dossal is from 1235, of Francis; the earliest extant women's dossal is probably one of Mary Magdalene completed a few years before Clare's, around 1280, by the Magdalen Master. Here Mary Magdalene is shown as a hermit holding an open scroll proclaiming, "You who have sinned do not despair, but return to God by following my example."[59] Mary, like Clare, is surrounded by eight narrative vignettes of her life; in one Mary is preaching. It is evident, therefore, that society included women from the beginning of this new form for religious art.

A few decades after the dossal made its appearance, frescoes were painted in the church of Santa Chiara on the main vaults above the high altar. These were filled with other illustrious spiritual women. The Madonna with Child and Clare have the place of honor directly above the roundel of the Pantocrator over the main altar, Agnes of Assisi and Agnes of Rome are on another, Lucy and Cecilis on a third, and Margaret (or Mary Magdalene) and Catherine of Alexandria are featured on the fourth fresco. All of the women are presented in spiritual and human perfection, enclosed on thrones and in tabernacles, enjoying their celestial rewards in heaven. Angels pay court to them and their accomplishments, some kneeling before and above them in respectful awe. Elsewhere in the church women are seen fulfilling various roles. One fresco in the right transept contains two narrative scenes, the funeral of St. Clare and her transport. Agnes of Assisi and Abbess Benedetta, Clare's successor, are probably two of the Poor Clares seen grieving at the funeral, while unidentified towns-women also grieve. Two other frescoes, now lost, represented the miracles of Clare and the birth of Mary. One fresco depicts the creation of Eve. Above the high altar is the Santa Chiara crucifix, a painting probably commissioned by the Poor Clares soon after Clare's death; at the feet of Jesus is Abbess Benedetta, with these words inscribed in the left corner: "Lady Benedette, abbess after Clare, had me made." Mary is seen with John the Apostle on the left arm of the crucifix and in the center. An earlier crucifix, the Talking Crucifix (late twelfth century), probably placed in the women's choir after 1263, displays the role of the Three Marys in Jesus's passion. A painted panel has Agnes of Rome, Clare, and Agnes of Assisi at the crucifixion. On the entrance wall of the Chapel of the Sacrament is the Annunciation and the Nativity. The left wall pictures Madonna with child enthroned with Clare, John the Baptist, Michael, Francis, and an unknown nun. The altar wall has depictions of Catherine of Alexandria, Mary Magdalene, Clare, Francis, and Agnes of Assisi, while the right wall (now lost) pictured Lucy. The entrance wall of the Chapel of the Crucifix includes portrayals of Clare and Anne, among others. There is no mistaking the fact that the Church of Santa Chiara in Assisi is dedicated to the spiritual perfection of women.[60]

Women in all their spiritual dignity are also quite visible in another medium favored by medieval society, the illuminated manuscript. During the High Middle Ages numerous manuscripts were produced that are pertinent to our topic. Besides images of women created by male artists for male audiences, we also have manuscripts with female figures painted by women, and some commissioned by and for women, which allow us to see women's perception of women. Manuscripts illuminated by women are not that numerous,[61] but there are enough for us to be able to draw some conclusions. The first generalization about all representations of women in illuminated manuscripts is obvious to the eye yet rarely observed. Women are not portrayed as devils; men are. Starting in the sixth century the devil began to appear in manuscript as a human or humanoid. He was an old man; a dark, muscular, young man; a male imp; part man, part beast; a naked, misshapen man. Just as the devil rarely took on the feminine form in literature, was given a female gender, or was discussed as a woman, so too the devil was rarely envisioned as a woman in pictorial art.[62] Second, the overwhelming majority of women who are identifiable as individuals are those who played major salvific roles in the Old and New Testaments. Third, the nonidentifiable generic woman who is frequently portrayed fulfilling everyday tasks is presented with her spiritual dignity intact.

When we examine the few manuscripts associated with women we learn even more. The St. Albans Psalter[63] probably was commissioned by Christina of Markyate; apparently she was its first owner, and the illuminations picture the main events and people in her life.[64] The bulk of the paintings concern themselves with the life of Christ (thirty-nine full-page drawings tell the story), but some of the historiated initials are of interest. One has Christina approaching Christ, with a group of monks following closely behind. As Madeline Caviness points out, this presents Christina as an imitator and follower of Mary Magdalene, who elsewhere in the Psalter is seen telling the eleven apostles that Christ has risen.[65]

Recently the manuscript of Hildegard of Bingen's *Scivias* has received much attention despite the disappearance of the original during World War II.[66] Its thirty-five illuminations are unsophisticatedly unique, even in the golden age of illumination. The identity of the artist is unknown, although some posit Hildegard herself. At the bottom of the illumination relating Hildegard's vision of Caritas an insert shows Hildegard receiving the fire of love emanating from Caritas and simultaneously transcribing this vision onto wax tablets,[67] while her amanuensis Volmar writes the text into a book. Female illuminators and scribes, while not the norm, were not unheard of. We know of at least one contemporary of Hildegard, a woman named Guta, who collaborated with a canon to produce an illuminated manuscript in 1154; another contemporary from the Rhine area also named Guta painted a self-portrait in her manuscript.[68] Regardless of the gender of Hildegard's illuminator, whoever did it kept meticulously close to the texts and made Hildegard's revelations visible to the reader. Hildegard's theology of the feminine is clearly reflected in the personification of the church, wisdom, the soul, virginity, the synagogue, and the Mystical Body as women and the devil and tempter as abstract objects with men closest to them and women farthest. The first of the Five Virtues is personified as a woman with a bishop's miter on her head. All the representations of women in the illuminations are positive and have the women as their central focus, except for Hildegard's vision of the Last Days. While her theology is certainly not a precursor of feminist theology, the illuminations that accompany her most famous work certainly communicate the full spiritual parity of women in the eyes of God.[69]

Probably more significant, because they are missing the idiomatic marks of Hildegard's singular genius, are the more mainstream illuminations of the *Hortus deliciarum*, also surviving only in facsimile. Abbess Herrad of Landsberg commissioned this illustrated instructional handbook, containing 636 illuminations, for the women in her monastery of Hohenburg. Here we see nuns placed above the prophets, the patriarchs, the martyrs, and even the apostles in heaven; women coming to confer with Mary and John the Evangelist; women busy founding their monastery of Hohenburg; and a female Philosophia proclaiming the origin of Wisdom; and the Old Testament issuing forth the seven liberal arts and four cardinal virtues while Plato and Socrates sit at her feet. The final page presents Herrad in all her spiritual equanimity, accompanied by sixty women from the monastery, each identified by name. One of the more interesting illuminations shows women progressing up the ladder of virtues toward heaven as male devils try to injure them and male clergy falter in their journey to salvation. One cleric already fallen from the ladder is seen offering a woman money to abandon her spiritual quest. The women all persevere.[70] The *Horus deliciarum* is one of the most explicit reminders we have of medieval women's strong self-image and perception of their spiritual worth.

Women were present in yet another area of the arts that underwent an extraordinary rebirth during the period, the drama. Medieval drama and the music that accompanied it had its origin in the liturgy, and its earliest expressions are in liturgical drama. The trope, the elaboration of the words of the liturgy, was probably the first step taken toward liturgical drama. The oldest known trope is the famed *Quem quaeritis* (*Whom do you seek*), in a question-and-answer format originally sung before the Easter Introit. By the late tenth century this trope was transformed into a musical liturgical drama. The change entailed little more than the singers consciously impersonating the historical characters asking and answering questions. The earliest known reference to the *Quem queritis* is found in an English document, *Regularis Concordia* (ca. 965-975), written for monks. In the directions given for the liturgical drama, the monks were to play all the roles, even the Marys who came to the tomb to anoint Jesus's body. By the eleventh century the play was being performed in Germany, England, and France, and was much longer.[71] The *Visitatio sepulchre* (*The Visit to the Sepulchre*), as the *Quem queritis* came to be known, was vastly popular, if extant manuscripts are an accurate indication. Its manuscripts outnumber others ten to one.[72]

This first liturgical drama had as its leading character a woman, Mary Magdalene. She was designated as "the first of them" in stage directions and had solo scenes at the sepulcher, one with Jesus as the gardener, and a soliloquy. She sang fifteen of the nineteen solos in the play, and more than half of the substance of the drama revolved around her.[73] Manuscripts from St. Quentin, Barking, Troyes, Essen, and Bresci show that by the end of the thirteenth century, women were playing the female roles.[74]

Another popular liturgical drama was *The Lament of Mary*, and it was also predominantly a women's play. The three Marys and John were the only actors, and John was not given a major role. Mary Magdalene was again a major character in *The Raising of Lazarus*, with Martha having an equally important role. Out of the fourteen singing roles in *The Wise and Foolish Maidens*, ten were women. *The Three Daughters*, *The Annunciation*, and *The Purification* all had women in the leading roles. Significant female roles also existed in dramas whose themes would not automatically demand them. In *The Slaughter of the Innocents*, for example, the laments of Rachael, accompanied by female consolers, formed the greater part of the climax, as did the laments of Euphrosina for her captive son in *The Son of Getron*.[75] The more religious and liturgical the theme, the more the women within were portrayed as admirable.

Women were not completely absent from the production of these dramas either. Hrotsvitha, from the noted monastery of Gandersheim, was a prolific and creative writer and is credited with being the first Western dramatist since antiquity and the first German poet. Hrotsvitha wrote in an age prior to the development of the liturgical drama; instead she wrote didactic dramas, six in all. While their theatrical appeal may rightly be questioned,[76] their theological content was rich and sophisticated. No matter how great the sin of humans, God's grace is greater and can redeem all. This theology was embodied in the play *Abraham*, a dramatization of the early monastic desert legend of the ascetic Abraham and his niece Mary. Brought up to follow in her uncle's footsteps, Mary was seduced by a man and eventually went to live in a brothel. Years later Abraham found her, and while she wanted to repent she feared rejection by God, until Abraham

reminded her that "the mercy of Heaven is greater than all living creatures."[77] Not only did such mercy apply equally to women, but in Hrotsvitha's eyes women's triumphs over sin were actually more meritorious. In
her preface she confessed that her goal in writing these dramas was "to
celebrate according to my ability the praiseworthy chasteness of godlike
maidens" whose triumph over evil is "so much more glorious," in particular
when men attempt to seduce women into illicit love. "So much greater is the
glory" of God when "woman's weakness triumphs and man's shameless
strength is made to succumb." Hrotsvitha was also aware that her creative
powers may not have been as great as those of Terence, her model from
classical Rome, but her sense of spiritual equality allowed her to continue.
"All I am bent on is, however insufficiently, to turn the power of the mind
given to me to the use of Him who gave it. I am not so enamored of myself,"
Hrotsvitha explains, "that I should cease from fear of criticism to proclaim
the power of Christ which works in the saints in whatever way it grants it."[78]

Hildegard of Bingen was born after liturgical dramas became popular,
and one of her writings, *Play of Virtues*, was a variation of that form. It is
different enough, though, for some critics to claim that this musical drama
has no medieval parallel.[79] As interesting as the play is, it is Hildegard's
reflection on music and women's participation in singing that is more
relevant to us, for here we meet her underlying presupposition again, the
spiritual equality of women and their equal participation in salvific history—
regardless of whether every man can see it. When the hierarchy forbade
Hildegard's monastery to sing or hear mass as a punishment for a perceived
wrong, Hildegard argued that "my sisters and I have been greatly distressed"
by the prohibition, because only the devil could be the "inspiration of such
a command." The women sang "through God's inspiration," and those who
tried to "prohibit the singing of God's praises . . . will lose their place among
the choir of angels."[80]

While Hildegard was expounding her theology of sacred song and
attacking hierarchical interference with any man or woman's right to engage
in such song, other devotions were gaining popularity with the hierarchy's
support. One of the most dominant devotions of the Late Middle Ages was
directed toward the Eucharist; the roots of this devotion are in the High
Middle Ages and in the spirituality of northern European women. The
groundbreaking work of Herbert Grundmann first brought attention to the
fact that in the thirteenth-century "religious movement in the North, it is
always the female element which is central."[81] Except for the work of Ernest
McDonnell on the beguines[82] (whom Robert Grosseteste said were "the
most perfect and the holiest in religion"),[83] little had been done to follow

through with Grundmann's observation until recently. Thanks chiefly to Bynum, we now have a more thorough understanding of how and why Grundmann's thesis is valid. Moreover, the factors revealed in Bynum's analysis of thirteenth-century northern European women and their spirituality have vast implications for how we look at all other women in the Christian tradition.

Bynum points out numerous indicators of women's devotion to the Eucharist: Women were instrumental in the institutionalization of the eucharistic feast of Corpus Christi; they often changed their affiliation with religious orders to satisfy their desire for frequent reception of the Eucharist; eucharistic vision and miracles were largely a female phenomenon; texts recommending frequent reception of the Eucharist often were directed explicitly to women; sermons and treatises on the Eucharist or the related theme of the humanity of Christ were disproportionately addressed to women; and even in narratives written by males for males, the Eucharist and the humanity of Christ were associated with women. When women themselves wrote, the Eucharist was a major theme incorporated into their spirituality.[84] For some women reception of the Eucharist was itself the ultimate union with Christ, as we see in Mechtild of Magdeburg's words: "Yet I, least of all souls, take Him in my hand, eat Him and drink Him, and do with Him what I will! Why then should I trouble myself as to what the angels experience?"[85]

Eucharistic devotion is probably most associated with the diocese of Liege, for it is there that it culminated in the feast of Corpus Christi. Juliana of Mont-Cornillon is credited with being the impetus behind the foundation of the feast. "From her youth whenever Christ's virgin gave herself to prayer," Juliana received a vision, a "full moon in its splendor, yet with a little breach in its spherical body," we are told in her vita. Her first reaction was to ignore it, and thus she "tried with all her might to make it go away," to no avail. After her efforts to banish it from her thoughts failed, "she finally began to wonder if perhaps, instead of trying so hard to drive it away, she should seek to discover some mystery in it." Once she directed her attention thus, "Christ revealed to her that the moon was the present Church, while the breach in the moon symbolized the absence of a feast which he still desired." What Christ wanted was simple: "That once every year, the institution of the sacrament of his Body and Blood should be recollected more solemnly and specifically than it was at the Lord's Supper." Christ also had a more difficult command, "that she herself should inaugurate this feast and be the first to tell the world it should be instituted." In confusion and humility Juliana "replied that she could not do what she had been commanded." Her visions persisted, and every time she prayed for Christ to "release me" and give the task to scholars "who would know how to promote such a great affair," Christ refused. Instead, "He responded that by all means, she should be the one to initiate this feast, and from then on it should be promoted by humble people."[86]

For twenty years this internal struggle raged, Juliana maintaining herself all the while unworthy "to proclaim so great a feast to the world" because of her "lack of experience and power," and Christ maintaining that she, above everyone else "who loves and teaches humility," was in fact most worthy. Finally Juliana told John of Lausanne, a canon of St. Martin's, because "he knew many great scholars and religious" and thus would be in a position "to find out what great theologians might think of such a feast." This tactic of Juliana's impressed her hagiographer, who holds it up as "a lesson for men and women" to imitate: "She does nothing rashly, approaches nothing without counsel but does everything in due time and with the utmost deliberation." In due course the appropriate people "pronounced with one mind that they could find no valid reason in divine law to preclude a special feast of the venerable Sacrament."[87]

Members of the hierarchy were not the only ones Juliana told. She confided in Isabella of Huy, after "often test[ing] her in conversation . . . to find out whether God had shown Isabella any of the celestrial mystery concerning the institution of a new feast of the Sacrament." But Isabella had not yet "received the comfort of a similar revelation," so she prayed for understanding, which finally came to her in ecstasy. After the revelation she decided "she alone would work to establish this feast in the Church even if the whole world would oppose it." After Isabella told Juliana that she too now shared in Juliana's vision, the two "talked frequently and intimately, in honeyed speech, about the institution and promotion of this holy festival."[88]

Next, the hagiographer wrote that Juliana set about arranging for the composition of an office for the feast. She turned to her confessor John Lausanne, who, unfortunately, "lacked literary knowledge." Because of this "at first he was diffident and began to excuse himself on the ground of his ignorance," but Juliana confidently bolstered her confessor's faith by promising divine assistance for completion of the task. In the face of such assurances John "was overcome by the prayers and authority of the virgin, whose sanctity he well knew," and so he agreed, but only after Juliana likewise "agreed that when he began to write, she would begin to pray." After he composed each section he submitted it to her to inspect for errors; "after her examination and correction, even the greatest master did not need to polish it any further."[89]

In 1246 the bishop of Liege established Corpus Christi as a feast within his diocese, and in 1251 the cardinal-legate to Germany began promoting the feast after being exposed to its devotion while passing through Liege on his legatine procession. With the election of Jacques of Troyes, one of the first persons Juliana and John of Lausanne consulted about the feast, as Pope Urban IV in 1261, it became a feast in the Roman church with the issuance of the bull *Transiturus*. The spread of the feast experienced a temporary setback with Urban IV's death in 1264, but when the bull *Transiturus* was included in the canon law collection, the Clementines, in 1317, its future was sealed. Not only was it the first universally observed feast in the Roman church, but it was the first to originate from the devotion of a woman.

In the years to come the feast of Corpus Christi was to dominate the culture of religious communities throughout Europe. Probably the best-known aspect of its celebration was the Corpus Christi processions and the dramatic performances created for the celebration. Within decades of the first performance of a Corpus Christi play (ca. 1335), cycles of these plays were being produced by a variety of organizations and peoples.[90] Town councils, craft guilds, church wardens, fraternities, parishes, clergy, and even professional actors participated in the production of these public dramas from the Iberian peninsula, to England, to Germany. As celebration of the eucharistic feast spread, the subject of the plays broadened to include a number of biblical and apocryphal themes, but the overall focus of the preaching, the teaching, the processions, and the liturgy remained focused on the Eucharist. Indeed, the cult of the Eucharist became, in Miri Rubin's words, "the central symbol of a culture,"[91] and in the establishment of the dominance of the Eucharist women contributed more than simply their visions; women created a spiritual environment that nourished eucharistic devotions to their maturity.

While the feast of Corpus Christi and the accompanying eucharistic devotions were probably the most popular and best-known of the devotions born in the High Middle Ages, women promoted others as well. They also played a major role in popularizing other specific forms of piety that sprang from the new spirituality. They were particularly important in the spread of devotions to the Passion and to the Sacred Heart. Angela of Foligno's *Book* had as its central theme her love for Christ crucified, who often appeared in vivid images, such as "looking as if he had just then been taken down from the cross. His blood flowed fresh and crimson as if the wounds had just recently been opened." During one vision "her whole body and soul felt pierced anew from the painful impact of this divine vision."[92] While still enraptured, "suddenly a multitude of the sons of this holy mother appeared" around the crucified Jesus who then "embraced them and pressed them to his sacred wound."[93] The author (who confessed that it was only after badgering Angela "that I, the writer, could get her to tell me about them. For she maintained the most astonishing and absolute reserve about the divine gifts she had received")[94] shared his reflections on Angela's devotion to the Passion and the role she played in promoting this devotion among others. It is clear the author considered her "an expert and a teacher of these things," worthy of imitation: "I believe that the friars whom the Most High gave her as sons of her heart should pay close attention to what this holy mother told me. Generally speaking, the gifts she received—that is, the kind just mentioned—begin in her own elevations and her being set afire, and find their fulfillment in our reproduction of them. By such means, the blessed God clearly shows us that in her is the root from which comes everything we receive, and we are her crown and joy in the Lord."[95]

Clare of Assisi hinted at a nascent devotion to the Sacred Heart when she advised Agnes of Prague to "place your heart in the figure of the divine substance and transform your whole being into the image of the Godhead Itself."[96] Hildegard of Bingen strongly believed in the centrality of the Passion in salvific history: "When Jesus Christ, the true Son of God, hung on the tree of His Passion, the Church, joined to Him in the secret mysteries of Heaven, was dowered with His crimson blood. . . . What does this mean? That when blood flowed from the wounded side of [Jesus], at once salvation of souls came into being."[97] Hadewijch reminded one of her correspondents that "you should bear God in your heart with constant remembrance, and embrace him lovingly with an open and expectant heart; and always long for the sweetness coming from his Heart."[98] Mechtild of Hackenborn rose each morning to recite the prayer, "Praise, benediction, glory, and salvation to the most gentle and benevolent heart of Jesus, my true lover." Her short salutation ended with the declaration "And now I offer you my heart like a fresh rose that its fragrance may delight your divine heart."[99]

It was Gertrude the Great, however, who articulated some of the most ardent extant expressions of this devotion. When discussing the source of her devotion (which she did willingly, for she believed "that the fervour of my devotion is increased by this kind of communication"), she repeated a prayer she found in a prayer book: "O Lord Jesus Christ, Son of the living God, grant that I may aspire towards Thee with my whole heart . . . engrave Thy wounds upon my heart with Thy most precious Blood, that I may read in them both Thy grief and Thy love; and that the memory of Thy wounds may ever remain in my inmost heart, to excite my compassion for Thy sufferings and to increase in me Thy love." Frequent repetition of the prayer increased her devotion and soon led to her prayer being answered. Gertrude was in the refectory "when I perceived that the grace which I had so long asked by the aforesaid prayer was granted to me, unworthy though I am; for I perceived in spirit that Thou hast imprinted in the depth of my heart the adorable marks of Thy sacred Wounds, even as they are on Thy Body."[100] Her devotion to the wounded heart grew unabated during the ensuing years, and seven years after she received the spiritual stigmata she asked a friend to "say this prayer every day for me before a crucifix, 'O, most loving Lord, by Thy pierced Heart, pierce her heart with the arrow of Thy love, so that nothing earthly may remain therein, and that it may be entirely filled with the strength of Thy Divinity.'" Once again Gertrude "soon perceived that my words had reached Thy Divine Heart," which answered her plea. To Gertrude, this devotion was not something to be kept secret. Again she repeated her belief that it was her duty and role in salvific history to spread this devotion. "The reason why I have written these things," Gertrude insisted, "is that I have profited so little by Thy liberality, that I cannot believe they were made known to me for myself alone." She implored God, therefore, to grant "that whoever reads these things may be touched with tenderness and compassion for Thee," as she had been through her devotion to Jesus's pierced heart.[101] Popular modern devotions to the Sacred Heart and the Passion grew slowly from all these small stirrings of pietistic attention by medieval women.

As we can readily see, the tradition of women's spiritual equality fared well in the High Middle Ages. Many aspects of medieval culture not only reflected this tradition but served as a vehicle for its communication. With the enduring presence of medieval culture—Marian Gothic cathedrals are still the center of many major European cities—the tradition entered the public discourse in a new and undeniable way.

10

Late Medieval Mysticism and the Devotio moderna

OF THE THREE TRADITIONAL WAYS OF KNOWING GOD—natural theology, dogmatic theology, and mystical theology[1]—by the late medieval period mystical theology was already the most popular and pervasive. The mystical movement continued to grow throughout the Late Middle Ages and involved all sorts of people and places. While remembering (as many generations did not) the crucial role women played in the movement, we must not neglect the presence of men, for through their preaching mysticism received a great deal of exposure. We shall take a deeper look into the mysticism of both men and women in the hope that it will deepen our knowledge of the tradition of women's spiritual parity.

All definitions of mysticism share some fundamental premises. First, there is the belief that, in the words of the author of *The Cloud of the Unknowing*, humans possess "one principal working power, the which is called a knowing power, and another principal working power, the which is called a loving power." With the first God remains "evermore incomprehensible," but with the second He is "all comprehensible to the full."[2] Meister Eckhart states it thus: "I accept God into me in knowing; I go into God in loving."[3] Mystics believe, in other words, that their experience of God is complete, that they attain the unattainable. All other ways of approaching God are sorely inadequate. "A staggering amount of things could be said" about the Trinity to help us understand "how the supreme superabundant Unity unfolds into Trinity," John Tauler offers as an illustration, but "to experience the working of the Trinity is better than to talk about it."[4]

Second, when mystics experience God in this complete manner, they experience a state "so simple and so modeless that in it every essential act of gazing, every inclination, and every distinction of creatures pass away," according to John Ruusbroec.[5] The distinctions that loom so large in the eyes of the world are obliviated in the mystical union. "I am so changed into him," wrote Eckhart, "that he produces his being in me as one, not just similar"; there is simply "no distinction."[6] According to the author of *The Epistle of Privy Counsel*, it was the obligation of the mystic to prepare for union with God by consciously striving to abandon all unique characteristics. One must "strip, spoil, and utterly unclothe thyself of all manner of feeling of thyself" in order to prepare for the mystical experience.[7]

Being stripped includes separation from the physical distinctions of sex. "When God made man, he made woman from man's side, so that she might be equal to him," Eckhart preached, repeating the now-familiar interpretation of the Genesis story. "He did not make her out of man's head or his feet, so that she would be neither woman nor man for him, but so that she might be equal." Eckhart applied this revelation to the mystical union. "So should the just soul be equal with God and close beside God, equal beside him, not beneath or above. Who are they who are thus equal? Those who are equal to nothing, they alone are equal to God. The divine being is equal to nothing, and in it there is neither image nor form. To the souls who are equal, the Father gives equally, and he withholds nothing at all from them."[8] Here we come face to face with Christianity's core belief in the spiritual equality of all persons. Before God all souls are indisputably equal. A person's class or gender or age is in no way responsible for, nor does it contribute to, the mystical union. It is wholly a God-given, God-initiated gift. "What art thou, and what hast thou deserved, thus to be called by our Lord?" the author of *The Cloud* asks. "He asketh no help but only thyself. He wills thou do but look upon him and let him alone."[9]

The impact a movement with these characteristics could have on women is not merely a matter of speculation; it is documented. Women such as Hildegard of Bingen, the women of Helfta, Clare and Agnes of Assisi, and the women religious of the Low Countries were among the early proponents of mysticism, and they all left sources. Indeed, some of the most profound mystical literature in Christianity is written by the women mystics of this period. Given the Christian belief that the soul's mystical union with God was complete and perfect, given the deep-seated deference and esteem in which the mystic was held by society because of this belief, and given the explicit inclusion of women on an equal basis with men, the female mystic was in a position of power indeed.

Even when male mystics were not referring to the naked, ungendered soul, they still did not talk disparagingly about women. Twice the author of

The Cloud wrote that we "wert lost in Adam," which the author of the *Privy Counsel* also believed.[10] Tauler wrote that "for all that is in man has gone estray through Adam's fall," that the internal powers of the soul are all in "disorder following the fall of Adam," and that "in Adam all die."[11] Eve was not mentioned in these texts, nor was she given primary blame.[12] Henry Suso offered us Mary Magdalene as the model repentant sinner to be imitated in *The Life of the Servant* and in *Wisdom's Watch upon the Hours.*[13] In *The Cloud* Mary Magdalene was one of the chief examples illuminating the ways of contemplation. She was the dominant subject of chapters 17 through 23, discussed so the "many wonderful points of perfect love written of her for our example" could be known. "And if a man will but see written in the Gospel the wonderful and special love that Our Lord had for her . . . he shall find that Our Lord might not suffer any man or woman—yea, not her own sister—to speak a word against her, but that he answered for her himself."[14]

Of greater import than the occasional presence of positive female models is the fact that much of the great male mystical literature was written expressly for women or was written by men working with female mystics. In Germany, in particular, the influence of the women over the men was so ubiquitous that one is left doubting the centrality traditionally given men within the mystical movement. True, many of their writings contain more of a speculative, theological analysis of mysticism than do the women's experiential writings, but their inspiration and comprehension of mysticism owes too much to the women to be viewed independently. At the very least, the motivation for the writings stems from women's demand for them, for as Evelyn Underwood long ago pointed out, "mysticism only thus becomes articulate when there is a public which craves for the mystic's message."[15]

In this case the public was overwhelmingly female. Two of the pioneers in the historical study of German mysticism, Heinrich Denifle and Herbert Grundmann, agree that these male writings owe their existence first and foremost to "the mission imposed on them by their [Dominican] order to care for a large number of women as pastors and preachers." Furthermore, only when this pastoral care was joined with vernacular preaching and female piety were conditions set "for the rise of a 'German Mysticism.'"[16] In other words, not only did the mysticism of the Late Middle Ages explicitly endorse the spiritual parity of women, but it also accepted direction and input from women and, when appropriate, acknowledged their spiritual authority and leadership.

The three greatest fourteenth-century German mystics—Eckhart, Tauler, and Suso—were Domincan friars whose pastoral duties included the spiritual direction of nuns, and they all wrote with women in mind. Suso wrote his autobiography[17] because Elsbeth Stagel "asked of him that he tell her from his own experience something about his sufferings so that her own stricken heart might take strength from it." When they met she "would draw him out with personal questions" and then secretly write "it all down as a help for herself and for others." When he found out he "burned everything he got hold of," but much of it escaped his destruction and became the core of his vita. Suso tells us "what follows [in the vita] remained unburned, as she wrote most of it with her own hand."[18] While scholars debate precisely how much and what part of the vita was written by whom, for our purposes the answer changes little. Regardless of authorship, it is indisputable that Suso and Elsbeth were of one mind, that they influenced each other, and that the beliefs were so similar that scholars have difficulty telling them apart. When their spiritual friendship first began Elsbeth asked that Suso grant her one request, that he share all his "good teaching."[19] The sharing became mutual, though, for when Elsbeth was struck down with her last illness, the spiritual equality upon which their friendship rested was evident. "Dear daughter," Suso wrote, "God has struck not only you with this. By striking you he has struck me as well. I have no one else who has been as helpful with such industry and devotion to God, as you were while still in good health, in bringing my books to completion."[20]

Suso's perception of the spiritual equality of women was not limited to specific women but is generalized in his writings and applied to all things spiritual. Wisdom was personified as the "greatest mistress of the heavenly disciples," a "most loving mother," a "gentle lady," and the like, not as a mere literary device but as the basis of his spirituality.[21] In his vita he confirmed that after his first mystical experience, his life "in its interior activity was a constant effort to achieve intense awareness of loving union with eternal Wisdom." He also wrote about the origin of his devotion to this female Wisdom. "One morning when he was sitting as usual at table," he heard Wisdom call him and tell him that "if you wish to devote yourself to sublime love, you should take gentle Wisdom as your dearly beloved." When he finally decided to do so, "he was able to imagine her through the explanatory examples of scripture with his inner eyes."[22]

As much as he wrote about Wisdom as a woman, his vision of Wisdom betrayed that articulation: "The minute he thought her to be a beautiful young lady, he immediately found a proud young man before him."[23] He knew that the spiritual realm is not gendered. Thus his spirituality was based on the belief in the equality of men and women in the spiritual realm. His remarks about the elect being "found in great number, men and women of every class and religious order and age"[24] and about the witness of "'young men and virgins' (Ps 148:12) and married women too and most devout widows through all the wide regions where the faith is kept [who] suffer for the love of God"[25] are but logical extensions of his understanding of things spiritual. That Suso's *Wisdom's Watch* was one of the most popular devotional treatises in the late medieval West and that only one other book from the period, *The Imitation of Christ,* is found in more extant manuscripts makes these beliefs just that much more significant.[26]

John Ruusbroec, the greatest Flemish male mystic, used a different female personification as his focus and theme, humanity as bride. In the opening passage of *The Spiritual Espousals,* his masterpiece, Ruusbroec writes, "'See, the bridegroom is coming. Go out to meet him' (Mt 25:6). These words, written for us by St. Matthew the Evangelist, were spoken by Christ to his disciples and to all persons in the parable of the virgins. The Bridegroom is Christ and human nature is the bride, whom God created according to his own image and likeness." The treatise is an analysis of the verse and its application in people's active, interior, and contemplative lives. The identification of humanity as Christ's bride is constant throughout. The Incarnation is when "the Son wedded this bride, our nature, and united her with his own person through the purest blood of the noble Virgin."[27]

Ruusbroec was, of course, only one of many medieval writers who discussed bridal mysticism. Women as well as men employed the imagery frequently,[28] and contemporary historians offer various explanations for its usage. Popularized by Bernard of Clairvaux's commentary on the Song of Songs and found more in male than female writings in the early days, some scholars posit that the imagery was basically a straitjacket men used to bind women to domestic, inferior roles. Other scholars argue that when men applied it to themselves it was an image of reversal, signifying renunciation rather than elevation.[29]

Both interpretations have weaknesses. First, it is hard to accept that medieval people understood any intimate relationship with Christ to be inferior. Second, the fact that men eagerly aspired after union with the Bridegroom as the bride makes it hard to argue that women's union with the Bridegroom is anything less than every Christian's goal; few cultures, if any, possess the ability to allow one symbol to communicate two different meanings in the same instance without confusion. Third, analysis of the passages in which men personify themselves, humanity, or all souls as brides in their full and proper context does not reveal motives of renunciation. Nowhere, for example, in the work of Ruusbroec does one get a sense of his adoption of the female persona of bride as being an exercise in humility, a ritual of renunciation, or a demeaning role reversal. Rather, the wedding of the bride and Bridegroom is the means by which Ruusbroec believes that "Christ, our faithful Bridegroom, [did] unite our nature with himself."[30] Constantly throughout his work he argued that "the wise virgin, that is, the pure soul" must listen to his spiritual advice and prescriptions, because it was "the end and purpose of all this work, namely, a meeting with Christ our Bridegroom in the blessed Unity of the Godhead."[31]

Perhaps instead of understanding bridal imagery as a stereotype communicated to all women to further anchor them to an inferior position, we should contemplate with Barbara Newman the possibility that "rather than stepping neatly into the role designed for them, some women forged a more complicated, less stereotypical way that allowed them a wider emotional range."[32] At a minimum, it should be noted that the bridal imagery and the feminization of humanity and souls by mystics is consistent with the main tenets of mysticism: the spiritual equality of all persons and God's freedom to offer the mystical experience to both women and men.

Certainly, in the lives and works of the great female mystics of the Late Middle Ages we find no evidence that they limited themselves to so-called female roles. Catherine of Bologna addressed this issue in her treatise on the spiritual formation of women, *The Seven Weapons of the Spirit*, by intertwining two major spiritual metaphors, the soldier and the bride, one masculine and the other feminine, and by advising women to embrace and imitate both. Even though sometimes "the bride of Christ, by God's permission, may find herself in such dreadful and fierce storms," she must never lay down her "weapons, because our enemies never sleep."[33] "The dowry that Christ Jesus wants from you is that you be stalwart in battle, strong and constant combatants," and thus "keep with you your nuptial regalia" as the women "await the grand and glorious embassy that your spouse will send to you."[34]

Indeed, this was a unique age in which roles often overlapped. For example, mystics, including female mystics, frequently intruded into the political world and were accepted there. The names of Catherine of Siena and Birgitta of Sweden need only be mentioned to prove that point. Both exercised an authoritative voice in the politics of their native countries and of the church because of society's recognition of their mystical status.[35] Both believed that they were acting under the direct instructions of God and showed no hesitancy in assuming a variety of roles. After "Jesus Christ appeared to me and began to speak," Birgitta reported, she composed a rule for a religious order for women.[36] To get the rule approved she had to inject herself into the political world of the papacy, again by following the instructions of Christ. "'Go and tell [Pope Urban V] on My behalf,' Christ told her that 'I want you not only to confirm it through a mandate, but also to strengthen it through your blessing.'" If that message was not persuasive or if Birgitta could not get a letter from the pope, she was not to worry: "My blessing is more than enough for you. For I will approve and confirm My word, and all the saints will be My witnesses."[37]

Birgitta's spiritual authority was clearly superior to any earthly author-ity, including papal. It is this belief that allowed her to confront two popes when she thought them to be in error. She did not hesitate to write Urban V the harsh message she received from Mary. "I am the Mother of God," Mary told Birgitta, whose prayers led Urban back to Rome from Avignon. "But what does he do now? Now he turns his back to me" and makes plans to return to Avignon, because it "wearies him to do his duty, and he is longing for ease and comfort" and "for his own country." Birgitta does not shrink from adding her own dire warning: "If he should succeed in getting back to his own country he will be struck such a blow that his teeth will shake in his mouth." When Gregory XI, the next pope, refused to leave Avignon, Birgitta again says boldly in Mary's voice: "This is God's will, that the Pope shall without delay come to Rome, or at least to Italy, and that he shall come now . . . if he desires at all to have me for his mother in heaven. But if he proves himself disobedient I will not later do anything for him and after death he must answer for not having willed to obey the commandment of God."[38]

This is not a case of one woman having inflated ideas of her power. Society as a whole recognized the superiority of Birgitta's spiritual authority over male ecclesiastical authority. Her popularity in Rome as a religious authority extended to rich and poor, clerical and lay. When her prophecy of 1348 (that the Avignon pope Urban V and Emperor Charles would come to Rome at the same time) actually came true in 1368, she received increased respect in the political world and, eventually, became a cult object among the Romans, impossible to ignore.

During her canonization process the designated adversarius appar-ently questioned the probability of God granting a woman such spiritual favors as a monastic rule dictated by God. Adam Easton, the appointed defender of her orthodoxy, answered that it was "so that to both sexes of mankind he would give the privileges of his grace."[39] In the years following her canonization, debate over some of her pessimistic visions arose, and the question of her sex and spiritual authority surfaced again. Johannes Tortsch argued that Birgitta was the chosen representative of Mary on earth whose function it was to channel God's grace to humanity and effect redemption.[40]

Birgitta herself had no problem with bypassing the church as a channel for grace, because the church had too often been led astray.[41]

Bishops, even archbishops, went to her for spiritual direction, as did friars, hermits, queens, and lords,[42] and she did not hesitate to offer her spiritual advice concerning all human activity. She prophetically warned the leaders of the kingdom of Cyprus "that if you will not correct yourself and amend your life," then God will destroy them so quickly that it will be "as if you had never been born."[43] She vehemently attacked Naples and its archbishop for allowing some Neopolitians to "keep their female servants and slaves in extreme abjection and ignominy, as if they were dogs" and others to "consult wicked fortune-tellers."[44] No activity was beyond her reach. As Eric Colledge comments in his study of Birgitta's political importance, we must not forget "that the politicians of the Middle Ages, avaricious, greedy for power, venal, and corrupt, still believed in the Four Last Things" and rarely ignored the warnings of those who prophesized about them, be they male or female prophets.[45]

Catherine of Siena's spiritual reputation brought her into the political arena even more than Birgitta. Besides her well-known role in getting the papacy back to Rome, Catherine was repeatedly asked to intervene in local politics by those who lived in daily contact with her spiritual presence. She counseled politicians from Lucco and Florence on alliances, preached a crusade, mediated between Bologna and Rome, comforted political prisoners, traveled to Avignon to intercede on behalf of the Florentines regarding a papal interdict, and negotiated peace between Florence and Rome.[46] Uneducated and a member of the *populo minuto*, the lower class, Catherine's origins did not earn her a political voice; her spirituality did. Catherine discussed her concept of authority in a letter to Bernabò, *visconti* of Milan.

> No lordship that we possess in this world allows us to consider ourselves lords. I don't know what sort of lordship that would be, that could be taken away from me and would not be within my control. It seems to me that no man ought to consider or call himself lord, but rather administrator. And this administration is not for always, but only for a time—as it pleases our gentle Lord. And if you should ask me, "Then don't we have any lordship at all on this earth?" I would answer, yes, we have the most satisfying, most gratifying, most mighty lordship there is—lordship over the city of our own soul.[47]

She had, in summary, a firm, balanced view of the source of her power.

She also had a solid grasp of who she was in the eyes of God. "Most beloved daughter," God the Father calls her in *The Dialogue*, "whom I have made in my image and likeness with such tender love."[48] Catherine repeated this fact continually throughout the work.[49] She also repeated her belief that "humankind was spoiled by the sin of the first man, Adam"; when she mentioned Eve it was as passive victim of "the lie with which the devil deceived."[50] She saw no reason for a woman to be considered less of a spiritual authority than a man, for "this greatness [creation in the image and likeness] is given to every person in general."[51]

Even when discussing the spiritual dignity of priests, Catherine placed the discussion in the context of the spiritual equality of all humanity. God has "dignified my ministers" because they administer "the body and blood of my only-begotten Son,"[52] not because of some inherent superior worth of the men themselves: "The reverence you pay to them is not actually paid to them but to me, in virtue of the blood I have entrusted to their ministry." Likewise, irreverence must not be shown them, not because they were spiritually superior but because "you are really sinning not against them but against me."[53] That being said, Catherine proceeded to call the clergy to task for their sins, which have "poisoned the whole world, as well as the mystic body of holy church."[54]

She was even less hesitant to chastise lay rulers. Her purpose in writing *The Dialogue* was to address "four petitions to the most high," the third of which was "for the whole world in general and in particular for the peace of Christians."[55] She reminded Bernabò that those who abuse their temporary administration of power "will be held accountable every time" and that "neither God nor his divine law will excuse you on the plea of any good intention you may have. No, you will be liable to the sentence of eternal death."[56] Like Birgitta, Catherine spoke with such conviction because her instructions came directly from God. After telling Gregory XI that she longed "to see you a courageous man, free of any cowardice," she quickly asked him to "forgive my presumption in saying what I've said—what I am compelled by gentle First Truth to say."[57]

Such conviction allowed her to speak with utmost authority: "I am telling you: come, and conquer our enemies with the same gentle hand. In the name of Christ crucified I am telling you."[58] Even her preaching mission came directly from God. "You must know," she wrote her mother in defense of her preaching activities, "that I, you miserable daughter, have not been put on earth for anything else: my Creator elected me to this."[59] As in Birgitta's case, Catherine's society acknowledged the source and supremacy of her authority;[60] her extensive correspondence with the leaders of the secular and the religious worlds and with common people clearly supports this conclusion.[61] Her influence after death only grew, culminating in the Roman church's recognition of her as a doctor of the church in 1970.

At first glance two English mystics, Julian of Norwich and Margery Kempe, appear to have little in common with Birgitta and Catherine. Neither Julian nor Margery are canonized saints, were visible outside their local world, exerted political influence, or had a cult develop around them immediately after death. Indeed, Margery's autobiography, the first written in English, was discovered only in the 1930s. These differences are helpful, for they give us access to an entirely different milieu. Birgitta and Catherine flourished in Italy, a major center of power during the late medieval period. Julian and Margery lived quiet lives in a country much removed from the controlling activities of the era. Identification of common spiritual perceptions among the four, therefore, would allow us to consider the universality of the perceptions.

The most striking theme in Julian's work was her feminization of God, which until recently had been considered unique. Current scholarship has unearthed a long tradition of this theme, however, and most now posit that Julian is rather the most original within the tradition.[62] To Julian the sexes reflected the mystery of the Trinity. Without the three Persons there is no God, just as without the union of male and female there is no human: "I saw and understood that the high might of the Trinity is our Father, and the deep wisdom of the Trinity is our Mother, and the great love of the Trinity is our Lord; and all these we have in nature and in our substantial creation. . . . And so our Mother is working on us in various ways, in whom our parts are kept undivided; for in our Mother Christ we profit and increase."[63]

Julian drew no radical conclusions from this realization, but it did reinforce her adherence to yet another tradition, the spiritual equality of women. "God showed the very great delight that he has in all men and women who accept, firmly and wisely the preaching and teaching of Holy Church."[64] Like Catherine, Julian said that "Adam's sin was the greatest harm ever done or ever to be done," not Eve's; Julian basically rewrote the Fall by removing Eve from the scene.[65] And like Catherine and Birgitta, Julian claimed that her message came directly from God, "who showed it to me without any intermediary."[66] Julian reflected at length on this and the contradiction between the earthly assumptions about women and God's.

> But God forbid that you should say or assume that I am a teacher, for that is not and never was my intention; for I am a woman, ignorant, weak, and frail. But I know very well that what I am saying I have received by the revelation of him who is the sovereign teacher. But it is truly love which moves me to tell you, for I want God to be known and my fellow Christians to prosper, as I hope to prosper myself, by

hating sin more and loving God more. But because I am a woman, ought
I therefore to believe that I should not tell you of the goodness of God,
when I saw at that same time that it is his will that it be known?[67]

Scholars debate what Julian meant when she claimed that she was "a
simple creature unlettered,"[68] but Denise Baker argues persuasively that the
sophistication of Julian's theology shows she was quite familiar with traditional theology.[69] The depth of her knowledge also contradicts those who
hold that women were rigorously restricted from the study of theology. This
is all the more puzzling, since nothing we know about Julian's life points to
exceptional educational opportunities.

Margery's story about her own education could possibly shed light on
how other women received their theological training. Although illiterate,
Margery was familiar with many works. While commenting on the nature
of knowledge received directly from God, she said that it was better than
anything else she had "heard [in] a book, not Hilton's book, not St. Bridget's
[Birgitta's] book, not the *Incendium Amoris* or any other which she had listened
to." Apparently, a priest she befriended "read to her for some seven years,"
including, besides those already mentioned, the Bible, commentaries, and
Bonaventure.[70] How many other women received informal training through
oral recitation is a matter of speculation, but there is no reason to think
Margery was unique.

Margery also offered evidence of the important role women saints
played in the life of a merchant-class mother of fourteen. She mentioned
holy women frequently and with knowledge of the particulars of their lives.
She was especially attached to Birgitta of Sweden, repeatedly referred to her
and her works, and even interviewed Birgitta's maid and landlord while on
a pilgrimage to Rome. After being told Birgitta "was courteous and humble
towards every creature, and that she had a smiling face," Margery went to
the room where Birgitta died to hear "a German priest there preaching about
her," and then, finally, knelt upon the stone where Christ told Birgitta when
she was to die.[71] Margery also talks about the lives of Elizabeth of Hungary,
Mary of Oignies, and Mary Magdalene. Mary Magdalene, whom Susan
Eberly contends was Margery's spiritual guide, appeared to Margery while
she was in Jerusalem and during a Good Friday vision.[72]

Margery availed herself to living exemplars as well. There was "an
anchoress in the same city, who was called Dame Julian," and since Julian
"was experienced in such things, and knew how to give good advice,"
Margery asked the woman to judge whether her revelations were fraudu-
lent.[73] That these two women's works have survived the ravages of time may

be a historical coincidence, but that two women mystics lived in the same town and shared many of the same ideas about women's spiritual nature indicate this is not an mere chance. Certainly their common socialization in the tradition of women's spiritual equality must have contributed somewhat to their similar assessment of their spiritual worth. Margery's faith in this tradition was extraordinary. When called upon to defend her orthodoxy at Leicester, "the mayor abused her vehemently," so she calmly retorted, "'Sir, you are not fit to be a mayor, and I shall prove it by Holy Scripture.'" When she was summoned to appear before the Archbishop of York, he "said to her: 'I have received bad reports about you. They tell me you are a very wicked woman.' And she replied: 'Sir, they tell me that you are a wicked man.'"[74] Infuriated, the archbishop told her to leave the diocese "'and swear that you will neither teach the people in my diocese, nor argue with them.'" This provided Margery with an opportunity to defend her preaching mission.

> "No, sir, I will not swear that," she said, "because I shall teach about God, and reprove those who blaspheme, everywhere I go, until the day when the Pope and the Holy Church decree that no one shall be so bold as to talk about God, for, sir, Almighty God does not forbid us to talk about Him. And it is also said in the Gospel that when the woman had heard our Lord preach, she stood in front of Him and said in a loud voice: 'Blessed be the womb that bore you' . . . and therefore, sir, it seems to me that the Gospel allows me to talk about God. . . ." Straight away an important cleric produced a book, and quoted St. Paul against her, saying no woman ought to preach. She in reply said: "I am not preaching, sir, I do not get up in a pulpit. I only use conversation and holy talk, and I intend to do that as long as I live."[75]

That this lengthy defense came from an uneducated woman of no known political, social, or economic distinction—in other words, one of the masses—is indeed food for thought.

Another spiritual movement arose in the late medieval period, the *devotio moderna*. This movement combined a new spirituality with a life of service in the world and was quite different from the mystical movement. At the same time, it has much in common with mysticism. Both movements placed few limits on membership: Cleric, nun, monk, married, single, male, and female were all welcome. Both operated within the boundaries of the church without direct, immediate hierarchical control. Both knew no geographical limits but were more popular in the Low Countries and Germany. Both advocated private meditation as the basic approach to God, and, finally, both promoted women's spiritual equality. The movements were not exclusive. Many members of the *devotio moderna* were mystics, although theoretically the two were not wholly compatible.

The *devotio moderna* began with the preaching of Geert Grote of Deventer around 1380. Men and women organized into informal congregations of brothers and of sisters, without vows or intentions of becoming a religious order. Within a century there were some ninety houses for women and forty for men in the Low Countries and Germany alone.[76] Throughout the history of the movement women continued to outnumber the men, a fact hard to remember given the attention the men receive. The brothers' fame was spread chiefly through their writings; *The Imitation of Christ*, probably authored by Thomas à Kempis, but definitely by someone in the movement, has been called "the most widely read work ever composed in Europe."[77] The women did not write popular literature, but they did write, and thus we can look at both male and female perceptions of women's spiritual nature within the movement.

Probably the most noticeable characteristic of the literature in regard to our topic is the lack of gendered spirituality, despite the fact that much of the literature was written by men for men. The literature is not built on either male or female analogies[78] but reflects a bare spirituality stripped of nonessentials, as can be seen through an analysis of *The Imitation of Christ*: "In all things I would find you naked and poor, and bereft of your own will," says Christ to Thomas. "Endeavor, therefore, to gain this freedom of spirit of which I speak. Pray for it, study for it and always desire it in your heart— that is to say, that you may be clearly deprived and bereft of all possessions and of your own will, and that, stripped of all worldly things, you may follow Me, who hung naked for you upon the cross."[79] The spirituality of *The Imitation* is individualistic ("The more you withdraw yourself from the consolation of all creatures, the sweeter and more blessed consolations you will receive from your Creator"); simple ("Man is borne up from earthly things on two wings: simplicity and purity"); universal ("I still do not cease to speak to every creature"); and private ("The most holy men and women who ever lived . . . chose to serve God in the secret of their hearts"). Moreover, it makes a frontal attack on the assumption that religious life has a monopoly on sanctity ("The religious habit and the tonsure help little; the changing of one's life and the mortifying of passions make a person perfectly truly religious") or that the highly intelligent have an advantage ("My words are spiritual and cannot be comprehended fully by man's intelligence").[80]

These characteristics explain in part *The Imitation's* wide appeal even into our own century; they also are the reason why it has appealed to both men and women. In Gerard Zerbolt's *Spiritual Ascents*, a work that John van Engen claims is the natural summary of all the *devotio moderna* literature and a work that all their houses probably possessed,[81] the movement's goal is clearly stated. A person is "a noble and rational creature" with a natural desire "to ascend toward the heights of your original dignity." Since such ascent "is possible only if you advance in your heart by way of the ascents and steps of the virtues," the task of the movement is to provide guidance for the journey.[82] "Even though Christ's most precious death redeemed us from original guilt" when Adam "fell grievously, and we in him," he left us with the job of reforming our souls "through holy exercises."[83] These Zerbolt spells out in structured form: "Carefully examine and consider what suits you, what is most useful. . . . Then order the steps, exercises, and means by which to reach that end."[84] And while this devotion is structured, it is also flexible enough for one to find "images of that celestial homeland adjusted to suit our capacities."[85]

Such a spirituality also possesses an inclusiveness that could not be missed by any man or woman: "Look upon all the divine benefits conferred generally on the human race as if they were to be bestowed on you alone, and think: Behold for me he created the whole world."[86] This inclusiveness is emphasized in other *devotio moderna* literature. "We all have one nobility, which is that we are the children of God en route toward our fatherland. We are all together one body," Gerlach Peter writes to his sister. "Therefore we should be most loving among ourselves and wholly united in all things."[87]

We find these same characteristics when we examine the women's writings. The commemorative lives of the sisters relate stories of women "poor by birth, but made rich in virtue," which were in no worldly way extraordinary. They were merely "humbly and simple children of God" who faithfully "did their exercises," sometimes "so secretive and hidden," but, ultimately, to such perfection that they became "the columns which helped to hold up this house."[88] Sister Wibbe Arnts "was a plain and simple creature . . . walked about simply and plainly"; Trude van Breda "was industrious at work and never seem to be idle during work time"; Heylewich van Grolle believed "that we were made rational creatures" who were individually "shaped according to his good pleasure"; although Katherine Hughen "had once lived with people who were great in the world's eyes" she willingly gave up her social status "when she came to join the sisters" and acted "as if she neither had nor had ever had great possessions in the world."[89]

These types of portraits were passed on from generation to generation to remind the "innumerable other virgins and women" drawn to the movement that "these poor sisters [were] their original root and lineage"[90] whose story would rouse more women "to mortify themselves in imitation."[91] The women also were quite aware that the portraits helped immortalize holy women, for "when we describe and take in the lives and morals of good people, they seem in a certain sense to go on living after death."[92]

The theme of witness by example is replete throughout the literature. The sisters argued ardently that if they "keep in mind these things as an example and realize that imitating them will make a great enough demand on our weakness," then their goal of sanctity will be met. One sister even hoped "that everyone who reads this or to whom it is read will say a short prayer for me" in thanksgiving for the benefits received.[93] What we have here, then, in these lives and in the *devotio moderna* movement in general is a glimpse of how, in the words of van Engen, "the higher ideals of the medieval Church [reached] into the lives of ordinary men and women."[94] Absent are the dramatic miracles and the highly charged prophecies of the extraordinary mystics; present are the examples "in obedience, another in humility, a third in resignation, and a fourth in sisterly love"[95] of the ordinary laywoman. And present also is a fairly reliable glance into a segment of society's ideas about women's spiritual nature.

11

Women in Late Medieval Sermons, Literature, and the Arts

WHILE THE RISE of vernacular secular literature during the latter part of the thirteenth century is well known, the spread of vernacular religious literature and the women providing the impetus for its germination it is often overlooked.[1] Many of the mystical works by and for women referred to in chapter 9 were written originally in or translated into the vernacular soon after composition,[2] and there is scattered evidence that the cleric Lambert translated parts of Scripture and legenda into the vernacular for women religious. These isolated instances of translation remained exceptional until the trend toward the vernacular also surfaced within the Dominican Order's ministry to women religious. We know that the first prior, Henry of Cologne, maintained devotional correspondence with women and that another Dominican prior, Henry of Basel, composed vernacular religious poetry for women.[3] Obviously some Dominicans believed that the German provincial's mandate to provide women religious with "the refreshment of the Word of God . . . according to the educational level of each convent"[4] meant preaching in the vernacular to those uneducated in Latin. Fortunately for us, many of their sermons were preserved in collections, providing us with the nearest we can get to a medieval oral tradition.

Sermons were always, of course, given in the vernacular. When "sermons" of church leaders prior to the Late Middle Ages were preserved, they were copied not as delivered but as translated into Latin and, in all likelihood, altered and polished in order to serve as aids for parish priests' own sermon preparation.[5] With the new demand for vernacular religious literature after the thirteenth century, sermons began to be copied as given. These sermons are an especially significant genre to examine, for we know the theology contained therein reached a great many people in an active and, it is hoped, commanding manner.

Most of the preserved sermons were given to congregations of both sexes and all classes in urban areas;[6] Michele Menot, a fifteenth-century French Franciscan, comments that "you will find four women for every man" and "also a lot of children" at his sermons.[7] Sermons at morning mass and afternoon services were originally the staple of the preacher, but preaching became more extraliturgical after the mendicants revitalized it as a major form of communication. By the sixteenth century almost any communal event warranted a sermon.

After analyzing twenty-three preachers' attitudes toward women in 1,657 sermons, Larissa Taylor challenges the stereotyped interpretation of preachers as antifeminist. She states that such a view is too simplistic and is contradicted by "a surprising number of late medieval preachers [who] stressed the dignity of woman and her equal role in Christian life."[8] Some preachers even questioned the prohibition against women preachers with arguments that go right to the heart of spiritual versus earthly standards. When discussing Mary Magdalene's legendary preaching, Guillaume Pepin, one of the staunchest defenders of women's spiritual parity, considered those who uphold Paul's mandate against women preaching: "[I]t must be answered that this is normally the case. But God is not bound by human laws, and can make women, just like men, assume the office of preaching." The sentiment is echoed by Josse Clichtove, famed Parisian theologian and preacher, and often found in practice.[9] Catherine of Siena wondered if she should wear male attire when assuming her role as preacher so as to abide with theory, until a revelation reminded her that He "who has created both sexes and all sorts of men" would not have created her a woman by accident.[10]

It is not simply God's whim that justifies a woman's leadership role but the worth of the woman herself. While Michel Menot and Robert Messier both pointed to the virtues of women who "studied well in the school of Christ"[11] as the reason why women were the first preachers of the Resurrection, Pepin waxes eloquent.

> It is proven that women are more devout than men, and this through the example of those learned women who were so devoted to Christ. Although during his time on earth, Christ found certain men agreeable, never did he find such perseverance and constancy among his disciples as he found in these women. These were the women who followed him as he traveled through the countryside preaching, and who ministered to his needs according to their abilities. . . . And so women announced

the triumph of the resurrection, for Christ knew that above all grace was the grace of a woman.[12]

When discussing Eve, Olivier Maillard placed himself in the tradition of Augustine and Peter Lombard by emphasizing that she was taken from Adam's side to remind all that husband and wife are meant to be companions.[13] Menot resolved the argument over who was more responsible for the first sin in Eve's favor: "After sinning, Adam excused himself by blaming his wife, saying: it was the woman who gave it to me, etc. So by this ruse he thought to escape; but instead he made things worse."[14] Pepin placed equal blame, but in his explanation he also revealed that contemporary women were not simply ingesting inferior images of women that men may hold. "There was extraordinary discord between men and women, who reproached each other for the transgressions of the first parents, with the men saying that the woman had seduced the man. For their part," Pepin added, "the women claimed that Adam was stupid to have behaved in such a way, wanting to please his wife more than God."[15] Even when preachers put the blame on Eve, they often couched it with a warning for those who project her guilt onto all women. "That woman should not be ashamed in that she made Adam trespass," preached one English cleric, "therefore through Christ Adam was amended. For no man should have woman in despite; for it is no wisdom to despise that God loveth."[16] Famed Sienese preacher San Bernardino likewise blamed Eve for the first transgression but tempered it with a reminder of Mary: "If some men say, it was woman who made us fall, I say that it is true, but it was also woman who raised us up again. And another man may say, 'If you think it over, it was woman who was the beginning of all evil'—but I reply, 'Woman was the beginning of all good.'"[17]

Pepin even turned the advantage men supposedly have over women, their higher intelligence, on its head by commenting that on a spiritual scale, such earthly advantages actually could be detrimental. Women were frequently "gravely stung" by the sermons of preachers, but "only rarely and always late in the day that we see evil men change their lives. And this is at least partially because men presume too much in their abilities and trust their reason. It is not that way with women."[18] Most preachers were keenly aware that women were more responsive to their preaching than men. Johannes Nider made a collection of his Nuremberg sermons at the request of "the honourable women" of that town.[19] Maillard rhetorically queried, "My ladies, do you not have your French bibles in your bedchambers?" and "Do you not study theology? O, that you would be good theologians and love

God."[20] Pepin commented on the fact that women's piety often led to charitable acts that surpassed men's. While preaching on Christ's sorrow for the death of sinners, he draws attention to the fact "that women are more compassionate to the sick and infirm than men, about whom we do not read such things. On account of this you find kindly nuns ministering to the needs of the sick in the great hospitals."[21] In the world of the spiritual, preachers acknowledged women's equality, often going further by noting their superior progress in spiritual matters.

The sentiment expressed in sermons found their echo in other forms of devotional literature produced during the period. A perennial favorite of the genre was the saint's life. The Late Middle Ages established Jacobus de Voragine's *Golden Legend* as the most popular collection of saints' lives ever produced. Compiled in the last quarter of the thirteenth century as a homiletic aid, its phenomenal publishing history bears witness to its success. Some 800 Latin manuscripts have been identified in this century alone, but more striking is the fact that the complete Latin manuscripts are only one of many variations of the *Legend*. It was abridged almost immediately, and then both the complete and the abridged editions were translated into numerous languages. When printing arrived it quickly became a staple of the industry.[22] Between 1470 and 1500 as many as 173 editions were published throughout Europe.[23]

Here in an accessible form clergy and laity read about the great women saints of old. Agatha, Agnes, Barbara, Cecilia, Dorothy, Katherine, Lucy, Mary of Egypt, Mary Magdalene, Martha, Paula, and Ursula were among the women from antiquity whose stories are kept alive by the *Legend*, along with more contemporary saints such as Clare and Elizabeth of Hungary. The *Legend* is a compilation, not an original composition, so we have met much of its content before. "S. Pauline [sic] was a much noble widow of Rome, of whom S. Jerome wrote the life, and saith first thus: . ."[24] is the beginning of Paula's legend, and it continues to make references to other sources throughout. Two of the longest legends are about women, Genevieve and Katherine. The four stories of the great feasts of Mary are included.

Since the bulk of the *Legend* are stories from late antiquity, it is not surprising to see an emphasis on the miraculous and the dramatic rather than on the everyday virtues emphasized in the *Books of the Sisters*. The story of Genevieve's prophetic saving of Paris from Attila by admonishing "the good women of the town that they should wake in fastings and in orisons by which they might assuage the ire of our Lord" is told at length, for example, as well as "many other miracles without number" wrought by this "mediatrix unto God."[25] The portrait of Mary Magdalene, on the other hand, includes miraculous elements that dominated earlier legends but emphasizes another dimension more, her preaching. Mary Magdalene is found "preaching with her disciples" in Marseilles while the people "marvelled of the beauty, of the reason, and of the fair speaking of her" and concluded that she was "inspired with the word of God."[26] Her preaching ultimately ends in the Christian-ization of Gaul, after which she retires to the desert for thirty years. This portrait of Mary Magdalene is preserved in various Renaissance paintings, the most exact being the Magdalene dossal by the Magdalene Master. Of the eight narratives painted on his dossal, two are of her preaching.[27]

The *Golden Legend* was the most popular example of its genre, but by no means was it unique. Osbern Bokenham's *Legends of Holy Women* was unique, for it is the first hagiographical collection in any language compiled that included only women.[28] It is openly dependent on Voragine's work and others, including such phrases as "as I find written in a book called the *Golden Legend*,"[29] but Bokenham's focus and tone isolated the women's spiritual essence more sharply than Voragine's. Women's physical nature was empha-sized, not denied, and used by the women to express their spiritual dignity, all the while men gaze upon them in admiration. Bokenham started his catalog with the life of Saint Margaret, upon the request of a man whom he calls "son and father."[30] Bokenham acknowledged Margaret's physical attributes, but rather than dwell on them he made a transparent excuse that he lacked "both eloquence and ability to amplify such matters."[31] Instead he stated that "she was also inwardly endowed with virtues, for she had faith, hope, and charity—the divine virtues—and also the four great cardinal virtues."[32] When a secular ruler was attracted to her physical body and not her virtues, she was imprisoned after she refused him. In prison she was tempted by a demonic dragon, whom she easily defeated, only to have another devil take its place. This devil managed to say only two sentences before "Margaret caught him by his long hair and threw him under her right foot."[33] As she faced death her final prayer reveals how fully she accepted woman's physical nature as inseparable from her spiritual being; one of her four pleas was for a "quick and safe delivery" for all "women in labor" when they pray to her.[34]

Bokenham included Elizabeth of Hungary's vita at the request of a woman, although the intended audience is both male and female, and the focus is again on the nongendered three divine virtues, which "Elizabeth had in excellent degree, as every intelligent person may ponder who diligently reads her legend."[35] This is a particular challenge, because Elizabeth was a member of a growing category of saints, married women. Bokenham was obviously aware of the limited acceptance this new category may have had, so he made uncharacteristic digressions to identify specific behavior he believed all should imitate. After discussing the extremes Elizabeth endured to submit to her spiritual director, Bokenham exclaimed, "O blessed obedience! What woman could now obey such a commandment without offense as did this mirror of patience: Behold! Scarcely a nun would do it meekly; and, to tell the truth, I believe that neither priest nor monk, canon nor friar would hear it without murmur."[36] Bokenham was trying to make sure that the audience did not think that Elizabeth was a mirror of spiritual perfection just for married women, but for all women and all men.

Lest one think that devotional literature remained under the purview of the male intelligentsia, descriptions of the reading habits of the laity remind us how thoroughly such literature permeated society. The household ordinances of Cecily of York at the end of the fifteenth century report that upon rising she prayed "the matins of the day, and the matins of our Lady," attended a private mass, ate breakfast, and attended mass again. "From there, she goes to dinner at which time she has a reading of some holy material, either Walter Hilton's book on the contemplative and active life, [pseudo-] Bonaventure's 'On the Nativity of our Savior,' the *Golden Legend*, the life of Saint Mary Magdalene, the life of Saint Catherine of Siena, or the *Revelations* of Saint Brigdit of Sweden."[37] Recent studies on reading all have reinforced the thesis that men and women from many different backgrounds read, owned, and promoted much of the vernacular religious literature produced during the era. Sylvia Thrupp claims that 40 percent of English merchants could read Latin, more than 50 percent could read English, and most merchant class wives could read and write English.[38] Examination of wills, inventories, purchasing records, and libraries show that by the fifteenth century, people were literate enough and books were plentiful and cheap enough to be owned by even the lower bourgeoisie. The overwhelming majority of these books were religious and increasingly in the vernacular.[39] It is therefore important to assess the image of women contained therein.

One of the more surprising facts to emerge from the pioneering work done on this subject is the role women played as audience in determining the contents of these books. Katherine Gill goes so far as to claim that "almost all the Italian vernacular authors and translators had some sort of close connection with religious women."[40] Susan Bell argues that these roles influenced the iconography in the books, producing innumerable illuminations of women reading. Mary reading at the Annunciation became a favorite theme, often with the female patron looking on.[41] Without known exception the portraits are positive representations, uniting women, spirituality, and reading into uplifting images. One is left wondering which had the greater impact on the reader, the text or the illuminations. When one remembers that mothers frequently used these books as textbooks for their children, they take on added importance: "When her daughter is of the age of learning to read, and after she knows her 'hours' and her 'office,'" Christine de Pizan advises, "one should bring her books of devotion and contemplation and those speaking of morality."[42]

Implicit in the acknowledgment by male authors of the need to consider their audience was the admission that women in that audience were as spiritually capable as men, and that the male author could even benefit from women's spiritual advances. "Remembering your request, I have tried, my sister, to write to you this *Ammonizione*, as you have asked," an anonymous fourteenth-century author wrote. "I do not profit from doing what your charity has taken care to ask; but if through this work you advance in divine love, and then I will have a part of your profit."[43] Sometimes the male author willingly acknowledged his spiritual inferiority: "Also, my sister, I am greatly afraid to write of such lofty matters," wrote the anonymous author of *The Chastising of God's Children*, "for I have neither the affective capacity nor the intellectual powers to declare them plainly, neither in English nor in Latin."[44] Or he may humbly ask for the woman's help, as does the author of *The Tree*: "Oh good sister, I pray thee then desire of thy spouse for me a drop of that devotion, I would also thou should desire of him such devotion for all my friends, and namely, my ghostly friends."[45] Occasionally an author explicitly stated the principle determining spiritual knowledge: "And thus thou may learn after the simple to write a fair, true book and better know Holy Writ than any master of divinity that loves not God so well as thou; for who loves best God, can best Holy Writ."[46]

Anne Bartlett's examination of Middle English devotional literature shows that the authors rejected many antifeminist stereotypes, including the myths that women often mistake hallucinations for visions, that women are more loquacious than men, and that women are more vulnerable to sins of the flesh.[47] In a retelling of John Cassian's tale of a desert father, the author of *The Chastising* rejected gynephobia and presented it as a transgression against monastic observances; after exhibiting near hysterics after contact with a woman, abba Paul was struck with palsy, and till death "no keeping might suffice him but the keeping of women."[48] Instead of perceiving women as inherently evil, the devotional literature often promoted healthy spiritual relationships between people, regardless of sex. "Another affection there is that falls to our purpose," the translator of *The Chastising* preached. "This reasonable affection of inward beholding of another man's virtue, as when a virtue or an holiness known of any man or woman be common fame or by reading of any man's life."[49]

One of the more reasoned, methodical examinations of spiritual misogynism is found in the fifteenth-century *Dives and Pauper,* where the clerical Pauper corrected various views of the worldly Dives. Here Eve was created from Adam's rib, "for the rib is next to the heart, in token that God made her to be man's fellow in love and his helper," and not from Adam's foot "to be man's toiler." When Dives reminded Pauper that Eve deceived Adam and concluded that, therefore, no man "may then be safer from woman's guile?" Pauper pontificated:

> Many men have been deceived by wicked women—more be his own folly than be through deceit of woman—but many more women have been deceived by the malice of men than ever were men deceived by malice of women. Therefore the lecherous is called the snare of the fiends that hunt after man's soul. . . . But men be called not only the snare of the fiend but also they be called his net spread abroad on the hill of Thabor for to take many at once (Osee 5:1). Man's malice is called a net spread abroad on a hill for it is open and boldly done, not in a few but in many, and therefore when Holy Writ reproves the malice of man he speaks in the plural number as to many, but when he reproves the malice of woman he speaks in the singular number as to few. . . .
>
> This false excuse that man so excuses his sin be the malice of woman began in Adam and has Adam and all mankind, for sinfully he excuses his sin be woman when God reproved him of his sin and put woman in default. . . . And so notwithstanding that he was more in default than woman yet he would not acknowledge only default but he puts woman and God principally that made woman in default.[50]

The discussion continued for some length, with Pauper reminding Dives that since Eve "was tempted by the fiend" and admitted "her guilt but she asked no mercy," and Adam "had less temptation than woman and thereto in nothing would accuse himself," he sinned more. Thus, "Christ became not woman but he became man to save mankind that as mankind was lost by man so mankind should be saved by man." In his Incarnation "he did great worship to woman, for only of woman's kin he made medicine to the sin of Adam and to help mankind of the hard sickness of Adam's sin."[51]

Secular vernacular literature also concerned itself with attacks on women. No one came to the defense of women more strenuously than Christine de Pizan, but she did not focus on women's spiritual nature. Her concern was woman's natural rights, and her defense was specific to contemporary attacks on women. "The ladies mentioned here complain of many clerks who lay much blame to them, composing tales in rhyme, in prose, in verse, in which they scorn their ways with words diverse," Christine wrote. What is worse is that "they give these texts out to their youngest lads, to schoolboys who are young and new in class, examples given to indoctrinate." Christine was obviously complaining about the same popular sentiments that concerned preacher Menot and the author of *Dives and Pauper:* "Thus, 'Adam, David, Samson, Solomon,' they say in verse, 'a score of other men, were all deceived by women morn and night, so who will be the man who can escape?'" Christine's strategy was to attack the logic of the misogynist literature. "If [women] are the fickle, foolish, faithless lot that certain clerks maintain they are, then why must men pursuing them resort to schemes, to clever subterfuge and trickery?" One thing was for certain, Christine concluded, "if women, though, had written all those books, I know that they would read quite differently. For well do women know the blame is wrong. The parts are not apportioned equally."[52]

In 1401 Christine became involved in a debate over what she considered to be the slanderous content of *The Romance of the Rose* with three royal secretaries and Jean Gerson, chancellor of the University of Paris, and with this argument we must acknowledge we have strayed from the tradition we are supposed to be documenting. Christine was arguing with male Christians about female Christians in a Christian setting, yet none rested arguments on spiritual dimensions. In *The Book of the City of Ladies* Christine examined herself "as a natural woman" and wondered why, given what "so many famous men" say about the vileness of women, God created such "monstrosities" in nature. "Oh, God, how can this be?" she lamented. "Did you yourself not create woman in a very special way and since that time did You not give her all those inclinations which it pleased you for her to have? And how could it be that You could go wrong in anything?" Stymied, she continued: "Alas, God, why did You not let me be born in the world as a man, so that all my inclinations would be to serve You better, and so that I would not stray in anything and would be as perfect as a man is said to be?" Her answer arrived when three ladies—Reason, Rectitude, and Justice—appear "to straighten out men and women when they go astray," this time, "to vanquish from the world" the wrongful attacks against women "by men."[53] The Lady Virtues, however, were not spiritual virtues per se, and Christine's evidence to support her contention concerning women's equality came from the secular world. Another work of Christine's, *The Treasury of the City of Ladies,* was also a kind of instruction manual or guide for women and is based on the same type of arguments.

Overall, Christine's attacks addressed the abuses developing in the fading feudal society and expressed in the courtly love literature of the day[54] rather than beliefs about women's spiritual nature. This may be attributable to the fact that *The Romance of the Rose* and other popular vernacular literature did not attack the spiritual equality of women directly either. Even Gerson, Christine's partner in the *querelle des femmes*, did not address the issue of spiritual equality, although his arguments are theologically based. His concern was public morality and the danger that *The Rose* posed to it. "Who deceives by fraud and perjury honest girls?" Gerson asked in his allegorical treatise. "Whence come robberies to maintain extravagances, bastardry or the suffocation of infants . . . in short, all wickness and all folly?"[55] His answer to that question was *The Fool of Love*, the summation of the courtly love literature represented by *The Rose*. Elsewhere, however, Gerson did talk about women's spiritual dignity, placing the chaste woman above even chaste men: "You will be singled out and crowned with a divine crown in paradise. . . . You are the most beautiful part of holy church."[56]

Still, one must note this is the beginning of the end of an era. Christianity's definition of a woman as a human being spiritually equal to man did not fully satisfy the participants in the discussion. Humanist arguments appeared contemporaneously with Christine's pioneering defense of women with social, intellectual, and commonsense arguments. Like Christine, humanists' main concern was not spiritual but earthly equality. Like Christine, their arguments assumed women's spiritual equality and society's acceptance thereof, hence they mention it only in passing. Humanist Baldesar Castiglione's apology in *The Book of the Courtier* is often quoted and was an example of this new approach and goal. Castiglione assumed throughout that women's spiritual equality was beyond debate. "That women are imperfect creatures and therefore of less dignity than men and incapable of practicing the virtues practiced by men, I would certainly not claim now," Castiglione's Gaspare proclaimed after listening to the arguments of Guiliano. "Male and female always go naturally together, and one cannot exist without the other," Guiliano continued, this time turning to Genesis for evidence. "And since one sex alone shows imperfection, the ancient theologians attribute both sexes to God . . . and we read in Holy Scripture that God made male and female in His own likeness."[57] Later when Frisio blamed Eve for leaving "the human race a heritage of death, travails and sorrows," Guiliano retorted impatiently, "[D]on't you know that the transgression you mentioned was repaired by a woman who won for us so much more than the other had lost," employing the Eve-Mary dichotomy. "[H]ow inferior are all other human creatures to Our Lady," and how many women have died for Christ or "in learned disputation have confounded so many idolators," he asked in frustration. "And you can discover many more women besides, who are less talked about, especially if you read St. Jerome, who celebrated certain women of his time with such marvellous praise that it would suffice for the holiest of men." Women are, Guiliano concluded, "naturally capable of the same virtues as men."[58]

Both Christine and Castiglione employed what literary critics call catalogs, and it was the catalog writing of Jerome that Castiglione is referring to here. Catalogs list historical examples of people who best exemplify the virtue or vice being discussed; they were common in ancient literature but lay dormant until found in such notable works as Chaucer's *Canterbury Tales,* Boccaccio's *De claris mulieribus,* and the literature of the *querelle des femmes* literature during the late medieval period.[59] The catalogs' revival is not surprising, for they addressed, just like hagiography, an audience that, in Glenda McLeod's words, "wanted edification, a moral example to imitate, and (in an age when books were expensive items) ample erudition and facts."[60]

The medieval reader certainly found those goals fulfilled in Dante Alighieri's *The Divine Comedy.* Possessor of a multitude of accolades, it is universally acknowledged to be a masterpiece of world literature, the culmination of medieval civilization, and the ultimate statement of the Christian worldview. Like all great works, it reflects its own age and influences all subsequent ages. What Dante said about women must be weighed accordingly. For Dante, women possessed the fullness of human nature, the fullness of human intellect, and, most significantly, the fullness of spiritual dignity. Through woman and only with woman could any creature be united with the Creator. Whether it be Beatrice or Mary, woman was the means to salvation. "'Now to the face which most resembles Christ direct thine eyes,'" Bernard of Clairvaux told Dante as they approach Mary, "because its spotless light alone can make thee fit to look on Christ.'"[61]

One of the first characteristics to strike the reader of the *Comedy* is the presentation of women in their own right. Women are not mere reflections of or complements to men, but independent humans responsible for their own destiny. If anything, Dante warned of the dangers involved when women forgot this reality; they inhabit Hell. Dante placed few women in Hell, but those that were there abdicated their responsibilities. Dido, "the self-slayer," who committed suicide, the definitive act of abdication, was there, as were Semiramis, Cleopatra, and Helen, queens who abandoned their responsibilities and consequently lost control of their own destinies.[62]

Women were more visible in Purgatory, and their essential role in the redemption of all humanity clearly emerged there when Beatrice explained the reason for Dante's journey: "So low he fell, that insufficient were by then all means of saving him, except to show him those who of being saved despair. For this I visited the portal kept for the dead."[63] The goal was, of course, to get Dante to Paradise: "Awhile, my face was both his strength and shield: and, showing him my youthful eyes, I led him with me, in the right direction held."[64] Women went to extraordinary ends to aid men in their journey to salvation, whether it was Mary's "Thy will be done" or Beatrice's altruistic help.

Virgil, the personification of reason, resigned his role as guide in Purgatory as he "reached a place where vision of mine no farther may intrude."[65] Dante could proceed no longer using only reason (viewed as masculine in classical and medieval thought), for it was "madness to hope that human reason knows how the unending pathway may be track'd by which one Substance in three Persons goes."[66] He must approach God with love, that is, with Beatrice by his side. "'Dante, for all that Virgil goes his way, not yet, weep thou not yet'"; Beatrice lectured him, "'for needs must thou weep when thou feel'st another sword in play.'"[67] Indeed, Beatrice questioned, "'How durst thou approach the mountain'" without love—without woman?[68] It was Beatrice "who cannot err," who led Dante to wisdom, not Virgil.[69] Man without woman was incomplete and therefore barred from Paradise. True wisdom came only when reason and love, male and female, worked together.

We know that Beatrice was not a mere symbol to Dante but a real, flesh-and-blood woman whose love taught him more about life than his intellect did. Love also made approach to God possible. In Paradise Mary, another real, historical woman, served as the means by which all see God. "But stop we here," Bernard advised Dante as they neared Mary, before they "to the primal Love direct our eyes." First, "we needs must pray for grace, and grace may get from her who hath the power to aid thee so."[70] As Joan Ferrante summarizes for us, "the vision Dante offers of mankind saved and glorified is a vision of the perfect integration of the human race with God and with itself. And Dante, a man, achieves that vision through the inspiration and active help of three women: Mary, through whom Christ brought salvation to all men; Lucy, the patron saint . . . and Beatrice, the lady Dante loved in life."[71]

Dante's vision was not the only one offered in late medieval society, but all of them included his basic thesis, salvation for all humanity achieved through the active role of woman in the salvific plan. Ferrante's use of the word *vision* reminds us of an important reality. Late medieval culture was still very much a visual culture.[72] The increase in literacy and the number of books was not an isolated event. There was a similar development in visual arts, and during the Late Middle Ages these two trends were wedded together in illuminated books. Devotional literature, particularly literature focused on saints, provided artists both with a popular medium for their craft and with subject matter. The growth of lay confraternities, the beguine and beghard movement, the *devotio moderna*, tertiary orders, and lay patronage help form new audiences for both the religious book and religious art. Often religious art was used to narrate the origins of a group or to commemorate a founder's life. As in previous periods, this era's art was a mirror of society's opinion of women, with one additional characteristic. Late medieval religious art was funded, commissioned, and enjoyed at a local level and by the laity to a greater degree than ever before; it therefore reflected and informed a larger and more diverse audience.

One of the obvious features of this art was the humanization of Jesus, Mary, and the saints. We have already noted the influence *The Golden Legend* had on vernacular literature, but it also had a great impact on art. Its narratives inspired visualization. In England Bokenham's *Legends of Holy Women* likewise inspired imitation; all of the surviving East Anglican rood screens, for instance, have paintings of the saints included in Bokenham's collection. Nine life-size portraits of saints included in Bokenham's *Legends* are also found on the screen at North Elmham and eight each at Litcham and Westhall. "His book reads like programme notes" for the artists of these screens, writes Eamon Duffy.[73] The art inspired by Mary Magdalene's legend alone was overwhelming. Beginning in the thirteenth century hers was the most popular image reproduced in Italy. As patron of many confraternities, lay associations, and guilds, Mary Magdalene's portrait was found in various mediums in churches, hospitals, and monasteries.[74]

Society's acceptance of women's spiritual authority is discernible in the role Birgitta of Sweden played in art, for it is Birgitta's vividly described vision of the birth of Jesus that became the standard representation of the Nativity, a representation still dominating Western faith and art today.

> With [Mary] there was a very dignified old man; and with them they had both an ox and an ass. When they entered the cave, and after the ox and the ass had been tried to the manger, the old man went outside. . . . [W]hile she was thus in prayer, I saw the One lying in her womb then move; and then and there, in a moment and the twinkling of an eye, she gave birth to a Son. . . . Then his mother took him in her hands and pressed him to her breasts, and with cheek and breast she warmed him with great joy and tender maternal compassion.[75]

In one of the most influential passages in Western art, we see the spiritual dignity of woman completely and utterly united with the physical dignity of woman. Fra Angelico, Niccolo di Tommaso, Turino Vanni, and Lorenzo Monaco are just some of the early painters to use Birgitta's imagery as the basis of their Nativity portrayal. To a lesser degree Birgitta also influenced Western portrayals of the crucifixion with her detailed revelation of the Passion, a description that possessed the same unforgettable imagery as the Nativity. Simple, ordinary moments in the Passion were rendered unforgettable under Birgitta's sway, as in this description of Jesus as he awaited death: "Thus his body was as if supported by the nails with which his feet had been crucified. Moreover, his fingers and hands and arms were now more extended than before; his shoulder blades, in fact, and his back were as if pressed tightly to the cross." The Pietà depiction also changed after Birgitta's description of Jesus "all torn as he was and wounded and black and blue" being laid on Mary's knee became well known.[76]

Other women exerted influence on art too, and they were present enough in the process of book production for us to consider their own perceptions of women. Women's patronage of literate works is common knowledge, but their patronage of art is not as well known.[77] The famed anecdote involving Buonamico Buffalmacco and some Florentine nuns and included in Vasari's Le Vite concerns a humorous struggle between the artist and female patrons for control of the work. The nuns are ridiculed throughout, but in the end they are the ones who determine the subject matter and even the colors.[78]

Individual women such as Isabel of Portugal were famous for their patronage, but most women's patronage came from communities, which had to house themselves and provide their own liturgical books, devotional reading, interior decor, and images. The Poor Clare community at Perugia left a detailed account of artistic patronage within their monastery, and here we see the abbess in firm control of the process, as in the case of commissioning Raphael to paint the Assumption.[79] When we examine the Dominican monastery of San Dominico in Pisa and the Franciscan monastery of Sant' Anna in Foligno, we find that in both houses female saints were quite common and placed in dominant positions. Both houses commissioned paintings of contemporary female saints; both possess thematic art on the humanity and Passion of Jesus; both display art that reflects contemporary devotional literature known for its positive images of women's spiritual nature; and both preserve images of women as intercessors, learned, authoritative, and, most important, spiritually blessed by union with God. The refectory of Sant' Anna, a house for nonenclosed tertiaries, is decorated with four lunettes, all of which picture food. One is of the house of Mary and Martha; another of Martha, the example par excellence of the active life, working alone in her kitchen; one of the wedding feast at Cana with two female saints seated at Jesus's table; and the final, the Last Supper. In San Dominico the altarpiece in the outer, public church displayed the details of Birgitta's life on the predella—commissioned a mere two generations after her death and only one after her canonization.[80] As Dominique Rigaux concludes in her study of Sant' Anna, "all these pictures served not only to teach or influence the nuns but to affirm their new power. And not only religious power."[81]

Catherine Vigri of Bologna, a true Renaissance women and abbess of the Poor Clare monastery of Corpus Domini, is one of the more impressive figures of the period. Brought up and educated in the d'Este court at Ferrara, where she served as lady-in-waiting to Margarita d'Este, Catherine entered a Ferrarese monastery after Margarita married, and in her later years she accepted the office of abbess at the new foundation in Bologna. She obviously never left her education behind, for once installed at Corpus Domini she quickly established an impressive library for the women[82] and actively contributed to the culture of all religious women both before and after her move to Corpus Domini. In 1438 she completed a treatise on spiritual direction for women where she explained her understanding of the relationship between spirituality and culture. Not only are all humans given talent, but "we shall have to render an account to Him of the talent of good will given to us to use in His praise and for the salvation of our soul and that of our neighbors."[83] That talent may manifest itself in ways not commonly associated with asceticism, such as exuberant dancing and singing: "Every lover who loves the Lord come to the dance singing of love," Catherine writes. "Come dancing and be utterly ablaze."[84]

Catherine's own talents were many. Besides being a spiritual director of women, writer of spiritual treatises, and administrator of a women's institution, she was a poet, musician, and artist. She utilized all her gifts because "each creature should strive to make itself laudable in its Creator," and it would be terribly selfish "if I fail to say what may help others."[85] The Word is what will help others, so Catherine spread the Word through various media. "Gladly, in the books and in many places of the monastery of Ferrara she painted the Divine Word," Illuminata Bembo, Catherine's closest friend and biographer wrote.[86] Catherine's paintings of the Madonna show her holding the Incarnate Word, and her painting "Redeemer" depicts the Incarnate Word holding a book, the Divine Word, with two roundels above of the Annunciation, when the Word was made flesh. Meditation on the Word was one of the weapons women must use to overcome temptation, Catherine wrote in *Seven Weapons of the Spirit*. "As we read of that prudent and holy virgin Saint Cecilia, where it reads, 'she always carried the gospel of Christ hidden in her breast,'" so must the women do likewise. "Do not allow those daily lessons read in choir and at table to be in vain . . . is not the teaching of the gospel the very Word of the honeyed mouth of Christ?"[87] The breviary Catherine illuminated preserves her theology, her artistic talents, and her understanding of women's spiritual destiny in a way that few artists have been able to do. It was written for the women, addressing them throughout, and its histrionic capitals and marginalia are filled with images reflecting Catherine's theology rather than empty decoration. "What can flowers and branches do there? Would not Jesus Christ be better in the initial letters as he is in prayers and lessons?" asked Illuminata.[88]

Catherine of Bologna's love of the Incarnate Word was shared by many during the late medieval period, and this manifested itself in devotion to the humanity of Jesus. Women fared well in such a theology. A major problem in the West regarding women was the nearly unchallenged tradition of negative perceptions of their physical nature. The late medieval pietistic stress on the Incarnation and humanity of Jesus came close to developing an opposing tradition. With Jesus's body being nourished directly and undeniably by Mary's body, it was logically inconsistent to maintain the inferiority of women's bodies. Thus the period saw the production of Visitation sculpture. Typically the figures would be Mary and Elizabeth greeting, with a slit in their wombs to allow the viewer to see Jesus and John thriving in their bodies. The startlingly graphic nature of the portrayal left little room for doubt about the worth of a woman's physical nature, no less her spiritual nature. The statues were popular throughout Bohemia, Austria, and southern Germany,[89] and paintings on maternal themes were popular everywhere in the West. Madonna portraits, many of them Renaissance masterpieces, and the paintings of the Child Jesus shed favorable light on the physical nature of woman via her spiritual function. Particularly popular were Madonna of Mercy images in which Mary's outspread arms and body protected whole families.[90] The Opening Virgin statues were also popular. These sculptures envisioned Mary as a tabernacle: Side hinges allowed the statues to open up and reveal the Trinity residing within her body.[91] Saint Anne images flourished, often depicting the physical relationship women had to Jesus, as did Holy Kindred paintings and depictions of the Three Marys and their children.[92] The incorrupt body of Catherine of Bologna was a favorite pilgrimage destination where all could see a woman's body so singularly exalted. "From a thousand directions the people run to see your body," wrote

Savonarola in his poem honoring Catherine's spiritual and physical natures. "O would any heart be so savage that it would not melt in tears of sweetness when it saw the holy deeds, the humble face?"[93] The stigmata of Catherine of Siena was the subject of art and literature; possessing the marks of the crucified Jesus is an intensely intimate identification between Jesus's body and the stigmatic's.[94]

New liturgical feasts and devotions reflect the seriousness in which society allowed beliefs concerning women's spiritual equality to influence their attitudes about women's physical being. Feasts such as the Compassion of the Virgin, instituted in 1423, and the Seven Sorrows of Mary, begun in the fourteenth century, and devotions like the Sorrowful Mysteries of the rosary were all part of society's realization that woman's physical body is part of the redemption story.[95] Unfortunately, however, the tradition of women's spiritual equality was not strong enough to completely break down society's prejudices about women's bodies or other aspects of their lives. In fact, in the coming age the power of this spiritual tradition actually weakened further as all things spiritual became compartmentalized. The tradition remained vocal and was certainly a major voice in the discourse on women, but it was a diminished voice.

12

Reformation, Counter-Reformation, and Enlightenment Opinions of Women

THE SIXTEENTH CENTURY has long been called a turning point in the history of Christianity, and this judgment is no less true for the history of Western society's perceptions of women. As we shall see, Christianity continued to maintain a tradition of women's spiritual equality, but many other things changed in the society in which the tradition was proclaimed. The tradition no longer carried the same weight. In a religious society one's religious status is the most significant status. In a secular society one's religious status is often the least significant status. During the sixteenth century Western society's journey toward secularism accelerated somewhat, and consequently less attention was paid in some quarters to the spiritual dignity of persons. In discussions of women's worth, spiritual equality was still stated or presupposed, but arguments now focused on other dimensions. We saw the focus begin to shift with Christine de Pizan and humanists such as Boccaccio. By the time we reach Rousseau and the Enlightenment *philosophes* such as physician Pierre Roussel, the change is quite pronounced. Women's spiritual equality is not negated but rather considered one aspect of a nature defined by organic functions, as evident in the title of Roussel's work: *Physical and Moral System of Woman, or Philosophical Portrait of the Constitution, Organic State, Temperament, Morals, and Functions Peculiar to the Sex.*[1]

The period opened, however, with Martin Luther proclaiming loudly Christianity's positive and negative traditions concerning women and, like many theologians before him, seeing no need to reconcile the two. In his commentary on Genesis Luther stated that "God created male and female in order to indicate that Eve, too, was made by God as a partaker of the divine image and of the divine similitude, likewise of the rule over everything. Thus even today the woman is the partaker of the future life, just as

Peter says that they are joint heirs of the same grace." Yet, in the same breath, he reminded all that "although Eve was a most extraordinary creature— similar to Adam so far as the image of God is concerned, that is, in justice, wisdom, and happiness—she was nevertheless a woman." To Luther, man is the sun while woman is the moon. Even while he was arguing strongly for the spiritual equality of woman, Luther could not forget that the female "is inferior to the male sex."[2] Never, however, did he lose sight that both "man and woman are the work of God,"[3] and he did follow through with at least some of the implications of this truth. Education of both boys and girls was "essential and beneficial" so that they could "in the fear of God, take their own place in the stream of human events."[4]

John Calvin wrote not about Eve's Fall but about "Adam's Fall" and "Adam's sin" repeatedly,[5] yet he included Eve when referring to "the primeval dignity [God] gave to Adam and Eve."[6] The image in which all humanity was made "includes anything which has relevance to spiritual and eternal life," not physical life. Woman and man, therefore, "can bear the same image in knowledge, purity, righteousness and true holiness."[7] For Calvin, Galatians 3:28 ("neither male nor female") was Paul's fundamental statement of universal spiritual equality where he made it plain that "none of us must advance himself as though he were better worth than his fellows" in God's eyes. Spiritual equality did not eliminate "diversity of degree as in respect of worldly policy," however, so Calvin saw no contradiction in maintaining both women's spiritual equality and her domestic inequality, "for we know there are masters and servants, magistrates and subjects: in a household there is the good man which is the head and the good wife which ought to be subject," an order that is "inviolable." When Paul said "that there is neither master not servant, man nor woman, he meaneth that to be sure of their salvation men must not set up their tails like peacocks." Once women "understand that all this came of Eve," then they will "bear patiently the subjection that God hath laid upon them."[8]

Huldreich Zwingli told the story of the Fall as if Eve never existed; "the cradle of religion" was the day Adam sinned. He "saw he deserved nothing but wrath," but God, having the "loyal devotion of the father to his undutiful son," ran "to him in spite of his obstinacy."[9] All humans, though, were made in God's image "in order to have fellowship with him," but it was only the soul, "our inward man—which is created in the divine image."[10] Balthasar Hubmaier also retold the story of the Fall principally through Adam, whose disobedience "lost this freedom for himself and all of his descendants."[11] Dietrich Philips emphasized the dual role of Adam and Eve in the Fall but immediately followed his comments with a reminder that "the reconstruction of the ruined church occurred in the promise of the coming seed (Gen 3:15) of a woman."[12]

This sampling of reformers' comments is representative of their overall ambivalent attitude toward women. None of them denied the spiritual equality of women, but none of them were particular champions of it either; almost all of them attacked institutions within Christianity that fostered women's visibility and high status, specifically, monasticism, saints, and Mariology. It is difficult to assess what the loss of these institutions had on women, but it is even more difficult to maintain that it was insignificant. All that historians have learned in the last few decades about the importance of one's environment, socialization, and role models in the formation of popular culture contradicts such an assertion.

This is not to say that the reformers muted the tradition of women's spiritual equality. To the contrary, it was alive and well, but it did manifest itself in new, more self-conscious ways. The reformers called for a reexamination of the two chief vocations women identified themselves with, marriage and religious life. In the eyes of Erasmus, one of the first to articulate dissatisfaction with both, "much reverence is due [marriage], which was instituted by God" before all the other sacraments. "The rest were instituted upon earth, but this in paradise; the rest for a remedy, this for partnership in happiness." Eve was created "out of Adam's ribs, so that we might clearly understand that nothing should be dearer to us, nothing more closely joined, nothing more tightly glued to us than a wife."[13] Moreover, husband and wife are close because they are spiritually equal. "Jesus who presides at weddings," Erasmus reminds us in this powerful passage, "made us equal in so many ways. He redeemed us by the same death, he washed us in the same blood. . . . Forget about your birth, and hers: what about your rebirth? Can you consider her beneath you, when God accepts her as a daughter, and Christ as a sister?"[14]

Corollary to a reevaluation of the spiritual status of marriage is a reevaluation of religious life, which Erasmus believed should be forthcoming. "Let the swarms of monks and virgins exalt their own rule of life as they will, let them boast as much as they like of their liturgical functions and their acts of worship, in which they excel all others; the holiest kind of life is wedlock." Erasmus did not go so far as to condemn religious life but did insist that "virginity is certainly worthy of praise, but on the condition that this praise is not transferred to the majority of mankind."[15]

Luther had no such reservations: "Monastic life is to be condemned." He contemptuously considered monasticism "really a lazy, secure, and good life" and monastics to be "of no use at all." Monks and nuns "neglect the gospel and instead go around making vows" and "hid[ing] themselves forever in monasteries."[16] A woman who pledges herself to a life of virginity "blasphemes and despises God" by her vows.[17] To Luther such celibacy was against God's ordinances; "therefore, priests, monks, and nuns are duty-bound to forsake their vows whenever they find that God's ordinance to produce seed and to multiply is powerful and strong within them. They have no power by any authority, law, command, or vow to hinder this which God has created within them;" if anyone disagrees, "it is certainly your own fault, you neither understand nor believe God's word and work."[18] In his personal life Luther realized these beliefs in his support of women who left monasteries, his role as matchmaker in their subsequent marriages, and his own marriage to one such nun, Katherine von Bora.

Whether women actually benefited from this theological reassessment of marriage is still being debated. The older, more popular view that it did indeed improve women's lot is seriously challenged today by those who maintain that familial patriarchy was reinforced once husbands' control over wives was no longer shared with priests.[19] Both interpretations marshal convincing evidence. The benefits women reaped by the elimination of religious life, on the other hand, are harder to identify. That almost all women did leave their monasteries when disbanded by men or when they adopted Protestantism is easily documented, but whether their plight improved or worsened is nigh impossible to analyze, because most women disappeared from records once they left their monasteries.[20] Gone also is the correspondence, devotional literature, and spiritual records by and about these communities of women in the areas where Protestantism dominated. Fortunately, in areas were the Roman church remained entrenched, our sources multiple dramatically, especially sources by women.

One of the richest fields to plow for insight into perceptions of women's spiritual dignity is in Spain. When the sixteenth century opened, Spanish women were enjoying society's endorsement of their spiritual dignity, thanks in no small way to Isabella of Castile. Through her insistence on education for women and men and on reformed religious orders, and through her chief advisor Cardinal Ximenes, an atmosphere was created where women flourished within the spiritual realm. *Beatas* (pious women self-dedicated to prayer) were found everywhere, sometimes living in groups resembling beguines or tertiaries, sometimes living alone. Their status within local communities was quite high, and Ximenes did much to elevate it even more. He corresponded with some, fostered their spirituality by having the vita of Catherine of Siena and Angela of Foligno's *Book* translated and published,[21] and saw to it that the judges of the famous *beata* Maria de Santo

Domingo acquitted her when she was accused of heresy. Not all of the women attracted to the movement were orthodox (some became involved with *alumbrados,* a heretical sect), but many of the autobiographies and vitae of the *beatas* disclose a spirituality consistent with the tradition we have been documenting. There is within an assumption of women's spiritual worth.

Maria de Santo Domingo's confessor testified at her trial that upon meeting Maria, he implored her to pray for his true conversion, and that soon after he experienced "a degree of fervor and repentance that he had never felt before;"[22] he obviously had no doubts about her spiritual potential. Few of these women's confessors did. In the mutually advantageous relationship that was developing between women and confessors who acted also as spiritual directors,[23] confessors frequently gave the women free rein in their spiritual life, because they recognized the women's high spiritual status. Maria Vela tells us that after "I placed myself under the direction of my confessor," he insisted that instead she should "have my aunt, who is now in heaven, act for him" and regulate her spiritual practice "in respect to prayer and penance" and communion.[24] Her confessor, in other words, placed himself and his directee under the constrains of a woman's direction. So serious did he consider the direction that he never "dared order that I do more than my aunt wished."[25] Years later Maria confided that "the *Works* of Holy Mother Teresa of Jesus" inspired her to begin "to lead a new life," not her confessor.[26] Maria also turned to another woman, Catherine of Siena, this time "to imitate her virtues" and behavior as precisely as she could, even praying to Christ "to give me, as He had given her, a new heart."[27] When her confessor concluded that Maria's mystical experiences were beyond his experience, he sought other men's opinions, but "never doubted that my guidance was from God."[28]

Teresa of Avila never doubted that her guidance was from God either. "I spent a good many years doing a great deal of reading and understanding nothing of what I read," Teresa tells us in her autobiography, until "God suddenly gave me a completely clear understanding."[29] Although we do not always possess an equivalent understanding of Teresa, for she is a complex genius, her writings, like those of Augustine before her, do make her one of the most accessible persons in Western culture; she had an uncanny ability "to set down what has happened to me with all the simplicity and truth at my command."[30] Always she spoke plainly, without pretension: "I used unexpectedly to experience a consciousness of the presence of God, of such a kind that I could not possibly doubt that He was within me or that I was wholly engulfed in Him. This was in no sense a vision: I believe it is called mystical theology."[31] Teresa's *Life* is a rare autobiographical and religious masterpiece, as is

Augustine's *Confessions,* and the similarity between the two books and the two saints did not escape her. Right in the beginning of *Life* Teresa compared herself to Augustine. "When I started to read the *Confessions* I seemed to see myself in them," and "it seemed exactly as if the Lord were speaking in that way to me,"[32] Teresa wrote, thus using the comparison to establish her fundamental belief in the equality of men and women before God.

Teresa, of course, was aware that the world did not treat men and women the same way, and certain passages, when isolated, might lead the reader to conclude that she agreed with the unequal treatment. Parenthical comments such as "as we women are not learned or fine-witted," and "women, especially so, since we are very weak"[33] are strewn throughout her works, but when studied in context Teresa's true intent becomes clear. As Alison Weber argues so persuasively, "Teresa wrote as she believed women were perceived to speak."[34] Teresa's short yet groundbreaking *Conceptions of Love of God* provides a dramatic example of this use of "the rhetoric of femininity" to communicate her belief in women's spiritual parity. First of all, the work was a commentary addressed to women on the Song of Songs, a most difficult book to gloss and a task traditionally reserved to men. When Teresa "showed [her confessor] a book on the *Songs* that she had written," Maria de San José testified at Teresa's canonization procedures, "he had ordered it to be burned, because it did not seem suitable to him that a woman should write on the Songs."[35] But we know from the work itself that Teresa anticipated such reaction and dismissed it as irrelevant. In fact, it was the very fact that the Song of Songs was difficult for women to comprehend that led her to write the commentary. She approached her task, therefore, careful not to offend some by her innovation, and intent upon persuading all of the wisdom of her goal. "When you read some book or hear a sermon or think upon the mysteries of our sacred Faith and find you cannot properly understand the subject, I strongly recommend you not to tire yourselves or strain your powers of thought by splitting hairs over it; it is something not meant for women"—and here she inserts her gentle qualifier—"and many such things are not meant for men either!" It is up to the Lord "to explain the matter to us" through people, male or female, whom He "has chosen to expound such things,"[36] like Teresa. "As I love learning what the Lord has to teach me when I hear any part of the Canticles, my hope is that, if I tell you something about it, you may be perhaps be comforted by it, as I am." She respectfully acknowledged the limitations men had imposed on women, but again subtly reminded all that ultimately God's law was the only one that counted: "I shall interpret these in my own way; for, providing I do not depart from what is held by the Church and the Saints (and very learned men will examine my book from this standpoint before you see it), the Lord,

I think, allows this." Teresa even confessed to some personal satisfaction from her undertaking. She did it willingly because "we women need not entirely refrain from enjoyment of the Lord's riches," and because "I like telling you about my meditations, as you are my daughters."[37]

Teresa's contributions to the tradition of spiritual equality, however, cannot be fully appreciated by citing a passage here, a passage there. Her entire life—her theology, her reform work, her literary accomplishments, her personal relationships, her spiritual direction—is an essential witness to the tradition. In her mystical ecstasy she was fully aware of her spiritual dignity, but she still had moments of doubt about her activity, especially her establishment of new monasteries. After "wondering if the people were right who disapproved of my going out to make foundations," Teresa repeated God's answer. "It seemed to me that, considering what Saint Paul says about women keeping at home (I have recently been reminded of this and I had already heard of it), this might be God's will. He said to me: 'Tell them they are not to be guided by one part of Scripture alone, but to look at others; ask them if they suppose they will be able to tie My hands.'"[38] Men might limit women, but God did not.

That she was aware of the attitudes of the times and of the unreconciled differences between the two Christians traditions toward women is evident in her earnest plea for the positive tradition in the preamble of *Way of Perfection*. The work contains Teresa's description of the prayer of quiet,[39] but first she stated her position about women's spiritual worth in prayer form.

> . . . when Thou were in the world Lord, Thou did not despise women, but did always help them and show them great compassion. Thou did find more faith and no less love in them than in men. . . . We can do nothing in public that is of any use to Thee, nor dare we speak of some of the truths over which we weep in secret, lest Thou should not hear this our just petition. Yet Lord I cannot believe this of Thy goodness and righteousness, for Thou are a righteous Judge, not like judges in the world, who, being, after all, men and sons of Adam, refuse to consider any woman's virtue as above suspicion. Yes, my King, but the day will come when all will be known . . . when I see what the times are like, I feel it is not right to repel spirits which are virtuous and brave, even though they be the spirits of women.[40]

Times were changing, and proponents of women's spiritual equality such as Teresa were responding by defending the tradition more explicitly and with greater zeal.

The women within Teresa's reformed Carmelite Order continued to respond after her death, sometimes even surpassing her in determination. In fact, some of the most powerful apologies of the period came from Carmelite women. Unlike Teresa's works, few of them circulated in their own day, and so they are more representative than influential. From them we gain a sense of the everyday frustrations that women experienced in this time of religious upheaval. The women learned very quickly that "the heroic virtues of so many weak women" were bewildering to men "in these flowering times of renewal."[41] In Maria de San José's *Recreations* the main character Gracia recalled how a visiting priest "grew very angry when he saw us crossing ourselves in Latin," and "scolding us," told them "women should on no account meddle in all sorts of erudite babble." When another woman, Justa, dismissed the comment as inconsequential because "he must have been a bit simple" if he did not know that nuns were obligated to recite the Office, Gracia responded exasperatingly, "Simple, Sister! He didn't act as a simpleton, for he was very far indeed from any such thing; but there are people who are shocked by a puff of wind, and if I were to relate to you all the trials and persecutions we underwent in that foundation [of their new monastery], with all sorts of dispositions, I would never finish telling them all." Gracia had enough sense to know that discussing "matters of faith which every Christian is obliged to know" was not heresy, but other women "suffered mightily, being made to think they were heretics." As what they say "is given no credence at all because we are women," Gracia wondered whether they should even bother to record the life of Teresa, but Justa put things in their proper spiritual perspective. "What does that matter to us? Those for whom this is written"—Carmelite women—"will believe it," and, more important, it will "please God." God chose Teresa, a woman, to do his work, and she did; she "shamed the men, and dragged them out to the field of battle, and when they had turned their backs on discipline and primitive virtue, made them follow the banner of their woman Captain."[42] For men living in an increasingly secular world that possessed no tradition of women's equality, abiding by spiritual standards of women's equality was difficult at best.

The women's sense of spiritual independence rather than inferiority was also communicated in their writing. Ana de San Bartolomé wrote that when her confessor thought that her prayer was from the devil, she simply bypassed him and went to Teresa for advice. "She told me not to worry, that it was not the Devil, for she had gone through that same way of prayer, with confessors who did not understand it."[43] Later when Ana was sent to Paris to establish a monastery there, her spiritual independence from the Carmelite Order's patron, Pierre Bérulle, was a source of friction. "And for a whole hour he was disputing points in the Constitution and the Rule (of the Order) about some things he wanted to change. I contradicted him, and he said he knew these things quite as well as I. I told him that was not so; that he must be great in book-learning, but that he had no experience, as I did, of matters concerning the Order, and that I would never agree to it."[44]

With the overpowering example of Teresa before them, these women were quite confident of their spiritual status. "I know that what I say is true," proclaimed Cecilia del Nacimiento, "and that One who can do so puts me in this state, for He is the Lord, who can work His divine will in all things as He pleases."[45] Men could not restrict God's gifts to women, nor should they want to, for it contradicted God's wishes and Christianity's tradition of spiritual equality. "How are we to view the fact that the Church permitted a Gertrude, a Teresa, a Birgitta, the nun of Agreda, and so many others to write" about God's gifts, Juana Inés de la Cruz herself wrote in New Spain, if it was wrong? "Men, who merely for being men, believe they are wise," are not the only ones in whom God worked his will.[46]

In the post-Gutenburg world literature achieved a new importance, and women like Juana were quick to note that the Pauline prohibition against women's church activities did not specifically include writing. Now that the written word was challenging the dominant position of preaching in communication to the masses, women's literature took on new significance. Juana used an argument in Arce's *Bibliorum* to bolster her case for women authors; Juana and Arce both argued that the injunction in 1 Corinthians was tempered by other passages, especially those in Titus, and that, therefore, for women "to study, write, and teach privately not only is permissible, but most advantageous."[47] Juana then quoted numerous examples from Jerome's letters ("Eustochium and Fabiola, and Marcella her sister, and Pacatula, and others whom the Saint honors") as evidence of his agreement with her.[48] Maria de San José commented that women "also have the duty, as do men, of recording the virtues and good works of their mothers and teachers," which in all probability "will be better suited to the women in days to come, than if they were written by men."[49] Marie Dentière, a French abbess turned Calvinist, argued in a letter to Marguerite, Queen of Navarre, the case for women authors even more strenuously, rooting her defense in women's spiritual equality and, at the same time, proving the issue was not solely a Catholic Hispanic concern.

> For we ought not, any more than men, hide and bury within the earth that which God has given you and revealed to us women. Although we are not permitted to preach in assemblies and public churches, never-

theless we are not prohibited from writing and advising one another in all charity. . . . Even to the present day this has been so hidden that one would not dare say a word and it seemed that women ought not read anything or listen to the Holy Scripture. This is my principal cause, my lady, that which has moved me to write to you. . . . If God has given graces to some good women, revealing to them something holy and good through His Holy Scriptures, should they, for the sake of the defamers of truth, refrain from writing down, speaking, or declaring it to each other? Ah, it would be too impudent to hide the talent which God has given us, we who ought to have the grace to persevere to the end. Amen![50]

The French religious situation was, however, considerably different from the Hispanic, and hence the tradition of spiritual equality manifested itself in different ways. Teresian reform revived the contemplative life in Spain, and while her reform spread north of the Pyrenees, it was the active life that caught the imagination of the French. The seventeenth century saw pioneers such as Jane de Chantal, Marguerite Naseau, Louise de Marillac, and Madame Goussault institutionalize new areas of spiritual ministry. Religious orders for women interested in nursing and teaching were first found in Italy during the Late Middle Ages[51] but did not catch fire throughout the West until the societal need for them increased in the early modern period. Urbanization made the need to care for the indigent sick more visible and pressing.[52] "The situation in Paris is so bad," wrote Vincent de Paul, "that Mademoiselle Le Gras [Louise] does not have enough sisters to care for the sick and the poor refugees in all the places where people are requesting them. Soup is prepared for them in a large number of parishes; our Sisters at Saint-Paul distribute it daily to almost eight thousand poor persons, both the bashful poor and the refugees, not counting the sixty to eighty patients they have on their hands."[53] The Reformation also spurred denominations to educate their children according to their own beliefs. The need in England was so acute that parents sent children abroad, as we see in this memorial: "Barbara Babthorpe, Anne Gogs, and Mary Ward declare that, seeing the necessities of the Catholics in England, and the difficulty they lie under of bringing up their children in the Catholic faith, and desiring to offer themselves to the service of God for the education and instruction of such children . . . have settled themselves with other young English ladies" in St. Omer to await the daughters "many Catholic nobles intend to send" so they can be "brought up as Catholic under the care of the said Ladies."[54]

There was no ready institution or profession to educate or to nurse the needy, and Catholic women responded by creating religious orders to meet those needs. Since women had no legal, social, or economic parity with which they could establish their credibility, they used the tradition of spiritual equality to break across old barriers into those previously forbidden realms of service. It was an uphill struggle with many discouraging moments, but by the end of the seventeenth century there were dozens of active religious communities throughout Europe and thousands of women teachers and nurses.

Acceptance of novel forms of spiritual activity in a period when all behavior was scrutinized for orthodox religious motives was accomplished most often by men and women working together. Women took on the roles of practical organizers, policy makers, and implementers, while men became the defenders, advocates, and promoters in the drive to gain approval of the church and society. Two of the more famous of these relationships were Jane de Chantal and Francis de Sales, and Louise de Marillac and Vincent de Paul, but there were many, many more in this age of spiritual friendship.[55] Fundamental to the relationships was an acknowledgment of spiritual equality. The most convincing evidence of this equality is found in the fruits of these friendships; approximately eighteen new teaching orders were established in France alone by 1640.[56] Prohibited from teaching about religious matters when schools were few, women ironically were the mainstay of religious education when schools became plentiful. How many girls and boys received their religious instruction from women during the period is unknown, but it goes against common sense to suppose that pupils did not subliminally receive a message from their female teachers about women's spiritual equality along with the doctrine.

Correspondence among the men and women involved in this movement is marked with references to spiritual equality and even the abandonment of secular inequality. When Noel Brulart, a well-connected French ambassador to Spain and Rome, wrote and asked Jane to be his spiritual director, he recognized that her spiritual state indeed overshadowed any other consideration, a point Jane comments on: "I see plainly by the gracious, candid tone of your letter that you are writing, not according to your rank in the world, but as a true servant of God."[57] One of the earliest orders of women to engage in the active life, the Ursulines, enshrined this principle in their rule: "God is not a discriminator of persons, but gives His grace to all with free hand . . . and often many of those who are deemed noble in the eyes of men, are little and vile in the sight of the Divine Majesty."[58] Even ecclesiastical ranks were shunned. "I have nothing else to say about that except that you should not write 'bishop' or any other formality in your letters," wrote Francis de Sales to Madame de Limojon. "I am not someone who stands on ceremony, but I am someone who loves and honors you with my whole heart for many reasons."[59] Worldly categories of class, gender, and rank should not enter into spiritual relationships, because in the spiritual realm all are equal. "Write to me whenever you wish, without ceremony or fear; do not let respect stand in the way of the love that God wants us to have for each other," wrote Francis to Angelique Arnauld and likewise to Madame de Villesavin.[60] If anything, God's standings run counter to worldly status. "Remember, my daughters, that God began the Church with poor people," not with the rich and the powerful, as Vincent preached.[61] The Rule of Angela Merici argues the case for the superiority of one's spiritual status thus: "Since to you, my most dear Daughters and Sisters, God has given grace to withdraw from the darkness of this miserable world and to work together for His Divine Majesty, you owe Him infinite thanks that to you specially He has conceded so singular a gift: because how many great persons there are, empresses, queens, duchesses, and the like, that would wish to be considered one of the least of your handmaids, esteeming your condition so much more worthy, so much better than their own?"[62]

As we can see, one of the results of early modern Europe's social needs meeting head on with Christianity's tradition of women's spiritual equality in the Roman church was that women became even more active in church ministries. "The end for which God sent" Daughters of Charity into parishes, according to their rule, was "to serve the sick poor not only corporally, by giving them food and medicine, but spiritually also"; this ministering "shall consist principally in consoling and encouraging salvation, teaching them to make acts of Faith, Hope, and Charity towards God and their neighbor, of contrition for their sins . . . to prepare them to make a good general confession."[63] As the Rule of Angela Merici succinctly put it, "All of them must carry on some charitable work, especially that of Christian instruction";[64] and as Vincent told the Daughters of Charity, "The lives of 10,000 persons depend perhaps on your fidelity. . . . You may perhaps be the cause of the salvation of many who would otherwise be lost."[65] Although physical situations precipitated society's need for nurses, the justification for women's involvement in nursing still remained rooted in the spiritual: "You are not to attend their bodies solely, you are also to help them to save their souls."[66]

The Counter-Reformation world where these activities flourished popularized an individualized spirituality for the masses. There were variants of Counter-Reformation spirituality—Salesian, Teresian, French School, Ignatian—but common to all was a humanistic emphasis on the dignity of the person individually called by God "to bring forth the fruits, each one according to its kind," in Francis de Sales's words. "Devotion ought, then, to be not only differently exercised by the gentleman, the tradesman, the servant, the prince, the widow, the maid, and the married woman, but its practice should be also adapted to the strength, the employments, and obligations of each one in particular."[67] Counter-Reformation spirituality was also flexible: "It is an error or rather a heresy, to say that devotion" is limited only to the contemplative, monastic, and religious. "Besides these three kinds of devotion, there are several others proper to conduct to perfection those who live in the secular state," Francis continued. Ignatius of Loyola specifically stated that his "spiritual exercises must be adapted to the nature of those who wish to undergo them."[68]

Women were not incidentally included in this democratic spirituality. "Woman," Francis wrote, "no less than man, enjoys the favour of having been made in the image of God: the honour is done equally to both sexes; their virtues are equal; to each of them is offered an equal reward; and if they sin, a similar damnation. I would not want woman to say: I am frail, my condition is weak. This weakness is of the flesh, but virtue which is strong and powerful is seated in the soul."[69] Women themselves also rebut the idea of their inherent inferiority in spiritual matters. "Let not your Reverence fear my woman's weakness," wrote Juana de Cardona to Ignatius, "because when the Lord sets his hand, he makes the weak strong, and when he removes his hand, the strong become weak."[70]

Furthermore, women were actively involved in the formation of the new spirituality. Even Ignatian spirituality, the only one not influenced by Teresa (it predates her), still had marks imprinted by Ignatius's women friends.[71] The French School's roots were Teresian, and it was nourished by Madame Acarie, Marguerite de Gondi, Marie Lumagne, Madeleine de Saint-Joseph, and informal pious groups of women such as the Saints and the *dévotes*. Wendy Wright and Joseph Power argue that Salesian spirituality was a misnomer, that it was the product of Jane de Chantal as much as Francis;[72] this is in addition to Teresa's long-acknowledged influence on Salesian spirituality.[73] Models of female sanctity were held up by both men and women for imitation. Teresa was, of course, referred to probably by every spiritual writer of the period, just as she referred to women saints who preceded her and to saintly contemporary women "beloved by so many important persons."[74] Bérulle possessed a particularly intense devotion to Mary Magdalene, and his attraction was to her authority. Just as a woman was the first person Jesus saw when born, a woman was first when he was reborn. "Your first words were to Magdalene. The first name you pronounced was her name," wrote Bérulle, and "the first commission you gave" was to Magdalene, "making her an apostle" above all other apostles: "An apostle to your apostles." He continues: "In this case, you make Magdalene your apostle in your state of glory. In this new state you make her alone an apostle, an apostle of your life only, for she will proclaim and make public only your life, power, and glory. You make her an apostle not to the world, but to the very apostles of the world and to the universal pastors of your church because you are so pleased to highlight the honor and the love of her soul."[75] One can see how such an image of Mary Magdalene reinforced and justified women's new venture into the active apostolate.

Not everyone, though, was interested in extending women's religious activities. Many tried to restrain them, sometimes even by persecution. England presents us with two examples, one Protestant, the other Roman, in which women's religious activities were repressed violently. What is telling is the women's defense.

The first example concerns numerous women martyred under Catholic Queen Mary of England for their Protestant leanings. John Foxe's record of their history, trial, and defense leaves us with many impressions, not the least of which is the spiritual conviction of these women. "You be not able to resist the Spirit of God in me, a poor woman," Alice Driven proclaimed at her examination. "In the defense of God's truth, and in the cause of my master Christ, by his grace I will set my foot against the foot of any of you all, in the maintenance and defense of the same."[76] Woman after woman announced the same. "Do what ye will; for if Christ were in error, then am I in an error," Elizabeth Warne challenged.[77] Identification with Christ is what mattered, not gender. "Are not we created of the same matter, that men are? Yea, after God's image and similitude are we made, as lyvely as they,"[78] Foxe reported an early Christian martyr saying. When supporters of a woman called "Prest's wife" tried to gain her release from execution by claiming she was but "an unlearned woman," she retorted indignantly, "I am not." Furthermore, "I will never turn from my heavenly husband to my earthly husband; from the fellowship of angels, to mortal children."[79] As strong as her temporal identification as wife and mother was, stronger still was her spiritual identification.

The second example is the recusant Mary Ward. Although her spiritual activities did not lead to execution, she was imprisoned briefly because of them. Founder of the English Ladies, Mary often was frustrated in her attempt to get formal approval for her teaching order. Part of the problem was her desire to model the group after the Jesuits[80] and part was the general uneasiness that all women's religious behavior engendered in the seventeenth century. Mary's celebrated Verity speech is often cited for good reason; while it summarizes well the beliefs driving much of women's religious activity in the period, it also is an excellent testimony to Christianity's tradition of spiritual equality and to the challenge confronting the tradition in Mary's day. When some of the English Ladies questioned Mary about a remark a priest made about their community being doomed to failure because "their fervour will decay . . . when all is done, they are but women!" Mary answered:

> Fervour is a will to do good, that is, a preventing grace of God, and a gift given gratis from God, which we could not merit. It is true fervour does many times grow cold, but what is the cause? Is it because we are women? No, because we are imperfect women. There is no such difference between men and women. Therefore it is not because we are women, but, as I have said before, because we are imperfect women, and love not verity. . . . It is not *veritas hominis,* verity of men, nor verity of women, but *veritas Domini,* and this verity women may have as well as men. If we fail, it is for want of this verity, and not because we are women.[81]

In previous eras we have proceeded from a discussion of the opinions of Christian leaders to an exploration of the religious culture of the day, but we will not do so here; conditions in the West after the Reformation make the value of such an approach questionable. The cultural unity of the West and of Christianity was dramatically affected by the disagreements within Christianity, by the loss of Rome as a focal point, and by the rise of the national state. In previous periods we could assume most Christians were exposed to the elements being discussed, but we can no longer make such assumptions. Roman Catholics developed a culture distinct from Protestants, Lutherans developed a culture distinct from Anabaptists, Swiss Calvinists' culture was distinct from Scottish Calvinists', and so on. The tradition of women's spiritual equality continued unabated within each group, but now it was rigidly compartmentalized and restricted to that group.[82] More significant than even this loss of cultural unity was religion's loss of dominance. The Age of Reason began replacing the Age of Faith. The question of women's religious equality was still important, but more important was the question of women's equality in general. For an answer to this question an increasing number of people turned to reason rather than to faith.

An example of these developments can be seen in the polemic literature produced in England on the subject of women's worth during the late sixteenth and early seventeenth centuries. While such debates had been occurring since antiquity,[83] analysis of the writings reveal that three new factors were added during this period. First, women were active debaters in the controversy. The spread of literacy and the availability of publishing helped make women's entrance into the debate possible, but anger was also a factor. Playing on her name, Jane Anger trumpeted that "it was ANGER that did write" her pamphlet, *Protection for Women to defend them against Scandalous Reports*,[84] while Esther Sowernam wrote because the author of *The Arraignment of Women* did "rage and rail generally against all the whole sex of women;" she "in defense of our Sex, began an answer to that shameful Pamphlet."[85] Second, the debate now included more participants from the burgeoning middle class than from the religious or intellectual class, and took place in everyday life rather than in universities or monasteries. Sowernam gave us a sense of how widespread the debates were when she described the setting for one debate: "[B]eing at supper amongst friends where the number of each sex were equal, as nothing is more usual for table talk, there fell out a discourse concerning women, some defenders, others objecting against our sex."[86] Finally, the discourse was concerned primarily with debating society's views of women in matters concerning this world. Mary Tattlewell and Joan Hit-him-home claimed most pamphlets were composed simply to blame women for all men's problems: "Some they have taxed with incontinence, some with incivility, some with scolding, some with drinking, some with backbiting and slandering their neighbors, some with a continual delight in lying, some with an extraordinary desire of perpetual gossiping."[87] They were, in other words, secular debates. Religious arguments and scripture were ostensively included in the literature, but they were rarely central to the debate. Sowernam claimed Joseph Swetnam misused Scripture deliberately and "wrested out of Scripture" only those passages that he could quote "to dishonor and abuse all women."[88] In *The Schoolhouse of women*, the author (probably Edward Gosynhill) made reference to Eve being created out of Adam's rib—"Crooked it was, stiff and sturdy"—in order to prove that in his day "of that condition all women be, Evil to rule, both stiff and sturdy."[89] Swetnam likewise used Eve's creation to denigrate women in his own day. "Let us consider the times past with the time present," he wrote, after stating that Genesis "Saith that [women] were made of the rib of a man, and that their forward nature showeth; for a rib is a crooked thing good for nothing else, and women are crooked by nature."[90] Because Esther Sowernam believed Swetnam "hath been long unanswered," she retorted thus: "Woman was made of a crooked rib, so she is crooked of conditions; Joseph Swetnam was made as from Adam of clay and dust, so he is of a dirty and muddy disposition."[91] This indeed is a clever reply but certainly not a religious argument. Adam and Eve served more as an authoritative literary allusion in the controversy than a definitive part of Revelation. In all of the controversy's pamphlets the writers' goals were similar, to promote their own particular interpretation of women's position relative to men's position in this world. If a more effective argument could be made by recalling aspects of Scripture, so be it. Tattlewell and Hit-him-home accused their detractors of just that when they complained that women "are set only to the Needle, to prick our fingers, or else to the Wheel to spin" by men who designate women "by the name of weaker Vessels," a favorite reference to 1 Peter 3:7.[92]

It is with the French of the seventeenth century that the shift in emphasis becomes undeniable. We know now that the attack upon Christianity was not nearly as complete or victorious as many Enlightenment *philosophes* themselves, or many scholars since, have thought. Much of Christianity was incorporated into Enlightenment programs, albeit severed from its religious roots. The process by which the *philosophes* secularized Christian ideas was in many instances highly successful,[93] but in matters concerning women it was not. Christian theology and Christian culture had provided society with a foundation for women's equality. True, it was equality only within that theology and culture, but it was an equality couched in a strong and enduring tradition. As long as Christian theology articulated society's self-understanding and as long as Christian culture was synonymous with society's culture, women had a tradition within which they could function and find a degree of respite from misogynist attitudes. When *philosophes* and Enlightenment society attacked religion and advocated reason in its place, the tradition of spiritual equality remained central to that religion but peripheral to the larger society. Unfortunately, society had no strong and enduring tradition of women's equality in realms other than religion, and the position of women suffered accordingly.

Enlightenment philosophies dealt with the question of women's worth directly and in the context of their two chief tenets: faith in reason and reverence for nature. The *philosophes* reasoned that humanity was by nature inherently free, and they recognized that women were half of humanity. Beyond those statements, however, they held few enlightened positions on the nature of woman. In the scientific realm they possessed only a tradition that promoted the inferiority of women. "In physique," wrote Voltaire, "woman is weaker than man on account of her physiology."[94] In sexuality, "there is no parity between the two sexes," according to Rousseau.[95] In psychology, he explained, "the search for abstract and speculative truths, principles, axioms in the sciences, and everything that tends to generalize ideas is not within the compass of women."[96] In intellectual matters, the *philosophes* inherited traditions that believed women did not possess the ability to participate in rational discussions. "Reason is never found," Montesquieu wrote in agreement with that tradition, "among those with beauty,"[97] nor was logic within the grasp of women, according to Diderot: "Logic is a rare possession: an infinite number of men do not possess it, and hardly any women at all."[98] Likewise, argued Boucher d'Argis, women's frailty did not allow them to be active politically: "Men, because of the prerogatives of their sex and the strength of their temperament, are by nature capable of all types of jobs and occupations, while women, as a result of the frailty of their sex and of their natural delicacy, are excluded from some functions and incapable of performing certain occupations. . . . [Consequently] women are not admitted to public office; thus they are not able to become judges, nor perform as magistrates, nor function as advocates or prosecuting attorneys."[99] Women were soon to discover that if they wanted equality in a secularized world, they must pioneer in the establishment of new traditions suited for that world. It was an arduous task that to date has not been completed.

Epilogue

As WE CAN NOW CONFIDENTLY ASSERT, Christianity did indeed possess a strong and enduring tradition of women's spiritual equality. Are we then to praise Christianity for its ability to establish and maintain the one lone tradition of equality that Western women possessed for a millennium and a half, or to fault it for its failure to force the whole of society to adopt similar traditions of equality in all other realms? Perhaps we should do both. That Christians adopted, promoted, defended, and preserved such a unique tradition is an outstanding contribution in the history of humanity, and this fact should be proclaimed more frequently and vigorously than it has in the past. The very real effects this tradition had on the lives of innumerable women throughout the centuries often is overlooked because we no longer live in a predominantly religious society. To those who lived in a religious world, though, the effects were quite clear; one's religious status was ultimately the only status that mattered. No, spiritual equality did not alleviate the sufferings women had to endure because of inequalities in all other realms. Even at the height of its power, the tradition was never strong enough to permeate more than a few areas of society, nor did its proponents try very hard, and for that Christians should be duly chastised. Spiritual equality for Christian women should have led to their social equality in a Christian society, and it did not. To be fair and balanced in our historical judgments, however, we must give Christianity credit for what it did accomplish. If a woman lived deep within the culture of Christian society, she could—and a vast number of women did—experience real social benefits from her spiritual equality, above and beyond the spiritual benefits promised. More important, the Christian tradition of women's spiritual equality broke new ground, and from any perspective this was a positive contribution to the history of women. Yes, Christian culture and theology also nurtured and protected a misogynist tradition, but in this Christianity was not a pioneer. Rather, it reinforced and borrowed from already existing misogynist traditions, and when it tolerated and even contributed to their presence, Christianity unfortunately strengthened many of them. Nevertheless, the existence of misogynist voices in the public discourse must not negate the historical value of the tradition we have been documenting here. We must acknowledge that Christians had more than one voice in the discourse on women, and that that voice was indeed a penetrating, powerful, and positive one.

Abbreviations

AASS   *Acta sanctorum.* Edited by Jean Carnandlt. 2nd ed. Paris: V. Palme, 1863.

ANF   *The Ante-Nicene Fathers: Translations of the Fathers down to A.D. 325.* Edited by Alexander Roberts and James Donaldson. Vols. 10. American reprint of the Edinburgh edition. New York: Charles Scribner's Sons, 1903.

MGH   *Monumenta Germaniae historica.* Hannover and Leipzig, 1826-.

NPNF   *The Nicene and Post-Nicene Fathers of the Christian Church.* Second series. Edited by Philip Schaff and Henry Wace. Vols. 14. New York: Charles Scribner's Sons, 1904.

PL   *Patrologicae cursus completus, series latina.* Edited by Jean-Paul Migne. Vols. 221. Paris, 1844-1864.

Notes

Introduction

1. See, for example, Martin Marty's foreword to Alvin Schmidt, *Veiled and Silenced* (Macon, GA: Mercer University Press, 1989), vii-ix, where he tells us that "the author pursues evidence—as if anyone needed it" to prove the church misogynist.

2. Examples of such works would be: Stephen Benko, *The Virgin Goddess* (Leiden: E.J. Brill, 1993); Patricia Miller, "The Devil's Gateway: An Eros of Difference in the Dreams of Perpetua," *Dreaming* 2:1 (1992), 45-63; and introductions to texts in Brigitte Cazelles, *The Lady as Saint* (Philadelphia: University of Pennsylvania Press, 1991).

3. Carolyn Walker Bynum, *Fragmentation and Redemption* (New York: Zone Books, 1991), 16.

Chapter 1
The Spiritual Nature of Woman in Scripture
and Early Christian Writings

1. The beginning of the verse, "Notwithstanding she shall be saved in childbearing," refers to Genesis 3:16-19, where Yahweh is meting out the physical punishments for Adam's and for Eve's transgression.

2. Elizabeth Schussler Fiorenza, *In Memory of Her* (New York: Crossroad, 1984), 226-229.

3. Eusebius, *The History of the Church from Christ to Constantine*, trans. G. A. Williamson (Harmondsworth: Dorset Press, 1965), 3:16.

4. *First Epistle of Clement to the Corinthians*, 33, in *ANF*, 1:13-14.

5. *Epistle of Barnabas*, 6, in ibid., 1:140.

6. This is the argument of Douglas J. Hall, *Imaging God* (Grand Rapids, MI: Wm. B. Eerdmans Publishing Co., 1986).

7. Clement of Alexandria, *Stromata*, 1:5, in *ANF*, 2:305.

8. Clement of Alexandria, *The Instructor*, 1:3, in *ANF*, 2:210-211.

9. Ibid.,1:4, in *ANF*, 2:211.

10. Clement of Alexandria, *Stromata*, 4:8, in *ANF*, 2:419-421.

11. Ibid., 2:420.

12. Clement of Alexandria, *Exhortation to the Heathen*, 6, in *ANF*, 2:203.

13. Clement of Alexandria, *Stromata*, 4:19, in *ANF*, 2:431.

14. Ireneaus, *Against Heresies*, 3:23.1-2, in *ANF*, 1:455-456. See also 5:1; 4:20.1; 1:24.1; 1:30.6; 4:20.1; and 5:16.1, in *ANF*, 315-567.

15. Ibid., 5:16.2, in *ANF*, 1:544.

16. Ibid., 5:6.1, in *ANF*, 1:531-32.

17. Ibid., 5:6.1 in *ANF*, 1:532.

18. Ibid., 5:6.2 in *ANF*, 1:532.

19. Ibid., 4:20.2 in *ANF*, 1:488.

20. Ibid., 4:20.5 in *ANF*, 1:489.

21. Athenagoras the Athenian, *Treatise on the Resurrection of the Dead*, 15, in *ANF*, 2:157.

22. Ibid.

23. Ibid., 27, in *ANF*, 2:105.

24. Ibid., 28, in *ANF*, 2:105.

25. Tertullian, *Against Marcion*, 1:24, in *ANF*, 3:290.

26. Tertullian, *To His Wife*, 1:4, in *ANF*, 4:41.

27. Jean LaPorte, *The Role of Woman in Early Christianity* (New York: The Edwin Mellen Press, 1982), 27.

28. Tertullian, *Wife*, 2:7, in *ANF*, 4:48.

29.   Origen, *Homilies on Genesis*, 1.13, in Origen, *Homilies on Genesis and Exodus*, trans. Ronald E. Heine (Washington, DC: Catholic University of America Press, 1981), 63. This distinction is made repeatedly throughout Origen's works. See H. Crouzel, *Theologie de l'image de Dieu chez Origène* (Paris: Aubier, 1956), 148-153.

30.   Origen, *Homilies in Joshua*, 9: 9, in George H. Tavard, *Woman in Christian Tradition* (Notre Dame, IN: University of Notre Dame Press, 1973), 68.

31.   See comments in Joan Ferrante, *Women as Image in Medieval Literature* (New York: Columbia University Press, 1975), 5-6; and Jaroslav Pelikan, *Eternal Feminine* (New Brunswick, NJ: Rutgers University Press, 1990), 36-37.

32.   Some later commentators disagreed. A few English reformers, for example, believed in a literal interpretation. See Matthew's Bible's heading for the book: "A mystical device of the spiritual and godly love between Christ, the spouse, and the church or congregation, his spouse. Solomon made the ballad or song by himself, and his wife, the daughter of Pharaoh, under the shadow of himself, figuring Christ, and under the person of his wife, the church."

33.   *Epistle of Polycarp to the Philippians*, 3, in *ANF*, 1:33.

34.   *Martyrdom of Justin Martyr*, 3, in *ANF*, 1:306.

35.   Irenaeus, *Against Heresies*, 5:35, in *ANF*, 1:566.

36.   Tertullian, *Against Marcion*, 3:25, in *ANF*, 3:342.

37.   Origen, *De principiis*, 4:1.22, in *ANF*, 4:371.

38.   Hippolytus, *Refutation of All Heresies*, 5:2.2, in *ANF*, 5:52.

39.   Recorded by Eusebius, *Church History*, 5:1.45. Some modern scholars believe *The Shepherd of Hermes* contains the first symbolism of woman as church. See LaPorte, *Role of Women*, 138-139.

40.   Hippolytus is also the first to use the term scripture as we do today. See *Treatise on Christ and AntiChrist*, 67, in *ANF*, 5:204-219.

41.   Ibid., 61, in *ANF*, 5:217.

42.   Irenaeus, *Against Heresies*, 24.1, in *ANF*, 1:458.

43.   Cyprian, *Treatise 1: On the Unity of the Church*, 5, in *ANF*, 5:423; *Treatise 2: On the Dress of Virgins*, 3, in *ANF*, 5:431; and *Treatise 3: Of the Lapsed*, 2, in *ANF*, 5:437.

44.   Cyprian, *Of the Lapsed*, 9, in *ANF*, 5:439.

45.   Ibid., 6, in *ANF*, 5:423.

46.   Tertullian, *To the Martyrs*, 1:1 in Tertullian, *Disciplinary, Moral and Ascetical Works*, trans. A. Arbesmann, E. J. Daly, and C. A. Quain (New York: Fathers of the Church, 1959), 17.

47.   Tertullian, *Prayer*, 2:6, in ibid., 160.

48.   Tertullian tells us in *Against Marcion*, 3:25, in *ANF* 3:342, that he wrote "at length how the figurative interpretation is spiritually applicable to Christ and His Church," in a lost treatise, *De Spe Fidelium*.

49.   Tertullian, *On the Soul*, 43:10, in Tertullian, *Apologetical Works and Minucius Felix Octavius*, trans. A. Arbesmann, E. J. Daly, E. A. Quain (Washington, DC: Catholic University of America Press, 1950), 277.

50.   Ibid., 11:3, in *Apologetical Works*, 203.

51.   Methodius Olympus, *Banquet of the Ten Virgins*, in *ANF*, 6:332-339.

52.   Ibid., 8:8, in *ANF*, 6:337.

53.   Tertullian, *The Apparel of Women*, 1:2, in Tertullian, *Ascetical Works*, 118.

54.   Venantius Honorius, *On Easter*, in *ANF*, 7:330.

55.   Origen, *Homily* 1:15, in *Origen on Genesis*, 68.

56.   Origen, *Commentary on the Song of Songs*, 1:1.2 in Origen, *The Song of Songs: Commentary and Homilies*, trans. K. P. Lawson (New York: Newman Press, 1957), 58-61.

57.   Origen, *Homily* 6:1, in *Genesis*, 123.

58.   Ibid., 6:1, in *Genesis*, 122; and *Homily* 11:1, in *Genesis*, 168-169.

Chapter 2
Women in Early Christian Communities

1.   James T. Burtchaell, *From Synagogue to Church: Public Services and Offices in the Earliest Christian Communities* (Cambridge: Cambridge University Press, 1992), 346.

2.   Ibid., 350.

3.   Clement of Rome, *The Letter to the Corinthians*, 37, in *The Apostolic Fathers*, trans. Francis X. Glimm, Joseph Marique and Gerald Walsh (Washington, DC: Catholic University of America Press, 1947), 39.

4.   *Didache, or Teaching of the Apostles*, 4, in ibid., 175.

5.   Tertullian, *Against Marcion*, 5:8, in *ANF*, 3:446. See also Clement of Alexandria's commentary on 1 Corinthians 12 in *The Instructor*, in *ANF*, 2:217-218.

6.   Origen, *Homily 7 on Leviticus*, n. 2, trans. in Henri de Lubac, *Catholicism* (New York: New American Library, 1964), 239.

7.   Clement of Rome, *The So-Called Second Letter*, 14, in *Apostolic Fathers*, 74.

8.   Irenaeus, *Against Heresies*, 5:6.1, in *ANF*, 1:532.

9.   Origen, *Commentary*, in Origen, *Song of Songs*, 26.

10.   *The Shepherd of Hermes*, parable 9:17.4: "[A]ll the nations that dwell under the heavens, after hearing and believing, are called by one name, that of the Son of God. So, when they receive the seal, they have an understanding and one mind. Their faith and love make them one. . . ." In *Apostolic Fathers*, 337. Also see Ignatius of Antioch, *To the Trallians*, 11-12, in ibid., 105.

11.   Clement of Alexandria, *Instructor*, 1:6, in *ANF*, 2:217.

12. Lactantius, *The Divine Institutes*, 7:4, trans. M. F. McDonald (Washington, DC: Catholic University of American Press, 1964), 480-481.

13. Cyprian, *On the Unity of the Church*, 4-5, in *ANF*, 5:422-423.

14. Cyprian, *On the Lord's Prayer*, 8, in *ANF*, 5:449.

15. Ibid., 5, in *ANF*, 5:448-449. See below, n. 27-29.

16. Orazio Marucchi, *Christian Epigraphy*, trans. J. A. Willis (Chicago: Ares Publishers, repr. 1974), 169.

17. Ibid., 160 (cemetery of Callistro), and 163 (cemetery of SS. Peter and Marcellinus).

18. Ibid., 161.

19. Ibid., 162.

20. Many first- and second-century writings, however, often were read to the assembly, and so a significant number of Christians probably were exposed to them.

21. The description itself is Acts 4:32-35, and medieval Christians used it as the model for the *vita apostolica*. Acts 5:12 also uses the phrase "with one accord" (*homolhumadin*).

22. For example, the prayers in Acts 4:24-30 just cited; the Our Father; the Benedictus; the Magnificant; Matthew 11:25-26; Luke 10:21; Romans 1:8-9; and 2 Corinthians 1:3.

23. *Didache*, 8:3, in *Apostolic Fathers*, 178.

24. Paul F. Bradshaw, *Daily Prayer in the Early Church* (New York: Oxford University Press, 1982), 45.

25. Tertullian, *Prayer*, 2:2-4, in *Ascetical Works*, 159-160.

26. Ibid., 2:5-7, in *Ascetical Works*, 160.

27. Cyprian, *On the Lord's Prayer*, 5, in *ANF*, 5:448.

28. Ibid., 36, in *ANF*, 457.

29. Cf. Clement, *Corinthians*, 61-64, in *Apostolic Fathers*, 56-58, and *Didache*, 9:2-4, in *Apostolic Fathers*, 178-179.

30. *The Treatise on the Apostolic Tradition of St. Hippolytes of Rome*, ed. Gregory Dix (London: Society for Promoting Christian Knowledge, 1937), 36 ff. The same themes are found in *The First Apology of Justin*, 61, in *ANF*, 1:183.

31. *Didache*, 9-10, in *Apostolic Fathers*, 178-180.

32. Justin Martyr, *The First Apology of Justin*, 67, in *ANF*, 1:185-186.

33. Examples are numerous. See Deuteronomy 10:18, 14:29, 16:11; 24:17-22; 26:12-13; Psalms 68:5; and Exodus 22:20-23.

34. Polycarp, *To Philadelphians*, 4:3, in *Apostolic Fathers*, 137.

35. *Constitution of the Holy Apostles*, 3:1.6, in *ANF*, 7:428. The whole of Book 3, section one, discusses widows.

36.   *Didascalia et Constitutiones Apostolorum,* ed. F. X. Funk (Paderborn: F. Schoeningh, 1905), 1:50. For later commentaries, see J. P. Arendzen, "An Entire Syriac Text on the *Apostolic Church Order," Journal of Theological Studies* 3 (1902), 59-80, and *The Testament of Our Lord,* 40-43, trans. James Cooper and A. J. Maclean (Edinburgh: T. and T. Clark, 1902), 105-111. In *The Testament* we have a rite of installation.

37.   The noun *martus,* witness, and the verb *martutein,* to bear witness, are used twenty-four times in Acts. See Allison A. Trites, *The Concept of Witness in New Testament Thought* (Cambridge: Cambridge University Press, 1977) and Patricia Ranft, "The Concept of Witness in the Christian Tradition from Its Origin to Its Institutionalization," *Revue bénédictine,* 102:1-2 (1992), 9-23.

38.   James C. Sherman, *The Nature of Martyrdom* (Paterson, NJ: St. Anthony Guild Press, 1942), 3-28, identifies four stages of the diachronistic change; Allison A. Trites, *"Martus* and Martyrdom in the Apocalypse: A Semantic Study," *Novum Testamentum* 15:1 (January 1973), 72-80, identifies five.

39.   Clement, *Corinthians,* 5, in *ANF,* I:6.

40.   *Martyrdom of Polycarp,* 19, in *ANF,* 1:43.

41.   Cf. the sermons of the apostles after Pentecost: Acts 2:32; 3:15; 5:32; 10:39; and 13:31.

42.   Cf. the lengthy introduction in *The Acts of the Christian Martyrs,* trans. and intro. Herbert Musurillo (Oxford: Clarendon Press, 1972), xi-lxxiii.

43.   *The Martyrdom of Pionius the Presbyter and His Companians,* 1, in ibid., 137.

44.   Eusebius, *Church History,* 8:7.6.

45.   *The Marytrydom of Perpetua and Felicitas,* 1, in *Acts,* 107.

46.   Eusebius, *Church History,* 8:9.4.

47.   Ibid., 8:12.1.

48.   See Stuart G. Hall, "Women among the Early Martyrs," in *Martyrs and Marty-rologies,* ed. Diana Wood (Oxford: Blackwell Publisher, 1993), 1-21; and Chris Jones, "Women, Death and the Law during the Christian Persecutions," in ibid., 23-34. Hall admits he sailed into unknown waters when he researched this period, and his conclusions should be judged accordingly. My presentation here of women martyrs is somewhat at odds with his conclusions, which I believe are too negative.

49.   *The Martyrdom of Agapê, Irenê, Chionê, and Companions,* 5:1, in *Acts,* 287.

50.   Ibid, 5:8, in *Acts,* 291.

51.   *Pionius the Presbyter,* 7:6, in *Acts,* 147.

52.   *Agapê,* 3, in *Acts,* 285.

53.   *The Martyrs of Lyons,* 1, in *Acts,* 81.

54.   Eusebius, *Church History,* 6:41.18.

55.   *Agapê,* 3:7, in *Acts,* 285.

56. *The Martyrdom of Saints Carpus, Papylus and Agathonicê*, 6, in *Acts*, 35.
57. *Lyons*, 1, in *Acts*, 67.
58. Ibid., 75.
59. Ibid., 79.
60. *The Martyrdom of Saint Crispina*, 3, in *Acts*, 307.
61. Ibid.
62. Ibid., 4:1, in *Acts*, 307.
63. *Agapê*, 1, in *Acts*, 281.
64. Ibid., 4, in *Acts*, 287. An example of the influence of women martyrs on future generations is seen in the work of Hrosvitha of Gandersheim (ca. 935-973). Hrosvitha wrote the first original dramas in the West in the medieval period, and one of her plays is an adaptation of the Acts, entitled *Dulcitus* in *Hrotsvithae Opera*, ed. K. Strecker (Leipzig: B. G. Teubneri, 1906).
65. *Agapê*, 5, in *Acts*, 287-291.
66. Ibid., in *Acts*, 289.
67. Ibid., 3, in *Acts*, 285.
68. Ibid., xxv.
69. See *The Passion of SS. Perpetua and Felicity. A new edition and translation of the Latin text, together with the Sermons of S. Augustine*, trans. W. H. Shewring (London: Sheed and Ward, 1931), 45-49.
70. *Perpetua*, 3-5, in *Acts*, 109-113.
71. Ibid., 6, in *Acts*, 115.
72. Ibid., 3, in *Acts*, 109-111.
73. Ibid., 6, in *Acts*, 115.
74. Ibid., 4, in *Acts*, 111.
75. Ibid., 7, in *Acts*, 117.
76. Ibid, 10, in *Acts*, 117. For analysis of this complex vision see E. R. Dodds, *Pagan and Christian in an Age of Anxiety* (Cambridge: Cambridge University Press, 1965); Mary Ann Rossi, "The Passion of Perpetua, Everywoman of Late Antiquity" in *Pagan and Christian Anxiety: A Response to E. R. Dodds*, ed. Robert C. Smith and John Lounibos (Lanham, NY: University Press of America, 1984); and Miller, "Devil's Gateway", 62.
77. *Perpetua*, 10, in *Acts*, 119.
78. Saturas, a fellow martyr, also writes a brief account of a vision he had while imprisoned, and it is included in the act between Perpetua's account and the compiler's conclusion.
79. *Perpetua*, 15, in *Acts*, 123-125.
80. Ibid., 20, in *Acts*, 129.
81. Ibid., 21, in *Acts*, 131.
82. Ibid., 18, in *Acts*, 127.

83. Ibid., 16, in *Acts*, 125.
84. Ibid., 18, in *Acts*, 127.
85. Ibid., 4, in *Acts*, 111.
86. Ibid., 20, in *Acts*, 129.
87. Ibid., 10, in *Acts*, 117-119.

Chapter 3
Fourth-Century Theologians

1.   Gregory of Nyssa, *On the Making of Man*, 16:2, in *NPNF*, 5:404.
2.   Ibid., 16:4.
3.   Ibid., 16:5.
4.   Ibid., 5:1, in *NPNF*, 5:391.
5.   Ibid., 5:2.
6.   Ibid., 16:2, in *NPNF*, 5:404 (quote above, n.1).
7.   Ibid., 16:9, in *NPNF*, 5:405.
8.   Ibid., 16:11.
9.   Ibid.
10. Ibid., 16:17, in *NPNF*, 5:406.
11. Ibid., 16:16 and 16:18. Gerhart B. Ladner argues for the Platonic influence in Gregory of Nyssa's understanding in "The Philosophical Anthropology of Saint Gregory of Nyssa," *Dumbarton Oaks Papers* 12 (1958), 59-94.
12. Gregory, *Making*, 16:16, in *NPNF*, 5:406.
13. Ibid., 16:18.
14. Ibid., 17:1.
15. Ibid., 17:4, in *NPNF*, 5:407.
16. Ibid., 16:4, in *NPNF*, 5:404.
17. Gregory of Nyssa, *The Life of St. Macrina*, trans. W. K. Lowther Clarke (London: Society for Promoting Christian Knowledge, 1916), 966C-D.
18. Ibid., 970C.
19. Ibid., 972C-D.
20. Ibid., 970A-B.
21. Gregory of Nyssa, *On the Soul and the Resurrection*, in *NPNF*, 5:430.
22. Gregory, *Macrina*, 978B-D.
23. Cf. Arnaldo Momigliano, "The Life of St. Macrina by Gregory of Nyssa," in *The Craft of the Ancient Historian*, ed. John N. Eadie and Josiah Ober (New York: University Press of America, 1985), 443-458.
24. Gregory, *Soul*, in *NPNF*, 5:433.
25. Ibid., 5:436.

26. Ibid., 5:436-437.

27. Ibid., 5:437.

28. Ibid., 5:457.

29. Ibid., 5:448.

30. Ibid., 5:449.

31. Ibid., 5:441.

32. Ibid., 5:450.

33. Athanasius, *Against the Heathen*, 2:2, in *NPNF*, 4:5.

34. Leo the Great, Sermo 66:1, in *PL* 54, 204.

35. Hilary of Portiers, *De Trinitate*, 11, 49, in *PL* 10, 432.

36. John Chrysostom, Letter to Theodoros, 14, quoted in Tavard, *Woman*, 82.

37. John Chrysostom, letter 6:599, quoted in Rosemary Rader, "The Role of Celibacy in the Origin and Development of Christian Heterosexual Friendship," Ph.D. diss., (Stanford University, 1977), 119.

38. John Chrysostom, letter 8:12, quoted in Tavard, *Woman*, 90.

39. Jerome, letter 39, in *NPNF*, 6:49.

40. Jerome, letter 32, in *NPNF*, 6:46.

41. Jerome, letter 31, in *NPNF*, 6:45.

42. Rosemary Rader, *Breaking Boundaries. Male/Female Friendship in Early Christian Communities* (New York: Paulist Press, 1983), 5.

43. Rader, "Role of Celibacy," 24.

44. Gregory Nazianzen, *Homily 37 on Matthew*, quoted in Tavard, *Woman*, 91.

45. Theodoretos of Cyrrhos, *Therapy of Hellenic Diseases*, 5, quoted in ibid., 90.

46. Ambrose, *Hexameron*, 43 and 45, in *Saint Ambrose. Hexameron, Paradise, and Cain and Abel*, trans. John J. Savage (New York: Fathers of the Church, 1961), 256-257.

47. Ibid., 259.

48. Ambrose, *Paradise*, 73, in ibid., 351.

49. Ibid.

50. Ibid., 350.

51. The literature is vast. See, for example, Elaine Pagels, *Adam, Eve and the Serpent* (New York: Vintage Books, 1988).

52. For example, F. Ellen Weaver and Jean LaPorte, "Augustine and Women: Relationships and Teachings," *Augustinian Studies* 12 (1981), 115-132; and Kari E. Børresen, "In Defence of Augustine: How *Femina* is *Homo*," *Collectanea Augustiniana* (1990), 411-428.

53. For example, see Tavard, *Woman*.

54. See Augustine, *The Catholic and Manichaean Ways of Life*, trans. Donald A. and Idella J. Gallagher (Washington, DC: Catholic University of America Press, 1966).

55. Augustine, *The Trinity*, trans. Stephen McKenna (Washington, DC: Catholic University of America Press, 1962), 12:7.10.

56. Augustine, *The Literal Meaning of Genesis*, trans. John H. Taylor (New York: Newman Press, 1982), 3:22.

57. Augustine, *Trinity*, 12:7.12.

58. Augustine, *Eighty-Three Different Question*, trans. David L Mosher (Washington, DC: Catholic University Press, 1982), 11.

59. Augustine, *Confessions*, trans. R. S. Pine-Coffin (New York: Penguin Books, repr. 1988) 13:32.

60. Augustine, *Literal Meaning*, 3:22.

61. Augustine, *Retractions*, trans. Mary Bogan (Washington, DC: Catholic University of America Press, 1968), 2:48.2.

62. Ibid., 2:79.

63. Augustine, *Literal Meaning*, 9:37.50, quoted in Tavard, *Woman*, 117.

64. Augustine, *Confessions*, 9:8.

65. See ibid., 9:9.

66. Ibid., 1:6.

67. Ibid., 2:3.

68. Ibid., 5:8.

69. Ibid., 3:11.

70. Ibid., 5:9.

71. Ibid., 6:2.

72. Ibid., 3:11.

73. Ibid., 9:10.

74. Ibid.

75. Ibid., 4:2.

76. Ibid., 6:15.

77. Gregory Nazianzen, *On the Death of His Father*, 8, in *NPNF*, 7:257.

78. Ibid., 11, in *NPNF*, 7:258.

79. Gregory Nazianzen, *Funeral Oration on His Sister Gorgonia*, 5, in *NPNF*, 7:239.

80. Ibid., 8, in *NPNF*, 7:240.

81. *Saint Basil Letters*, trans. Agnes C. Way (Washington, DC: Catholic University of America Press, 1951), letter 52.

82. Nyssa, *Macrina*, 982D.

83. *The Letters of Paulinus of Nola*, vol.1, trans. P. G. Walsh (New York: Newman Press, 1967), 29:5.

84. *Palladius*, 46:6.

85. Quoted in Haye van der Meer, *Women Priests in the Catholic Church?*, trans. Arlene and Leonard Swidler (Philadelphia: Temple University,1973), 63. See *NPNF*, 8:69, for commentary on homily.

Chapter 4
Fourth-Century Women

1. The exceptions are Perpetua, Proba, Eudokia, and Egeria. See Patricia Wilson-Kastner and others, *A Lost Tradition* (Lanham, NY: University Press of America, 1981).

2. The debate was not limited to Christians either; the moral lapse within the Empire had brought forth a debate throughout the Mediterranean. Jovinian, Tatian, Marcion, the Manichaeans, and the Encratites presented what many thought were extreme opinions about marriage and celibacy, and theologians like Jerome, Cyprian, Origen, and Augustine formulated interpretations in response to the former group. See Denise Grodzynski, "Ravies et coupables," *Mélanges de l'école française de Rome: Antiquité* 96 (1984), 697-726.

3. In particular, see Peter Brown, "The Notion of Virginity in the Early Church," in *Christian Spirituality*, ed. Bernard McGinn, John Meyendorff, and Jean Leclerq (New York: Crossroad, 1987), 427-443; Peter Brown, *The Body and Society: Men, Women and Sexual Renunciation in Early Christianity* (New York: Columbia University Press, 1988); and Carolyn Walker Bynum, *The Resurrection of the Body in Western Christendom, 200-1336* (New York: Columbia University Press, 1995).

4. These interpretations dominate the literature from the 1960s onward. See *Religion and Sexism*, ed. Rosemary R. Ruether (New York: Simon and Schuster, 1974); *Women of the Spirit*, ed. Rosemary R. Ruether and Eleanor McLaughlin (New York: Simon and Schuster, 1979); Elizabeth Clark, *Ascetic Piety and Women's Faith* (Lewiston, NY: Edwin Mellon Press, 1986); Elizabeth Clark, "Sexual Politics in the Writings of John Chrysostom," *Anglican Theological Review* 59 (January 1977), 3-20; Jane Simpson, "Women and Asceticism in the Fourth Century: A Question of Interpretation," *Journal of Religious History* 15:1 (June 1988), 38-60. See Michel Foucault, *The History of Sexuality*, trans. Robert Hurley (New York: Pantheon Books, 1978), for insight into modern problems in interpretating the past with twentieth century's sex-obsessed colored glasses.

5. Brown, "Notion of Virginity," 428.

6. Ibid., 429.

7. Ibid., 432.

8. Ibid., 434-435.

9. Ibid., 435.

10. Ibid., 436.

11. Ibid., 435.

12. As Bynum herself notes, Brown treats the body as a locus of sexuality; she treats it as the locus of biological process. See Bynum, *Resurrection*, xviii.

13. Ibid., 13.

14. Carolyn Walker Bynum, *Holy Feast and Holy Fast* (Berkeley: University of California Press, 1987), 217.

15. The quote is from ibid., 218, originally applied to late medieval women. However, Bynum refers the reader to this opinion in her discussion of Western Christianity in general in *Resurrection*, 11, n. 17.

16. *Palladius: The Lausaic History*, trans. Robert T. Meyer (New York: Newman Press, 1964), 6:3.

17. Ibid., 34:3.

18. Ibid., 34:6.

19. Ibid., 66:2.

20. Ibid., 66:1.

21. Ibid., 67:1-2.

22. Ibid., 41:3-4.

23. Ibid., 41:1.

24. Ibid., forward, 1. See Arthur Fisher's calculations, "Women and Gender in Palladius' *Lausaic History*," *Studia Monastica* 33 (1991), 23-50, where he says there are 18,900 men and 3,095 women mentioned in the *Lausaic History*.

25. At least most of the current literature so states. Terminology is vague and imprecise, and exactly why scholars call this the first women's monastery while knowing about the sisterhood that Anthony's sister entered is not quite clear.

26. *Palladius*, 32:1.

27. Ibid., 32:8.

28. Ibid., 33:1.

29. Ibid. By Palladius's time the word *virgin* was increasingly restricted to mean a woman celibate. See also a different version, *The Bohairic Life of Pachomius* in *Pachomian Koinonia*, vol. 1, *Life of St. Pachomius*, trans. A. Veilleux (Kalamazoo: Cistercian Publication, 1980), 1:50.

30. Bynum, *Resurrection*, 59-114.

31. Ambrose, *Concerning Virgins*, 1:12.65, in *NPNF*, 10:373.

32. Jerome, Letter 127:5, in *NPNF*, 6:254.

33. Letter 127:2, in *NPNF*, 6:253.

34. Letter 127:3, in *NPNF*, 6:254.

35. Letter 127:5, in *NPNF*, 6:254-255.

36. Letter 127:9, in *NPNF*, 6:256. The controversy was over Rufinus of Aquileia's alterations of Origen's heretical passages in *On First Principles*. Jerome became involved when Rufinus claimed he was merely continuing the work begun by Jerome. Bitter and personal accusations flew back and forth for years. Cf. Angelo di Bernardino, ed., *Patrology*, vol. 4: *Golden Age of Latin Patristic Literature*

From the Council of Nicea to the Council of Chalcedon (Westminster, MD: Christian Classic, Inc., 1986), 212-254.

37. Jerome, letter 127:10, in *NPNF*, 6:256-257.
38. Ibid.
39. Letter 127:7, in *NPNF*, 6:255.
40. *Palladius*, 55:3.
41. Ibid., 56:2.
42. Nyssa, *Resurrection*, in *NPNF*, 5:432.
43. Letter 39:1, in *NPNF*, 6:49.
44. Jerome, letter 108:27, in *NPNF*, 6:210.
45. Jerome, *Preface to the Psalms*, in *NPNF*, 6:494.
46. Jerome, preface to Book of Ester, trans. in anonymous, "The House on the Aventine," *The Catholic World* (August 1898), 640-641.
47. Jerome, letter 77:7, in *NPNF*, 6:161.
48. *Palladius*, 46:1.
49. *Letters of Paulinus*, letter 29:10.
50. Gerontius, *The Life of Melanie the Younger*, trans. Elizabeth Clark (Lewiston, NY: Edwin Mellon Press, 1984), 1.
51. Ibid., 3-6.
52. Ibid.
53. Ibid., 7.
54. *The Life of Olympias*, 3, trans. in *Maenads, Martyrs, Matrons, Monastics*, ed. Ross S. Kraemer (Philadelphia: Fortress Press, 1988), 196.
55. Ibid., 4.
56. Ibid., 5, in *Maenads*, 197.
57. Jerome, letter 128:5, in *NPNF*, 6:231.
58. Jerome, *The Pilgrimage of the Holy Paula*, trans. Aubrey Stewart (London: Palestine Pilgrims Text Society, 1887), 2.
59. Jerome, letter 77:6, in *NPNF*, 6:160.
60. Because of the size of her fortune, she was, of course, restricted by the political implications that all concentrated wealth brought. This problem was solved, however, when Patriarch Nectarius ordained her deaconess, an office that contained the obligation to support the church as much as possible. Also, it is interesting to note that the deep friendship that existed between Olympias and John Chrysostom was nurtured early on by a unique partnership concerning her wealth; she had the money, and he had the business acumen to distribute it: "Perceiving that she bestowed her goods liberally on any who asked her for them," John approached her. "I applaud your intentions; but would have you know that those who aspire to the perfection of virtue according to God, ought to distribute their wealth with economy." He offered

to help regulate her donations "to the wants of those who solicit relief" and thus enable her "to extend the sphere of your benevolence." *Sozomen*, 8:9, in *NPNF*, 2:405.

61. Gerontius, *Melanie the Younger*, 12.
62. Jerome, letter 108:5, in *NPNF*, 6:197.
63. Letter 108:31, in *NPNF*, 6:211.
64. *Palladius*, 54:1-2.
65. Ibid., 54:4.
66. Ibid., 54:5-6.
67. Nyssa, *Macrina*, 972C.
68. Ibid., 970C.
69. Jerome, letter 24:3, in *NPNF*, 6:43.
70. Letter 127:5, in *NPNF*, 6:255.
71. *Palladius*, 46:2-3.
72. Jerome, *Paula*, 18.
73. *Egeria's Travels*, trans. John Wilkinson (London: SPCK, 1971), 19:5.
74. Ibid., 20:7.
75. Ibid., 23:6.
76. Ibid., 19:5.
77. Ibid., 19:19.
78. Ibid., 21:3.
79. Ibid., 23:2-4.
80. Gregory of Nyssa, *On Virginity*, 2, in *NPNF*, 5:345.
81. Pseudo-Athanasius, *Canons of Athanasius, Patriarch of Alexandria*, ed. and trans. W. Riedel and W. E. Crum (Amsterdam: Philo Press, repr. 1973), 98.
82. *Palladius*, 31:4.
83. Nyssa, *Macrina*, 1000A.
84. Gerontius, *Melanie the Younger*, 8.
85. *Palladius*, 38:8-9.
86. *Syncletica*, 7, in *The Sayings of the Desert Fathers. The Alphabetical Collection*, trans. Benedicta Ward (Kalamazoo, MI: Cistercian Publications, 1975), 232.
87. Theodora, 2, in ibid., 83.
88. Ibid., 3.
89. *Syncletica*, 24, in ibid., 234-235.
90. Jerome, letter 24:4, in *NPNF*, 6:43.
91. Theodora, 4, in *Sayings*, 83.
92. *Palladius*, 55:1-2.
93. Syncletica, 15, in *Sayings*, 233.
94. Jerome, letter 127:4, in *NPNF*, 6:254.
95. Letter 24:5, in *NPNF*, 6:43.

96. Gerontius, *Melanie the Younger*, 8-9.
97. Nyssa, *Macrina*, 970C.
98. Jerome, letter 23:2, in *NPNF*, 6:42.
99. Letter 77:6, in *NPNF*, 6:160.
100. Olympias, 7, in *Maenads*, 198.
101. Jerome, letter 77:6, in *NPNF*, 6:160.
102. Even to the extreme of talking to them; see Cyrus, 1, in *Sayings*, 118-119.
103. *Palladius*, 59:1.
104. Ibid., 63:3-4.

Chapter 5
Devotional Life and Mary in Late Antiquity

1. Augustine, *Confessions*, 5:9.
2. Ibid., 6:2.
3. Ibid., 5:9.
4. Ibid., 6:1.
5. Ibid., and throughout the whole of 6.
6. Ibid.
7. Ibid., 6:13.
8. That is, with the exception of women martyrs' last words.
9. Nyssa, *Macrina*, 984C.
10. Ibid., 984D-986A.
11. Ibid., 984D.
12. Ibid., 986A.
13. Ibid., 992B.
14. Ibid., 990C.
15. This is basically the argument of Bynum, *Holy Feast*, in her analysis of late medieval female mystics. Their own physicality brought them closer to Jesus's humanity.
16. Gerontius, *Melanie the Younger*, 64.
17. *Egeria's*, 10:7.
18. Ibid., 5:12.
19. Ibid., 3:6.
20. Ibid., 4:3.
21. Ibid., 10:7.
22. Ibid., 11:3.
23. Ibid., 13:2.
24. Ibid., 14:1.

25. Ibid., 24:1.

26. Ibid, 24:1-14.

27. Ibid., 45-46.

28. Quoted in Pierre Batiffol, *The History of the Roman Breviary*, trans. A. M. Y. Baylay (London: Longmans, Green and Co., 1912), 19.

29. *Basil Letters*, letter 207, 2:83-84.

30. *The Hymns of the Breviary and Missal*, ed. Matthew Britt (New York: Benzigen Brothers, new ed., 1948), 364-365.

31. Ibid., 374-375.

32. Ibid., 33-34.

33. Ibid., 36-37.

34. Gerontus, *Melanie the Younger*, 42, 46, and 47.

35. Jerome, letter 108:20, trans. in *Maenads*, 157.

36. *Augustine Letters (204-270)*, trans. W. Parsons (New York: Fathers of the Church, 1956), letter 211, 5:43.

37. Ibid.

38. For a fuller analysis of the rule, see Patricia Ranft, "The Rule of St. Augustine in Medieval Monasticism," *Proceedings of the PMR Conference* 11 (1986), 143-150.

39. Nyssa, *Macrina*, 986B.

40. Ibid., 992D-994A.

41. Augustine, *Confessions*, 9:7.

42. Ibid., 9:6. Augustine is not consistent on this point, though, and elsewhere in *Confessions* he accuses himself of being too taken in by the sensual aspects of music and thus being distracted from worship. He admits "I waver between the danger that lies in gratifying the senses and the benefits which, as I know from experience, can accrue from singing." Ibid., 10:33.

43. Augustine quoted in E. Mersch, *The Whole Christ. The Doctrine of the Mystical Body of Christ in Scripture and Tradition*, trans. J. R. Kelly (London: D. Dodson, 1962), 427.

44. Ibid., 430.

45. Ibid., 424.

46. Gregory of Nyssa, *On the Formation of Man*; Theodore of Mopsuestia, *Sixth Liturgical Homily*; Hilary, *On the Trinity*; Eusebius of Caesarea, *On the Theology of the Church*; and Paulinius of Nola, *Letter 38*, are just some of the works that deal with the unity of the church.

47. Augustine quoted in Mersch, *Mystical Body*, 428-429.

48. Ibid., 424.

49. Ibid., 436-437.

50. *Egeria*, 26.

51. Ignatius of Antioch, *Letter to Ephesians*, short version, 7, in *ANF*, 1:52.

52. Justin Martyr, *First Apology*, 33, in *ANF*, 1:174.

53. Justin Martyr, *Dialogue with Trypho*, 100, in *ANF*, 1:249.

54. Irenaeus, *Against Heresies*, 3:10, 16, 19, 22; 4:33 in *ANF*, 1:423-454; 506-511.

55. Tertullian, *On the Flesh of Christ*, 17, in *ANF*, 3:536.

56. Ibid., 23, in *ANF*, 3:541; and *Against Marcion*, 4:19, in *ANF*, 3:376-378.

57. Clement of Alexandria, *Stomata*, 7:16, in *ANF*, 2:551.

58. Origen, *Against Celsus*, 1:34-35, in *ANF*, 4:410-411; and *Commentary on Matthew*, 10:17, in *ANF*, 9:424-425.

59. Socrates, *Ecclesiastical History*, 7:32, in *NPNF*, 2:171, argues that Eusebius used it in his life of Constantine, as did Origen in his commentaries on Romans and 1 John, as "written in the ancient copies."

60. Quoted in Vasiliki Limberis, *Divine Heiress* (London: Routledge, 1994), 104.

61. Sozomen, *The Ecclesiastical History*, 7:5, in *NPNF*, 2:379.

62. Limiberis, *Heiress*, 107.

63. *Ephrem the Syrian Hymns*, trans. and intro. Kathleen E. McVey (New York: Paulist Press, 1989), 3,5.

64. They were translated into Greek as early as the end of the fourth century. Cf. Limberis, *Heiress*, 91.

65. *Ephrem Hymns*, 29.

66. *Hymns on the Nativity*, ibid., 149 and 153.

67. Ibid., 108.

68. Ibid., 131.

69. Ibid., 132.

70. Ibid., 149.

71. Ibid., 102.

72. Ibid., 132.

73. Ibid., 122.

74. Ibid., 137.

75. Ibid., 121.

76. Ibid., 122.

77. Ibid., 203.

78. Ibid., 189.

79. Ibid., 102.

80. Ibid.

81. Hilda Graef, *Mary: A History of Doctrine and Devotion* (New York: Sheed and Ward, 1963), 133.

82. Epiphanius of Salamis, *Panarion*, 78, quoted in R. L. P. Milburn, "The Historical Background of the Doctrine of the Assumption," in *Women in Early Christianity*, ed. David M. Scholer (New York: Garland Publishing, Inc., repr.1993), 55-56.

83. Cf. *The "Panarion" of St. Epiphanius, Bishop of Salamis. Selected Passages,* trans. Philip R. Amidon (New York: Oxford University Press, 1990), 78:23.

84. Ibid., 79:1.1.

85. Ibid.,79:5.1-2.

86. Ibid., 79:5.4

87. See below, p. 97.

88. Sozomen, *Ecclesiastical History,* 8:22, in *NPNF,* 2:413.

89. Ibid., 8:20, in *NPNF,* 2:412.

90. Ibid., 9:1 in *NPNF,* 2:419.

91. Socrates, *Ecclesiastical History,* 7:32, in *NPNF,* 2:170-171.

92. A. Loofs, *Nestoriana,* quoted in Graef, *Mary,* 104.

93. Cyril of Alexandria, Letter 4, trans. in W. F. C. Frend, *The Rise of Christianity* (Philadelphia: Fortress Press, 1984), 756.

94. Leo D. Davis, *The First Seven Ecumenical Councils (325-787)* (Wilmington, DE: Michael Glazier Inc., 1987), 156.

95. Limberius, *Heiress,* 106, suggests that Pulcheria established the festival herself.

96. Nestorius, *Bazaar of Heracleides,* 96-97, quoted in ibid., 55.

97. Proclus, quoted in ibid., 55-56.

98. Ibid., 60.

99. Graef, *Mary,* 111-114.

100. The discourse is attributed to Cyril of Jerusalem by E. A. Wallis Budge in *Miscellaneous Coptic Texts* (London: Longmans and Co., 1915). See R. L. P. Milburn, "Assumption" in Scholer, *Women,* 189.

101. *St. Leo. The Great Letters,* trans. E. Hunt (New York: Fathers of the Church Inc., 1957), letter 28.

102. Labbe and Cassant, *Concilia,* Tom. IV, col. 343, trans. in Council of Chalcedon, session II, in *NPNF,* 14:253.

103. Limberius, *Heiress,* 89-90.

104. *The Akathistas Hymn,* trans. in ibid., appendix, 152.

105. Ibid., 157.

106. Ibid., 156.

107. Venantius Fortunatus, in *Hymns,* ed. Britt, 349-350.

108. Jaroslav Pelikan, *Mary through the Centuries. Her Place in the History of Culture* (New Haven, CT: Yale University Press, 1996), 220 and 219, respectively.

Chapter 6
Early Medieval Saints East and West

1. *Ephrem,* 1.

666

2. Graef, *Mary*, 57.
3. Sebastian P. Brock and Susan A. Harvey, *Holy Women of the Syrian Orient* (Berkeley: University of California Press, 1987), 2-3.
4. Ibid., 13.
5. John of Ephesus, *Mary and Euphemia* in ibid., 124.
6. Ibid., 126.
7. Ibid., 124-125.
8. Ibid., 125.
9. Ibid., 126.
10. Ibid., 127.
11. Ibid., 126.
12. Ibid., 127.
13. Ibid., 131.
14. Ibid., 132.
15. *Susan* in ibid., 133.
16. Ibid., 134.
17. Ibid., 139-141.
18. John of Ephesus, *Lives of the Eastern Saints*, 19,187, 562, quoted in Susan A. Harvey, *Asceticism and Society in Crisis: John of Ephesus and "The Lives of the Eastern Saints"* (Berkeley: University of California Press, 1990), 127.
19. Ibid.
20. Ibid., 128.
21. Ibid., 129.
22. Ibid., 126.
23. Second letter from Simeon of Beth Arsham in Brock, *Holy Women*, 105.
24. Ibid., 109.
25. Ibid., 110.
26. Ibid.
27. Ibid., 115.
28. Ibid., 111.
29. Ibid., 113.
30. Ibid., 111-112.
31. Ibid., 112-113.
32. Ibid., 113.
33. Ibid., 114.
34. Martyrios, *Book of Perfection*, in Brock, *Holy Women*, 178.
35. Ibid., 180.
36. Ibid., 179.
37. Ibid., 181.

38. James C. Russell, *The Germanization of Early Medieval Christianity* (New York: Oxford University Press, 1994), 121.

39. Otto of Bamberg's missionary work is a prime example. He was rejected the first time when he arrived in full regalia to convert the Germanic people; his later attempt was unpretentious and successful. Poverty was a more effective witness than wealth. See Ranft. "Witness," 16.

40. *Sainted Women of the Dark Ages*, ed. and trans. Jo Ann McNamara and John E. Halborg with E. Gordon Whately (Durham, NC: Duke University Press, 1992), 280.

41. *Life of Austreberta*, in ibid., 314.

42. *Life of Balthild*, in ibid., 276.

43. *Life of Waldetrude*, in ibid., 259.

44. *Life of Gertrude*, in ibid., 229 and 222, respectively.

45. Quotes taken from preceding discussion.

46. Some scholars argue that they were written by Radegund with Fortunatus's help. See Karen Cherewatuk, "Radegund and Epistolary Tradition," in Karen Cherewatuk and Ulrike Wiethaus, ed., *Dear Sister* (Philadelphia: University of Pennsylvania Press, 1993), 21; her argument is explained more thoroughly on pages 41-42, n.3. Bibliography for the debate is included with the note.

47. Venantius Fortunatus, *The Life of Holy Radegund*, in *Sainted Women*, 70.

48. Ibid., 75.

49. Ibid., 71.

50. See Cherewatuk, "Epistolary Tradition," 20-45.

51. Baudonivia, *Life of Radegund*, in *Sainted Women*, 87.

52. Fortunatus, *Life*, in ibid., 72.

53. Gregory, Bishop of Tours, *The History of the Franks*, trans. Ernest Brehaut (New York: Columbia University Press, 1916), 57.

54. Fortunatus, *Life*, in *Sainted Women*, 75.

55. Baudonivia, *Life of Radegund*, in ibid., 89.

56. Ibid., 91.

57. Ibid., 90.

58. Ibid., 91.

59. Fortunatus, *Life*, in ibid., 80.

60. Ibid., 77.

61. Baudonivia, *Life of Radegund*, in ibid., 87.

62. Ibid., 99, 104, 100, 100, 103, 104-105, and 94, respectively.

63. Gregory of Tours, *The Glory of the Confessors*, trans. Raymond van Dam (Liverpool: Liverpool University Press, 1988), 104.

64. *The Life of the Blessed Queen Balthild*, in *Sainted Women*, 270.

65. See introductory remarks in ibid., 265-267.

66. *Balthild,* in ibid., 271.
67. Ibid., 274.
68. Ibid., 277.
69. Gregory of Tours, *Life of the Fathers,* trans. Edward James (Liverpool: Liverpool University Press, 2nd ed., 1991) 19: pref. The Pauline paradox of strength-in-weakness is obviously in play here.
70. Ibid., 19:2.
71. Ibid., 19:3.
72. Gregory, *Confessors,* 103.
73. Ibid., 34.
74. Ibid., 24.
75. Ibid., 33
76. *The Life of Gertrude,* in *Sainted Women,* 222.
77. *The Life of Aldegrend,* in ibid., 237.
78. *The Life of Bertilla,* in ibid., 280.
79. *The Life of Austreberta,* in ibid., 306.
80. Sean Connolly and J. M. Picard, "Cogitosus: *Life of Saint Brigit,*" *Journal of the Royal Society of Antiquaries of Ireland,* 117 (1987), 11.1, 3.
81. Kim McCone, "Brigit in the Seventh Century: A Saint with Three Lives?" *Peritia,* 1 (1982), 107.
82. For the history of double monasteries, see Patricia Ranft, *Women and the Religious Life in Premodern Europe* (New York: St. Martin's Press, 1996), 24-29.
83. "Cogitosus," 11-12.
84. Ibid., 18.
85. Ibid., 13.
86. Sean Connolly, trans., "*Vita Prima Sanctae Brigitae,*" *Journal of the Royal Society of Antiquaries of Ireland,* 119 (1989), 39:3-5.
87. *Bethu Brigte,* ed. Donncha O' hAodha (Dublin: Dublin Institute for Advanced Studies, 1978), 31.
88. The author used the imagined meetings and conversations between Brigit and Patrick that fill the *Vita Prima* to further his understanding of the jurisdiction between the Armagh-Kildare sees.
89. "*Vita Prima,*" 75:5.
90. Ibid., 84; cf. also 68; 83; 85.
91. Ibid., 96:1.
92. Ibid., 30:4; 33:3; and 52:1, respectively.
93. Ibid., 15:3.
94. *AASS,* January 15, 1:1062-1068.
95. Letter 22 (735-736) in *The Letters of Saint Boniface,* trans. Ephraim Emerton (New York: Octagon Books, 1973), 60-61.

96. Letter 26 in ibid., 64-65.

97. Letter 19 in ibid., 57; Letter 77 in ibid., 170-172.

98. Letter 53 in ibid., 122.

99. Letter 39 in ibid., 77-78.

100. Rudolf of Fulda, *The Life of Saint Leoba* in *Anglo-Saxon Missionaries in Germany*, ed. and trans. C. H. Talbot (New York: Sheed and Ward, 1954), 222.

101. Ibid., 222-223.

102. Ibid., 211.

103. Letter 21 in *Letters of Boniface*, 59-60.

104. *Life of Leoba*, 218 and 221.

105. Ibid., 214.

106. Ibid., 223.

107. Ibid., 215.

108. Ibid.

109. Ibid., 214.

110. Ibid., 216.

111. Letter 6 in *Letters of Boniface*, 37.

Chapter 7
Early Medieval Monasticism and Church Life

1. Philibert Schmitz, *Historie de l'ordre de Saint Benoît* (Liege: Editions de Maredsous, 1948-56), argues that the earliest use of the term *abbatissa* was in the fourth century. Caesarius's use of the term probably contributed greatly to its popularity.

2. See *Pachomian Koinonia*, vol. 2: *The Chronicles and Rules*, trans. A. Veilleux (Kalamazoo, MI: Cistercian Publications, 1980-1982).

3. Athanasius, *The Life of St. Anthony the Great* (Willits, CA: Eastern Orthodox Books, n.d), 1:1.

4. It should be noted that Augustine and Basil both wrote monastic rules that may have been used in women's monasteries, but since the rules were not intended specifically for women they are not discussed here. For a history of the rule, see Ranft, "The Rule of St. Augustine."

5. Caesarius of Arles, *The Rule for Holy Virgins*, in Maria McCarthy, *The Rule for Nuns of St. Caesarius of Arles. A Translation with a Critical Introduction* (Washington, DC: Catholic University of America Press, 1960), 170.

6. Ibid., 171.

7. Leander of Seville, *The Training of Nuns and the Contempt of the World* in *Iberian Fathers*, vol. 1: *Martin of Braga, Paschasius of Dumium, Leander of Seville*, trans. Claude W. Barlow (Washington, DC: Catholic University of America Press, 1969), 188.

8. Ibid., 189.

9. For example, ibid., 190.

10. Jo Ann McNamara and John E. Halborg, "The Rule of Donatus of Besançon, a Working Translation," *Vox Benedictina* 2:2 (April, 1985), prologue. See also *PL* 87:273-298.

11. Caesarius, *Rule for Virgins*, 2.

12. See analysis in the following: *RB 1980: The Rule of St. Benedict*, ed. Timothy Fry (Collegeville, MN: The Liturgical Press, 1981); McCarthy, *Caesarius of Arles*; Gerhard Ladner, *The Idea of Reform* (Cambridge, MA: Harvard University Press, 1959); and Luc Verheijen, *La régle de Saint Augustin*, 2 vols. (Paris: Etudes Augustinennes, 1967).

13. Caesarius, *Rule for Virgins*, 1 and 65, in McCarthy, *Caesarius of Arles*, 170 and 192.

14. Caesarius's rule is "approved and signed" by seven other men. See ibid., 73.

15. Leander, *Training*, prologue, in *Iberian Fathers*, 1:189.

16. Braulio of Saragossa, Letter 18, in *Iberian Fathers*, vol. 2: *Braulio of Saragossa, Fructusosus of Braga*, trans. Claude W. Barlow (Washington, DC: Catholic University Press, 1969), 2:45-47.

17. Leander, *Training*, 3, in *Iberian Fathers*, 1:199.

18. McNamara and Halborg, "Rule of Donatus," 1.

19. Caesarius, *Rule for Virgins*, 35, in McCarthy, *Caesarius of Arles*, 182.

20. Ibid., 64, in ibid., 191-192.

21. Ibid., 27, in ibid., 179.

22. Ibid., 61, in ibid., 190.

23. Bede, *A History of the English Church and People*, trans. Leo Sherley-Price, rev. R. E. Latham (Harmondsworth: Penguin Books, rev. ed., 1968), 3:8.

24. Jane Tibbetts Schulenburg, "Women's Monastic Communities, 500-1100: Patterns of Expansion and Decline," *Signs* 14:2 (1989), tables 1 and 2, claims that forty-seven new monasteries were founded during the seventh century.

25. Bede, *History*, 4:23.

26. Ibid., 3:25.

27. Ibid., 4:23.

28. Affiliated monasteries would be adjacent to, founded by, or have juridicial ties to one another. A double monastery may or may not have one or all the above traits plus one more: The men's monastery ministers to the women's. For many monasteries discussed below sources are incomplete, and thus it is hard for the historian to classify them. The terms, therefore, are used less technically

here, although most historians agree with the labels I have given them. See the still magistered work of Mary Bateson, "Origin and Early History of Double Monasteries," *Transactions of the Royal Historical Society* 13 n.s. (1899), 137-198.

29.   *Palladius*, 33:1.

30.   "Cogitosus," 32:2-3.

31.   Bateson, "Double Monasteries," 148-149.

32.   *Life of Sadalberga*, in *Sainted Women*, 183.

33.   Suzanne F. Wemple, *Women in Frankish Society* (Philadelphia: University of Pennsylvania Press, 1981), 161.

34.   Bede, *English Church*, 4:23.

35.   Bateson, "Double Monasteries," 173.

36.   Bede, *English Church*, 4:10.

37.   Huneberc of Heidenheim, The *"Hodoeporicon" of St. Willibald*, in *Anglo-Saxon Missionaries*, 153.

38.   Cf. M. Emmanuel, "Saint Walburga, Benedictine Abbess and Missionary (710-799)," *Word and Spirit* 11 (1989), 50-59.

39.   Bateson, "Double Monasteries," 188-190, mentions some possible ones.

40.   Ibid., 190.

41.   Fructuosus of Braga, *General Rule for Monasteries*, 4, in *Iberian Fathers*, 2:183.

42.   Ibid., 2:184.

43.   A. de Yepes, *General de la Orden de S. Benito*, quoted in Bateson, "Double Monasteries," 196.

44.   Bateson, "Double Monasteries," 190-196.

45.   II Council of Nice, canon xx in *The Seven Ecumenical Councils of the Undivided Church, Their Canons and Dogmatic Decrees*, ed. Henry R. Percival, in *NPNF*, 14:568.

46.   Wemple, *Frankish Society*, 170.

47.   See M. A. Meyer, "Women and the Tenth Century English Monastic Reform," *Revue bénédictine* 87 (1977), 34-61.

48.   John Godfrey, "The Double Monastery in Early English History," *The Ampleforth Journal* 79 (1974), 32.

49.   Cf. Schulenburg, "Monastic Communities," *Signs*, 281, for a partial listing of these houses in Britain, France, and Belgium.

50.   Council of Vernense 11, in *MGH* 1, 35, quoted in Wemple, *Frankish Society*, 166.

51.   Charlemagne's edict of 789 so stated. See *Duplex legations edictum*, 19, in *MGH* 1 ,69, quoted in Wemple, *Frankish Society*, 167.

52. Hefele, *Conciliengeschichte*, III, 692, quoted in Mary Pia Heinrich, *The Canonesses and Education in the Early Middle Ages* (Washington, DC: Catholic University of America Press, 1924), 26.

53. Council of Paris (829), 45, quoted in Wemple, *Frankish Society*, 167.

54. *Capitula missorum generale*, 802, quoted in Franceen S. Hoyt, "The Carolingian Episcopate: Concepts of Pastoral Care as Set Forth in the Capitularies of Charlemagne and His Bishops (789-822)," Ph.D. diss. (Yale University, 1975), 40.

55. Ibid., 88-89.

56. Gregory Dix, *The Shape of the Liturgy* (London: Dacre Press, repr. 1970), 375.

57. Cyrille Vögel, *Medieval Liturgy*, trans. W. G. Storey and N. K. Rasmissen (Washington, DC: Pastoral Press, 1986), 34-35.

58. Joseph A. Jungmann, *The Mass of the Roman Rite*, 2 vols., trans. F. A. Brunner (Dublin: Four Courts Press, replica ed. 1986), 1:62.

59. Ibid., 2:170-179 and 2:248-259.

60. Prudentius, quoted in Batiffol, *Roman Breviary*, 58.

61. Gerontius, *Melanie the Younger*, 5.

62. Sidonius Apollinarius, letter 107:9, quoted in Batiffol, *Roman Breviary*, 59.

63. *Ecumenical Councils*, in *NPNF*, 14:463.

64. Batiffol, *Breviary*, 30-31. There were twenty-five title churches in sixth-century Rome. Only the patriarchal churches were more important.

65. Cf. ibid., 57-66, for a discussion of stational churches, and Jungmann, *Mass*, 1:67-74. The association of saints' tombs and relics with the liturgical celebration of the saint probably accounts for the lateness of Mary's feasts; she had neither.

66. Cf. Batiffol, *Breviary*, 68-71.

67. *Aldhelmi opera*, in *MGH* 15:17, 59-65, trans. in Mary Clayton, "Feasts of the Virgin in the Liturgy of the Anglo-Saxon Church," *Anglo-Saxon England* 13 (1984), 213-214.

68. Bede, *De temporum ratione liber*, 323, trans. in ibid., 220, n. 45.

69. Some scholars hold that the *Kyrie eleison* after the Introit was originally a litany; others say it developed independently. See the discussions in Dix, *Liturgy*, 453-457, and Edmund Bishop, *Liturgica Historica* (Oxford: Clarendon Press, repr. 1962), 137-164.

70. John T. McNeill and Helena M. Gamer, *Medieval Handbooks of Penance* (New York: Columbia University Press, repr. 1990), 291.

71. *Anglo-Saxon Litanies of the Saints*, ed. Michael Lapidge (London: Henry Bradshaw Society, 1991), 16.

72. Bishop, *Liturgica*, 161, says there is only one exception "in which the name of the Blessed Virgin does not come first."

73. *Anglo-Saxon Litanies*, 41.

74. Ibid., 42.

75. There are 157 saints listed in all, but when angels, biblical figures, and popes are eliminated, the ratio of men to women is surprisingly low. Cf. ibid., 110-114.

76. Ibid., 193-202; 203-209; 225-230; 210-211; and 75, respectively.

77. See Carolyn Walker Bynum, *Docere Verbo et Exemplo: An Aspect of Twelfth Century Spirituality* (Missoula, MT: Scholars Press, 1979).

78. J. B. L. Tolhurst, *Introduction to the English Monastic Breviaries* (Suffolk: The Boydell Press, repr. 1993), 70. Prime was followed by a litany.

79. Chance remarks in the custumals of Lincoln cathedral and in the Sarum tractate *de officiis* tell us that in the thirteenth century it was recited daily in these churches; Radulphus de Rivo tells us that in the fourteenth century, daily recital of the office was the custom of all peoples and obligatory. See Bishop, *Liturgica*, 233-234.

80. *Peter Damian. Letters*, vol. 1:1-30, trans. Owen J. Blum (Washington, DC: Catholic University of America Press, 1989), 17:22.

81. *PL* 151, 183.

82. Tolhurst, *English Breviaries*, 113-114.

83. J. D. Crichton, "The Office in the West: The Early Middle Ages," in *The Study of Liturgy*, ed. Cheslyn Jones, G. Wainwright, and Edward Yarnold (New York: Oxford University Press, 1978), 369-378.

84. J. Gelineau, "Music and Singing in the Liturgy," in ibid., 445-446.

85. *Hymns*, ed. Britt, 119-121.

86. Ibid., 323-327.

87. Ibid., 358-365.

88. Graef, *Mary*, 174.

89. *Hymns*, ed. Britt, 347-349.

90. Graef, *Mary*, 170-171.

91. Ibid., 166.

92. Ambrose Autpert, quoted in ibid., 169-170.

93. Graef, *Mary*, 169-170.

94. The literature on the subject grows daily. See Friedrich Prinz, "Heiligenkult und Adelsherrschaft in Spiegel merowingischer Hagiographie," *Historische Zeitschrift* 204 (1967), 529-544; F. Graus, *Volk, Herrscher und Heiliger im Reich der Merowinger* (Prague: Nakladatelstvi Ceskoslovenské Akádemie Ved, 1965); and James C. Russell, *The Germanization of Early Medieval Christianity* (New York: Oxford University Press, 1994).

95. Charles T. Wood, *The Quest for Eternity* (Hanover, NH: University Press of New England, 1983), 38.

96. James A. Brundage, "Sex and Canon Law: A Statistical Analysis of Samples of Canon and Civil Law," in *Sexual Practices and the Medieval Church*, ed. Vern L. Bullough and James Brundage (Buffalo, NY: Prometheus Books, 1982), 91.

97. Canons of a Synod of Patrick, Auxilius, and Iserninus, 22, in McNeill, *Handbooks of Penance*, 79.

98. The Penitential of Theodore, 22 and 23, in ibid., 210.

99. Penitential of St. Columbanus, 23 in *Scriptores Latini Hibernial*, vol. 5: *The Irish Penitentials*, ed. Ludwig Bieler (Dublin: The Dublin Institute for Advanced Studies, 1963), 104-105.

100. Ibid., 16 in *Irish Penitentials*, 102-103.

101. Ibid., 8 in *Irish Penitentials*, 100-101.

102. James A. Brundage, *Law, Sex and Christian Society in Medieval Europe* (Chicago: University of Chicago Press, 1987), 153.

103. Penitential of Theodore, 36, in McNeill, *Handbooks of Penance*, 211.

104. Ibid., 37.

105. Second Synod of Patrick, 27, in ibid., 85.

106. The Canons of Adamnan, 45, in ibid., 137.

107. Penitential of Finnian, 18, in ibid., 90.

108. Canones Wallic, 37, in *Irish Penitentials*, ed. Bieler, 143.

109. Penitential of Finnian, 34, in McNeill, *Handbooks of Penance*, 93-94.

Chapter 8
The High Middle Ages: Hermits and Scholars

1. Cf. L. R. Ménager, "La 'byzantinisation' religieuse de l'Italie meridionale (ixe-xii^{e}s) et la politique monastique des Normandi l'Italie," *Revue d'Histoire Ecclesiastique* 53 (1958), 747-774.

2. Cf. *AASS*, February 2, and *PL* 144, 953-1008 for Romuald's vita.

3. David Knowles, *The Monastic Orders in England* (Cambridge: University Press, 1940), 200. Romuald apparently had no trouble finding one to be his abba (*PL* 144, 958).

4. *PL* 204, 1013.

5. Cf. *PL* 144, *PL* 145, and the recent English translations in *Peter Damian*, trans. Blum.

6. Cf. *AASS*, October 6, and *PL* 152, 555-606; *PL* 153, 11-568.

7. Cf. *AASS*, February 3, and *PL* 162, 1079-1082; *PL* 162, 1017-1078.

8. Cf. *AASS*, Apr. 2, and *PL* 172, 1363-1446.

9. E. P. Sauvage, ed., "Stephen of Fulga, *Vita B. Vitalis Saviniacensis*," ed. E. P. Sauvage, *Analecta Bollandiana* 1(1882), 13:355.

10. *PL* 172, 1380.

11. *Peter Damian*, 28: 4.

12. He advised Hildebrand to consult poets and philosophers for deeper under-standing of scripture (*PL* 145, 560) and extended this advice to the laity (*PL* 144, 541). He sent his nephew to Cluny for education in the trivium and quadrivium (*PL* 144, 373), and insisted that clergy and bishops must be educated in secular knowledge (*PL* 144, 345; 353; *PL* 145, 98; 126). For a detailed analysis of these apparent contradictions, see Patricia Ranft "The Role of the Eremitic Monk in the Development of the Medieval Intellectual Tradition" in *From Cloister to Classroom*, ed. E. Rozanne Elders (Kalamazoo, MI: Cistercian Publications, 1986), 80-95.

13. Cf. I. S. Robinson, "The 'Colores Rhetorici' in the Investiture Contest," *Traditio* 32 (1976), 209-38. Related to this is women's use of the rhetoric of humility; see below, ch.12.

14. *Peter Damian*, 31.

15. Ibid., 80: 28.

16. Ibid., 61:12.

17. Giovanni Miccoli, "Theólogie de la vie monastique chez Saint Pierre Damien (1007-1072)," in *Theologie de la vie monastique: Etudes sur la tradition patristique* (Paris: n.p., 1961), 463.

18. *Peter Damian*, 28:11-21.

19. Ibid., 28:20.

20. Ibid., 28:12-24.

21. Ibid., 19:8.

22. Ibid., 51:3-4.

23. For discussion and analysis of the sources, see n.a., *L'Eremitismo in Occidente nei secoli Xle-Xlle* (Milano: Societa Editrice Vita et Pensiero, 1965); and Bede K. Lackner, *Eleventh-Century Background to Citeaux* (Washington, DC: Cistercian Publications, 1972).

24. *PL* 162, 1051.

25. *PL* 162, 1052-1053.

26. Cf. A. Wilmart, "Eve et Goscelin," *Revue bénédictine* 46 (1934), 414-438; ibid., 50 (1938), 42-83.

27. Ann K. Warren, *Anchorites and Their Patrons in Medieval England* (Berkeley: University of California Press, 1985), table 1. Terms used to describe women living the eremitic life varied: hermit, recluse, anchorite, inclusa. As the Middle Ages progresses the word *anchorite* becomes more restrictive. Here we

will use the word *hermit* to refer to a person who lived the religious life outside an institution in a solitary or relatively solitary setting.

28. A complete but occasionally confused source for female hermits in Francesca M. Steele, *Anchoresses of the West* (London: Sands & Co., 1903). See also Rotha Mary Clay, *The Hermits and Anchorites of England* (London: Methuen, 1914).

29. *The Book of St. Gilbert*, ed. Raymonde Foreville and Gillian Keir (Oxford: Clarendon Press, 1987), 31-35.

30. Penny Schine Gold, *The Lady and the Virgin* (Chicago: University of Chicago Press, 1985), 113.

31. Warren, *Anchorites*, 18-29.

32. Aelred of Rievaulx, "A Rule for Life for a Recluse," in *The Works of Aelred of Rievaulx*, vol. 1, *Treatises, The Pastoral Prayer* (Spencer, MA: Cistercian Publications, 1971), 1:7.

33. Ibid., 1:3, 8, 9, 11.

34. Ibid., 1:28.

35. Ibid., 1:2, 4.

36. Ibid., 1:28.

37. *Ancrene Wisse* in *Anchorite Spirituality: "Ancrene Wisse" and Associated Works*, trans. Anne Savage and Nicholas Watson (New York: Paulist Press, 1991), 76-77.

38. Ibid., 200.

39. Ibid., 176.

40. Ibid., 186.

41. Ibid., 101.

42. *The Life of Christina of Markyate. A Twelfth Century Recluse*, ed. and trans. C. H. Talbot (Oxford: Clarendon Press, repr.1987), 103-105.

43. Cf. Nikolaus M. Häring, "Abelard Yesterday and Today," in *Pierre Abélard, Pierre le Vénérable*, ed. René Louis, Jean Jolivet and Jean Châtillon (Paris: CNRS, 1975), 341-403.

44. *Christina*, 145.

45. Ibid., 125-127.

46. See James M. Garnett, "The Latin and the Anglo-Saxon *Juliana*," *Publications of the Modern Language Association* 14 (1899), 279-298.

47. *The Life of Saint Juliana* in Brigitte Cazelles, *The Lady as Saint* (Philadelphia: University of Pennsylvania Press, 1991), 205. Cazelles's interpretation of this genre is at variance with the one offered here.

48. See introductory remarks in *Anchorite Spirituality* 11-12, and 285-287.

49. Ibid., 288.

50. Ibid., 306.

51. Ibid., 299.

52. Ibid., 300.

53. Ibid., 303.

54. Anselm, *Monologuim*, in *St. Anselm Basic Writings*, trans. S. N. Deane (La Salle, IL: Open Court Publishing Co., 2nd ed., 1968), 138.

55. Ibid., 134.

56. Ibid., 139.

57. Anselm, *Cur Deus Homo*, in ibid., 249.

58. Ibid.

59. Anselm, *Orator*, 7, quoted in Graef, *Mary*, 212-214.

60. Anselm, *Monologium*, in *St. Anselm Writings*, 105.

61. Letter 4 in *The Letters of Abelard and Heloise*, trans. Betty Radice (London: Penguin Books, 1974), 150.

62. C. M. Buytaert, "Abelard's *Expositio in Hexaemeron*," *Antonianum* 43:2-3 (1968), 180.

63. Letter 7, *Letters of Abelard*, 196.

64. Letter 6, quoted in Mary McLaughlin, "Peter Abelard and the Dignity of Women: Twelfth-Century 'Feminism' in Theory and Practice," in *Pierre Abélard*, 301.

65. Letter 2, *Letters of Abelard*, 122.

66. Abelard, Sermo 13, *PL* 178, 448 and 488-489.

67. McLaughlin, "Women," 304.

68. Letter 5, *Letters of Abelard*, 160.

69. Letter 6, in McLaughlin, "Dignity," 297.

70. Ibid., 298.

71. Letter 4, in *Letters of Abelard*, 150.

72. Letter 3, in ibid., 131.

73. Letter 5, in ibid., 162-163.

74. Ibid., 174.

75. Ibid., 166. Earlier she states: "I think it should be sufficient for our infirmity if the virtue of continence and also of abstinence makes us the equals of the rulers of the church themselves and of the clergy who are confirmed in holy orders. . . . It would also be thought a great thing if we could equal religious laymen. . . ." Ibid., 164.

76. Häring, "Yesterday," 403.

77. 1 Corinthians 14:34-40; 1 Timothy 2:12-15, and 1 Timothy 3.

78. *PL* 191, 1672.

79. *PL* 192, 341-342.

80. *PL* 191, 1585-1597.

81. Brundage, *Law*, 264-265.

82. Petri Lombardi, *Sententiae in IV Libris Distinctae* (Grottaferrata: Collegii S. Bonaventurae ad Claras Aquas, 3rd ed., 1981), L. II, d. 16, c. 3:6; and *PL* 192, 283.

83. Petri Lombardi, *Sententiae,* L. II, d. 18, c. 2.

84. *PL* 145, 660-661, quoted in Brundage, *Law,* 189. Much of what follows is dependent on Brundage.

85. Brundage, *Law,* 256-278.

86. Petri Lombardi, *Sententiae,* L. IV, d. 27, c. 3.

87. Ibid., L. IV, d. 26, c. 6.

88. Ibid. Lombard put great emphasis on this metaphor throughout distinction 26: "For as between husband and wife there is union in the harmony of their spirits and in the joining of their bodies, so the Church is joined to Christ by will and nature."

89. Joffe-Ewald, *Regestum Pontificium Romanum,* 2870, quoted in Jane Bishop, "Bishops as Marital Advisors in the Ninth Century" in *Women in the Medieval World,* ed. Julius Kirshner and Suzanne Wemple (Oxford: Basil Blackwell, 1985), 82.

90. See Seamus P. Heany, *The Development of the Sacramentality of Marriage from Anselm of Laon to Thomas Aquinas* (Washington, DC: Catholic University of America Press, 1963).

91. See Guiseppe Ferroglio, "Raptus in parentes," *Annali della Fàcolta giuridica dell' Università di Camerino* 19 (1952), 3-34.

92. See R. H. Helmholz, *Marriage Litigation in Medieval England* (Cambridge: Cambridge University Press, 1974). For an opposing view of the above discussion, see Paulette l'Hermite-Leclercq, "The Feudal Order," in *A History of Women in the West,* vol. 2: *Silences of the Middle Ages,* ed. Christiane Klapisch-Zuber (Cambridge, MA: Harvard University Press, 1992), 202-249, esp. 213-220.

93. Thomas Aquinas, *Summa Theologica,* trans. Fathers of the English Dominican Province (Westminster, MD: Christian Classics, rev. ed., repr. 1981), Part 1: q. 78, a.1; q.76, a.1; q.83, a.1; and q.90, a.4, respectively.

94. Ibid., Part 1, q. 92, a. 4. Kari Børresen, *Subordination and Equivalence: The Nature and Role of Woman in Augustine and Thomas Aquinas* (Washington, DC: Catholic University of America, 1982) is an excellent guide through the works of Aquinas on these matters.

95. Ibid., Part 1, q. 92, a. 3. See Petri Lombardi, *Sententiae,* L. II, d. 18, c. 3-4; and L. II, d. 28, c. 3.

96. *Summa,* Part 1, q. 93, a. 6.

97. Ibid., Part 1, q. 93, a. 1, and intro., respectively.

98. Ibid., supp., q. 47, a. 4.

99. Ibid., Part III, q. 29, a. 2.

100. Ibid., supp, q. 45, a. 1. Thomas's entire discussion on marriage is a commentary on Lombard's *Sentences*, again showing the importance of Lombard's opinions.

101. Ibid., supp. q. 47, a. 6.

102. Ibid., supp. q. 47, a. 3.

103. Brundage, *Law*, 414.

104. Cf. Elizabeth Robertson, *Early English Devotional Prose and the Female Audience* (Knoxville: University of Tennessee Press, 1990), 32-43.

105. *Summa*, Part 1, q. 92, a. 1

106. See, respectively, summaries of these debates: Joan Gibson, "Could Christ Have Been Born a Woman?" *Journal of Feminist Studies in Religion* 8:1 (Spring 1992), 65-82; Francine Cardman, "The Medieval Question of Women and Orders," *The Thomist* 42 (1978), 582-599; Charles T. Wood, "The Doctors' Dilemma: Sin, Salvation and the Menstrual Cycle in Medieval Thought," *Speculum* 56:4 (October 1981), 710-727.

107. Quoted in Brundage, *Law*, 354.

108. Brundage repeats this thesis continually throughout *Law*.

Chapter 9
The New Spirituality and Medieval Culture

1. Carolyn Walker Bynum, *Jesus as Mother: Studies in the Spirituality of the High Middle Ages* (Berkeley: University of California Press, 1982), 130.

2. Anselm, *Prosloguim* in *St. Anselm Writings*, 23.

3. Ibid., 22.

4. Ibid., 24.

5. Ibid., 29.

6. *The Letters of St. Bernard of Clairvaux*, trans. Bruno Scott James (Chicago: Henry Regnecy Company, 1953), letter 119.

7. Ibid., letter 110:2.

8. Ibid., letter 116:1.

9. The differences in influence is evident in the interrogation transcripts of inquisitional investigations. See examples from *Le registre d'inquisitión de Jacques Fournier*, in Peter Dronke, *Women Writers of the Middle Ages* (Cambridge: Cambridge University Press, repr. 1994), 265-274.

10. Bynum, *Jesus*, 172.

11. Bernard, *On Loving God*, trans. Robert Walton, in *The Works of Bernard of Clairvaux*, vol. 5, *Treatises II* (Washington, DC: Cistercian Publications, 1974), 2 and 3.

12. Hadewijch, *Visions* in *Hadewijch: The Complete Works*, trans. M. Columba Hart (New York: Paulist Press, 1980), vision 9.

13. Bynum, *Jesus*, 143.

14. Jane Tibbetts Schulenburg, "Sexism and the Celestial Gynaeceum from 500 to 1200," *Journal of Medieval History* 4 (1978), 122, 127 and 131 n.11, reports that in the latter half of the eleventh-century women saints comprised 9.8 percent; by 1449 they were 29 percent. Bynum, *Jesus*, 137, also reports that there were more female than male lay saints between 1215 and 1500 and a great increase in married women saints.

15. By the thirteenth century the papacy was suppressing unofficial, local cults of saints. The decretals of 1234 gave absolute jurisdiction over canonizing saints to the pope, thereby making all future saints common to the universal church.

16. Hildegard of Bingen, *Causae et curae*, 104a, trans. in Dronke, *Women Writers*, 176 (English) and 244 (Latin).

17. *The Book of the Blessed Angela of Foligno* in *Angela of Foligno: Complete Works*, trans. Paul Lachance (New York: Paulist Press, 1993), 175.

18. *Hadewijch*, vision 14.

19. Thomas de Cantimpré, *The Life of Margaret of Ypres*, trans. Margot King (Toronto: Peregrina Publishing Co., 1990), 19.

20. Ibid., 23 and 17, respectively.

21. *Hadewijch*, vision 3.

22. Ibid., poem 16:31-33.

23. Ibid., vision 11.

24. Margaret Ebner, *Revelations* in *Margaret Ebner: Major Works*, trans. and ed. Leonard P. Hindsley (New York: Paulist Press, 1993), 166.

25. *The Letters of Hildegard of Bingen*, trans. Joseph L. Baird and Radd K. Ehrman (New York: Oxford University Press, 1994), letter 52r.

26. *Angela*, 168. See also Catherine M. Mooney, "The Authorial Role of Brother A. in the Composition of Angela of Foligno's *Revelations*" in *Creative Women in Medieval and Early Modern Italy*, ed. E. Ann Matter and John Coakley (Philadelphia: University of Pennsylvania Press, 1994), 34-63, for discussion of her "voice."

27. *Letters of Hildegard*, letter 1.

28. Ibid., letter 2.

29. Mechtild of Magdeburg, *Das fliessende Licht der Gottheit*, trans. Margot Schmidt (Einsiedeln: Benziger, 1956), 2:26, 1-9.

30. Ibid., 4:2, 130.

31. *The Life of Blessed Juliana of Mont-Cornillon*, trans. Barbara Newman (Toronto: Peregrina Publishing Co., 2nd ed. 1989), 126.

32. *Letters of Hildegard*, letters 61, 62.

33. Thomas de Cantimpré, *The Life of Lutgard of Aywières*, trans. Margot H. King (Toronto: Peregrina Publishing Co., 1989), 40.

34. Ibid., 36-37.

35. Mechtild of Hackeborn, *Le Livre de la Grâce Spéciale* (Tours: Mame, 1928), quoted in Mary J. Finnegan, *The Women of Helfta* (Athens: University of Georgia Press, 1991), 42.

36. Jordan of Saxony, Letter 9, in *Early Dominicans: Selected Writings*, ed. Simon Tugwell (New York: Paulist Press, 1982), 402.

37. *Lutgard*, 40.

38. *Juliana of Mont-Cornillon*, 65.

39. *Lutgard*, 17.

40. Clare of Assisi, letter 2:11-14, in *Francis and Clare: The Complete Works*, trans. Regis J. Armstrong and Ignatius C. Brady (New York: Paulist Press, 1982), 196.

41. Emile Mâle, *Art and Artists of the Middle Ages*, trans. S. S. Lowe (Redding Ridge, CT: Black Swan Books, Ltd., 1986), 150-156.

42. C. S. Jung, *Collected Works* (Princeton, NJ: Princeton University Press, 1964), 10:803.

43. Painton Cowen, *Rose Windows* (San Francisco: Chronicle Books, 1979), 10.

44. John Baker, *English Stained Glass of the Medieval Period* (London: Thames and Hudson Ltd., 1978), passim. An example of St. Catherine is found in the priory church in Gloucestershire (west window) and Mary Magdalene in West Horsely church in Surrey (east window).

45. Otto von Simpson, *The Gothic Cathedral* (New York: Pantheon Books, 1956), 8.

46. Henry Adams, *Mont-Saint-Michel and Chartres* (Princeton, NJ: Princeton University Press, repr. 1981), 91.

47. *PL* 179, 1606.

48. *Hymns*, ed. Britt, 275-280.

49. Ibid., 66.

50. Graef, *Mary*, 308.

51. See Patricia Ranft, "An Overturned Victory: Clare of Assisi and the Thirteenth-Century Church," *Journal of Medieval History* 17 (1991), 123-134.

52. The dossal was commissioned for the first church ca. 1281-1285; Thomas of Celano wrote the vita immediately after Clare's canonization and was probably finished in 1256.

53. *Legend and Writings of S. Clare of Assisi: Introduction; Translation; Studies*, ed. Ignatius Brady (St. Bonaventure, NY: Franciscan Institute, 1953), *Legend*, 4:7-8.

54. Ibid., 5:9.

55. Ibid., 16:24-26.

56. Ibid., 5:9.

57. See Jeryldene M. Wood, *Women, Art, and Spirituality: The Poor Clares of Early Modern Italy* (Cambridge: Cambridge University Press, 1996), 11-33.

58. *Legend*, 6:10a.

59. Reproduced in Susan Haskins, *Mary Magdalen: Myth and Metaphor* (New York: Harcourt Brace and Company, 1993), plate 46.

60. The work of Jeryldene M. Wood has formed the basis of the summary presented here. Besides *Women, Art*, see "Perceptions of Holiness in Thirteenth-Century Italian Painting: Clare of Assisi," *Art History* 14:3 (September 1991), 301-328.

61. See Annemarie Weyl Carr, "Women Artists in the Middle Ages," *Feminist Art Journal* 5:1 (Spring 1976), 5-9, and 26.

62. Jeffrey Burton Russell, *Lucifer* (Ithaca, NY: Cornell University Press, 1984), 129-158. Occasionally a masculine devil is "supported by female spirits, whom folklore transposes into witches" (149).

63. There is currently a struggle among art historians to rename it the Psalter of Christina of Markyate. See discussion in Madeline H. Caviness, "Anchoress, Abbess and Queen: Donors and Patrons or Intercessors and Matrons?" in *Cultural Patronage*, ed. McCash, 105-154, esp. n.8.

64. See Otto Pächt, C. R. Dodwell, and Francis Wormald, *The St. Albans Psalter (Albani Psalter)* (London: The Warburg Institute, 1960); and C. J. Holdsworth, "Christina of Markyate" in *Medieval Women*, ed. Derek Baker (Oxford: Basil Blackwell, 1978), 189-195.

65. Caviness, "Anchoress," 111-112, fig. 5 and fig. 6.

66. In 1927 a photocopy was made and from 1927 to 1933 women artists at the monastery at Eibinger painted a facsimile on parchment. See ibid., 147, n.31.

67. Probably the most available reproduction of *Scivias'* illuminations are in Matthew Fox, *Illuminations of Hildegard of Bingen* (Santa Fe, NM: Bear and Co., 1985), although the text is of debatable value.

68. Jonathan J. G. Alexander, *Medieval Illuminators and Their Methods of Work* (New Haven: Yale University Press, 1992), 18-19.

69. See Barbara Newman, *Sister of Wisdom* (Berkeley: University of California Press, 1987).

70. See *Hortus deliciarum*, ed. Rosalie Green et al (London: The Warburg Institute, 1979).

71. Richard Donovan, *The Liturgical Drama in Medieval Spain* (Toronto: Pontifical Institute of Medieval Studies, 1958), 13.

72. Fletcher Collins, *The Production of Medieval Church Music-Drama* (Charlottesville: University Press of Virginia, 1972), 57.

73. Ibid., 61.

74. Karl Young, *The Drama of the Medieval Church*, 2 vols. (Oxford: Oxford University Press, 1933), 1:221, 333, 381, 603, 605.

75. Ibid., 2:102-124.

76. See M. M. Butler, *Hrotsvitha: The Theatricality of Her Plays* (New York: Philosophical Library, 1960).

77. Quoted in Bert Nagel, "Dramas of Hrotsvit von Gandersheim" in *The Medieval Drama and Its Claudelian Revival*, ed. E. Catherine Dunn, T. Folitch, and Bernard M. Peebles (Washington, DC: Catholic University of America Press, 1970), 22.

78. *Die Werke der Hrotsvitha*, ed. K. A. Barack (Nürnberg: Bauer U. Raspe, 1858), 137-139.

79. J. Míchele Edwards, "Women in Music to ca. 1450," in *Women and Music: A History*, ed. Karen Pendle (Bloomington: Indiana University Press, 1991), 23.

80. *Letters of Hildegard*, letter 23.

81. Originally published in 1935, it has only recently been translated into English. See Herbert Grundmann, *Religious Movements in the Middle Ages*, trans. Steven Rowan (Notre Dame, IN: University of Notre Dame Press, 1995), 77.

82. Ernest McDonnell, *Beguines and Beghards in Medieval Culture* (New York: Octagon Books, 1969).

83. Quoted in Miri Rubin, *Corpus Christi* (Cambridge: Cambridge University Press, 1991), 171.

84. Bynum, *Fragmentation*, 122-125.

85. Mechtild of Magdeburg, *The Flowing Light of the Godhead* (London: Longmans, 1953), 48, quoted in ibid., 126.

86. *Juliana of Mont-Cornillon*, 94-95.

87. Ibid., 95-98.

88. Ibid., 98-100.

89. Ibid., 100-102. The office was used locally, but an office written by Thomas Aquinas was the one eventually used throughout the Roman church.

90. Rubin, *Corpus Christi*, 273.

91. Ibid., 347.

92. *Angela*, 245.

93. Ibid., 247.

94. Ibid., 244.

95. Ibid., 247.

96. Clare, letter 3:13 in *Francis and Clare*, 200.

97. *Hildegard of Bingen: Scivias*, trans. Columba Hart and Jane Bishop (New York: Paulist Press, 1990), 238.

98. *Hadewijch*, letter 24. See also letters 9, 15, 18, 22, 28, and 30.

99. Mechtild, *Livre*, 3.17, 21-22, quoted in Finnegan, *Helfta*, 136.

100. Gertrude the Great, *The Life and Revelations of Saint Gertrude* (Westminster, MD: Newman Press, repr. 1952), 2:4.

101. Ibid., 2:5.

Chapter 10
Late Medieval Mysticism and the *Devotio moderna*

1. These approaches are noted at least as far back as Maximus the Confessor. See Lars Thurnberg, *Microcosm and Mediator: The Theological Anthropology of Maximus the Confessor* (Copenhagen: Munksgaard, 1965), 363-374. For late medieval use of them, see Joannis de Gerson, *De mystica theologia*, ed. André Combes (Lucconi: In aedibus Thesauri Mundi, 1958), cons. 2.

2. *The Cloud of the Unknowing*, 4, in *The Cloud of the Unknowing, together with the Epistle of Privy Counsel by an English Mystic of the XIVth Century*, ed. Justin McCann (London: Burns and Oates, 1964), 10.

3. Meister Eckhart, Sermon 6, in *Meister Eckhart: The Essential Sermons, Commentaries, Treatises and Defense*, trans. Edmund Colledge and Bernard McGinn (New York: Paulist Press, 1981), 188.

4. *Johannes Tauler: Sermons*, trans. Maria Shrady (Mahwah, NJ: Paulist Press, 1985), 103-108.

5. John Ruusbroec, *The Little Book of Clarification* in *John Ruusbroec: The Spiritual Espousals and Other Works*, trans. James A. Wiseman (New York: Paulist Press, 1985), 265.

6. *Meister Eckhart*, 188.

7. *Privy Counsel*, 8, in *Cloud with Epistle*, 126.

8. *Eckhart*, 187.

9. *Cloud*, 2, in *Cloud with Epistle*, 6-7.

10. *Cloud*, 2 ,25, and *Privy Counsel*, 3, in *Cloud with Epistle*, 6, 42, and 112.

11. John Tauler, *The Following of Christ*, trans. J. R. Morell (London: T. Fisher Unwin, 1910), 2:44, 46, and 44, respectively.

12. *Henry Suso: The Exemplar, with Two German Sermons*, trans. and ed. Frank Tobin (New York: Paulist Press, 1989), 366; and *Eckhart*, 108-109, both mention Eve's role at the fall as the possessor of inferior reason and, therefore, not responsible. Elsewhere, however, *Henry Suso* (374) does place blame at Eve's feet. *John Ruusbroec*, 41, narrates it thus: "But then came an evildoer, the enemy from hell, who . . . deceived the woman. They both deceived the man, in whom human nature existed in its entirety."

13. *Henry Suso*, 134, and Henry Suso, *Wisdom's Watch upon the Hours*, trans. Edmund Colledge (Washington, DC: Catholic University of America Press, 1994), 286.

14. *Cloud*, 22, in *Cloud with Epistle*, 38.

15. Evelyn Underwood, *The Mystics of the Church* (New York: Schocken Books, 1964), 54.

16. Grundmann, *Religious Movement*, 239, and Henrich Denifle, "Meister Eckhart lateinische Schriften und die Grundanschauung seiner Lehre," *Archiv für Litteratur und Kirchengeschichte des Mittelalters* 2 (1886), 417-615.

17. Scholars acknowledge that Elsbeth Stagel may well have written a good deal of the vita. See discussion of authorship and of its classification as autobiography in *Henry Suso*, 38-44.

18. Ibid., 63.

19. Ibid., 134.

20. Ibid., 141.

21. Suso, *Wisdom's Watch*, 141; 222; *Henry Suso*, 267, respectively.

22. *Henry Suso*, 67-69.

23. Ibid., 69.

24. Suso, *Wisdom's Watch*, 106.

25. Ibid., 190.

26. The other two devotional works, according to Edmund Colledge, were Pseudo-Bonaventure's *Meditations on the Life of Christ* and Ludolph of Saxony's *Life of Christ*. See Suso, *Wisdom's Watch*, 15-30, for discussion and bibliography.

27. *Espousal*, prologue, in *John Ruusbroec*, 41.

28. See John Bugge, *Virginitas* (The Hague: Martinus Nijhoff, 1975), 59-79; and Bynum, *Jesus as Mother*, for discussion of writers.

29. Bynum, *Fragmentation*, 171.

30. *Espousal*, prologue, in *John Ruusbroec*, 41.

31. Ibid., 71.

32. Barbara Newman, *From Virile Woman to WomanChrist* (Philadelphia: University of Pennsylvania Press, 1995), 138.

33. Catherine of Bologna, *The Seven Weapons of the Spirit* in *Women Writers of the Renaissance and Reformation*, ed. Katherina M. Wilson (Athens: University of Georgia Press, 1987), 89 and 87, respectively.

34. Ibid., 94.

35. Birgitta was a noblewoman, and it was her nobility that gave her a political voice in her native home at first. After her husband's death in 1344 she received her first vision and her influence in Sweden only increased from that point on, even after her move to Rome in 1349.

36. *Regula Salvatoris*, 29: 283-286, in *Sancta Birgitta Opera Minora I: Regula Salvatoris*, ed. Sten Eklund (Stockholm: Almqvist and Wiksell International, 1975), 134-135.

37. *Extrauagancium* 44, 1-7, in *Den Heliga Birgittas Reuelaciones, Extrauagantes*, ed. Lennart Hollman (Uppsala: Almquist and Wiksells Boktryckeri, 1956), 160-161.

38. *Reuelaciones* 4.138, trans. in Johannes Jørgensen, *Saint Bridget of Sweden*, 2 vols., trans. I. Lund (London: Longmans, 1954), 2:221-226.

39. *Defensorium St. Birgittae*, Bodleian ms. Hamilton 7. Oxford University, F. 233v., quoted in James Schmidtke, "'Saving' by Faint Praise: St. Birgitta of Sweden, Adam Easton and Medieval Antifeminism," *American Benedictine Review* 33:2 (June 1982), 160.

40. Johannes Tortsch, *Onus mundi, id est prophecia de malo futuro ipsi mundo superventuro*, in *Das Werk der Heiligen Birgitta von Schweden in oberdeutschen Überlieferung* ed. Ulrich Montag (Munich: Beck, 1968), 260.

41. *Reuelaciones*, 4.141.

42. See *Revelations*, 7:12; 7:27-29 (for bishops); 7:11; 7;27 (queen); 7:20 (friar); 7;5 (lords) in *Birgitta of Sweden: Life and Selected Revelations*, ed. Marguerite Harris, trans. A. Kezel (New York: Paulist Press, 1990).

43. Ibid., 7:19.24-25.

44. Ibid., 7:28.18.

45. Eric Colledge, "Epistola solitarii ad reges: Alphonse of Pecha as Organizer of Brigittine and Urbanist Propaganda," *Medieval Studies* 18 (1956), 49.

46. See for Bologna, letter 63; Lucco, letter 53; Crusade, letters 30, 78,79; prisoner, letter 31; Florentine negotiations, letters 70, 72, 82; interdict, letter 64; Siena and Lucco, letter 41, in *The Letters of St. Catherine of Siena*, vol. 1, trans. Suzanne Noffke (Binghamton, NY: Medieval and Renaissance Texts and Studies, 1988).

47. Ibid., letter 17.

48. *Catherine of Siena: The Dialogue*, trans. Suzanne Noffke (New York: Paulist Press: 1980), 283.

49. Ibid., 26, 49, 50, 53, 58, 114, 165, 205, 208, 273, 276, 277, 283, 288, 290, and 324.

50. Ibid., 51 and 67.

51. Ibid., 205.

52. Ibid., 212.

53. Ibid., 216.

54. Ibid., 234.

55. Ibid., 26.

56. *Letters of Catherine*, letter 17.

57. Ibid., letter 71.

58. Ibid., letter 63.

59. Letter 117, trans. in Karen Scott, "'So Catarina': Catherine of Siena," in *Dear Sister: Medieval Women and the Epistolary Genre*, ed. Karen Cherewatuk and Ulrica Wiethaus (Philadelphia: University of Pennsylvania Press, 1993), 112.

60. See Thomas Luongo, "Catherine of Siena: Rewriting Female Holy Authority," in *Women, the Book and the Godly*, ed. Lesley Smith and Jane Taylor (Cambridge: D.S. Brewer, 1995), 89-103.

61. Extant correspondence includes letters to leaders of Siena, Lucco, Florence, Milan, Bologna, Pisa, Naples, Hungary and France, and to various monks, nuns and members of the papal court as well as the pope.

62. Cf. introduction in *Julian of Norwich: Showings*, ed. Edmund Colledge and James Walsh (New York: Paulist Press, 1978), and Denise Baker, *Julian of Norwich "Showings": From Vision to Book* (Princeton, NJ: Princeton University Press, 1994).

63. *Showings*, ed. Colledge, 294.

64. Ibid., 235-236.

65. Ibid., 227-228. See Helen Phillips, "Rewriting the Fall: Julian of Norwich and the *Chevalier des dames*," in *Women, Book*, ed. Smith and Taylor, 149-156.

66. *Showings*, ed. Colledge, 181.

67. Ibid., 135.

68. See Grace Jantzen, *Julian of Norwich: Mystic and Theologian* (New York: Paulist Press, 1988), 15-20, for historiography of the debate. More than likely it is a conventional rhetorical disclaimer of authors.

69. Baker, *From Vision to Book*, 6-14.

70. *The Book of Margery Kempe*, in *Medieval Mystics of England*, ed. Eric Colledge (New York: Charles Scribner's Sons, 1961), 288 and 292.

71. Ibid., 294. Birgitta was also a favorite of two other contemporary holy women, Clara Gambacorta and Dorothy of Montau. See Richard Kieckhefer, *Unquiet Souls* (Chicago: University of Chicago Press, 1984), 22-49.

72. Susan Eberly, "Margery Kempe, St. Mary Magdalene and Patterns of Contemplation," *Downside Review* 107 (July 1989), 209-223.

73. *Book of Margery*, 285.

74. Ibid., 300-301.

75. Ibid., 302.

76. John van Engen, "The Virtues, the Brothers and the Schools," *Revue bénédictine* 98 (1988), 178; and Wybren Scheepsma, "'For hereby I hope to rouse some piety': Books of Sisters from Convents and Sister Houses Associated with the *Devotio Moderna* in the Low Countries" in *Women, Book* ed. Smith and Taylor, 30.

77. Albert Hyma, *The Christian Renaissance: A History of the "Devotio Moderna,"* 2nd ed. (Hamden, CT: Archon Books, 1965), 512.

78. This is not to say such analogies are never used. See, for example, a sermon addressed to the laity by Geert Grote in which he compares an earthly marriage to a heavenly marriage. *Devotio Moderna: Basic Writings,* trans. John van Engen (New York: Paulist Press, 1988), 96-97, and Gerlach Peter's letter, ibid., 222.

79. Thomas à Kempis, *The Imitation of Christ,* trans. Richard Whitford, ed. Harold Gardiner (Garden City, NY: Doubleday and Company, 1955), 3:37.

80. Ibid., 3:12; 2:4; 3:3; 1:20; 1:17; and 3:3, respectively.

81. *Devotio Moderna,* 56.

82. Gerard Zerbert, *The Spiritual Ascents,* in ibid., 245.

83. Ibid., 249.

84. Ibid., 255.

85. Ibid., 268.

86. Ibid., 270.

87. Ibid., Letter to Lubbe, 218. See also John Brinckerink's collation on conversion, ibid., 223-234.

88. *Edifying Points of the Older Sisters,* in ibid., 121-122.

89. Ibid., 126, 134, 133, 126, respectively.

90. Ibid., 121.

91. Salome Sticken, *A Way of Life for Sisters,* in ibid., 181.

92. *Edifying Points,* 122-123.

93. Diepenveen, *Book of Sisters,* prologue and epilogue, trans. in Scheepsma, "Book of Sisters," 37.

94. *Devotio Moderna,* 45.

95. Ibid., 121.

Chapter 11
Women in Late Medieval Sermons, Literature, and the Arts

1. Grundmann, *Religious Movements,* 187-201.

2. Hadewijch and Beatrice of Nazareth wrote in the vernacular; the vita of Juliana of Mont-Cornillon was originally written in French; the vita of Lutgard of Aywieres was translated early on into German; and Mechtild of Magdeburg's *The Flowing Light of the Divinity* was the first great religious prose in German.

3. Grundmann, *Religious Movements,* 192-196.

4. Ibid., 396, n. 54.

5. Ibid., 187-188.

6. H. Leith Spencer, *English Preaching in the Late Middle Ages* (Oxford: Clarendon Press, 1993), 65; and Larissa Taylor, *Soldiers of Christ: Preaching in Medieval and Reformation France* (New York: Oxford University Press, 1992), 15-16

7. Michele Menot, "Second Careme de Paris," quoted in Taylor, *Soldiers*, 31. Bishop Brunton made similar claims; see G. R. Owst, *Preaching in Medieval England* (New York: Russell and Russell, reissue 1965), 173.

8. Taylor, *Soldiers*, 157.

9. Pepin, *Conciones de sanctis*, 292, quoted in ibid., 176-177.

10. *AASS*, April 3, 884, cited in Bynum, *Fragmentation*, 169.

11. Messier, *Super epistola*, in Taylor, *Soldiers*, 174.

12. Pepin, *Rosareum aurem*, in ibid., 175.

13. Maillard, *Sermones de adventu*, in ibid., 162.

14. Menot, *Paris*, 290, in ibid., 158.

15. Pepin, *Conciones quadragesimales*, 342, in ibid., 158.

16. Quoted in G. R. Owst, *Literature and Pulpit in Medieval England* (Oxford: Basil Blackwell, 1961), 20.

17. Quoted in Iris Origo, *The World of San Benardino* (New York: Harcourt Brace & World, 1962), 72.

18. Pepin, *Quadragesimales*, 517, in Taylor, *Soldiers*, 172.

19. John Dalmus, "Preaching to the Laity in Fifteenth-Century Germany: Johannes Nider's 'Harps,'" *Journal of Ecclesiastical History* 34:1 (January 1983), 59.

20. Maillard, *Opus Parisius*, in Taylor, *Soldiers*, 173-174.

21. Pepin, *Rosareum*, 352, in ibid., 171.

22. Sherry L. Reames, *The Legenda aurea* (Madison: University of Wisconsin Press, 1985), 3-5.

23. Robert Seybolt, "Fifteenth-Century Editions of the *Legenda aurae*," *Speculum* 21 (1946), 327-338.

24. Jacobus de Voragine, *The Golden Legend or Lives of the Saints as Englished by William Caxton* (London: J. M. Desk and Co., 1900), 3:1.

25. Ibid., 3:289, and 303-304.

26. Ibid., 4:82, and 76.

27. Haskins, *Magdalen*, 223-228.

28. *A Legend of Holy Women: Osbern Bokerham's Legends of Holy Women*, ed. Sheila Delaney (Notre Dame, IN: University of Notre Dame Press, 1992), xxvii.

29. Ibid., 8. See comments on Gower, Chaucer, and Lydgate, 193.

30. Ibid., 6.

31. Ibid., 10.

32. Ibid.

33. Ibid., 16.

34. Ibid., 17-18.

35. Ibid., 175.

36. Ibid., 182.

37. *Collection of Ordinances and Regulations for the Government of the Royal Household*, ed. J. Nichols (London: London Society of Antiquaries, 1790), quoted in Anne C. Bartlett, *Male Authors, Female Readers* (Ithaca, NY: Cornell University Press, 1995), 10-11.

38. Sylvia Thrupp, *The Merchant Class of Medieval London, 1300-1500* (Ann Arbor: University of Michigan Press, 1962), 158.

39. Susan Groag Bell, "Medieval Women Book Owners," in *Sisters and Workers in the Middle Ages*, ed. Judith Bennett et al. (Chicago: University of Chicago Press, 1989), 137-145.

40. Katherine Gill, "Women and the Production of Religious Literature in the Vernacular, 1300-1500," in *Creative Women in Medieval and Early Modern Italy*, ed. E. Ann Matter and John Coakley (Philadelphia: University of Pennsylvania Press, 1994), 70.

41. Bell, "Book Owners," 153-156.

42. Christine de Pizan, *Le Trésor de la Cité de Dames*, quoted in ibid., 149.

43. Quoted in Gill, "Production," 71.

44. *The Chastising of God's Children and the Treatise of Perfection of the Sons of God*, ed. Joyce Bazine and Eric Colledge (Oxford: Basil Blackwell, 1957), 95, quoted in Bartlett, *Male, Female*, 98.

45. *A Devout Treatyse Called the Tree and the xii Frutes of the Holy Goost*, ed. J. J. Vaissier (Groningen: J. B. Wolters, 1960), 26-27.

46. *Book to a Mother*, ed. Adrian J. McCarthy (Salzburg: Institut für Anglistik und Amerikanistik, 1981), 39.

47. Bartlett, *Male, Female*, 102-103.

48. *Chastising*, 165.

49. Ibid., 194.

50. *Dives and Pauper*, ed. Priscilla Barnum (London: Oxford University Press, 1980), 81.

51. Ibid., 81-84.

52. Christine de Pizan, *The Letter of the God of Love*, in *The Writings of Christine de Pizan*, ed. Charity C. Willard (New York: Persea Books, 1994), 145-149.

53. *Book of the City of Ladies*, in ibid., 171-177.

54. Charity C. Willard, "A Fifteenth-Century View of Women's Role in Medieval Society: Christine de Pizan's *Livre des Trois Vertus*," in *The Role of Women in the Middle Ages*, ed. Rosemarie Morewedge (Albany: University of New York Press, 1975), 90-120.

55. Quoted in Charity C. Willard, *Christine de Pizan: Her Life and Works* (New York: Persea Books, 1984), 83.

276   WOMEN AND SPIRITUAL EQUALITY IN CHRISTIAN TRADITION

56. Quoted in Margaret King, *Women of the Renaissance* (Chicago: University of Chicago Press, 1991), 93.

57. Baldesar Castiglione, *The Book of the Courtier*, trans. George Bull (Baltimore: Penguin Books, 1967), 217 and 220.

58. Ibid., 223-225.

59. See Glenda McLeod, *Virtue and Venom* (Ann Arbor: University of Michigan Press, 1991), 1-9 and 141, for discussion of catalogs.

60. Ibid., 3.

61. Dante Alighieri, *The Divine Comedy*, trans. Geoffrey L. Bickersteth (Cambridge, MA: Harvard University Press, 1965), Paradiso 32:85-87.

62. Ibid., Inferno 5:58-66.

63. Ibid., Purgatorio 30:136-140.

64. Ibid., 30:121-123.

65. Ibid., 27:128-129.

66. Ibid., 3:34-36

67. Ibid., 30:55-57

68. Ibid., 30:74

69. Ibid., Paradiso 7:19-24.

70. Ibid., 33:1-21.

71. Ferrante, *Women as Image*, 152. One cannot but wonder why so few works in women's studies utilize Dante as a source.

72. See Pamela Sheingorn, "'The Wise Mother': The Image of St. Anne Teaching the Virgin Mary," *Gesta* 32:1 (1993), 78.

73. Eamon Duffy, "Holy Maydens, Holy Wyfes: The Cult of Women Saints in the Fifteenth- and Sixteenth-century England," in *Women in the Church*, ed. W. J. Sheils and Diana Wood (Oxford: Basil Blackwell, 1990), 185.

74. Haskins, *Magdalen*, 232.

75. *Birgitta: Revelations*, 7:21.1-16. James Hall, *A History of Ideas and Images in Italian Art* (New York: Harper & Row, 1983), 214, notes that Birgitta may have previously viewed such a scene in an Italian painting but, given the popularity of her work, this still does not diminish her role in its spread.

76. *Birgitta: Revelations*, 7:715.26-27 and 32.

77. See, for example, *Cultural Patronage*, ed. McCash, where literary patronage is well represented but not artistic.

78. Giorgio Vasari, *The Lives of the Painters, Sculptors and Architects*, ed. William Gaunt (London: J. M. Dent and Sons, 1963), 1:111-113.

79. Jeryldene M. Wood, "Breaking the Silence: The Poor Clares and the Visual Arts in Fifteenth-Century Italy," *Renaissance Quarterly* 48 (Summer 1995), 266-272.

80. See Ann M. Roberts, "Chiara Gambacorta of Pisa as Patroness of the Arts," in *Creative Women*, ed. Matter and Coakley, 120-154; and Dominique Rigaux, "The Franciscan Tertiaries at the Convent of St. Anna," *Gesta* 31:2 (1992), 92-98.

81. Rigaux, "Tertiaries," 96.

82. See Serena Spanò Martinelli, "La biblioteca del 'Corpus Domini' bolognese: l'inconsueto spaccato di una cultura monastica femminile," *La Bibliofiliá* 88:1 (1986), 1-23.

83. Catherine, *Seven Weapons of the Spirit*, in *Women Writers*, ed. Wilson, 91. She did not make the treatise public until on her deathbed.

84. Ibid., 87.

85. Ibid., 86.

86. Illuminata Bembo, *Lo specchio de illuminazione*, quoted in Wood, *Women, Art*, 134.

87. In *Women Writers*, ed. Wilson, 93.

88. Quoted in Wood, *Women, Art*, 130-131.

89. See example and discussion in Gail McMurray Gilson, *The Theater of Devotion* (Chicago: University of Chicago Press, 1989), 7-10.

90. For example, see Ghirlandaio's Madonna of Mercy in Hall, *Ideas and Images*, 223.

91. Gilson, *Devotion*, 144 and fig. 6.2.

92. Eamon Duffy, *The Stripping of the Altars* (New Haven, CT: Yale University Press, 1992), 181.

93. Quoted in *Women Writers*, ed. Wilson, 84-85.

94. Hall, *Ideas and Images*, 214.

95. R. W. Pfaff, *New Liturgical Feasts in Later Medieval England* (Oxford: Clarendon Press, 1970), 97-115.

Chapter 12
Reformation, Counter-Reformation, and Enlightenment
Opinions of Women

1. Pierre Roussel, *Systeme physique et moral . . .* (Paris: Vincent, 1803).

2. *Luther's Works*, ed. Jaroslav Pelikan (St. Louis, MO: Concordia Publishing House, 1958), 1:69.

3. Ibid., 45:37.

4. Ibid., 45:367, 369.

5. John Calvin, *The Institutes of Christian Religion*, ed. Tony Lane and Hilary Osborne (Grand Rapids, MI: Baker House, 1986), 85-94.

6. Ibid., 87.

7. Ibid., 62.

8.   John Calvin, "Sermon on Epistle of St. Paul to Galatians," in *Renaissance Women: A Sourcebook*, ed. Kate Aughterson (London: Routledge, 1995), 17; and John Calvin, "Sermon on Epistle of St. Paul to Ephesians," in ibid.

9.   Huldreich Zwingli, *On True and False Religion*, in *Great Voices of the Reformation. An Anthology*, ed. Henry Fosdick (New York: The Modern Library, 1952), 162. See also *An Account of the Faith*, in ibid., 183.

10. Huldrych Zwingli, quoted in W. P. Stephens, *The Theology of Huldrych Zwingli* (Oxford: Clarendon Press, 1986), 139-140.

11. Balthasar Hubmaier, *On Free Will*, trans. in *Spiritual and Anabaptist Writers*, ed. George H. Williams (Philadelphia: Westminster Press, 1957), 119.

12. Dietrich Philips, *The Church of God*, in *Spiritual and Anabaptist*, 230.

13. Erasmus, *In Praise of Marriage*, trans. C. Fantazzi, in *Erasmus on Women*, ed. Erika Rummel (Toronto: University of Toronto Press, 1996), 59.

14. Erasmus, *The Institution of Marriage*, trans. Michael Heath, in ibid., 117-118.

15. Erasmus, *In Praise*, in *Erasmus*, 67.

16. *Luther's Works*, 46:145-151.

17. Ibid., 46:147.

18. Ibid., 45:19 and 45:37.

19. See Steven Ozment, *When Fathers Ruled* (Cambridge, MA: Harvard University Press, 1983); M. Lucille Marr, "Anabaptist Women of the North: Peers in Faith, Subordinate in Marriage," *The Mennonite Quarterly* 61 (October 1987), 347-362; Paul Russell, *Lay Theology in the Reformation* (Cambridge: Cambridge University Press, 1986); and Lyndal Roper, *The Holy Household* (Oxford: Clarendon Press, 1959).

20. Merry E. Wiesner, "Nuns, Wives, and Mothers: Women and the Reformation in Germany," in *Women in Reformation and Counter Reformation Europe*, ed. Sherrin Marshall (Bloomington: Indiana University Press, 1989), 10. See also Joyce Youings, *The Dissolution of the Monasteries* (London: Allen and Unwin, 1971).

21. Milagros Ortega Costa, "Spanish Women in the Reformation," in *Women in Reformation*, ed. Marshall, 92; and *Angela*, 114.

22. Quoted in Jodi Bilinkoff, "Confessor, Penitents, and the Construction of Identities in Early Modern Avila," in *Culture and Society in Early Modern Europe (1500-1800)*, ed. Barbara Diefendorf and Carla Hesse (Ann Arbor: University of Michigan Press, 1993), 86.

23. See Patricia Ranft, "A Key to Counter Reformation Women's Activism: The Confessor-Spiritual Director," *Journal of Feminist Studies in Religion* 10:2 (Fall 1994), 7-26.

24. *The Third Mystic of Avila: The Self-revelation of Maria Vela*, trans. Frances P. Keyes (New York: Farrar, Strauss and Cudahy, 1960), 41-42.

25. Ibid., 43.

26. Ibid., 47-48.

27. Ibid., 50.

28. Ibid., 49.

29. Teresa of Avila, *The Life of the Holy Mother Teresa of Jesus,* in *The Complete Works of Saint Teresa of Jesus,* trans. and ed. E. Allison Peers (London: Sheed and Ward, 1957), 1:73.

30. Ibid., 1:299.

31. Ibid., 1:58.

32. Ibid., 1:56.

33. *Way of Perfection,* in *Complete Works,* 2: 117; and *Life,* in *Complete Works,* 1:150.

34. Alison Weber, *Teresa of Avila and the Rhetoric of Femininity* (Princeton, NJ: Princeton University Press, 1990), 11. Weber documents in an organized, scholarly manner what most readers instinctively perceive.

35. Quoted in *Complete Works,* 2:354.

36. *Conceptions of Love of God,* in ibid., 2:359.

37. Ibid., 2:362.

38. *Spiritual Relations,* 19, in *Complete Works,* 1:344.

39. In his introduction to *Way of Perfection* in *Complete Works,* 2:xvi, Peers calls this "the most beautiful and expressive exposition of this degree of contemplation to be found in any book on the interior life whatsoever."

40. Ibid., 2:13.

41. Maria de San José, *Recreations,* in Electa Arenal and Stacey Schau, *Untold Sisters: Hispanic Nuns in their Own Works,* trans. Amanda Powell (Albuquerque: University of New Mexico Press, 1989), 95.

42. Ibid., 94-96.

43. Ana de San Bartolomé, *Autobiography,* in *Untold Sisters,* 57.

44. Ibid., 64.

45. Cecilia del Nacimiento, "First Account of God's Favors," in *Untold Sisters,* 181.

46. Sor Juana Inés de la Cruz, *Poems, Protest and a Dream: Selected Writings,* trans. Margaret S. Peden (New York: Penguin Books, 1997), 59, 49.

47. Ibid., 49.

48. Ibid., 53.

49. Maria de San José in *Untold Sisters,* 94.

50. Marie Dentière, Letter, in *Women Writers,* ed. Wilson, 276-277.

51. See Ranft, *Women,* 96-106.

52. See Edward Udovic, "'Caritas Christi Urgent Nos': The Urgent Challenges of Charity in Seventeenth Century France," *Vincentian Heritage* 12:2 (1991), 85-87.

53. Letter to Sisters at Valpuiseaux in *Vincent de Paul and Louise de Marillac: Rules, Conferences, and Writings,* ed. Frances Ryan and John Rybolt (New York: Paulist Press, 1995), 162.

54. Translated in Mary Chambers, *The Life of Mary Ward, 1585-1645*, ed. Henry J. Coleridge (London: Burns and Oates, 1882-1885), 1:273-274. Commonly known as the English Ladies, their formal name was the Institute of the Blessed Virgin Mary.

55. See Wendy M. Wright, *Bond of Perfection* (New York: Paulist Press, 1985).

56. See Judith C. Taylor, "From Proselytizing to Social Reform: Three Genera-tions of French Female Teaching Congregations 1600-1720," Ph.D diss. Arizona State University, 1980, 679-693, for a complete history, and appendix 1 for a list of the orders. Numerous nonteaching orders also were founded by male-female partnerships. See discussion in *Bérulle and the French School: Selected Writings*, ed. William M. Thompson, trans. L. M. Glendon (New York: Paulist Press, 1989), 81 and 91, n. 6.

57. *Francis de Sales, Jane de Chantal: Letters of Spiritual Direction*, trans. Péronne M. Thibert (New York: Paulist Press, 1988), 186.

58. *Rule of St. Angela Merici*, trans. in M. Monica, *Angela Merici and Her Teaching Idea, 1474-1540* (New York: Longman Green and Company, 1927), 275.

59. *Francis, Jane*, 156.

60. Ibid., 174 and 179.

61. *Vincent and Louise*, 206-207.

62. *Rule of Angela*, 246.

63. "Particular Rules for the Sisters of the Parishes" in *Vincent and Louise*, 194.

64. *Rule of Angela*, 266.

65. *Vincent and Louise*, 206.

66. Ibid., 204.

67. Francis de Sales, *Introduction to a Devout Life* (Ratisborn: Frederick Pustet & Company, n.d.) 7-8.

68. Ignatius Loyola, *The Spiritual Exercises*, trans. Thomas Corbishley (Wheathamp-stead: Anthony Clarke, repr. 2nd ed., 1979), 18. We know women made the Exercises right from the beginning. See letter from Sebastiana Exarch, dated 1545, in Hugo Rahner, *Saint Ignatius Loyola: Letters to Women*, trans. Kathleen Pond and S. Weetman (New York: Herder and Herder, 1960), 301.

69. Francis de Sales, *Oeuvres*, 25:291-292, trans. in Elizabeth Rapley, *The Dévotes* (Montreal: McGill-Queens' University Press, 1990), 37.

70. Rahner, *Ignatius: Letters*, 307.

71. See ibid.; and James Reites, "Ignatius and Ministry with Women," *The Way*, supp. 17 (Summer 1992), 7-19.

72. *Francis, Jane*, 11-13.

73. See M. M. Rivet, *The Influence of the Spanish Mystics on the Works of Saint Francis de Sales* (Washington, DC: Catholic University of America Press, 1941).

74. Saints Catherine, Catherine of Siena, Angela of Foligno, Isabel of Portugal, Martha, Mary Magdalene, Gertrude, Monica, Merecendia, Anne, Paula, and Ursula are some of the women. In *Book of Foundations* Teresa writes at some length about various models of behavior, such as Cataline de Cardona. See *Complete Works*, 3:156-162, quote 3:161.

75. Pierre de Bérulle, "Elevation to Jesus Christ our Lord," in *Bérulle*, 178-179.

76. *The Acts and Monuments of John Foxe*, ed. Stephen Reed Cattley (London: Seeley and Burnside, 1838-1841), 8:496, quoted in Pamela J. Grace, "John Foxe's Protestant Women Martyrs: Bold Actors or Quintessential Victims?" M.A. thesis, Central Michigan University, 1997, 37. The discussion here derives much from this excellent, thorough study.

77. Cattley, 7:343, in Grace, "John Foxe," 93.

78. *Acts*, quoted in Ellen Macek, "The Emergence of a Feminine Spirituality in *The Book of Martyrs*," *Sixteenth Century Journal* 19:1 (1988), 78.

79. Cattley, *Acts*, 8:501-502.

80. For explanation see Ranft, *Women*, 124-128.

81. "Three Speeches of our Reverend Mother," trans. in Chambers, *Mary Ward*, 1:408-410.

82. In the Roman culture, for example, the tradition was expressed in the writings of women religious, particularly those who settled in the Americas. See S. Juana Inés, *Poems;* and *Marie of the Incarnation. Selected Writings*, ed. Irene Mahoney (New York: Paulist Press, 1989).

83. See Francis Lee Utley, *The Crooked Rib* (New York: Octagon Books, 1970), 3-90, for a history of such debates.

84. Jane Anger, *Protection for Women . . .*, in Katherine U. Henderson and B. F. McManus, *Half Humankind. Contexts and Texts of the Controversy about Women in England 1540-1640* (Urbana: University of Illinois Press, 1985), 173.

85. Ibid., 219.

86. Esther Sowernam, *"Esther hath hanged Haman . . ."* in ibid., 218-219.

87. Mary Tattlewell and Joan Hit-him-home, *The women's sharp revenge . . .*, in ibid., 308.

88. Sowernam, *Esther*, in ibid., 223.

89. Edward Gosynhill, *The Schoolhouse of Women . . .*, in ibid., 148.

90. Joseph Swetnam, *The arraignment of Lewd, idle, froward and unconstant women . . .*, in ibid., 193-194.

91. Sowernam, *Haman*, in ibid., 227, 222.

92. Tattlewell and Hit-him-home, *Revenge*, in ibid., 313.

93. See Peter Gay, *The Enlightenment: An Interpretation.* (New York: Vintage Books, 1966), 322-357.

94. Voltaire, *Philosophical Dictionary*, quoted in Michele Crampe-Casnabet, "A Sampling of Eighteenth-Century Philosophy," in *A History of Women in the West*, vol. 3, *Renaissance and Enlightenment Paradoxes*, ed. Natalie Zemon Davis and Arlette Farge (Cambridge, MA: Belknap Press of Harvard University Press, 1993), 326.

95. Jean Jacques Rousseau, *Emile*, quoted in ibid.

96. Ibid., 329.

97. Montesquieu, *The Spirit of Laws*, quoted in ibid., 328.

98. M. Diderot, *Oeuvres philosophiques*, ed. Paul Verniere (Paris: Garnier frères, 1961), 593.

99. *Encyclopedie, ou dictionnaire raisonne des sciences, des arts et des metiers, par une societe de gens de lettres*, ed. Denis Diderot and Jean LeRond d'Alembert (Paris: Briasson et al, 1751), s.v. "Femme (jurisp)" by Boucher d'Argis, 475, col. 1-2.

Bibliography

Primary Sources

Acts and Monuments of John Foxe. Vols. 8. Edited by Stephen Reed Cattley. London: Seeley and Burnside, 1838-1841.

The Acts of the Christian Martyrs. Translated by Herbert Musurillo. Oxford: Clarendon Press, 1972.

Alighieri, Dante. *The Divine Comedy.* Translated by Geoffrey L. Bickersteth. Cambridge, MA: Harvard University Press, 1965.

Ana de San Bartolome. *Autobiographia.* In Electra Arenal and Stacey Schau. *Untold Sisters: Hispanic Nuns in Their Own Works.* Translated by Amanda Powell, 46-65. Albuquerque: University of New Mexico Press, 1989.

Anchorite Spirituality: "Ancrene Wisse" and Associated Works. Translated by Anne Savage and Nicholas Watson. New York: Paulist Press, 1991.

Angela of Foligno: Complete Works. Translated by Paul Lachance. New York: Paulist Press, 1993.

Anglo-Saxon Litanies of the Saints. Edited by Michael Lapidge. London: Henry Bradshaw Society, 1991.

Anglo-Saxon Missionaries in Germany. Edited and translated by C. H. Talbot. New York: Sheed and Ward, 1954.

The Apostolic Fathers. Translated by Francis X. Glimm, Joseph Marique, and Gerald Walsh. Washington, DC: Catholic University of America Press, 1947.

Arendzen, J. P. "An Entire Syriac Text on the *Apostolic Church Order.*" *Journal of Theological Studies* 3 (1902), 59-80.

Athanasius. *The Life of St. Anthony the Great.* Willits, CA: Eastern Orthodox Books, n.d.

Augustine. *The Catholic and Manichaean Ways of Life.* Translated by Donald A. and Idella J. Gallagher. Washington, DC: Catholic University of America Press, 1966.

———. *Confessions.* Translated by R. S. Pine-Coffin. New York: Penguin Books, repr. 1988.

———. *Eighty-Three Different Questions.* Translated by David L. Mosher. Washington, DC: Catholic University of America Press, 1982.

———. *Letters.* Vols. 5. Translated by W. Parsons. New York: Fathers of the Church, 1956.

————. *The Literal Meaning of Genesis*. Translated by John H. Taylor. New York: Newman Press, 1982.

————. *Retractions*. Translated by Mary Bogan. Washington, DC: Catholic University of America Press, 1968.

————. *The Trinity*. Translated by Stephen McKenna. Washington, DC: Catholic University of America Press, 1962.

Bede. *A History of the English Church and People*. Translated by Leo Sherley-Price, revised by R. E. Latham. Harmondsworth: Penguin Books, rev. ed., 1968.

Bérulle and the French School: Selected Writings. Edited by William M. Thompson. Translated by L. M. Glendon. New York: Paulist Press, 1989.

Bethu Brigte. Edited by Donncha O'hAodha. Dublin: Dublin Institute for Advanced Studies, 1978.

Birgitta of Sweden: Life and Selected Revelations. Edited by Marguerite Harris. Translated by A. Kezel. New York: Paulist Press, 1990.

The Book of Margery Kempe. In *Medieval Mystics of England*. Edited by Eric Colledge. New York: Charles Scribner's Sons, 1961.

Book to a Mother. Edited by Adrian J. McCarthy. Salzburg: Institut für Anglistik und Amerikanistik, 1981.

The Book of St. Gilbert. Edited by Raymonde Foreville and Gillian Keir. Oxford: Clarendon Press, 1987.

Brock, Sebastian P. and Susan A. Harvey. *Holy Women of the Syrian Orient*. Berkeley: University of California Press, 1987.

Buytaert, C. M. "Abelard's *Expositio in Hexaemeron*." *Antonianum* 43:2-3 (1968), 163-194.

Calvin, John. *The Institutes of Christian Religion*. Edited by Tony Lane and Hilary Osborne. Grand Rapids, MI: Baker House, 1986.

————. "Sermon on Epistle of St. Paul to Ephesians." In *Renaissance Women: A Sourcebook*. Edited by Kate Aughterson, 15-17. London: Routledge, 1995.

————. "Sermon on Epistle of St. Paul to Galatians." In *Renaissance Women: A Sourcebook*. Edited by Kate Aughterson, 17-18. London: Routledge, 1995.

Castiglione, Baldesar. *The Book of the Courtier*. Translated by George Bull. Baltimore: Penguin Books, 1967.

Catherine of Bologna. *The Seven Weapons of the Spirit*. In *Women Writers of the Renaissance and Reformation*. Edited by Katherina M. Wilson, 86-95. Athens: University of Georgia Press, 1987.

Catherine of Siena: The Dialogue. Translated by Suzanne Noffke. New York: Paulist Press, 1980.

Cazelles, Brigitte. *The Lady as Saint*. Philadelphia: University of Pennsylvania Press, 1991.

Cecilia del Nacimiento. *First Account of God's Favors.* In Electra Arenal and Stacey
    Schau, *Untold Sisters. Hispanic Nuns in Their Own Works.* Translated by Amanda
    Powell, 179-181. Albuquerque: University of New Mexico Press, 1989.

The Chastising of God's Children and the Treatise of Perfection of the Sons of God. Edited by Joyce
    Bazine and Eric Colledge. Oxford: Basil Blackwell, 1957.

*The Cloud of Unknowing, together with the Epistle of Privy Counsel by an English Mystic of the
    XIVth Century.* Edited by Justin McCann. London: Burns and Oates, 1964.

Complete Works of Saint Teresa of Jesus. Translated and edited by E. Allison Peers. Vols.
    3. London: Sheed and Ward, 1957.

Connolly, Sean, translator. "*Vita Prima Sanctae Brigitae.*" *Journal of the Royal Society of
    Antiquaries of Ireland* 119 (1989), 5-49.

Connolly, Sean and J. M. Picard. "*Cogitosus: Life of Saint Brigit.*" *Journal of the Royal
    Society of Antiquaries of Ireland* 117 (1987), 5-27.

Dentière, Marie. *Letter.* In *Women Writers of the Renaissance and Reformation.* Edited by
    Katherina M. Wilson, 275-281. Athens: University of Georgia Press, 1987.

Devotio Moderna: Basic Writings. Translated by John van Engen. New York: Paulist Press,
    1988.

A Devout Treatyse Called the Tree and the xii Frutes of the Holy Goost. Edited by J. J. Vaissier.
    Groningen: J. B. Wolters, 1960.

Didascalia et constitutiones apostolarum. Edited by F. X. Funk. Paderborn: F. Scheningh,
    1905.

Diderot, D. *Oeuvres philosophiques.* Edited Paul Verniere. Paris: Garnier frères, 1961.

Dives and Pauper. Edited by Priscilla Barnum. London: Oxford University Press, 1980.

Early Dominicans: Selected Writings. Edited by Simon Tugwell. New York: Paulist Press,
    1982.

Egeria's Travels. Translated by John Wilkinson. London: SPCK, 1971.

*Encyclopedie, ou dictionnaire raisonne des science, des arts et des metiers, por une societe de gens de
    lettres.* Edited by Denis Diderot and Jean LeRond d'Alembert. Paris: Briasson
    et al, 1751.

Ephrem the Syrian: Hymns. Translated and introduced by Kathleen E. McVey. New
    York: Paulist Press, 1989.

Erasmus. *In Praise of Marriage.* Translated by C. Fantazzi. In *Erasmus on Women.* Edited
    by Erika Rummel, 57-77. Toronto: University of Toronto Press, 1996.

———. *The Institution of Marriage.* Translated by Michael Heath. In *Erasmus on Women.*
    Edited by Erika Rummel, 79-130. Toronto: University of Toronto Press,
    1996.

Eusebius. *The History of the Church from Christ to Constantine.* Translated by G. A.
    Williamson. Harmondsworth: Dorset Press, 1965.

Francis and Clare: The Complete Works. Translated by Regis J. Armstrong and Ignatius C.
    Brady. New York: Paulist Press, 1982.

Francis de Sales, Jane de Chantal: Letters of Spiritual Direction. Translated by Péronne M.
    Thibert. New York: Paulist Press, 1988.

Gerontius. *The Life of Melanie the Younger.* Translated by Elizabeth Clark. Lewiston, NY:
    Edwin Mellon Press, 1984.

Gerson, Joannis de. *De mystica theologia.* Edited by André Combes. Lucconi: In aedibus
    Thesauri Mundi, 1958.

Gertrude the Great. *The Life and Revelations of Saint Gertrude.* Westminster, MD: Newman
    Press, repr., 1952.

Gregory of Nyssa. *The Life of St. Macrina.* Translated by W. K. Lowther Clarke.
    London: Society of Promoting Christian Knowledge, 1916.

Gregory of Tours. *Glory of the Confessors.* Translated by Raymond van Dam. Liverpool:
    Liverpool University Press, 1988.

———. *The History of the Franks.* Translated by Ernest Brehaut. New York: Columbia
    University Press, 1916.

———. *Life of the Fathers.* 2nd ed. Translated by Edward James. Liverpool: Liverpool
    University Press, 1991.

Hadewijch: The Complete Works. Translated by M. Columbia Hart. New York: Paulist
    Press, 1980.

Half Humankind: Contexts and Texts of the Controversy about Women in England 1540-1640.
    Edited by Katherina U. Henderson and B. F. McManus. Urbana:
    University of Illinois Press, 1985.

Harvey, Susan A. *Asceticism and Society in Crisis: John of Ephesus and "The Lives of the Eastern
    Saints."* Berkeley: University of California Press, 1990.

Den Heliga Birgittas Reuelaciones, Extrauagantes. Edited by Lennart Hollman. Uppsala:
    Almquist and Wiksells Boktryckeri, 1956.

Henry Suso: The Exempler, with Two German Sermons. Translated and edited by Frank Tobin.
    New York: Paulist Press, 1989.

Hildegard of Bingen. *Causae et curae.* In Peter Dronke, *Women Writers of the Middle Ages.*
    Cambridge: Cambridge University Press, repr. 1994.

Hildegard of Bingen: Scivias. Translated by Columba Hart and Jane Bishop. New York:
    Paulist Press, 1990.

Hortus deliciarum. Edited by Rosalie Green, et al. London: The Warburg Institute, 1979.

Hrotsvithae Opera. Edited by K. Strecker. Leipzig: B. G.Teubneri, 1906.

Hubmaier, Balthasar. *On Free Will.* In *Spiritual and Anabaptist Writers.* Edited by George
    H. Williams. Philadelphia: Westminster Press, 1957.

Hymns of the Breviary and Missal. Edited by Matthew Britt. New York: Bennigen
    Brothers, new ed., 1948.

Iberian Fathers. Vol. 1, *Martin of Braga, Paschasius of Dumium, Leander of Seville.* Translated
    by Claude W. Barlow. Washington, DC: Catholic University of America
    Press, 1969.

————. Vol. 2, *Braulio of Saragossa, Fructuosus of Braga*. Translated by Claude W. Barlow. Washington, DC: Catholic University of America Press, 1969.

The Irish Penitentials. Edited by Ludwig Bieler. Dublin: The Dublin Institute for Advanced Studies, 1963.

Jacobus de Voragine. *The Golden Legend or Lives of the Saints as Englished by William Caxton*. London: J. M. Desk and Co., 1900.

Jerome. *The Pilgrimage of the Holy Paula*. Translated by Aubrey Stewart. London: Palestine Pilgrims Text Society, 1887.

Johannes Tauler: Sermons. Translated by Maria Schady. Mahwah, NJ: Paulist Press, 1985.

John Ruusbroec: The Spiritual Espousals and Other Works. Translated by James A. Wiseman. New York: Paulist Press, 1985.

Julian of Norwich: Showings. Edited by Edmund Colledge and James Walsh. New York: Paulist Press, 1978.

Juana Inés de la Cruz, Sor. *Poems, Protest and a Dream: Selected Writings*. Translated by Margaret S. Peden. New York: Penguin Books, 1997.

Jung, C. S. *Collected Works*. Princeton, NJ: Princeton University Press, 1964.

Lactantius. *The Divine Institutes*. Translated by M. F. McDonald. Washington, DC: Catholic University of America Press, 1964.

Legend and Writings of S. Clare of Assisi: Introduction, Translation and Studies. Edited by Ignatius Brady. St. Bonaventure, NY: Franciscan Institute, 1953.

A Legend of Holy Women: Osbern Bokerham's Legends of Holy Women. Edited by Sheila Delaney. Notre Dame, IN; University of Notre Dame Press, 1992.

The Letters of Abelard and Heloise. Translated by Betty Radice. London: Penguin Books, 1974.

The Letters of Hildegard of Bingen. Translated by Joseph L. Baird and Radd K. Ehrman. New York: Oxford University Press, 1994.

The Letters of Paulinus of Nola. Translated by P. G. Walsh. Vols. 2. New York: Newman Press, 1966-1967.

The Letters of St. Bernard of Clairvaux. Translated by Bruno Scott James. Chicago: Henry Regnecy Company, 1953.

The Letters of Saint Boniface. Translated by Ephraim Emerton. New York: Octagon Books, 1973.

The Letters of St. Catherine of Siena. Translated by Suzanne Noffke. Binghamton, NY: Medieval and Renaissance Texts and Studies, 1988.

The Life of Christina of Markyate. A Twelfth Century Recluse. Edited and translated by C. H. Talbot. Oxford: Clarendon Press, repr. 1987.

The Life of Blessed Juliana of Mont-Cornillon. Translated by Barbara Newman. Toronto: Peregrina Publishing Co., 1989.

Loyola, Ignatius. *The Spiritual Exercises*. 2nd ed. Translated by Thomas Corbishley. Wheathampstead: Anthony Clarke, repr. 1979.

Luther's Works. Edited by Jaroslav Pelikan. Vols. 55. St. Louis, MO: Concordia
    Publishing House, 1958.

Maenads, Martyrs, Matrons, Monastics. Edited by Ross S. Kraemer. Philadelphia: Fortress
    Press, 1988.

Margaret Ebner: Major Works. Edited and translated by Leonard P. Hindsley. New York:
    Paulist Press, 1993.

Maria de San José. *Recreations.* In Electra Arenal and Stacey Schaw. *Untold Sisters:
    Hispanic Nuns in Their Own Works.* Translated by Amanda Powell.
    Albuquerque: University of New Mexico Press, 1989.

Marie of the Incarnation: Selected Writings. Edited by Irene Mahoney. New York: Paulist
    Press, 1989.

McCarthy, Maria. *The Rule for Nuns of St. Caesarius of Arles. A Translation with a Critical
    Introduction.* Washington, DC: Catholic University of America Press, 1960.

McNamara, JoAnn, and John E. Halborg. "The Rule of Donatus of Besançon, a
    Working Translation." *Vox Benedictina* 2:2 (April 1985), 85-107; and 2:3
    (July 1985), 181-204.

McNeill, John T., and Helena M. Gamer. *Medieval Handbooks of Penance.* New York:
    Columbia University Press, repr. 1990.

Mechtild of Magdeburg. *Das fliessende Licht der Gottheit.* Translated by Margot Schmidt.
    Einsiedeln: Benziger, 1956.

Meister Eckhart: The Essential Sermons, Commentaries, Treatises and Defense. Translated by
    Edmund Colledge and Bernard McGinn. New York: Paulist Press, 1981.

Origen. *Homilies on Genesis and Exodus.* Translated by Ronald E. Heine. Washington,
    DC: Catholic University of America Press, 1981.

————. *The Songs of Songs: Commentary and Homilies.* Translated by R. P. Lawson. New
    York: Newman Press, 1957.

Pachomian Koinonia. Vol. 1, *Life of St. Pachomius.* Translated by A. Veilleux. Kalamazoo:
    Cistercian Publication, 1980.

————. Vol.2, *The Chronicles and Rules.* Translated by A. Veilleux. Kalamazoo:
    Cistercian Publication, 1980.

Pacht, Otto, C. R. Dodwell, and Frances Wormald. *The St. Albans Psalter: Albani Psalter.*
    London: The Warburg Institute, 1960.

Palladius. *The Lausaic History.* Translated by Robert T. Meyer. New York: Newman
    Press, 1964.

The "Panarion" of St. Epiphanius, Bishop of Salamis: Selected Passages. Translated by Philip R.
    Amidon. New York: Oxford University Press, 1990.

*The Passion of SS. Perpetua and Felicity. A New Edition and Translation of the Latin Text, together
    with the Sermons of S. Augustine.* Translated by W. H. Shewring. London:
    Sheed and Weed, 1931.

Patrology. Vol. 4, *Golden Age of Latin Patristic Literature from the Council of Nicea to the Council of Chalcedon*. Edited by Angelo di Bernardino. Westminster, MD: Christian Classic, 1986.

Peter Damian Letters. Vols. 3. Translated by Owen J. Blum. Washington, DC: Catholic University of America Press, 1989.

Petri Lombardi. *Sententiae in IV Libris Distinctae*. 3rd ed. Grottaferrata: Collegii S. Bonaventurae ad Claras Aquas, 1981.

Philips, Dietrich. *The Church of God*. In *Spiritual and Anabaptist Writers*. Edited by George H. Williams. Philadelphia: Westminster Press, 1957.

Pseudo-Athanasius. *Canons of Anthanasius, Patriarch of Alexandria*. Edited and translated by W. Reidel and W. E. Crum. Amsterdam: Philo Press, repr. 1973.

Rahner, Hugo. *Saint Ignatius Loyola: Letters to Women*. Translated by Kathleen Pond and S. Weetman. New York: Herder and Herder, 1960.

RB 1980: The Rule of St. Benedict. Edited by Timothy Fry. Collegeville, MN: The Liturgical Press, 1981.

Le registre d'inquisition de Jacques Fournier. In *Women Writers of the Middle Ages*. Edited by Peter Dronke, 265-274. Cambridge: Cambridge University Press, repr. 1994.

Roussel, Pierre. *Systeme physique et moral de la femme; ou, Tableau philosophique de la constitution de l'etat organique, du temperament, des moeurs, & des fonctions propres au sexe*. Paris: Vincent, 1775.

Saint Ambrose Hexameron, Paradise and Cain and Abel. Translated by John J. Savage. New York: Fathers of the Church, 1961.

St. Anselm Basic Writings. 2nd ed. Translated by S. N. Deane. LaSalle, IL: Open Court Publishing Co., 1968.

Saint Basil Letters. Translated by Agnes C. Way. Washington, DC: Catholic University of America Press, 1951.

St. Leo the Great Letters. Translated by E. Hunt. New York: Fathers of the Church, 1957.

Sainted Women of the Dark Ages. Edited and translated by JoAnn McNamara and John E. Halborg with E. Gordon Whately. Durham, NC: Duke University Press, 1992.

Sancta Birgitta Opera minora I: Regula Salvatores. Edited by Sten Eklund. Stockholm: Almqvist and Wiksell International, 1975.

The Sayings of the Desert Fathers: The Alphabetical Collection. Translated by Benedicta Ward. Kalamazoo, MI: Cistercian Publications, 1975.

"Stephen of Fulga. *Vita B. Vitalis Saveniacensis*." Edited by E. P. Sauvage. *Analecta Bollandiana* 1 (1882).

Suso, Henry. *Wisdom's Watch upon the Hours*. Translated by Edmund Colledge. Washington, DC: Catholic University of America Press, 1994.

Tauler, John. *The Following of Christ*. Translated by J. R. Morell. London: T. Fisher Unwin, 1910.

Tertullian. *Apologetical Works and Minucius Felix Octavius.* Translated by A. Arbesmann, E. J. Daly, and E. A. Quain. Washington, DC: Catholic University of America Press, 1950.

————. *Disciplinary, Moral and Ascetical Works.* Translated by R. Arbesmann, E. Daly, and E. Quain. New York: Fathers of the Church, 1959.

The Testament of Our Lord. Translated by James Cooper and A. J. Maclean. Edinburgh: T. and T. Clark, 1902.

The Third Mystic of Avila: The Self-revelation of Maria Vela. Translated by Frances P. Keyes. New York: Farrar, Strauss and Cudahy, 1960.

Thomas à Kempis. *The Imitation of Christ.* Translated by Richard Whitford. Edited by Harold Gardiner. Garden City, NY: Doubleday and Company, 1955.

Thomas Aquinas. *Summa Theologica.* Rev. edition. Translated by Fathers of the English Dominican Province. Westminster, MD: Christian Classics, repr. 1981.

Thomas de Cantimpré. *The Life of Lutgard of Aywières.* Translated by Margot H. King. Toronto: Peregrina Publishing Co., 1989.

The Life of Margaret of Ypres. Translated by Margot King. Toronto: Peregrina Publishing Co., 1990.

Tortsch, Johannes. "Onus mundi, id est prophecia de malo futuro ipsi mundo superventuro." Edited by Ulrich Montag. In *Das Werk der Heiligen Birgitta von Schweden in oberdeutschen Überlieferung.* Edited by Ulrich Montag. Munich: Beck, 1968.

The Treatise of the Apostolic Tradition of St. Hippolylus of Rome. Edited by Gregory Dix. London: SPCK, reis. 1937

Utley, Francis Lee. *The Crooked Rib.* New York: Octagon Books, 1970.

Vasari, Giorgio. *The Lives of the Painters, Sculptors and Architects.* Vols. 4. Edited by William Gaunt. London: J. M. Dent and Sons, 1963.

Verheijen, Luc. *La régle de Saint Augustine.* Vols. 2. Paris: Etudes Augustinennes, 1967.

Vincent de Paul and Louise de Marillac: Rules, Conferences, and Writings. Edited by Frances Ryan and John Rybolt. New York: Paulist Press, 1995.

Die Werke der Hrotsvitha. Edited by K. A. Barack. Nürnberg: Bauer U. Raspe, 1858.

Wilson-Kastner, Patricia, et al. *A Lost Tradition.* Lanham, NY: University Press of America, 1981.

The Works of Aelred of Rievaulx. Vol. 1, *Treatises, The Pastoral Prayer.* Spencer, MA: Cistercian Publication, 1971.

The Works of Bernard of Clairvaux. Vol. 5, *Treatise II.* Translated by Robert Walton. Washington, DC: Cistercian Publications, 1974.

The Writings of Christine de Pizan. Edited by Charity C. Willard. New York: Persea Books, 1994.

Zwingli, Huldreich. *On True and False Religion.* In *Great Voices of the Reformation: An Anthology.* Edited by Henry Fosdick, 161-178. New York: The Modern Library, 1952.

Secondary Sources

Adams, Henry. *Mont-Saint-Michel and Chartres.* Princeton, NJ: Princeton University Press, repr. 1981.

Alexander, Jonathan J. G. *Medieval Illuminators and Their Methods of Work.* New Haven, CT: Yale University Press, 1992.

Baker, Denise. *Julian of Norwich "Showings:" From Vision to Book.* Princeton, NJ: Princeton University Press, 1994.

Baker, John. *English Stained Glass of the Medieval Period.* London: Thames and Hudson Ltd., 1978.

Bartlett, Anne C. *Male Authors, Female Readers.* Ithaca, NY: Cornell University Press, 1995.

Bateson, Mary, "Origin and Early History of Double Monasteries." *Transactions of the Royal Historical Society* 13 n.s. (1899), 137-198.

Batiffol, Pierre. *The History of the Roman Breviary.* Translated by A. M. Y. Baylay. London: Longmans, Green and Co., 1912.

Bell, Susan Groag. "Medieval Women Book Owners." In *Sisters and Workers in the Middle Ages.* Edited by Judith Bennett et al., 135-160. Chicago: University of Chicago Press, 1989.

Benko, Stephen. *The Virgin Goddess.* Leiden: E. J. Brill, 1993.

Bilinkoff, Jodi. "Confessors, Penitents, and the Construction of Identities in Early Modern Avila." In *Culture and Society in Early Modern Europe (1500-1800).* Edited by Barbara Diefendorf and Carla Hesse, 83-100. Ann Arbor: University of Michigan Press, 1993.

Bishop, Edmund. *Liturgica Historica.* Oxford: Clarendon Press, repr. 1962.

Bishop, Jane. "Bishops as Marital Advisors in the Ninth Century." In *Women in the Medieval World.* Edited by Julius Kirshner and Suzanne Wemple, 53-84. Oxford: Basil Blackwell, 1985.

Børresen, Kari E. "In Defense of Augustine: How *Femina* Is *Homo.*" *Collectanea Augustiniana* (1990), 411-428.

———. *Subordination and Equivalence. The Nature and Role of Women in Augustine and Thomas Aquinas.* Washington, DC: University Press of America, rev. ed. 1981.

Bradshaw, Paul F. *Daily Prayer in the Early Church.* New York: Oxford University Press, 1982.

Brown, Peter. *The Body and Society. Men, Women and Sexual Renunciation in Early Christianity*. New York: Columbia University Press, 1988.

———. "The Notion of Virginity in the Early Church." In *Christian Spirituality*. Edited by Bernard McGinn, John Meyerdorff, and Jean Leclercq, 427-443. New York: Crossroad, 1987.

Brundage, James A. *Law, Sex and Christian Society in Medieval Europe*. Chicago: University of Chicago Press, 1987.

———. "Sex and Canon Law: A Statistical Analysis of Samples of Canon and Civil Law." In *Sexual Practice and the Medieval Church*. Edited by Vern L. Bullough and James Brundage, 89-101. New York: Prometheus Books, 1982.

Bugge, John. *Virginitas*. The Hague: Martinus Nijhoff, 1975.

Burtchaell, James T. *From Synagogue to Church: Public Services and Offices in the Earliest Christian Communities*. Cambridge: Cambridge University Press, 1992.

Butler, M. M. *Hrotsvitha: The Theatricality of Her Plays*. New York: Philosophical Library, 1960.

Buytaert, C .M., "Abelard's *Expositio in Hexaemeron*." *Antonianum* 43(1968), 163-194.

Bynum, Carolyn Walker. *Docere Verbo et Exemplo: An Aspect of Twelfth-Century Spirituality*. Missoula, MT: Scholars Press, 1979.

———. *Fragmentation and Redemption*. New York: Zone Books, 1991.

———. *Holy Feast and Holy Fast*. Berkeley: University of California Press, 1987.

———. *Jesus as Mother: Studies in the Spirituality of the High Middle Ages*. Berkeley: University of California Press, 1982.

———. *The Resurrection of the Body in Western Christendom, 200-1336*. New York: Columbia University Press, 1995.

Cardman, Francine. "The Medieval Question of Women and Orders." *The Thomist* 42 (1978), 582-599.

Carr, Annemarie Weyl. "Women Artists in the Middle Ages." *Feminist Art Journal* 5:1 (Spring 1976), 5-9 and 26.

Caviness, Madeline H. "Anchoress, Abbess and Queen: Donors and Patrons or Intercessors and Matron?" In *The Cultural Patronage of Medieval Women*. Edited by June Hall McCash, 105-154. Athens: University of Georgia Press, 1996.

Chambers, Mary. *The Life of Mary Ward, 1585-1645*. Vols. 2. Edited by Henry J. Coleridge. London: Burns and Oates, 1882-1885.

Cherewatuk, Karen. "Radegund and Epistolary Tradition." In *Dear Sister*. Edited by Karen Cherewatuk and Ulrike Wiethaus, 20-45. Philadelphia: University of Pennsylvania Press, 1993.

Clark, Elizabeth. *Ascetic Piety and Women's Faith*. Lewiston, NY: Edwin Mellon Press, 1986.

———. "Sexual Politics in the Writings of John Chrysostom." *Angelica Theological Review* 59 (January 1977), 3-20.

Clay, Rotha Mary. *The Hermits and Anchorites of England.* London: Methuen, 1914.

Clayton, Mary. "Feasts of the Virgin in the Liturgy of the Anglo-Saxon Church." *Anglo-Saxon England* 13 (1984), 209-233.

Colledge, Eric. "Epistola solitarii ad reges: Alphonse of Pecha as Organizer of Birgittine and Urbanist Propaganda." *Medieval Studies* 18 (1956), 19-59.

Collins, Fletcher. *The Production of Medieval Church Music-Drama.* Charlottesville: University Press of Virginia, 1972.

Costa, Milagros Ortega. "Spanish Women in the Reformation." In *Women in Reformation and Counter-Reformation.* Edited by Sherrin Marshall, 89-119. Bloomington: Indiana University Press, 1989

Cowen, Painton. *Rose Windows.* San Francisco: Chronicle Books, 1979.

Crampe-Casnabet, Michèle. "A Sampling of Eighteenth-Century Philosophers." In *A History of Women in the West.* Vol. 3, *Renaissance and Enlightenment Paradoxes.* Edited by Nataliie Zemon Davis and Arlette Farge, 315-347. Cambridge, MA: Belknap Press of Harvard University Press, 1993.

Crichton, J. D. "The Office in the West: The Early Middle Ages." In *The Study of Liturgy.* Edited by Cheslyn Jones, G. Wainwright, and Edward Yarnold, 369-378. New York: Oxford University Press, 1978.

Crouzel, H. *Theologie de l'image de Dieu chez Origène.* Paris: Aubier, 1956.

Dalmus, John. "Preaching to the Laity in Fifteenth-Century Germany: Johannes Nider's 'Harps'." *Journal of Ecclesiastical History* 34:1 (January 1983), 55-68.

Davis, Leo D. *The First Seven Ecumenical Councils (325-787).* Wilmington, DE: Michael Glazier, 1987.

De Lubac, Henri. *Catholicism.* New York: New American Library, 1964.

Denifle, Henrich. "Meister Eckhart lateinische Schriften und die Grundanschauung seiner Lehre." *Archiv für Litteratur und Kirchengeschichte des Mittelalters* 2 (1886), 417-615.

Dix, Gregory. *The Shape of the Liturgy.* London: Dacre Press, repr. 1970.

Dodds, E. R. *Pagan and Christian in an Age of Anxiety.* Cambridge: Cambridge University Press, 1965.

Donovan, Richard. *The Liturgical Drama in Medieval Spain.* Toronto: Pontifical Institute of Medieval Studies, 1958.

Duffy, Eamon. "Holy Maydens, Holy Wyfes: the Cult of Women Saints in Fifteenth- and Sixteenth-century England." In *Women in the Church.* Edited by W. G. Sheils and Diana Wood, 175-196. Oxford: Basil Blackwell, 1990.

———. *The Stripping of the Altars.* New Haven, CT: Yale University Press, 1992.

Eberly, Susan. "Margery Kempe, St. Mary Magdalene and Patterns of Contemplation." *Downside Review* 107 (July 1989), 209-233.

Edwards, J. Michèle. "Women in Music to ca. 1450." In *Women and Music: A History*. Edited by Karen Pendle, 211-257. Bloomington: Indiana University Press, 1991.

Emmanuel, M. "Saint Walburga. Benedictine Abbess and Missionary (710-799)." *Word and Spirit* 11 (1989), 50-59.

Engen, John van. "The Virtues, the Brothers and the Schools." *Revue bénédictine* 98 (1988), 178-217.

L'Eremitismo in Occidente nei Secoli XIe-XIIe. Milano: Societa Editrice Vita et Pensiero, 1965.

Ferrante, Joan. *Women as Image in Medieval Literature*. New York: Columbia University Press, 1975.

Ferroglio, Guiseppe, "Raptus in parentes." *Annali della Fàcolta giuridica dell' Università di Camerino* 19 (1952), 3-34.

Finnegan, Mary J. *The Women of Helfta*. Athens: University of Georgia Press, 1991.

Fiorenza, Elizabeth Schussler. *In Memory of Her*. New York: Crossroad, 1984.

Fisher, Arthur. "Women and Gender in Palladius' *Lausaic History*." *Studia Monastica* 33 (1991), 23-50.

Foucault, Michel. *The History of Sexuality*. Translated by Robert Hurley. New York: Pantheon Books, 1978.

Fox, Matthew. *Illuminations of Hildegard of Bingen*. Santa Fe, NM: Bear and Co., 1985.

Frend, W. F. C. *The Rise of Christianity*. Philadelphia: Fortress Press, 1984.

Garnett, James M. "The Latin and the Anglo-Saxon *Juliana*." *Publications of the Modern Language Association* 14 (1899), 279-298.

Gay, Peter. *The Enlightenment: An Interpretation*. New York, Vintage Books, 1966.

Gelineau, J. "Music and Singing in the Liturgy." In *The Study of Liturgy*. Edited by Cheslyn Jones, G. Wainwright, and Edward Yarnold, 440-453. New York: Oxford University Press,1978.

Gibson, Joan. "Could Christ Have Been Born a Woman?" *Journal of Feminist Studies in Religion* 8:1 (Spring 1992), 65-82.

Gill, Katherine. "Women and the Production of Religious Literature in the Vernacular, 1300-1500." In *Creative Women in Medieval and Early Modern Italy*. Edited by E. Ann Matter and John Coakley, 64-104. Philadelphia: University of Pennsylvania Press, 1994.

Gilson, Gail McMurrray. *The Theater of Devotion*. Chicago: University of Chicago Press, 1989.

Godfrey, John. "The Double Monastery in Early English History." *The Ampleforth Journal* 79 (1974), 19-32.

Gold, Penny Schine. *The Lady and the Virgin*. Chicago: University of Chicago Press, 1985.

Grace, Pamela J. "John Foxe's Protestant Women Martyrs: Bold Actors or Quintessential Victims?" Unpublished Master's thesis, Central Michigan University, 1997.

Graef, Hilda. *Mary: A History of Doctrine and Devotion.* New York: Sheed and Ward, 1963.

Graus, F. *Volk, Herrscher und Heiliger im Reich der Merowinger.* Prague: Nakladatelstvi Ceskoslovenské Akádemie Ved, 1965.

Grodzynski, Denise. "Ravies et coupables.' *Mélanges de l'école francaise de Rome: Antiquité* 96 (1984), 697-726.

Grundmann, Herbert. *Religious Movements in the Middle Ages.* Translated by Steven Rowan. Notre Dame, IN: University of Notre Dame Press, 1995.

Hall, Douglas J. *Imaging God.* Grand Rapids, MI: Wm. B. Eerdmans Publishing Co., 1986.

Hall, James. *A History of Ideas and Images in Italian Art.* Cambridge, MA: Harper & Row, 1983.

Hall, Stuart G. "Women among the Early Martyrs." In *Martyrs and Martyrologies.* Edited by Diana Wood, 1-21. Oxford: Blackwell Publisher, 1993.

Häring, Nikolaus M. "Abelard Yesterday and Today." In *Pierre Abélard Pierre le Vénérable.* Edited by René Louis, Jean Jolivet, and Jean Chatillon, 341-403. Paris: CNRS, 1975.

Haskins, Susan. *Mary Magdalen: Myth and Metaphor.* New York: Harcourt Brace and Company, 1993.

Heany, Seamus P. *The Development of the Sacramentality of Marriage from Anselm of Laon to Thomas Aquinas.* Washington, DC: Catholic University of America Press, 1963.

Heinrich, Mary Pia. *The Canonesses and Education in the Early Middle Ages.* Washington, DC: Catholic University of America Press, 1924.

Helmholz, R. H. *Marriage Litigation in Medieval England.* Cambridge: Cambridge University Press, 1974.

L'Hermite-Leclercq, Paulette. "The Feudal Order." In *A History of Women in the West.* Vol. 2: *Silences of the Middle Ages.* Edited by Christiane Klapisch-Zuber, 202-249. Cambridge, MA: Harvard University Press, 1992.

Holdsworth, C. J. "Christina of Markyate." In *Medieval Women.* Edited by Derek Baker, 185-204. Oxford: Basil Blackwell, 1978.

"The House of the Aventine." *The Catholic World* (August 1898), 636-643.

Hoyt, Franceen S. "The Carolingian Episcopate: Concepts of Pastoral Care as Set Forth in the Capitularies of Charlemagne and His Bishops (789-822)." Ph.D. diss., Yale University, 1975.

Hyma, Albert. *The Christian Renaissance: A History of the "Devotio Moderna".* 2nd ed. Hamden, CT: Archon Books, 1965.

Janzten, Grace. *Julian of Norwich: Mystic and Theologian*. New York: Paulist Press, 1988.

Jørgensen, Johannes. *Saint Bridget of Sweden*, Vols. 2. Translated by I. Lund. London: Longmans, 1954.

Jungmann, Joseph A. *The Mass of the Roman Rite*. Vols. 2. Translated by F. A. Brunner. Dublin: Four Courts Press, replica ed., 1986.

Kieckhefer, Richard. *Unquiet Souls*. Chicago: University of Chicago Press, 1984.

King, Margaret. *Women of the Renaissance*. Chicago: University of Chicago Press, 1991.

Knowles, David. *The Monastic Orders in England*. Cambridge: Cambridge University Press, 1940.

Lackner, Bede K. *Eleventh-Century Background to Cîteaux*. Washington, DC: Cistercian Publications, 1972.

Ladner, Gerhard B. *The Idea of Reform*. Cambridge, MA: Harvard University Press, 1959.

————. "Philosophical Anthropology of Saint Gregory of Nyssa." *Dumbarton Oaks Papers* 12 (1958), 59-94.

LaPorte, Jean. *The Role of Women in Early Christianity*. New York: The Edwin Mellen Press, 1982.

Limberis, Vasiliki. *Divine Heiress*. London: Routledge, 1994.

Luongo, Thomas. "Catherine of Siena: Rewriting Female Holy Authority." In *Women, the Book and the Godly*. Edited by Lesley Smith and Jane Taylor, 89-130. Cambridge: D. S. Brewer, 1995.

Macek. Ellen. "The Emergence of a Feminine Spirituality in *The Book of Martyrs*." *Sixteenth Century Journal* 19:1 (1988), 63-80.

Mâle, Emile. *Art and Artists of the Middle Ages*. Translated by S. S. Lowe. Redding Ridge, CT: Black Swan Books, 1986.

Marr, M. Lucille. "Anabaptist Women of the North: Peers in Faith, Subordinate in Marriage." *The Menonite Quarterly* 61 (October 1987), 347-362.

Martinelli, Serena Spanò. "La biblioteca del 'Corpus Domini' bolognese: l'in consueto spaccato di una cultura monastica femminile." *La Bibliofiliá* 88:1 (1986), 1-23.

Marucchi, Orazio. *Christian Epigraphy*. Translated by J. A. Willis. Chicago: Ares Publishers, repr. 1974.

McCone, Kim. "Brigit in the Seventh Century: A Saint with Three Lives?" *Peritia* 1 (1982), 107-145.

McDonnell, Ernest. *Beguines and Beghards in Medieval Culture*. New York: Octagon Books, 1969.

McLaughlin, Mary. "Peter Abelard and the Dignity of Women: Twelve-Century 'Feminism' in Theory and Practice." In *Pierre Abélard Pierre le Vénérable*. Edited by Rene Louis, Jean Jolivet, and Jean Chatillon, 287-334. Paris: CNRS, 1975.

McLeod, Glenda. *Virtue and Venom.* Ann Arbor: University of Michigan Press, 1991.

Ménager, L. R. "La 'byzantinisation' religieuse de l'Italie meridionale (ixe-xii^{e}s) et la politique monastique des Normands l'Italie." *Revue d'Historie Ecclesiastique* 53:4 (1958), 747-774.

Mersch, E. *The Whole Christ. The Historical Development of the Doctrine of the Mystical Body in Scripture and Tradition.* Translated by J. R. Kelly. London: D. Dobson, 1962.

Meyer, M. A. "Women and the Tenth Century English Monastic Reform." *Revue bénédictine* 87 (1977), 34-61.

Miccoli, Giovanni. "Theólogie de la vie monastique chez Saint Pierre Damien (1007-1072).' In *Theologie de la monastique: Etudes sur la tradition patristique*, 459-483. Paris: n.p., 1961.

Milburn, R. L. P. "The Historical Background of the Doctrine of the Assumption." In *Women in Early Christianity.* Edited by David M. Scholer, 55-86. New York: Garland Publishing, repr. 1993.

Miller, Patricia. "The Devil's Gateway: An Eros of Difference in the Dreams of Perpetua." *Dreaming* 2:1 (1992), 45-63.

Momigliano, Arnaldo. "The Life of St. Macrina by Gregory of Nyssa." In *The Craft of the Ancient Historians.* Edited by John N. Eadie and Josiah Ober. New York: University Press of America, 1985.

Monica, M. *Angela Merici and Her Teaching Idea, 1474-1540.* New York: Longman Green and Company, 1927.

Mooney, Catherine M. "The Authorial Role of Brother A. in the Composition of Angela of Foligno's *Revelations.*" In *Creative Women in Medieval and Early Modern Italy.* Edited by E. Ann Matter and John Coakley, 34-63. Philadelphia: University of Pennsylvania Press, 1994.

Nagel, Bert. "Dramas of Hrotsvit von Gandersheim." In *The Medieval Drama and Its Claudelian Revival.* Edited by E. Catherine Dunn, T. Folitch and Bernard M. Peebles, 16-26. Washington, DC: Catholic University of America Press, 1970.

Newman, Barbara. *From Virile Woman to WomanChrist.* Philadelphia: University of Pennsylvania Press, 1995.

———. *Sister of Wisdom.* Berkeley: University of California Press, 1987.

Origo, Iris. *The World of San Bernardino.* New York: Harcourt Brace and World, 1962.

Owst, G. R. *Preaching in Medieval England.* New York: Russell and Russell, reissue, 1965.

———. *Literature and Pulpit in Medieval England.* Oxford: Basil Blackwell, 1961.

Ozment, Steven. *When Fathers Ruled.* Cambridge, MA: Harvard University Press, 1983.

Pagels, Elaine. *Adam, Eve and the Serpent.* New York: Vintage Books, 1988.

Pelikan, Jaroslav. *Eternal Feminine.* New Brunswick, NJ: Rutgers University Press, 1990.

————. *Mary through the Centuries: Her Place in the History of Culture.* New Haven, CT: Yale University Press, 1996.

Pfaff, R. W. *New Liturgical Feasts in Later Medieval England.* Oxford: Clarendon Press, 1970.

Phillips, Helen. "Rewriting the Fall: Julian of Norwich and the *Chevalier des dames.*" In *Women, the Book and the Godly.* Edited by Lesley Smith and Jane Taylor, 149-156. Cambridge: D. S. Brewer, 1995.

Prinz, Friederich. "Heiligenkult und Adelsherrschaft in Spiegel merowingischer Hagiographie." *Historische Zeitschrift* 204 (1967), 529-544.

Rader, Rosemary. *Breaking Boundaries: Male/Female Friendship in Early Christian Communities.* New York: Paulist Press, 1983.

————. "The Role of Celibacy in the Origin and Development of Christian Heterosexual Friendship." Ph.D diss., Stanford University, 1977.

Ranft, Patricia. "The Concept of Witness in the Christian Tradition from Its Origin to Its Institutionalization," *Revue bénédictine* 102:1-2 (1992), 9-23.

————. "A Key to Counter Reformation Women's Activism: The Confessor-Spiritual Director." *Journal of Feminist Studies in Religion* 10:2 (Fall 1994), 7-26.

————. "An Overturned Victory: Clare of Assisi and the Thirteenth-Century Church." *Journal of Medieval History* 17 (1991), 123-134.

————. "The Role of the Eremetic Monk in the Development of the Medieval Intellectual Tradition." In *From Cloister to Classroom.* Edited by E. Rozanne Elders, 80-95. Kalamazoo, MI: Cistercian Publications, 1986.

————. "The Rule of St. Augustine in Medieval Monasticism." *Proceedings of the PMR Conference* 11 (1986), 143-150.

————. *Women and the Religious Life in Premodern Europe.* New York: St. Martin's Press, 1996.

Rapley, Elizabeth. *The Dévotes.* Montreal: McGill-Queens' University Press, 1990.

Reames, Sherry L. *The Legenda aurea.* Madison: University of Wisconsin Press, 1985.

Reites, James. "Ignatius and Ministry with Women." *The Way.* Supp. 17 (1992), 7-19.

Religion and Sexism. Edited by Rosemary R. Ruether. New York: Simon and Schuster, 1974.

Rigaux, Dominique. "The Franciscan Tertiaries at the Convent of St. Anna." *Gesta* 31:2 (1992), 92-98.

Rivet, M. M. *The Influence of the Spanish Mystics on the Works of Saint Francis de Sales.* Washington, DC: Catholic University of America Press, 1941.

Roberts, Ann M. "Chiara Gambacorta of Pisa as Patroness of the Arts." In *Creative Women in Medieval and Early Modern Italy.* Edited by E. Ann Matter and John Coakley, 120-154. Philadelphia: University of Pennsylvania Press, 1994.

Robertson, Elizabeth. *Early English Devotional Prose and the Female Audience.* Knoxville: University of Tennessee Press, 1990.

Robinson, I. S. "The 'Colores Rhetorici' in the Investiture Contest." *Traditio* 32 (1976), 209-238.

Robertson, Elizabeth. *Early English Devotional Praise and the Female Audience.* Knoxville: University of Tennessee Press, 1990.

Roper, Lyndal. *The Holy Household.* Oxford: Clarendon Press, 1959.

Rossi, Mary Ann. "The Passion of Perpetua, Everywomen of Late Antiquity." In *Pagan and Christian Anxiety: A Response to E. R. Dodds.* Edited by Robert C. Smith and John Lounibos, 53-86. Lanham, NY: University Press of America, 1984.

Rubin, Miri. *Corpus Christi.* Cambridge: Cambridge University Press, 1991.

Russell, James C. *The Germanization of Early Medieval Christianity.* New York: Oxford University Press, 1994.

Russell, Jeffrey Burton. *Lucifer.* Ithaca, NY: Cornell University Press, 1984.

Russell, Paul. *Lay Theology in the Reformation.* Cambridge: Cambridge University Press, 1986.

Scheepsma, Wybren. "'For hereby I hope to rouse some piety': Books of Sisters from Convents and Sister Houses Associated with the *Devotion Moderna* in the Low Countries." In *Women, the Book and the Godly.* Edited by Lesley Smith and Jane Taylor, 27-40. Cambridge: D. S. Brewer, 1995.

Schmidt, Alvin. *Veiled and Silenced.* Forward by Martin Marty. Macon, GA: Mercer University Press, 1989.

Schmidtke, James. "'Saving' by Faint Praise: St. Birgitta of Sweden, Adam Easton and Medieval Antifeminism." *American Benedictine Review* 33:2 (June 1982), 149-161.

Schmitz, Philibert. *Historie de l'ordre de Saint Benoit.* Liege: Editions de Maredsous, 1948-1956.

Scholer, David M. *Women in Early Christianity.* New York: Garland Publishing, 1993.

Schulenburg, Jane Tibbetts. "Sexism and the Celestial Gynaeceum from 500 to 1200." *Journal of Medieval History* 4 (1978), 117-133.

————. "Women's Monastic Communities, 500-1100: Patterns of Expansion and Decline." *Signs* 14:2 (1989), 261-292.

Scott, Karen. " 'So Catarina': Catherine of Siena." In *Dear Sister.* Edited by Karen Cherewatuk and Ulrica Wiethaus, 87-121. Philadelphia: University of Pennsylvania Press, 1993.

Seybolt, Robert. "Fifteenth-Century Editions of the *Legenda aurea.*" *Speculum* 21 (1946), 327-338.

Sheingorn, Pamela. "'The Wise Mother': The Image of St. Anne Teaching the Virgin Mary." *Gesta* 32:1 (1993), 69-80.

Sherman, James C. *The Nature of Martyrdom.* Paterson, NJ: St. Anthony Guild Press, 1942.

Simpson, Jane. "Women and Asceticism in the Fourth Century: A Question of Interpretation." *Journal of Religious History* 15:1 (June 1988), 38-60.

Spencer, H. Leith. *English Preaching in the Late Middle Ages.* Oxford: Clarendon Press, 1993.

Steele, Francesca M. *Anchoresses of the West.* London: Sands and Co., 1903.

Stephens, W. P. *The Theology of Huldrych Zwingli.* Oxford: Clarendon, 1986.

Tavard, George H. *Woman in Christian Tradition.* Notre Dame, IN: University of Notre Dame Press, 1973.

Taylor, Judith C. "From Proselytizing to Social Reform: Three Generations of French Female Teaching Congregations 1600-1720." Ph.D diss., Arizona State University, 1980.

Taylor, Larissa. *Soldiers of Christ: Preaching in Medieval and Reformation France.* New York: Oxford University Press, 1992.

Thrupp, Sylvia. *The Merchant Class of Medieval London, 1300-1500.* Ann Arbor: University of Michigan, 1962.

Thurnberg, Lars. *Microcosm and Mediator: The Theological Anthropology of Maximus the Confessor.* Copenhagen: Munksgaard, 1965.

Tolhurst, J. B. L. *Introduction to the English Monastics Breviaries.* Suffolk: The Boydell Press, repr. 1993.

Trites, Allison A. *The Concept of Witness in the New Testament Thought.* Cambridge: Cambridge University Press, 1977.

———. "Martus and Martyrdom in the Apocalypse: A Semantic Study." *Novum Testamentum* 15:1 (January 1973), 72-80.

Udovic, Edward. "'Caritas Christ Urgent Nos:' The Urgent Challenges of Charity in Seventeenth Century France." *Vincentian Heritage* 12:2 (1991), 85-104.

Underwood, Evelyn. *The Mystics of the Church.* London: Schocken, 1964.

Van der Meer, Haye. *Women Priests in the Catholic Church?* Translated by Arlene and Leonard Swidler. Philadelphia: Temple University, 1973.

Vögel, Cyrille. *Medieval Liturgy.* Translated by W. D. Storey and N. K. Rasmisser. Washington, DC: Pastoral Press, 1986.

Von Simpson, Otto. *The Gothic Cathedral.* New York: Pantheon Press, 1956.

Warren, Ann K. *Anchorites and Their Patrons in Medieval England.* Berkeley: University of California Press, 1985.

Weaver, F. Ellen and Jean LaPorte. "Augustine and Women: Relationships and Teachings." *Augustinian Studies* 12 (1981), 115-132.

Weber, Alison. *Teresa of Avila and the Rhetoric of Femininity.* Princeton, NJ: Princeton University Press, 1990.

Wemple, Suzanne F. *Women in Frankish Society.* Philadelphia: University of Pennsylvania Press, 1981.

Wiesner, Merry E. "Nuns, Wives, and Mothers: Women and the Reformation in Germany." In *Women in Reformation and Counter-Reformation Europe.* Edited by Sherrin Marshall, 8-28. Bloomington: Indiana University Press, 1989.

Willard, Charity C. *Christine de Pizan: Her Life and Works.* New York: Persea Books, 1984.

———. "A Fifteenth-Century View of Women's Role in Medieval Society: Christine de Pizan's *Livre des Trois Vertus.*" In *The Role of Women in the Middle Ages.* Edited by Rosemarie Morewedge. Albany: University of New York Press, 1975.

Wilmart, A. "Eve et Goscelin." *Revue bénédictine* 46 (1934), 414-438.

Women of the Spirit. Edited by Rosemary Ruether and Eleanor McLaughlin. New York: Simon and Schuster, 1979.

Wood, Charles T. "The Doctors' Dilemma: Sin, Salvation and the Menstrual Cycle in Medieval Thought." *Speculum* 56:4 (October 1981), 710-727.

———. *The Quest for Eternity.* Hanover, NH: University Press of New England, 1983.

Wood, Jeryldene M. "Breaking the Silence: The Poor Clares and the Visual Arts in Fifteenth-Century Italy." *Renaissance Quarterly* 48 (Summer 1995), 262-286.

———. "Perceptions of Holiness in Thirteenth-Century Italian Painting: Clare of Assisi." *Art History* 14 (September 1991), 301-328.

———. *Women, Art and Spirituality: The Poor Clares of Early Modern Italy.* Cambridge: Cambridge University Press, 1996.

Wright, Wendy M. *Bond of Perfection.* New York: Paulist Press, 1985.

Youings, Joyce. *The Dissolution of the Monasteries.* London: Allen and Unwin, 1971.

Young, Karl. *The Drama of the Medieval Church.* Vols. 2. Oxford: Oxford University Press, 1933.

Index

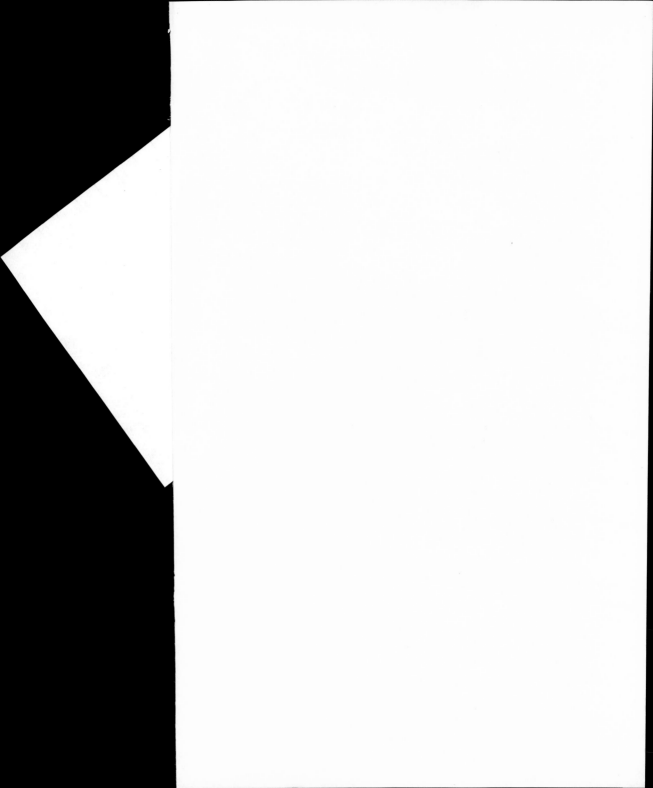

DATE

APR 03 2000

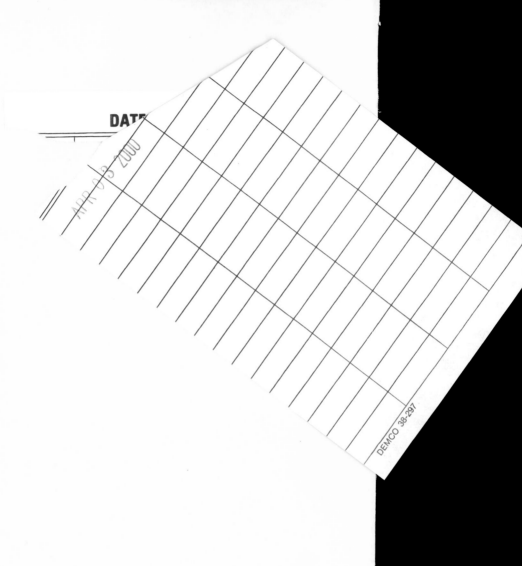

DEMCO 38-297

Lewis & Clark College - Watzek Library

3 5209 00652 3142